BOOKS BY

MAX FREEDOM LONG

The Secret Science Behind Miracles
The Secret Science At Work
The Huna Code in Religions
Growing Into Light
Self-Suggestion
Psychometric Analysis
What Jesus Taught in Secret

THE HUNA CODE IN RELIGIONS

The Influence of the Huna Tradition on Modern Faith

MAX FREEDOM LONG

DeVorss *Publications*

The Huna Code in Religions
Copyright © 1965
by Max Freedom Long

ISBN: 0-87516-495-1
Sixth Printing, 1998

For information about the author,
please write to:

Mrs. Dolly Ware
1501 Thomas Place
Fort Worth TX 76107

DeVorss & Company, Publisher
P.O. Box 550
Marina del Rey, CA 90294

Printed in The United States of America

To the *Huna Research Associates*
with warm appreciation for their continuing
help with the research and their sustaining
encouragement.

CONTENTS

Section Two:
1. A short dictionary of Hawaiian-English words
2. Addenda for the word list

FOREWORD

In the year 1953 the presence of coded Huna information in the Bible was discovered and a partial report on the hidden meanings incorporated in my book, THE SECRET SCIENCE AT WORK. Since that time the research work has progressed, with a number of additional pieces of coded information uncovered. This book gives not only the later findings, but further expands the study to show similar coded information in the religions of the ancient Egyptians, Israelites, Buddhists and practitioners of Yoga.

Interest in the coded material has increased to the point at which it has been found well to place in the hands of the reader a condensation of the 1865 Andrews HAWAIIAN DICTIONARY, with English equivalents. While some of the other languages used in Polynesia offer additional light on the multiple-meanings of words employed in the Huna code, the Hawaiian dialect has been found nearest to the form of the Code Language as used in inserting the secret meanings into parts of the Bible as well as into some of the contemporary Gnostic literature.

If the reader wishes to explore hidden meanings in the New Testament, this can be done by getting from the American Bible Society, 450 Park Ave., New York 22, N. Y., a copy of the New Testament with the English translation given beside the Hawaiian in parallel columns. The price is $2.00 post paid. As the Hawaiian language is very simple and does not have verbs changed to show tense, almost any word thought to be related to the code can be investigated and its roots looked into to get at the possible code significance. Unfortunately, the old Andrews dictionary has long been out of print and used copies are difficult to find, while the new $16.00 Hawaiian-English Dictionary (which may be obtained from the University of Hawaii, Honolulu, Hawaii) has been modernized and many of the root meanings to be found in the Andrews are omitted. Where the reader has access to a large library, copies of the Andrews dictionary may sometimes be found in the reference rooms, also the MAORI COMPARATIVE DICTIONARY, by Tregear which gives the vocabularies of the several dialects common to Polynesia, some of these being of value in running down special code meanings.

There are a number of books containing studies of early Christian writings and beliefs, Charles Guignebert's JESUS, now available in the English translation from University Books, being good. A much later book, THE RELIGION OF THE OCCIDENT, by Martin A. Larson, published by Littlefield & Adams, is the best and most inclusive source book, giving as it does, a full account of the manner in which outside beliefs were incorporated into Christianity in the formative centuries.

While I have tried in this book to give a sufficient outline of what was believed by the early Polynesians before they migrated from their homeland to the islands of the Pacific, the student who wishes the complete picture and story of the uncovering of the

"Secret" (which we call "Huna," which means "secret"), will do well to read my book, THE SECRET SCIENCE BEHIND MIRACLES. (In the back of this volume may be found a complete list of my books dealing with this subject, together with descriptions of the titles and the prices.)

The complete investigation of the Bible and Gnostic literature has not yet been finished, and the reader who wishes to do so may carry on for himself without much difficulty, once this book has been read and the research method is understood.

In the New Testament as translated by the Missionaries in Hawaii before the turn of the century, there are a few errors which were unavoidable because they did not understand the secret beliefs and code meanings of the Hawaiian native priests or kahunas. These priests were bound by a cult of secrecy which was even then perhaps three thousand years old, and so did not correct the Missionaries when they used the word *uhane* for God, although it actually had the meaning of what is called in modern Psychology, the "conscious mind." The word *akua* should have been used, and in the revised dictionary now in use, this mistake has been corrected.

From the historical angle, it may be said that the uncovering of the Huna lore had its beginnings in the hands of Dr. William Tufts Brigham, long curator of the Bishop Museum, in Honolulu. It began with his curiosity concerning the secret healing methods used by the kahunas (please add this word to your vocabulary), and was highlighted by a personal experience in which a fire-walk was done under the protection of three old priests, the barely cooled surface of a lava flow being used for the "walk." Dr. Brigham ran instead of walked, as did the kahunas, and unlike them, he wore heavy mountain boots and two pairs of heavy socks instead of a single layer of green *ti* leaves tied around each foot. The heavy boots and socks were burned from his feet, but his soles were not injured in any way.

In a search lasting for over forty years, Dr. Brigham accumulated much information concerning the beliefs and practices of the kahunas, but was unable to get any of them to share the heart of their ancient "Secret" with him. In this "heart" lore lay the key to instant healing, slow healing and such things as fire-immunity. In my turn, I, as a young man, became curious and was taken in hand by Dr. Brigham and given such information as he had been able to accumulate together with his ideas of what might lie behind the workability of the native magic. Sixteen years were to pass with the "Secret" not yet uncovered. Dr. Brigham passed on, and I continued the investigation—eventually discovering that the kahunas had been forced to name the various elements of their lore in order to be able to pass on their knowledge to the ones whom they chose to initiate.

Following this discovery, the vocabularies of the kahunas were combed, and by slow stages there came to light a system of psychology and religion, in combination, which was so fully developed that it could hardly be believed that it had been discovered by the ancestors of the Polynesians. Further studies, however, confirmed the opinion that the lore had not been a borrowing, or if it had been, a whole language had been borrowed with it and had been adopted by the ones who had inherited the knowledge from whatever source may be imagined.

At the time of this writing, we still do not know just how the kahunas performed their magic. We know many of the prayers they used, but we still are not certain about what additional action of mind was silently used to make the prayers miraculously effective. In due time, it is hoped, this last link in the chain will be discovered. Meantime, in so far as the joy of obtaining pure knowledge is concerned, we have in the present book the first new light to be thrown on Christianity (and some other religions), since the writing of the Four Gospels. At last we are privileged, thanks to the kahunas, to know what was contained in the Mystery Teachings which tradition has so long held to lie behind the Scriptures. As a bonus we have also the new light which is thrown on Yoga and Buddhism. The added understanding of the Gnosis is part of the benefits.

That this new information will find acceptance except by a very few, is to be expected. The most stubbornly resistant thing in the world is religion. Once a belief has been accepted and its dogmas established, the bars are up against all changes of every sort. We have seen the phrenetic struggle to prevent Protestant reforms in the heyday of the Churches of Rome and Greece. We have seen the savage resistance to change when it came to the discovery that the world was round and of an age much greater than specified in the Bible, and that there was such a thing as evolution.

In its turn, the information concerning the newly discovered Huna code will be rejected blindly if for no other reason that it suggests change. But, despite the natural conservatism of religions, we will, in time, have a renewal of the small band of initiates who took such pains to conceal their "Secret" in the Gospels in order to preserve it—possibly to preserve it for those of this age who may have been seen in prophetic vision as eventually to arrive upon the scene and to be ready.

Yesterday the unveiling of the coded knowledge would have been countered by the Church with burnings and any torture needed for the suppression of heresy. Today, happily, even the humblest Galileo is able safely to take up his telescope and peer into the realms of the new and strange . . . . . and still forbidden.

Max Freedom Long,
Vista, Calif., 1965

CHAPTER 1

FROM WHENCE CAME HUNA?

Years ago, when Dr. Brigham first recognized in the beliefs and practices of the Hawaiian native priests of Huna, a system which contained elements still unknown to modern Psychology and Religion, the question of the possible origin of this body of knowledge arose.

It seemed incredible that men as untutored and filled with superstitions as the remote ancestors of the Hawaiians must have been, could have been able to originate a system such as the one which enabled the kahunas to walk unharmed over very hot lava or over heated stones in the "Oven Ceremony," or to bring about instant healing at times, particularly the healing of broken bones—things which Dr. Brigham had investigated at first hand and verified.

So far as could be learned, the Polynesians had come to the Pacific Islands not earlier than the year 1 A.D., and had brought the secret knowledge with them. But from whence had they come? Their legends told of a homeland which had been blessed with "heavenly dew" and which had been overlooked by lovely blue mountains. But nothing in the legends gave definite place to the homeland or told why the several tribes of the Polynesians had decided to leave it in search of new homes in the Pacific.

Efforts to trace the path of migration through the language used by the Polynesians had been made by a number of able men, but nothing definite had been learned other than that there are many words to be found in Africa which are duplicated in the tongue of the New Zealand branch of the migrants, the Maories, and that an excellent dialect of the Polynesian general language is spoken on about half of the large island of Madagascar, off the east coast of South Africa. Judge Fornander, long a resident of Hawaii and an excellent student of the native culture, decided that the Coptic, or language of ancient Egypt, more closely resembled the Hawaiian than any other.

As Egypt became an advanced civilization at a very early time, it was natural that this place and age should be inspected eagerly to determine whether Huna had originated there. The lead showed that Huna had been known there, but nothing was found to indicate that it had not been brought in as a fully developed system and shared, at least in part, with the local priests and men of learning.

Even today the mystery remains unsolved, and at best we can only speculate concerning possible places and times which might have lent themselves to the working out of such a profound knowledge of man and his relation to entities and powers which have only been guessed at in the modern world.

To aid the speculation, we have two things to use as starting points. The first is that we must look for an ancient race which had a well established belief in spirits, and second, a belief in totems and the inevitable taboos which accompany such a belief.

We have the modern science of Geology to aid us

in our search before recorded history tells us much about the most primitive peoples and their beginnings. We peer curiously at the scars left by glaciers and know now that there were several glacial ages. During a period of about a million years, ice ages came and went. Oceans rose and fell as much as 450 feet, great depressions appear to have been made by the weight of ice, only to be filled with water when the ice melted.

There were periods of unusual warmth between times of glacial cold, and in the warm times tropical vegetation grew far above the tropics and left deposits of peat, coal and oil behind them when pushed back by the next ice age.

During this vast reach of time, mankind evolved and moved back and forth around the earth. The different races became distinct in color and character-istics, and began to divide themselves into people who lived inland on game animals and those who lived near the water and depended largely on fish for food. Fruit, roots and nuts were eaten when available, and in time seeds were added to the diet. Gradually the planting and harvesting of seed-bearing plants devel-oped into the earliest agriculture. Animals were do-mesticated and plants developed through the selection of the best types for use, into much better food sources.

The first tools were made of wood, then of bone, and finally of chipped flint. Eventually the shaping of stone by pecking with hard points or by grinding was learned. Flint points were also used to peck or cut pictures into the rock walls of caves, and it is there that we get our first glimpse of what our ancestors believed and what they did about it.

The first crude pictures of animals on cave walls

3

gave way in following periods to more elaborate drawings, even with the use of color. The first pottery was very crude, but in time it came to be smoothed and decorated.

In some way which is still a mystery, the black "Abos," or Arunta people, of Australia reached that southern continent and settled there. They may have been a fisher folk when they arrived, but some eventually became hunters living far from the sea. They had no tools other than a throwing stick for use in hunting, and a digging stick which also served to whip seeds from the tops of wild grasses into rough wooden trays. They did not weave or plant. All in all, they were the least cultured people on earth, but they had an elaborate religion based on totems, taboos and magic. They had good psychics and mediums in the clans, and some practiced hypnosis surprisingly well. They even had their own version of the "death prayer" which was familiar to the later Polynesians, and sent magical death to an enemy while pointing at him with a dagger of bone. They practiced circumcision, just as did the people of the Near East and the Polynesians. They knew the difference between good and bad conduct and had good and bad totem creatures.

We do not know as yet whether the Arunta people brought with them their beliefs and culture when they arrived in Australia, or whether they developed these for themselves over a long period of time. However, the similarity of beliefs and customs, when compared to those of other world inhabitants, suggests strongly an early contact.

Some cave remains and drawings in Africa have

recently been discovered, but to date our best information has been obtained from the caves in Alta Mara, in Spain. These appear to have been occupied for the first time after the Fifth Glacial Period, and on the cave walls can be seen drawings well executed and often in color, which indicate that at that very early time the belief in magic and totemism was well developed. Tools were made of wood, stone and bone.

Following the earliest evidence of developing cultures, as studied in the cave remains, we can trace the progress of inventions in various parts of the world. In some places the progress was much swifter than in others. Agriculture and animal husbandry advanced and better equipment was invented for hunting and fishing, with the spear, club and knife coming much sooner than the bow and arrow. Boats, hooks and lines for fishing, and, in time, nets, were evolved. The use of fire and the invention of tools for making fire marked a great step forward. Much later came the first use of metals.

Meantime, the peoples of the earth from the Arunta of Australia to the Cave Dwellers of the North had developed one thing in common, the beliefs in spirits and totems. Those who progressed rapidly with their inventions seemed to progress in the matter of religious beliefs as slowly as their more backward brothers. (This conservatism in such things as beliefs and customs is still with us. In Christianity, for instance, almost no changes have been made in beliefs and rituals in nearly twenty centuries, although our inventions are new and endless.)

In lands near the equator or parts which were not

reached by the glaciers or the glacial cold, the beginning steps of early civilization may have been made long before the caves in Spain were put to use. The valley of the Nile was greatly favored in many ways. Its climate suffered little change and its land was fertilized by the mud of the inundation year after year. This applied to a degree in the valley lands of the Euphrates and Tigris rivers where the Sumerian culture developed. In the southern parts of China the great river valleys also provided places for permanent residence and the development of a series of cultures. In the Americas the earliest men left little trace of their stay, but much later the lands were again inhabited and in the lower edge of modern times the complicated cultures of Central America developed, with, once more, the totem and taboo basic to the religious beliefs and practices.

In all parts of the world the knowledge of astronomy was mixed with the totems so that the sky of the night became filled with the outlines of starry creatures. Snakes became great dragons. Invisible powers, as in the wind and storms, became gods. The symbology was developed in which Light and Darkness were personified. The sun and moon were deified and worshiped both for themselves and as symbols of degrees of light and darkness. The year was divided into twelve parts and some parts were associated with the creatures of the totem class in early Egypt.

At some point in these formative millenniums, the ancestors of the Polynesians must either have developed their lore or had it given to them through some form of revelation, perhaps by an advanced spirit who taught through a living medium. The first definite indication that such a body of knowledge as that of Huna was known and used is to be found in a certain classical form of the totem pole which was used in New Zealand up to fairly modern times. This totem pole represents the belief that man has three spirits, the most advanced of which is a dual entity made up of a combined male and female unit. The lowest figure on the carved pole is usually large and gross, above it, and often with its legs folded around the neck and chest of the low figure, is a second and more human figure, while above it, often with a tiny body, is a figure with two faces placed back to back on a single head. The number three is made prominent by having only three fingers on each of the hands of the lower pair of figures.

If the guess is correct that the kahuna people, at a very early time, shared an outer and an inner system of religious beliefs with other clans and peoples with whom they made contact, then we can say that their inner or secret knowledge of the three selves of man, (the highest being dual) was not passed on in the outer teachings. Because of this, the spread of the use of totem poles, while covering a large part of the world, especially North America, did not include the knowledge of the dual self as represented on the original poles of the kahunas. Modern totem poles may contain up to eight figures, some of the lower ones animals.

A modification of the three-self totem pole was the carved scepter or wand of the priestly ruler or magician. This became also a staff, and in Aaron's rod in the Old Testament we have magic performed in which a rod was used. Moses used his rod to smite the rock in the wilderness to bring forth a flow of water.

While in the early Huna lore there was taught the doctrine that man is a trinity of three selves or spirits, there was also taught the doctrine of "duality," which covered the secret that the third and most evolved spirit in the make up of the triune man was dual—that is, made of a united male and female pair of selves or spirits. (We will return to this later.)

In my book THE SECRET SCIENCE BEHIND MIRACLES, I have presented in detail the beliefs of the Polynesians concerning their clan totems, also the magical practices in which sharks and turtles can be called, even by children standing on a cliff and reciting the ancient ritual chants.

Owing to the surprisingly complete and complicated system of beliefs found in even the earliest traces of Huna, it seems quite possible that in it were developed the first rituals by which the Intelligences acting as "Group Souls" to guide the evolution of living creatures might be persuaded to control their charges for the benefit of men. The Nature of the Group Spirit idea also included Intelligences presiding over winds and rain. Whether or not the first rites of magical approach to such Beings were developed by the ancestors of the Polynesians, we find that such rites are spread throughout the world. American Indians perform their Rain Dance in Arizona with live rattlesnakes held in their teeth, and later release the snakes after instructing them to carry the request for rain to the gods of rain.

Similar to the selection of an animal, fish or bird by the Huna people to stand as the friend and helper of a family or clan, is the selection of a totem Nature Spirit to watch over individuals. With the American Indians the older children were often encouraged to try to make contact with the Over-soul of some creature so that it could be called upon to give help when needed. The healing practices of some of the medicine men resembled closely the modern seances in which spirits materialize and winds are made to blow, people are levitated and apports are brought. One report on a healing ceremony, written in 1840, described a bear spirit as coming when called and making a great commotion inside the large teepee in which a badly wounded warrior was to be healed—with the result that the healing was swiftly and miraculously accomplished.

The use of a totem or clan animal to identify a tribe has been customary from the dawn of history, and even in our present materialistic and scientific age, we carefully preserve the practice. The British totem emblem is the lion, the Russian the bear, while that of the United States is the bald eagle.

One thing has been noted by famous scholars in studying ancient religions, and this is that once a belief has taken form, it tends to spread and to undergo changes. The beliefs become symbolized and develop rituals. One belief after another is added, with the accumulation usually lacking a rational over-all system. The nearest to a system which is to be found is the formation of the myth, but myths touch only on fragments of belief and cover only a fraction of the gods and spirits.

The lasting quality of these beliefs is amazing. Even

when the original significance of a ritual or symbol has been forgotten, it is carefully preserved in one form or another. Because each new religious myth or belief is manufactured from pieces borrowed from those which were older, it is quite probable that parts of Huna were added to current symbols, beliefs and myths in Egypt.

In 1882, a remarkable student of ancient religions, Gerald Massey, wrote, "The Jews were caught and confined in a complete net-work of symbolism, so closely woven round them that they were cramped and catalepsed into rigidity from long keeping of the same postures, and the interstices are almost too narrow for breath to pass through. So it is with the Muhammedan and Parsee ritual of rigid rule and ceremonial routine; a religion of form in which the trivial is stereotyped for all time because of its mystical, that is, emblematical character.

"The world of thought is thronged with false births and malformations which are entirely bred of perverted typology. The theological doctrines of evil, the depravity of matter, the fallen nature of the flesh have no other basis and no other beginning.

"Religion is itself sick and daily dying in the process of unliving and sloughing off that which has been imposed upon it by a misinterpretation of symbolism.

"It is not the ancient legends that lie; the creators of these did not deal falsely with us. The falsehood is solely the result of ignorantly mistaking mythology for 'revelation' and historic truths.

"They did not teach geology in the ancient mysteries. The Christian world assumed that they did, and therefore it was found in opposition to scientific geology.

"They did not teach the historic fall of man in the myths. Theologists have assumed that they did, and consequently were found to be utterly opposed to the *ascent of man* unveiled by the doctrine of evolution. The earliest limits of the human mind have been re-imposed upon it as the latest, in the name of religion, until it looks at last as if all that faith accepted is arrayed against and at enmity with everything that science affirms to be true.

"Nor are the symbolists insane as they appear to Max Muller. There is nothing of insanity, nothing irrational in the origins of mythology, when the subject is considered in the light of evolution. The irrationality arises from and remains with the non-evolutionist view. It may be affirmed here, for it will be proved hereafter, that the Ancient Wisdom is not made up of guesses at truth, but is composed of Truths which were carefully ascertained and verified; that the chief character of the myths in their primitive phases is a most perfect congruity and that they have the simplicity of nature itself." (From THE NATURAL GENESIS, Vol., 1, pages 13–14.)

To one reading the above excerpts, it would almost seem, at this late discovery date, that Massey had in mind the ancient Huna System and its doctrine of evolution, or the body of beliefs which have been known so slightly in outer circles and which have been so misinterpreted.

11

CHAPTER 2

HUNA IN ANCIENT EGYPT

The kahunas have left no written record of their Huna system of beliefs. So far as is known, they have never allowed their language to be subjected to recording in written form, although we shall see in due time that some kahuna initiates of about the beginning of the Christian era translated the pre-Polynesian tongue into the current Greek and used that language to insert coded Huna passages into the Bible, especially into the four Gospels.

However, to continue our survey, let us leave the period of the Gospels and go back to about the year 3,000 B.C. to look for evidence of the belief in totems and taboo magic in Egypt.

As the earliest cultures developed and progressed, Totemism took on more complicated forms and, following pictures painted on cave walls or cut into stones, as at Alta Mara, in Spain, and in the earliest tombs uncovered in Egypt, writing was slowly developed. At first it was always picture writing, but some of the pictures were gradually simplified for easier drawing. For instance, on the Nile it became necessary to indicate water simply by drawing three wavy lines one above another. Instead of drawing five pictures in a row to indicate five men, only one man was drawn and after him five straight lines to show that five men were meant. An invisible thing like the spirit body of a man could not be pictured, of course, but by common consent such an invisible body was indicated by a pair of arms and hands, uplifted from the shoulders, apparently holding up something which could not be seen.

At about this same time the art of picture writing was progressing in China, in India and in the valleys of the Tigris and Euphrates. There the same process of simplification was already beginning, with signs replacing pictures. But for some lands the development of alphabets was still millenniums away. In fact, the Chinese did not, until the present century, advance past the use of simplified pictures which stood for ideas rather than for the letter sounds making up words.

Writing materials were important in the development. In Egypt the papyrus plant supplied bark strips which could be used to make a rough but practical paper. Ink was invented in various colors, and a reed with a split end served as an admirable pen or brush. In Sumeria the lack of paper influenced the rapid change from pictures to signs. Clay tablets or cylinders of moist clay were used to write upon, and as the best instrument to mark on such material was a stick sharpened to a slanting, wedge-shaped point, the signs came to be made up of combinations of little indentations, all much alike in shape and allowing almost no picture drawing at all.

In Egypt, when the change to the use of signs for sounds was made, the old pictures were retained for some time and given letter meanings, but the system was clumsy, and in much of the writing which was done in early copies of THE BOOK OF THE DEAD, sentences had to be accompanied by one or more of the old pictures to act as aids in understanding what was written in the new mode. Eventually the signs were simplified and the writing became devoid of pictures. We now call this system the "Demotic."

While the invention of writing was moving ahead in Egypt, the Totem and Taboo system was retained, coloring all religious beliefs as well as the growing knowledge of the stars and their movements. But there came a day when the Sumerians moved in and conquered the Egyptians, forcing upon them much of their more advanced culture, including their views on religion. The old religion of Egypt was not easily displaced, however, and the Totem Creatures and gods, along with the worship of the sun as the symbol of Light and conqueror of Darkness, changed only enough to absorb the new elements brought in by the Aryan-Sumerians to the darker Egyptians. Thus some 5,000 years of Totemism on the Nile began to change by about 3,000 B.C. and to include elements similar to those in Huna.

Up to the time when the Aryan-Sumerians came into power in Egypt and introduced the belief in the god, Osiris, and his wife, Isis, with their son, Horus, the chief of the Totem gods had been Ra, the sun. (Ra or La is the sun in the Polynesian dialects of the code we are to study.) Ra had created the world when he was the totem god, Tem, and from his own substance he had also created a family of gods. Some totem abstractions such as the sky and earth were personified as gods with animal bodies and heads, or with human bodies and the heads of animals or birds.

14

Many legends had developed to tell about the acts of the gods and their relation to those over whom they ruled.

When the Sumerian belief in Osiris, as the creator god, was introduced, the Egyptians promptly identified him with their Tem or Ra. They did the same with Mother Isis and the divine son, Horus. In short order they had everything adjusted and the walls of religious belief were pushed out to accomodate the old creature gods as well as the new counterparts. Ra, the sun, had long been known as the "Father," for he had created the earth through a god produced from his own substance, one Toth, who was the "Word" (and who reappears as the "word" in the Gospels much later) and who issued the orders which caused the creation of things ordained by the Father.

With the two simpler religious systems of Egypt and Sumeria joined on the Nile, a surprisingly complex new set of beliefs resulted. The salvation offered the good and just man by Osiris, who was one with his wife, Isis, and their son, Horus, in some mystical way, was complicated by the necessity of getting past a "judgment" presided over by nothing less than a group of the old totem gods. The soul of the deceased, as we learn from THE BOOK OF THE DEAD, entered the Hall of Judgment and was weighed in a balance by Maat, whose feather of truth lay in one of the pans of the scales and must not be out-weighed by the sins clinging to the soul. A monkey god sat above the scales on the top beam, to supervise the weighing, while Toth, who had invented writing and most of the arts, stood by to write down the results of the test, his ibis head impressive on his human body. At the base of the scales lay a giant crocodile god waiting to devour the soul if it failed in the weighing.

While all of this was very primitive and heavy with superstition, there were, oddly enough, Huna elements associated with parts of the beliefs. Some of these elements have been identified even at this very late date. Where they came from, or when or how, we do not know, but they were there.

Even before the Sumerian conquest, the Egyptians had what now appears to have been a knowledge of the ten elements which make up the man in Huna. Evidently the full understanding was soon lost and ideas were garbled and one mixed with another, but fragments which are listed in THE BOOK OF THE DEAD speak of Huna either directly or in symbols. The famous students of ancient Egyptian lore have done their best to bring order out of the confusion at this point and to decide just what the Egyptians of the Pyramid Age believed went into the making of the human soul. They have been hindered by the modern Christian belief that man has but one soul, and none of them has thought to ask whether one of the parts listed by the dwellers on the Nile might have been our "subconscious part of mind." (The same difficulty confronted the Christian missionaries in Polynesia when they undertook to list the parts of man which were specified in the several words used by the kahunas. The missionaries counted only one soul or spirit, while the kahunas counted three in each man.)

The heiroglyphs used to write about "souls" by the Egyptians at the time of the VIth Dynasty, give us our

16

first clue to the fact that Huna knowledge was held at the time. In Huna any bird may symbolize a spirit or "self," and in the scenes depicting the burning of souls in the ovens of hell, as found on the walls of tombs, the souls are represented as long-legged birds—the same type of bird used in the picture writing to stand for souls. In accompanying scenes the "shadows" of the souls are also being burned, and the glyph for these is the parasol, appropriately enough, for parasols cast shadows and so make a shade. (We still speak of the "shades" of the dead.)

For the "subconscious" or "low self" of Huna, the Egyptians used the symbol of the human heart, and we see a jar containing a heart being placed on one pan of the scales in scenes showing the balancing of the soul against the Feather of Truth in the Judgment. The kahunas believed that the solar plexus or bowel region was the center from which the low self presided over the body. The head was the symbol of the "conscious mind" or middle self, as in Huna, and in the burning scenes just mentioned, this self is also being burned. It is pictured as three heads. The number three is significant in this connection as possibly standing in its way for the Huna belief in the triune nature of the man, he having three souls or "selves."

Max Muller, in his book, EGYPTIAN MYTHOLOGY, Chapter X, writes:

"The doctrine of life after death was so richly developed in ancient Egypt that here we can sketch only a few of its most remarkable features. It would take an entire volume to do justice to this chapter, for no people ever showed so much care for the dead as the Egyptians, or so much imagination about the life hereafter.

"Even in the earliest prehistoric times the soul was believed to be immortal, as is shown by the gifts of food, drink, and ornaments found in all graves of that period. There was only a large tray or pot placed over the bodies, which were interred in crouching position, or a few stones or mud bricks show the gradual efforts to guard the dead against animals of the desert; but the large tombs of the kings at the beginning of the Dynastic Period commence to betray precisely the same care for the existence of the departed as was manifested in later times. In the Pyramid Period embalming begins with the kings, increasing care is given to the tombs of private citizens, and rich inscriptions reveal to us most of the views about life after death which the Egyptians kept so faithfully. We see from them that in the earliest period as well as in the latest the most contradictory views reigned concerning life after death, in harmony with the general character of Egyptian religion, which desired to preserve the ancestral opinions as equally sacred without examining them too closely and without systematizing them.

"We may infer that the most primitive period held that the spirits of the dead haunted the wide desert where the graves were situated, filling the stony mountains of the inhospitable regions by night. In consequence of their miserable abode and hard existence such spirits were not very safe company for the wanderer in the desert. The best wish for the soul of one's relatives may have been that it might become the most dangerous among all those demons, feared and respected by the rest. The custom of placing all kinds of weapons beside the dead to protect him in this life of danger, in which he is hunted by the terrible demons of the desert or of the underworld, also looks like a remnant of such primitive ideas, although it survived until the New Empire."

The respected early mythology and the developing star lore of Astronomy, all came to mingle in the ideas expressed in THE BOOK OF THE DEAD as it grew in length and complexity century after century. The old gods of early mythology were grafted to the Osiris-Isis-Horus legends and beliefs. Nothing was thrown away, and magic increased the collection of charms, amulets and special markings mentioned as of value in the Ritual to be followed by the spirits of the dead.

The element of ancestor worship which seems to have developed directly from mediumistic contact with the dead in the earliest ages, was firmly established in Egypt and was part of the system of beliefs in China. However, in Egypt the ancestors were not so much worshiped as lovingly served with periodic gifts of food and drink to sustain their souls. In addition, priests were hired to recite sustaining magical formulae at the tombs on appropriate days.

* * * * *

Before we can go on to compare the ten elements of man in the Huna system to similar elements in the Egyptian system of the period under discussion, it is necessary to pause to explain what these elements were believed to be by the kahunas. For the reader who is already familiar with Huna, this section can be passed over or read as a review.

First let us list the ten elements and compare them with those parts of man as recognized in modern Psychology.

1. Huna: Three separate selves or spirits make up the man. They may be compared with the "subconscious and conscious" parts of mind discovered by Psychology at the turn of the century. In addition, Huna has a self which may be compared with the "Superconscious" which has been postulated in some unothodox schools of Psychology. This self may be compared to the "Guardian Angel" of some religions. For convenience sake the three selves of Huna are called, the low self, the middle self and the High Self. The low and middle selves live in the physical body,

19

which is controlled in large part by the low self. The High Self lives in a "halo" type of body which is invisible and which remains outside and above the physical body, but which is connected to it by an invisible cord made of the same thin substance as the "shadow" bodies about to be listed.

2. Each of the three selves, according to Huna, has its own invisible or "shadowy" (*aka* in Hawaiian) body. During life the shadowy bodies of the low and middle selves interblend with or closely surround the physical body. After death the selves live in their shadowy bodies. The High Self lives at all times in its shadowy body. In life it may contact the physical body, but it never resides in it. Psychology recognizes no such elements, but in Psychic Science these body-covers are known to exist and are sometimes called "etheric doubles" or just "doubles."

3. Huna recognizes three kinds of vital force, one kind for the use of each of the three selves. All of these are called *mana,* but while the low self uses its grade of mana as the life force of the body, or as a mesmeric force, the middle self uses its grade as "will" or hypnotic force, this being stronger than the mesmeric force which the low self can exert. The High Self uses the mana generated in the body (as does the middle self,) but changes it in some mysterious way for its particular uses. It can control elements and forces with this "high mana" to give protection in fire-walking, and it can also be used to produce instant healing or slower healing. It is used to create the future of its man as "patterns" in the shadowy substance of its level, this future gradually becoming "materialized"

as actual events or conditions. The future which has been made in conformance with the hopes and fears and acts of the lesser pair of selves in the body may be changed by the High Self by breaking down the "patterns" in existence and making new and better ones to replace them.

Including the physical body as one, we have ten elements:

Three spirits or selves, three manas or grades of vital force, three shadowy bodies, and, during life, the physical body.

The evolution of all forms of life from the lowest to the highest is a basic concept in Huna that must be kept well in mind. In contrast to the many religious systems which teach that God created the earth, then the living things to be placed on it, all starting at a definite beginning in time and all scheduled to end eventually in some form of final Judgment, Huna raises the curtain on Creation already in the third act of the great drama. No time is lost speculating on how life was first generated or made to evolve from the lowest single-cell form of life to the highest, or man. While the kahunas brought with them to Polynesia legends of the Creation which closely match the account given in the Old Testament, they believed that an animal spirit had evolved upward until it became the animal or low self of the man. This spirit, evolving slowly, eventualy became a middle self in a man, and this self evolved and in time became a High Self.

The prime value to the Huna system of the Creation legend was contained in the story of Adam, who was divided into two parts, male and female. The peculiarity of the Huna lore is that in it alone,—and in no religion—is to be found the teaching that the sexes were separated early in the evolutionary climb, and that, only when a self rises high enough to become a High Self, are the two halves of the symbolic Adam reunited to make a complete spirit containing both its male and female parts.

The kahunas called the High Self the *Aumakua* or "Utterly Trustworthy Parental Pair." It was recognized by all initiates as the inner or secret side of Ancestor Worship, for all High Selves were thought to be members of the clan or family, and to have once been middle selves living in a body with a low self. Behind this belief lies all the romance of the theory of "soul mates," and the inner meaning of the Yoga goal of "Union." The circle divided by an "S" curve in the Yin and Yang of China is the symbol of the High Self as composed of a male and a female self—these blended into one, but still retaining in some way their individuality and sex characteristics.

The evolutionary progress of Huna is thought to be made possible by the fact that the three-self man reincarnates a number of times. It may take a dozen incarnations for the low self of a man to be less like an animal and more like a middle self, but when the lesson is learned, the low self is next born in a body as a middle self, and after another dozen or so incarnations, this middle self steps up to the High Self level, is joined there to its "soul mate" and the blended and united pair become a new High Self.

To see the picture clearly, we must think of all three of the selves of a man incarnating as a team and note that when one of the team steps up a rung on the ladder of life, the others step up also, always at the same time, never separately. The team is never broken. At the top of the ladder the High Self steps up to the level above it, called that of the *Akua Aumakuas*, or "High Self gods." There are levels and more levels above this, but these are beyond the mental grasp of the middle self man. The Ultimate and Final God is something which he can hardly imagine.

When a man steps up a rung, this leaves the lowest rung empty, and, according to Huna, a creature spirit is selected and added to the team as a new low self when the next series of incarnations begins. The secret of the Totem lore is wrapped up in this belief, but, as has been noted, only the crude and mistaken outer aspects of Totemism now remain, so far as is known, from the Eskimos of the Arctic Circle to the Aborigines in the interior of Australia.

(Note: Please see the chapter on Reincarnation for further information as to how the theory came to be recognized in Huna.)

With this brief survey of the Huna beliefs, we can return to our comparison of Huna and Egyptian beliefs. Later, as we take up the study of the coded Huna information in religious writings, especially in the Gospels, there can be more discussion of the Huna lore and of its nature and significance as it appears in various passages.

❋ ❋ ❋ ❋ ❋

In Egypt as the picture writing was slowly adapted to use as an alphabet in which sounds were indicated by certain pictures which had been simplified, changes gradually took place in the religious beliefs and these were reflected in the inscriptions on tombs and monuments as well as in the continually recopied BOOK OF THE DEAD which was placed with the mummy to guide the spirit through the hereafter.

As a result of these changes it has been difficult to learn just what words stood for the counterparts of the ten elements in Huna which have just been listed. Sir Wallis Budge, one of the authorities on the subject, does not agree with the learned scholar, Max Muller, or with the findings of the great English investigator and student, Gerald Massey. All offer slightly different interpretations of words and symbolic pictures. Budge, in giving his list, warns that there have been changes which have made exact meanings difficult to decide upon, but we will use the list as he presents it, and later note what Muller and Massey had to say.

The first element in the Huna system as well as the Egyptian is the physical body. These are the *kino* and the *khat* respectively. Both words begin with a "k" sound, but beyond that there is little resemblance despite the fact that Massey was able to assemble pages of words from the language of the Polynesians and the Egyptians which had similar sounds and meanings.

The three spirits or "selves" or souls of Huna check well with the Egyptian. The low self of the kahunas lived in the intestines, as has been noted, or we can say as did the Egyptians, in the heart, however there is no resemblance between the Egyptian word *ab*, for heart, and the word *unihipili*, in Hawaiian, meaning the animal self which presides over the life in the body. The

24

word for the "heart," in Hawaiian, is *puu wai*, which has no meaning of a "self," but symbolizes the low self as the part, *puu*, filled with water, *wai*. Water is the symbol of mana or vital force and the low self manufactures the mana and shares it with the other two selves as the veritable "water of life" mentioned in THE BOOK OF THE DEAD.

For a further comparison of the two elements, we find a most interesting thing in the Egyptian. The lesser or heart soul came back at times to visit the mummified body in the tomb, and in doing so it assumed the form of a snake, a bee or a grasshopper. The word *unihipili* has a secondary meaning of "grasshopper" and a primary meaning of the remains of the deceased person, especially his preserved bones. (The roots of the word give the meaning of the low self, and also a fine description of its characteristics.) The snake was the emblem of vital force, and in India was pictured as a serpent of force sleeping at the base of the spine, which, with proper manipulation, could be caused to rise and vitalize the entire man with its "serpent fire"—the *kundalini* in Yoga. In Egypt the bee could bring temporary life back to the mummy because it carried honey, which was the nectar of the gods, and the *sa* of the Egyptians, the divine ichor which flowed in the veins of the gods and which could be used to give life to men in the body. The grasshopper also had a magic fluid in its mouth. The Hawaiian gods when needing an extra supply of mana were said to descend to earth and take it from green things, as the grasshopper takes its magic fluid. (The *sa-hu* which we will come to shortly, was a soul raised to the god level and in its glorified light-body had *sa*, the magical force or the high mana-power of the Huna system.)

When we come to the next element for comparison, we find in the Egyptian the *ka*. This is so much like the Hawaiian *aka* or "shadow" that one may guess that the "a" had been lost from the *ka* and with it part of its significance. We know that the Egyptian glyphs when later used for sounds or syllables in words, often gave the consonant sounds but left the reader to supply the vowels. At this late time we have no knowledge of the spoken language used then on the Nile, so we must guess at what vowel sounds should go with the consonants. It is quite in keeping with the problem of the *ka* soul to decide that it was really called *aka*, and was not a soul at all, but a general term for the shadowy body of the heart self or low self. This is made more conclusive by the knowledge we have of the nature of the Egyptian concept of the *ka*. Budge says that it was "the double attached to the physical body but had individual life and could come and go from the body." (This is correct when we know the Huna belief that each of the three "selves" lives in its own "shadowy" body or *kino aka* after death, and that the selves can come and go as they please, often being seen by people with psychic ability as ghosts. The *aka* has no life of its own and is never separated from its "self.") "It had the outline and characteristics of the body and was an abstract individuality or personality . . . possessed of absolutely independent existence." (The ghostly low self, usually accompanied by the middle self, is in form a duplication of the dead physical body, and can materialize enough to be seen or even touched, as modern Psychical Research has discovered.) "The *ka*, if not offered food and drink in the tomb, might starve." (This was a mistake made by the too-literal Egyptians in the early ages when they mummified the body in the belief that the resurrection was of the actual flesh and bone body. The Huna truth which must have been known even then to the initiates, was that the spirits drew the small amounts of mana needed after death, from living relatives, and that it was the *aka* or shadowy body which survived and so could be said to be resurrected and used by the souls or selves or the man.)

The word given in the Egyptian list for "shadow" is *khaibit*, and Budge writes that it was another part of the man which was mentioned frequently in connection with his soul, and in later ages was thought to be with or near it. As has been said, this element was pictured in the writings as a small parasol or sun shade which casts a shadow. It is seen in pictures from the tombs, in which the happy life in heaven is being enjoyed by the man and his wife after their arrival there as purified souls. The man usually has a slightly pointed parasol resembling a fan in size, while the wife has one with a more rounded top, but the symbol is unmistakable, and the "shadow" as a "body" for the souls has been taken along. As these are the *sahu* souls, and as man and wife are pictured, we may guess that we have a muddled outer meaning in which two middle selves have been united to make a single High Self.

In the Huna system the middle self was called the

uhane, or a "self" unique in that it alone could talk. In the Egyptian lore much was made of the ability of the man to talk, and there were ritual prayers made at the time of the birth of a child asking that it be allowed to speak. In the after-life, prayers were included in THE BOOK OF THE DEAD to insure the ability of the deceased to speak, and a special ritual was performed to bring about the "opening of the mouth." Otherwise the words *uhane* and *ba*, in the two systems, bear little resemblance in themselves. In fact, the reversal of the heartself name of *ab*, gives us the *ba*, and remembering the lack of vowels in the picture writing one is justified in suspecting that the two selves are the same. If this is true, the Egyptian list of elements is made shorter.

We turn to the next word for a "soul," the *khu*. Budge writes: "The spiritual intelligence of a man was called khu, (Muller thinks it may have been *iku*) and it seems to have taken form as a shining, luminous, intangible shape of the body; the *khu*, like the *ka*, could be imprisoned in the tomb, and to obviate this catastrophe, special formulae were composed and duly recited."

The above description which Budge has drawn from the various parts of the Egyptian writings, contains items belonging to each of the three "selves" of the man as specified by Huna. The "spiritual intelligence" and the "shining, luminous" elements fit the High Self, whose intelligence is a level higher than that of the middle self, and whose presence is never noted as a form, but only as a white light that comes to illuminate one's surroundings for a few moments. The High Self symbol is "Light" and the sun. The "intangible shape of the body" applies to the low self, but the shadowy (*aka*) bodies are always intangible for all three selves, except when that of the low self is in some way given a temporary filling of material or substance—is "materialized," as they say when spirits come in solid flesh to visit the living at seances. None of the three selves can be confined as ghosts outside the body. That is evidently a superstitious belief which developed in Egypt along with many other such beliefs. However, this idea of confining the spirit low self may have had its origin in a practice of a degraded sect of kahunas who carried on temple worship and who used hypnotic suggestion to cause the low self spirits of sacrificed victims to remain by the temple and in some way to guard . it. The supposed "curse" placed on certain tombs and thought by some to have exerted killing influence on the explorers of the tombs after thousands of years, may also have been linked to the traditional placing of spirit guards to protect the remains of the one buried in the tomb. (The most famous and most dreaded form of the "death prayer" used in Hawaii right up to modern times, was based on the ability of a kahuna of the *anaana* class who possessed inherited low self spirits as slaves, to control them hypnotically and send them to take the vital force or mana from a living victim for three days, so that he weakened and died. Dr. Brigham fought off with counter hypnosis such an attack on one of his native helpers who had accompanied him on a botanical collecting trip into the back country. The kahuna was killed when Dr. Brigham commanded the spirits to return to him and take his vital force instead of that of the selected victim.)

The third spirit of man in the Huna system, the High Self or *Aumakua*, compares well with the Egyptian *sahu*, which Budge does not list, but which Massey finds very important. Alvin Boyd Kuhn, in his book, THE LOST LIGHT, drew heavily on the studies made earlier by Massey. Kuhn wrote, page 251, that the highest spirits in the Egyptian heavens were as gods and associated freely with them. These were the "perfected mortals," and such descriptions of them as we have, indicates that they had risen through the various places of testing and purification and had managed to reach the highest heavenly level or state as purified single souls.

The last part of the man in the ancient Egyptian list was his name, *ren*. Although it was counted as a part of the man in Egypt, it was not in Huna. On the other hand, in Huna the ability to remember one's name, or anything at all, depended upon the remembering faculty, this belonging to the low self. It did all the remembering for the middle self, and so could not be allowed to get lost from it at death, otherwise, the middle self would not know who it was. The High Self had a different and superior thinking power and did not need the low self to do its remembering. What it wanted to know, it knew perfectly and immediately by what might be called a process of identifying itself with a thing, person or event, and learning all about it. The event could be of the past, and to a limited extent of the future, the latter feature accounting for prophesy as something made possible for a man who could gain the aid of his High Self. The Egyptians believed that if one knew the name of a god, a favor could be "asked in his name," and it could not be refused. Just calling the name of a person appears to have given one a certain power to demand favors of him. To curse him it was also necessary to know his name.

The High Self, after the graduation from the level of the middle self, was given a new name, and there seems to have been a lost lore connected with the learning of this name and "calling upon" the owner of the name, when requesting help in healing or other affairs of life.

Budge sums up the listing of the parts of man as follows. (Page 192 of the book already mentioned.)

"We have seen that the entity of a man consisted of a body, double, heart, soul, spiritual intelligence or spirit, power, shadow and name. These eight parts may be reduced to three by leaving out of consideration the double, heart, power, shadow and name, as representing beliefs which were produced by the Egyptian as he slowly ascended the scale of civilization, and as being the peculiar product of his race; we may then say that a man consisted of body, soul and spirit. But did all three rise and live in the world beyond the grave? The Egyptian texts answer this question definitely; the soul and the spirit of the righteous passed from the body and lived with the beatified and the gods in heaven; but the physical body did not rise again, and it was believed never to leave the tomb. There were ignorant people in Egypt who, no doubt, believed in the resurrection of the corruptible body, and who imagined that the new life would be, after all, something very much like a continuation of that which they were living in this world . . . in the Vth dynasty, about B.C. 3400, it was stated definitely: 'The soul to the heaven, the body to earth.' "

Budge goes on to say that the belief that mummification was necessary to preserve the soul by preserving the body, passed and was replaced by a belief that by the recitation of magic formulae the dead could cause a heavenly reconstruction of the earthly body and put it to use. THE BOOK OF THE DEAD was an elaboration of such formulae and a copy was buried with the deceased so he would be sure to recite the correct words and produce a new body. In still later times, especially after Christianity took form, the Egyptians became content to rely upon the promise that when the time came for the Last Judgment, all bodies would be resurrected.

Huna would have said that in the evolutionary progress of a man, his Egyptian *ab* or low self would rise to become the *khu* or middle self and then the *sahu* or High Self. But, if the Egyptians had lost the secret knowledge that the High Self was composed of a male and female, then Kuhn's conclusion that the *sahu* represented a single soul would be incorrect.

Gerald Massey said that the *sahu* was the soul, and that after full purification, and when in its highest state, it went to live forever in heaven as one of the Osirian gods as well as one with the various gods of the totem type, among whom was the sun, Ra, as the supreme god of the older days who had become identified with Osiris, the latter being triune in nature and composed of his wife, Isis, and his Son, Horus, and himself. Muller adds to the list of man's parts the *iku(u)*, which he calls the "illuminated soul."

The Egyptian word *sekhem* is given by Budge as meaning, "Mastery over something, or power." He lists it as an "important part of the man's entity which went into heaven with him." He explains, "The sekhem of a man, was, apparently, his vital force or strength personified, and the Egyptians believed that it could, and did, under certain conditions, follow him that possessed it upon earth into heaven."

Huna tells us that this "personification" of the mana-power is a mistake which was simple to make, for the three grades of mana are as much a part of the man as his three selves and their three shadowy bodies. Mana is the life force, and without it, there can be no entity.

In Egypt, in this connection, we read in the moral axims of Ani, "Pour libations of water for thy father and mother, who rest in the valley. . . . Thy son shall do the same for thee." The Huna symbol for mana or vital force was "water," and the libation poured with actual water, symbolizes to the initiates the sharing of mana by the living with the ancestors—they always needing a small amount of the life force to keep them alive as spirits.

* * * * *

While it is most significant to find such similarities in the Egyptian beliefs, it does not prove that the ancestors of the Polynesians lived there or developed the Huna knowledge there. Tradition does not tell us where these people came from before migrating to the Pacific, but an Englishman, Reginald Stewart, in about the year 1900, found a small Berber tribe living in the Atlas Mountains of North Africa which possessed a working knowledge of Huna. Their queen was the last of a long line of kahunas, and she told of the legend preserved in the tribe that their people had lived long before in Egypt, had helped build the Pyramids with their skill in the use of magic, and had moved west to find a new home. At the time this tribe moved west, she related, eleven other tribes of the same people had left by way of the Red Sea to find the new homes in the Pacific which had been seen in visions. This woman undertook to teach Stewart the Huna lore and made a good beginning, but was accidentally killed before the lessons had gone very far. In any event, Stewart had preserved in his notes the words she used to name most of the ten elements, and these were later recognized as from a dialect similar to the modern Tahitian. At the time, the members of the tribe knew little or nothing of the "secret language" and spoke the tongue used by the Berbers.

Anthropologists, in the last few years, making elaborate studies of the customs and languages of the eleven recognized branches of the Polynesians, have decided that they originated as a small coastal tribe of fishing folk in South China, and that they had been driven out by stronger peoples and forced to find new homes in the Pacific. They were of a backward civilization and reached far islands usually by being blown away from land when fishing in their dugout canoes. All in all, they have been put down as a very primitive people, having no written language, no pottery and only the beginnings of weaving. Little is offered to tell how they came to make paper cloth or *tapa*, just as the early Egyptians made paper upon which to write, nor is any very satisfactory explanation given for the fact that these people reached Easter Island in one direction and Madagascar in the other. The fact that they had brought from some place a knowledge of Psychology far more advanced than any we have developed in this century, is not recognized.

Just how the anthropologists could explain the fact that so much pure Huna was written into the Gospels in a code dependent on a Polynesian dialect, is hard to see. Perhaps they would happily ignore the evidence, just as they have the fact that the Polynesians, when discovered in modern times, already knew the story of the Creation, of the Flood, and even of Jonah and the whale. In passing, it is amusing to note that the early discoverers decided that the Devil or else some renegade Christian priest or monk had given them the stories. But that theory failed to cover the entire lack of a knowledge of the story of Jesus. However, it is generally agreed that if there had been a contact with people who knew the Old Testament, the time was before the beginning of the Christian era and the migration had commenced before Jesus was born.

In trying to find a clue to the origin of Huna, we get little comfort from the evidence which tends to show that traveling kahunas had been in India at a very early date and had left many of their secrets with local priests—who soon forgot them, retaining only the symbols of ideas. That one of the Maori tribes which settled in New Zealand had been in contact for a time with India seems certain because its members have some of the legends of that land well enough preserved to be identified.

If we make the guess that the kahunas and their people came to Egypt in ancient times, perhaps from a Lost Atlantis, we have then to account for many time discrepancies and for the discrediting of the Atlantis theory in recent years. If the very far-fetched theory of their origin on a lost continent of Lemuria in the Indian Ocean is considered, it poses even greater problems and almost no factual evidence has been found.

The picture as it now seems to take form is one in which the people knowing and using Huna appear to have come into the Near East at a very early time and to have left some of their secret lore in the keeping of local priests so that it entered the religious thought and practices of the people. That the ancestors of the Polynesians were exclusive, must be concluded when it is seen that they must have preserved their language at all costs. This "sacred language" had, evidently, been in use during the period in which the knowledge of Huna was developing, perhaps for many centuries, and perhaps when the Sahara Desert was well watered and offered a good place to live. The whole of the Huna or "Secret" code was built upon the language and many words were given a surprising number of different meanings. It became the world's finest "double talk," and was used in the tribes to enable the kahunas to instruct their sons and daughters without the laymen of the tribes being able to understand what was being said, even if instructions were overheard by accident.

To repeat, we have no way to ascertain just what may have happened at the time around the year 1 A.D. or earlier, when the tribes began their migrations, but from the evidence to be drawn from the coded Huna in the Bible, we can be sure that after the migration there remained at least a few very intelligent and influential men who had been initiated into Huna. These men must have written in Greek to be able to insert the coded passages into the Gospels, but they also must have had a good knowledge of the "sacred language," otherwise they could not have done what they did.

One puzzling thing remains to be considered. In the coded parts of the Gospels and Gnostic literature the Huna system is not completely revealed. For instance, there is no clear exposition of the fact that there are three selves needed to make up a man. The three shadowy bodies and three grades of mana, all of which are so important to a full understanding of Huna were left out. It may have been that these elements were too difficult to put into the code, or it may be that the authors of the Gospels were not fully initiated. The latter possibility is hard to accept when we find that they knew and coded the most secret and advanced part of the entire Huna lore, that of the final union of the male and female to make a new High Self. It is also hard to imagine men who were able to handle the code as they did being but partly initiated. They could not themselves have understood Huna properly unless they had been well grounded in the knowledge of all ten elements and the further knowledge of how to use them.

CHAPTER 3

HUNA IN ANCIENT INDIA

Turning from Egypt and the Near East, we come to the India of about the same general period, and remember that there was a brisk interchange of ideas as kings often invited the wise men of other realms to visit them and impart the knowledge which they might possess. In the days of Buddhism the Buddhist missionaries traveled far and wide, and, from the evidence we find in the traces of Huna which have survived in the beliefs of early India, we may conclude that one of two things happened.

Either the kahunas traveled to India and shared their secret knowledge with the wise men of that land, or the traveling wise men made contact with the kahunas in or around the Nile, and carried home the information which had been given them. It is evident that the sharing of initiate Huna knowledge was difficult because the kahunas spoke a language which was not at all like any of the dialects used in India. As there was no written form of the "sacred language" of the kahunas, and as oral transmission had to be made then translated and written in Sanskrit syllabic characters, the task was great, and the chance for mistakes and for making blundering changes in ideas was ever present.

In trying to trace the origin of Huna, the ancient

38

Vedas of Aryan India were examined, then the Upanishads, and still later, the earliest Yoga writings. For a time it was thought that the names of the ten elements of Huna might be found to be of Sanskrit origin, but no corresponding names were discovered.

The sacred literature of early India began with gods of the totem sort, but these were less confined to the animal-gods than in Egypt. Fire and the dawn, waters and winds and rain, all these and a host of others made up the pantheon. Centuries were to pass before some sage rose to teach that all the gods were, in essence, ONE. Very little was found in the Vedic material to correspond to Huna, but in the later Upanishads, especially the ones which may have been written late in the millenium antedating Buddhism, things begin to appear which take on at an increasing rate the flavor of Huna beliefs and practices.

After the coded Huna had been discovered in the Bible and in Gnostic writings, it was hoped that similar code units might be found in the later writings of India, but nothing of the kind has so far been located. However, as the literature of India is so vast, such a discovery might come later. It took six volumes to contain the Vedic hymns alone, after Max Muller had finished translating them from the Sanskrit, and there remains a considerable number of the sacred writings which are still to be translated and published in a Western language.

In the literature of the Theosophical Society, which was organized by Mme. Helena Blavatsky before the turn of the present century, there was made available to the lay student in the West a digest of the main beliefs of India. This digest, even with some items still not well understood, served one very important purpose: it listed the elements in Indian beliefs which will bear comparison to the ten elements of Huna and the similar ones of Egypt.

Instead of ten elements, as in Huna, the Theosophists listed seven and called them the "Seven Principles of Man." On one or two of these there was a lack of agreement as to the exact nature of the thing named, but on the whole, the list was excellent and offered an immediate opportunity for comparison.

Here is a rough listing as given in Powis Hoult's DICTIONARY OF THEOSOPHICAL TERMS.

(1) Atma, Spirit. (Basic meaning is "breath.") (This checks with the Egyptian Sahu and the Huna High Self.)

(2) Buddhi, spiritual soul. (This is evidently lower in quality than the Atma and checks nicely with the khu of Egypt and the middle self of Huna.)

(3) Manas, mind. (This, with the following "kama" element, combine to check with the ab-ka or heart-soul self of Egypt, and with the low self of Huna.)

(4) Kama, feeling. (The kahunas believed that the low self produced all feelings and all emotions as well as being capable of recording and reproducing all events as memories, but it had only inferior reasoning powers.)

(5) Prana, life. (This is a Sanscrit word and it has also the basic meaning of "breath." In this way it points to the Huna method of deep breathing to accumulate more mana or life force. (Mana was a poor word for the Sanskrit-speaking sages to use as it had the meaning of "to think," which does not fit Huna concepts. The Sanscrit word is basically the root "man." For the Yoga system prana remained a single element only for a short time. Soon the speculative tendency caused the division of the prana into a special kind for almost every act and thought of man. The resultant grades were a far cry from the three kinds of mana in Huna.)

(6) Linga-sharira, the etheric double. (Here we have the khaibit of Egypt and the aka or shadowy body of Huna. But where Huna had a shadowy body for each of the

40

three selves, the three became one in the other systems, unless the ka of Egypt may also have represented the shadowy body of the middle self khu.)

(7) Sthula-sharira, the physical body. (Here all three systems agree.)

Hoult continues, "But there is confusion here between the 'bodies' and 'principles,' between objective and subjective, and it would appear that it is to the fivefold universe—not to the sevenfold—that man, as thus described, is related. The analysis, then, is by no means satisfactory. Objectively considered, man is, perhaps, best described as consisting of a Mental Body —Causal or Manasic—, an Astral Body, and a Physical Body—Dense and etheric. These correspond with, and are in relation to, 'the three worlds'; and it is through, or by means of, these bodies that the 'Principles,' the Jivatmic expression, manifest themselves. Higher than these three worlds, existence is Arupa or formless, and the 'Principles' are Divine rather than human."

From the above quotations we can see how difficult it is to draw from the six great systems of thought and belief of Hinduism and reach agreement even on very general lines. The Taraka Raja Yoga system counts four divisions, the Vedanta five, Theosophy seven, and Huna, as we have seen, gives us ten. In addition to the parts of man, there are counted in some systems seven planes or levels of consciousness.

The term "astral" as applied to the aka or shadowy bodies of Huna, is misleading because it is derived from the word for "star" and connotes faint light from the stars. This fails to match the idea of a "translucent substance," and "etheric substance" serves little better. The word *aka*, in Hawaiian, means "the shadow of a person," just as *khabit* does in the early Egyptian, so the idea of dim light as from the stars might also do as a symbol, but not as a term descriptive of the invisible but actually material substance of the three shadowy bodies inhabited by the three selves of Huna.

The nearest counterpart word to be found in Sanskrit is *"akasha,"* which may in some way have made use of the root *aka*. The meaning here is "light" or "etheric substance," but, (explains Mme. Blavatsky) "this is not the ether of science." The Sanskrit word, *akara*, may use the *aka* root for it means, "Form; appearance; or substantial form," and this would cover the ghostly "materializations" at seances as well as the Huna theory that all things and events are first built in this tenuous substance before becoming materialized in the physical world.

In India we find the word *guna* in Sanskrit meaning "a string or cord," and an elaborate explanation has been offered to show in terms of such a cord how the many lives, or reincarnations, are "strung" on the enduring and invisible cord so that there can be a continuity of sorts, and so that the "karma" or "cause of results" can be allowed to function from one life to the next.

The Vedantists believed that their *manas-sutrama* or "thread soul" was the part of the man which was carried over from life to life. The "causal body," listed by some Theosophists, serves a similar purpose. Dr. Annie Besant was at pains to point out that the accumulated experience of many incarnations is retained in a special "body" which belongs to the one single Divine Self of which the lower expressions are transitory. The Divine Self is the "ego, the Thinker" and is "formed of matter in the three highest subdivisions of the mental plane. The growth of the permanent body which, with the divine consciousness, forms the Thinker, is extremely slow. Its technical name is the causal body because he gathers up within it the results of all experiences, and these act as causes, moulding future lives. It is the only permanent one among the bodies used during incarnation, the mental, astral and physical bodies being reconstituted for each fresh life; as each perishes in turn, it hands on its harvest to the one above it, and thus all the harvests are finally stored in the permanent body; when the Thinker returns to incarnation, he sends out his energies, constituted of these harvests, on each successive plane, and draws round him new body after new body suitable to his past."

This tendency to collapse the lower and middle selves into the High Self is entirely in keeping with the Yoga idea of later centuries in which the only real self is the High Self, the others all being unreal, temporal and part of the great illusion fostered by the Goddess Maya for the blinding of man. The early Vedic beliefs mixed poorly with the muddled ideas of Yoga which were perhaps drawn in part from Huna. The mixture that resulted was even farther away from the simplicity of Huna.

In Huna the memories are believed to be stored by the low self as thought-form clusters made of the shadowy aka substance and held together by mana. These clusters are stored in the shadowy body and are carried along when one dies, leaving the physical body. However, the elaborate *guna* idea or that of an endur-

43

ing "causal" body is not found in Huna. In Huna, as we have seen, the High Self is believed to have a far superior way of remembering anything and everything, and it is responsible for the circumstances of birth in each incarnation, placing the lesser selves in such surroundings as will best serve to allow them to continue to learn the lessons of life. The idea of "karma" is one of exact reward and punishment, but in Huna the belief on this point is that the High Self administers a more flexible form of justice.

It is a simple matter to make the elements of man as given for India conform to the ten in Huna. We can list the three selves as, "The Thinker" for the High Self; the "higher mind" self for the middle self; and the "lower self" for the low self.

The "astral" body can be divided into three varieties, one *aka* body to fit each of the three selves.

"Prana" (mana) can easily be divided according to the use made of the basic life force by each of the three selves, giving us simply three *pranas* (manas) or vibratory rates of the same force.

Many other things can be found in the beliefs and practices of India which seem to indicate an early contact with Huna, but the mention of these will suffice for the moment. Later we will come back to have a closer look at Buddhism.

CHAPTER 4

THE CODE AND ITS CONSTRUCTION AND USE

As the whole structure of this presentation of the mystery lore behind religions either stands or falls on the question of whether or not there was a code, and on the further question of whether we have learned the proper way to unravel it, we will do well to pause before going on, and to inspect with care the method used in constructing the code and in applying it.

The kahunas of old seem to have constructed a language to embody the code, and, in addition to placing secret meanings in words through the roots of which they were made, a series of words which contained no code roots were used as symbols—as in the case of the word *wai*, meaning "water," and symbolizing the kind of mana or vital force used by each of the three selves of the triune man.

The symbol words did not form a code which could be broken, but after the code section of the Huna mystery lore was broken, it made possible the understanding of the complicated meanings which were covered by the symbol words. The two parts of this verbal puzzle interlock so perfectly that it might be said that no more perfect code system has ever been evolved.

In addition to the construction of almost an entire language to carry the code words, it was necessary, we must conclude, to find a way to preserve that language by teaching it to an enduring race of people and causing it to become the everyday means of communication of the race. We can only speculate about how or where or when this feat was accomplished, for all we have now to work with is the end result in the language of the Polynesians and the code which is contained in the several existing dialects.

Despite the almost unbreakable nature of the code, once it has been broken and the secret meaning of the symbol words has been grasped, the system is charming in its simplicity and in the ease with which it can be used. The language was so constructed that there were almost no changes in words to indicate tense, time, gender and the like. Grammatical case and number were indicated also by adding small root words to the principal verbs, nouns, adjectives and adverbs. Only the pronouns changed, but aside from the word for "I," *au*, none of them were used as a part of the code. Owing to this simplicity of structure, a person with no knowledge of the Polynesian tongue can take the New Testament with its Hawaiian and English passages given side by side, and with the aid of a word list begin at once to hunt out the code words and test their root meanings for possible secret intimations.

The kahunas of old may well have considered the low self or "subconscious," as we have come to call it, one of the most important elements in their highly developed system of Psychology. In any event they took elaborate pains to construct a word to name this self, and managed in its roots to code meanings which give a remarkable description of its characteristics. The name given was *unihipili*, and in time the "a" was worn off at the beginning so that it must be replaced for study purposes to give us the original *aunihipili*, or the alternate form of the word *auhinipili*, which, when used, supplies a few more roots to carry code meanings. It will be noted also that the roots overlap, with borrowing often made from the sound at the end of one root part taken to add to the next. Remembering that *au* is "a self" or "I," we can go ahead with the analysis of the word and the discovery of the secret meaning built so expertly into it—with all of the secret values neatly hidden from the uninitiated by the simple common meanings which we will begin by listing.

1. *Unihipili* (or *uhinipili*): grasshopper. (Recall the Egyptian belief that the "soul" returned as a grasshopper to the tomb to visit the mummy, and that in the dark spittle of its mouth possessed a magic fluid to revive the remains.)

2. The second meaning is that of the arm and leg bones of a dead person, these being cleaned and preserved in Polynesia instead of the entire body in the form of the mummy. Chiefs who were thought to be so great that they became lesser gods soon after death, were often worshiped, with their preserved bones becoming objects of veneration. (This was the outer portion of the belief, the inner or secret part being the understanding that a good chief might have graduated to become an *Au-makua* or High Self. In this we can see the elements of the outer form of ancestor worship.)

With only these two common meanings attached to

47

unihipili, it can be seen how beautifully the secret meaning was protected. A century ago when the able linguists among the first Christian missionaries to visit Hawaii set about translating the Bible into the native tongue, they entirely overlooked the fact that three "selves" were recognized by the kahunas, and that each had its own special name. They selected the name for the middle self, *uhane*, and used it for all the "selves," even for God, as "the Holy Spirit," (*Hemolele* (A) *Uhane*). (The superiority of the Hawaiian dialect over the others used in Polynesia is to be seen in a number of instances in which words important to the code appear only in the Hawaiian, as in the case of *unihipili*, which is not listed even by Tregear in his inclusive dictionary of the several tribal variations of the language.)

Starting with the *u* or *au* root as found in the word for the low self, we can list the meanings and see how they identify the three selves, after which we can concentrate on the roots describing the low self and its nature.

1. *Au*, as in *Aumakua* has the literal translation of "I" plus "parents." This is the High Self or united pair of parental or older and more evolved selves.

2. (A)uhane or uhane, means a self, and the root *hane* means to whimper, cry or talk, so we may say that the middle self, which is named, is characterized as, "the self which talks." This is an excellent way of describing it in contrast to the low self, which, in common with all other animals, lacks the gift of speech. Neither does the High Self speak in words, so the self which we know in Psychology as the "conscious mind" is peculiar in this respect and one very much set apart.

48

3. The next root in *unihipili* takes a letter from the au root, and so we call such roots "overlapping." This root is actually taken from the alternate word, *uhinipili*, and is *uhi*, carrying the very important meaning of "a veil" or "to be veiled or concealed." And, as we well know, the low self is indeed the "veiled" or hidden self —being so hidden that modern Psychology is still uncertain of its existence and uncertainly classes it as a "part" of the conscious mind self. This root also repeats the information that the low self cannot speak. It has a secondary meaning of a voice which is smothered, hidden or drowned out.

4. *Uhini*, means "small," and also the young of an insect, the grasshopper. In this we are made to understand that the low self is the youngest of the three, the middle self adult, and the High Self "The Ancient of Days," or as Isaiah puts it, "The Time Father." In this we have the orderly growth in terms of evolution neatly inserted into the meanings of the whole word. (The alternate spelling of the word gives us this root as *unihi*, which also means "small."

5. *Hi*, means "to flow away," as water, also "to blow out with force any liquid from the mouth." In this root we have the low self as the one who, like the grasshopper which creates the magic fluid in its mouth, creates the mana or vital force which is symbolized by "water." The mana, therefore, may flow from the low self to the middle self in the natural and usual way, or it may be sent with force as a "flow" along the shadowy cord to the High Self. (By now it will be seen that the code was so constructed that unless one already knows something of the Huna mechanisms, it

will be almost impossible to understand the secret meanings given in words and roots.)

6. *Pili*, gives us first the root *pi*, which repeats the very important information that this self makes the "water" (or mana) "flow." It "sprinkles water" slowly and stingily, as a rule it can be made by the middle self to "throw water with the hand," or send it as mana to the High Self in generous portions. The meaning of "stingy" also shows that the low self is a selfish animal self which must be taught generosity by the middle self. The full root word, *pili*, has nineteen variations of meaning and gives in them the general meaning of two selves which interblend, match or coincide, like two boards joined together, then "To cleave to or adhere, to be united or joined," and this description of the relationship of the two selves fits them exactly. But the middle self is more evolved and much wiser. To it falls the duty of watching over and guiding the low self as a younger brother—a meaning we see in, "To become one's to account for or take care of." The meaning of "adhere" becomes "sticking to" in the doubled root, *pili-pili*, and because we know from other words and the general lore of Huna about the aka or shadowy cord and the threads of the same material, we are able to see why the low self is said to be "sticky." It is like a spider who spins out strands of web, these sticking to the things they touch and making a connecting strand between the spider and something else. Every time we touch someone, the low self fastens to it an invisible thread of the shadowy substance of its shadowy body, and in this way a contact

is made which could possibly be used for sending telepathic messages from one person to another.

7. *Nihi* is very descriptive of the low self of which we are so dimly aware. It is likened to someone hiding and working behind the scenes with the wish not to be discovered. The root gives these meanings: "To walk very softly and carefully," "To do a thing quietly, silently or secretly, unseen by others." Then there is the very significant meaning of, "To abstain from doing certain things for fear of the gods," in which we see that the low self, when it feels that it is guilty of sin, will refuse to do its part in praying to the High Self, who stands as a god in its relationship to the lesser pair of selves.

Having seen how the code was made and how we must handle it to get at its hidden meanings, we are ready to continue with the broader outlines of our study.

CHAPTER 5

THE CODED MYSTERY TEACHINGS
IN THE BIBLE

From the time of the writing of the Four Gospels (generally thought to have been from A.D. 80 to 90), the most learned Christians have striven to discover just what was contained in the "mysteries" which Jesus mentioned immediately after calling his Disciples and beginning to teach them as his "chosen" or "elect." We read, Mark 4:11, "Unto you it is given to know the mystery of the kingdom of God: but unto them that are without, all these things are done in parables."

Paul, who had never sat at the feet of the Master, was one of the first to embark on the work of deciding just what the "mysteries" might be. He drew heavily on the inspiration of his visions and his knowledge of the prophesies. His decision was that Jesus, in order to save mankind from the curse of Adam and the Fall, must offer himself as a blood sacrifice on the cross to atone for the sins of all such men as would accept his proffered salvation. (Or at least all such men as were "elected" by God to receive salvation as a gift.)

No one else seemed to have definite ideas concerning the mystery teachings, or, if thy did, they had been sworn to secrecy as was the custom of the time when one was initiated into the mysteries of any of the religious cults. In the face of the silence of the

Disciples on this crucial point, the Pauline conclusions were soon accepted on all sides, and the work of spreading the "Good Word" went forward on that basis. Nor did there come changes or corrections as century followed century. Today we have in all standard branches of Christianity the mysteries as Paul supposed them to be.

In a careful study of the outer meanings of the words of Jesus, as recorded in the Gospels, we fail to learn what the mysteries contained. Mark gives us several parables, and we read, 4:33-34, "And with many such parables spake he the word to them, but privately to his own disciples he expounded all things."

As a matter of fact, Jesus apparently expounded the meaning of the parables quite openly to all of those who gathered to hear him. He explained, Mark 4: 14-15, "The sower soweth the word. And these are they by the wayside, where the word is sown; and when they have heard, straightway cometh Satan, and taketh away the word which hath been sown in them."

We have nothing at all that we can say was taught as very secret and as reserved to be told only to the "elect" or the Disciples. There is not a single utterance in the recorded teachings which we may suppose was not also open to any who wished to listen and to try to understand.

It is upon the word "understand" that the explanation of the mysteries must hinge. He must have said something from time to time which had an outer meaning so open that it could safely be written into the Gospels when the time came, but which contained in the words or phrases some coded or hidden meaning.

For years, and especially in modern times, men have tried to find a key to the nature of the mysteries, and through the key the code which might unlock all doors. Several books have been written in which claims were made that a code had been discovered which unveiled the mysteries, but in every case arbitrary meanings were assigned to common words, and the only proof offered to show that the meanings were significant was that the writer vouched for his own claims. In every case these mystery codes could be made to apply to only a very few carefully selected passages. When a general application was attempted, the system inevitably broke down. What little was supposedly revealed by giving special meanings to certain words had no relation to a hidden teaching or to one not already made open to all in the Gospels.

It has long been recognized that very little is actually known as historical certainty concerning the life and work of Jesus. His appearance and characteristics are unknown.

After the Dead Sea Scrolls had been discovered at Qumran in 1947, it was hoped that their translation would turn up information on the mystery teachings, or at least give new insight into the origin of Christianity. But, although efforts were made to connect in some way the "Teacher of Righteousness," mentioned in one scroll, with Jesus, there was little or nothing to go on.

Slightly more fruitful was the discovery at Chenoboskion, in Egypt, of early Christian documents written in one of the Coptic dialects. These had been the property of a monastery and had been buried in jars in a cemetery. Several versions of the brief, "Sayings of Jesus" as well as the short, "Gospel According to Thomas" gave material which had not been included in the canon when the New Testament was frozen into the final form in which it has come down to us.

The Gnostic literature, which we will consider in more detail in a later chapter, contains accounts of what Jesus said, with slightly different material presented in different ways. The "TRICE GREATEST HERMES," "PISTIS SOPHIA" and "MYTHRAIC MYSTERIES" are often found to contain the mystery teachings which the Huna code reveals in the Bible, but with certain very important items left out.

The evidence of the existence of a mystery teaching behind the outer doctrines of early Christianity was mentioned by G. R. S. Mead, (whose writings we will draw upon later) in his book, FRAGMENTS OF A FAITH FORGOTTEN, pages 253–4. He wrote:

" . . . Basilides and his followers elaborated one of the most abstruse and consistent systems of the Gnosis. . . . Of the life of the great doctor of the Gnosis we know nothing beyond the fact that he taught at Alexandria. His date is entirely conjectural . . . flourishing between A.D. 120-130. . . . He was also well versed in the Hebrew scriptures. . . . The Gospel teaching was his delight, and he wrote no fewer than twenty-four books of commentaries thereon, although he does not appear to have used the subsequent canonical versions. He also quotes from several of the Pauline letters. . . . They were the first commentaries on Gospel-teachings written by a Christian philosopher.
"He also mentioned certain Traditions of Matthias, as held in great honour by the school. (Gnostic.) These purported to be teachings given to Matthias in secret by Jesus after the 'resurrection'. . . . Basilides presumably wrote a commentary on the Sayings and Doings of the Lord, which were in general circulation in many traditions, with or without the various historical settings; and his own elaboration of certain inner instructions that had been handed down by a secret tradition. . . . It is to be supposed that his commentaries aimed at explaining the

public Sayings and Parables by the light of the secret Gospel
. . . . (It is thought by some that) Matthias wrote the original
Sayings and Doings underlying our Synoptic accounts, and that
these accounts were expansions by various presbyters of the
outer churches in Egypt. The original draft was presumably a
Life intended for public circulation, and designed to be capable
of an interpretation according to the inner tenets of the
Gnosis."

One of the few bits of evidence which tends to confirm the belief that there was a mystery teaching in
the Gospels was described by Dr. Morton Smith, a
specialist in ancient religions, in a paper read before
the Society of Biblical Literature and Exegisis in the
latter part of the year 1960. (See TIME magazine,
issue of January 6, 1961.) Dr. Smith told of finding
in the back of an old book, in the library of a 5th
century monastery in the wilderness a dozen miles
from Jerusalem, a copy of a letter which purports to
have been handed down secretly from very early times.

The letter is a quotation rather than a complete
epistle, and is said to have been written by one of the
important Church Fathers, Clement of Alexandria, who
lived at the end of the 2nd century at a time when
the Gospels were in much their present form. One
Theodore, is addressed and told of a secret Gospel
account of the life and teachings of Jesus written by
Mark. The information was so secret that Clement
enjoins Theodore to deny knowledge of it even on
oath.

There was an exoteric version of the story, written
also by Mark, but given openly to anyone who might
be interested. In the secret account, it was said, certain things were divulged that were so secret that they
were not given even in the account which was reserved

for the initiate priests. This "truth" was said to be "hidden behind seven veils." (It is to be presumed that the parts omitted were passed on by word of mouth.)

* * * * *

In making this study of the Huna code in the writings which have a bearing on the life and teaching of Jesus, we are, fortunately, under no obligation to try to decide whether or not the historical version of the Life is to be relied upon. Our purpose is that of endeavoring to learn what additional light is thrown on the teachings by Huna.

In passing, it may be said that should the student decide that Jesus was not a real figure in history or that the belief that mankind must be saved because of the sins of Adam is erroneous, there is a comforting alternative. If there is no necessity for salvation from the sins of the "Fall," then there is no necessity for the sacrifice of Jesus on the cross to furnish that salvation. Removing these two necessities which have been so long stressed in Christianity, sets one free to search for a less dogmatic salvation which may be found in either the familiar outer teachings of Jesus or in the hidden teachings of the "mysteries" which Huna reveals through the code.

For the purposes of our study, a number of almost insurmountable problems can be avoided by dividing the life and the teachings of Jesus into two parts. If we accept Jesus as a living teacher and the account of his life as given in the Gospels as fairly accurate historically, we can place in the first part of the study everything, right through to the crucifixion, death and resurrection. We can look upon the resurrection as a new incarnation in living flesh, and then continue the life of Jesus into the second division, in which the experience of the Transfiguration on the mount can be lifted from the first part of the Gospel story and placed in the second.

If we conclude that the Life as given in the Gospels was a two-part mystery drama written for use in initiating candidates into the mysteries of Huna, we can at once discard the Pauline doctrine of the necessity of the blood sacrifice of Jesus. In addition, we can discard the theory that Jesus fulfilled the prophesies, accepting only what the code reveals of such fulfillment, but, as we shall soon see, the code gives no indication that the man, Jesus, had actually been forseen and the events of his life predicted, Matthew notwithstanding.

Treated as a drama used for initiatory purposes, as were many similar dramas in the several mystery cults current at the time, we find Jesus as a man who is in touch with his High Self and who heals, teaches and strives to perfect himself so that he can enter the "kingdom of heaven" which is the core of his inner teachings. Near the end of the first part or act of the drama he fails in a crucial test and loses contact with his High Self. This disaster is dramatized most impressively in his betrayal, trial and crucifixion between two thieves.

But he is resurrected in the flesh in the second part of the drama, and after further teaching, again goes up for his testing and initiation, this time being successful, and receiving the coveted Transfiguration, thus ending the drama by having him pass out of the physical world and into the "kingdom of heaven" or realm of the High Self.

The Transfiguration will be seen to be of the greatest importance in the Huna version of the Life, but for some unknown reason, its supreme value was lost in the writing of the Gospels. John, in his account, did not once mention it.

The coded material in the Bible, unfortunately, does not start at the beginning as would a teaching presenting the simple things first, then the more complicated and finally the most complicated and abstract concepts. Instead, it is given, "here a little, there a little," and whoever the writers were, they left the initiates for whom they recorded the "Secret" to fill in many places for themselves. The story of the Creation and of Adam and Eve and their fall from grace, belongs at the very end of the system as well as at the very beginning, for it explains the Transfiguration ending.

In order to make a clearer picture of the coded teachings, we can divide them into outer and inner parts. The outer teachings of the Gospels were open to all. Then came the first part of the secret teachings of the code, these covering what might be called the path to the First Salvation of Huna, after which comes the very heart of the hidden teachings, the Second or final Salvation being revealed.

We will be picking up a coded passage from any place in the Bible, especially the Four Gospels, at any time the need arises. In all cases we will be working

59

from English translations made from the Greek of the originals. The Old Testament was undoubtedly written in a Hebrew dialect in the first place, or in two or three of them. But our version dates back to the time when seventy learned Jewish scholars were brought together in Alexandria, Egypt, at the beginning of the Christian era, and put to work to translate into Greek the existing Jewish scriptures. The Gospels were written in the same Greek, that being the official language of the time. It has often been said that Jesus and those with whom he worked spoke Aramaic, but such versions of the Gospels as are to be found in that language undoubtedly were also translated from the original Greek. In a few instances one can find needed information when checking the Old Testament code passages by going back to see what Hebrew words may have been used in the original. STRONG'S BIBLE CONCORDANCE had been consulted in such cases.

For the translations from the Greek, the King James Bible is usually good, but now and then other and later translations are helpful, especially that of Fenton. In checking the code we will find all eleven dialects spoken in Polynesia helpful, but on the whole the Hawaiian seems to have been nearest to the one used in the code.

* * * * *

We are now ready to begin the study proper of the Huna code in the Bible and contemporary literature, but a word of explanation is needed. As the initiate writers of various accounts were at pains to present the basic tenets of Huna repeatedly, and from various angles lest it be overlooked, there is bound to be repetition. Once the idea of making the four-step prayer after the Huna method is grasped, the reader may be irked by finding the same thing turning up as part of the secret meaning in passage after passage. Patience must be exerted in this matter.

We found in the secret version of Mark, mentioned in the letter to Theodore a few pages back, the statement that the truths were hidden behind "seven veils," and this gives us a good point of departure for our consideration of the code.

To "veil" is to conceal, and we recall the description in the Old Testament, (Exodus: 26:31–37) of the veil which Moses was commanded to make and use in the tabernacle to separate the "holy place" from the "most holy place" in the Ark itself. This gives us two words in the Hawaiian dialect of the "sacred language" used in the code writings, and both are significant. The first, for "veil," is *pa-ku*, the 6th meaning of which is given in the dictionary which we are using as, "A uniting or joining or sewing (together) of two pieces of kapa (paper cloth)." The "most holy place" symbolized in code terms the High Self which is made up of a united male and female self, and which is the "Father-Mother" self of Huna. The sewing together of the two pieces of paper cloth gives us the symbol of the union of the two middle selves who have become a High Self. As this is probably the greatest mystery and hope of Huna, as well as the secret most revered, it is not surprising that its symbology should be found in the early Jewish tabernacle. The simple "holy place" was the place of worship outside the veil, and

61

symbolizes the initiate who is aware of the High Self hidden behind the "veil" as it is worshiped.

To be permitted to "raise the veil" had been symbolic in still earlier Egypt, where the goddess, Isis, was veiled as a statue in the temples and where only the most sacred of the high priests was allowed to lift the veil for a closer look. The second code word for "veil" is *uhi*, meaning simply "to conceal."

The "seven veils" indicate in the code seven things which were concealed, these being the three selves of the man and his three aka or shadowy bodies. These make only six, but in the seventh lies the secret of secrets, the fact that the High Self is made up of two united male and female selves, the doubling of the highest self thus making the full "seven." The first part of a kahuna's initiation covered only the knowledge that there were three selves and three shadowy bodies. The final initiation added the secret information concerning the nature of the High Self. (The three grades of mana or vital force were not classed definitely as "bodies" or "veils" in this symbology by the makers of the code.)

In the Biblical description of the building of the Tabernacle to house the Ark, the number "seven" is repeatedly found put to use in the same manner as was the single veil which was made of two parts united to make one. Outside the veil stood the altar and on it stood the seven-cupped candlestick, which was composed of a central stick from which branched out the six side pieces. The central candle, with its flame symbolizing the High Self, whose code symbol is "Light" (*la*), was, of course, most significant as well as most revealing to any who had been initiated into the secret lore.

We have seen that Huna was known in early Egypt and that its concepts have been preserved in the *ka, ba, sa, khabit* names applied to the several parts of the man. According to the Bible, Moses was born and reared in Egypt, and it is to be supposed that when he led the exodus of the Hebrews and gave them the Ten Commandments and a religion, he acted with the full knowledge of Huna as an initiate. We do not know whether he wrote the first two books of the Bible or not, but, as we are seeing, whoever wrote the originals or worked the accounts over later in copying them, inserted sections carrying the Huna code.

Much later, Jesus repeated the ascent of the mount and was there transfigured, much as Moses made his ascent and brought down the Ten Commandments as from Jehovah, himself. In Exodus 35:32–35, we have the veil mentioned again as a Huna symbol and the tale of a form of transfiguration which was experienced by Moses. We read:

" . . . and Moses talked with them. And afterwards all the children of Israel came nigh and he gave them in commandment all that the Lord had spoken with him in mount Sinai. And till Moses had done speaking with them, he put a veil on his face. But when Moses went in before the Lord to speak with him, he took the veil off, until he came out. And he came out and spoke unto the children of Israel that which he was commanded. And the children of Israel saw the face of Moses, that the skin of Moses' face shone: and Moses put the veil upon his face again, until he went to speak with him."

In his time and turn, Jesus also was in full contact with the Lord, or High Self in the person of the "Father," and, as did Moses, he spoke for the Father—

indeed, he often spoke AS the Father. Ordinarily, like Moses, he spoke for himself, the man.

So we see the thread of Huna tradition and the almost hidden Mystery coming down through the sacred literature or, as in the case of the Huna tribes who migrated to the Pacific without a written language, with the "Secret" being handed down by word of mouth. However, whether written or spoken, the language of the code had to be used to conceal the lore from the uninitiated.

CHAPTER 6

THE NATURE OF JESUS IN THE
MYSTERY TEACHINGS

Unquestionably the greatest controversy faced by the Christian fathers centered on the question of the exact nature of Jesus. All agreed that he was a man but at the same time must be God, for the scriptures were very plain on this point. Jesus had himself said, "I and the Father are one," and they thought "Father" meant God. However, there was a very strong tradition that called for this Duad to be expanded to a Trinity which would include the Holy Ghost.

The internal strife caused by this question raged for years and was finally settled by force rather than reason or scriptural authority, and the Trinitarian doctrine became supreme. It remains so today for the majority of Christians, although some have come to prefer Dualism, and a few have joined the Unitarians.

There was also the question of just when the man Jesus became the divine man. One faction insisted that the Holy Spirit and Father were born into the body of the child, Jesus. Another faction chose to believe that although Jesus had been begotten by God and not by a human father, he did not attain to his fully divine status until baptized by John. When he came up out of the water it was very clear, they held, that the Holy Spirit descended upon Jesus as the man, and abode in him from that time on. In modern times the German Theosophist, Rudolph Steiner, developed this theory in his extensive writings, coupled it with Buddhist beliefs, and won a large following. He, like many others, was confronted by the difficult question of whether God-the-Father entered Jesus at his baptism, or whether the Holy Ghost was alone involved. The argument remained as it had always been, that a male voice spoke from heaven as the Dove descended on Jesus, saying, "This is my beloved son, in whom I am well pleased. This day have I begotten him." The "begotten" idea pointed directly to a male divinity and God as the Father. But some versions of the story very plainly stated that it was the Holy Spirit or Holy Ghost that descended on him, and this kept alive the Trinitarian idea, leaving Jesus to stand as interchangeable with either the Father or the Holy Ghost. The argument for the Duad idea of God in the early Church was based largely on the statement made by Jesus (John 10:30), "I and my Father are one." But the argument is just as well grounded for the Trinitarian belief because Jesus also said, (Matt. 28:19) "Go ye therefore, and teach all nations, baptizing them in the name of the Father, and of the Son and of the Holy Spirit."

If the recovery of the knowledge contained in Huna and revealed through the coded passages of Holy Writ did no more than settle this question, the research effort would have been greatly worth while.

Let us return to Egypt for a moment to get a background against which to view the problem as a whole. The Egyptians, upon a part of whose early religion the concepts of Christianity may have been modeled, recognized a Triune God in the form of Osiris, the "Father," his wife, Isis, the Mother or "Holy Spirit," and Horus, their divine "Son." In a rather poorly defined way the three were "one," each with the other, and equal and interchangeable in being and power.

The Hebrews, under Moses, borrowed from the Egyptians but adopted a more simple concept of God. For them Jehovah, their tribal god, was a single unit, at least in so far as the outer teaching given to the masses was concerned. (The esoteric teaching is thought by some to indicate a Duad because both the Ark of Noah and of the Covenant were boat-shaped and may have been symbols borrowed from the Egyptian worship of Isis, or the worshipers of Asarte and Venus-Aphrodite elsewhere—these female deities being represented, as in India, by the use of the *Argha* or boat-shaped sign of the female generative organ.)

Huna comes into the picture when the Hebrews called their God, Jehovah, by the title of "Lord," or, in the Hebrew, *adow*, from which came the word *Adoni*. The basic meaning of the word is "to wash the body all over." In other words, the Lord was washed clean. He was the perfectly cleansed one, the anointed one, or, in terms of the Gospels, the baptized one. This cleansing was symbolic and belonged to certain religious rituals which cleansed one of sin and made one a part of a superior religious fraternity. The Egyptians came eventually to do their "anointing" with perfumed oil, and in the Greek this is to *chrisom*, and from that word came "Christ," or he who was cleansed, anointed and made superior.

None of this gives us a secret and greatly significant meaning other than in the ceremonial washing as a part of a priestly act of forgiving one his sins. In the Huna code, we get at the secret meaning. The code word for "Lord" is *haku*, and the meanings of the two root parts, *ha* and *ku* give us, roughly, "prayer" plus the meaning of "the one whom the prayer reaches." Filling in, as an initiate must, we know that all prayer is addressed under the Huna system to the High Self of the one making the prayer. No prayer is addressed to Ultimate God. If it is thought necessary to call for help which the High Self cannot give, as in the case of asking aid for an entire nation, the High Self is asked to pass the prayer on to as high a Power as is thought necessary. Praying in this manner ties in with the custom of "asking in my name," thought by many to have originated in the teachings of Jesus. In Huna one may address the Highest God but always through the intermediary High Self, in whose name the help is asked.

Owing to the partial acceptance of the Old Testament and its teachings by Jesus, a strange muddle ensued. The Christians possessed a single God in Jehovah to whom they prayed, and they possessed also the new God who was "Three in One"—a divine Trinity made up of the Father, the Holy Spirit and the Son, who was Jesus. This very apparent contradiction is almost entirely over-looked in the modern churches.

In Huna the High Self is the "Father," and he is called the *Aumakua*, or "I-Parent." The theory of evolution taught by Huna makes the High Self the oldest and most evolved of the three selves which make up the man. But, and here is a deep secret in Huna, a "parent" demands that there be a mother to match the father, so we have the Holy Spirit or female counterpart who is "one" with the "Father." The lesser man made up of the low and middle selves is their "son."

Huna composes all differences in a very simple manner by making the "Father" include the "Mother" or Holy Spirit, whose identity was lost in the outer teachings because she was made a blended and absolute part of the Father in the inner teachings—which were those of Huna.

The extremely troublesome contraindication found in the statement, "I and the Father are one," is, likewise, given its proper meaning when we learn from Huna that man is made up of three selves, and that the High Self or "Father-Mother Self," is "one" with the low and middle selves, just as they are with it. If any one of the selves were to be removed, there would be no man according to the belief.

The "oneness" has also the meaning of being in full contact with the High Self. Moses set the pattern when he made the contact and gave the children of Israel the "commandments" as the very words of the Lord. Jesus, as has been explained, made the same contact, according to both the outer teaching and the inner, and at times he spoke for the High Self or as if he himself were the High Self "Father." At other times he spoke as the lesser man made up of the low and middle selves. In the Gospel accounts there is nothing at any time to indicate whether Jesus is speaking for himself when standing before those he addressed, or for the High Self "Father."

In our study of the code we have to decide for ourselves, with the reading of the various passages, just which position Jesus is taking and whether he is speaking for the "Father" or for the "son of man," the lesser pair of selves.

There can also be some confusion produced if we do not understand that the word, "one" is a triple symbol in Huna. It stands for (1) the fact that the three selves are one in that they are joined to make the man, (2) the lesser pair of selves make a closer contact with the High Self during the Huna type of prayer action, and are said to be "one" when this contact is made, (3) the Father and Mother halves of the High Self are permanently united to make one self.

The Father-Mother idea is not strictly Egyptian in origin. It is similar to the Hindu concept of the gods and their wives. With the early Hebrews, the very thought of a human being saying that he was "one" with Jehovah would have been blasphemy, indeed. It was so considered when the listeners mistook the meaning of the words of Jesus as he said that he and the Father were one, and they took up stones and would have stoned him had he not managed to escape. In the Old Testament the term "father" is applied to Jehovah only a few times, and in this respect as the Father or Creator, not as an individual father, even for as great a priest as Moses.

Keeping in mind these several things revealed by

the code, let us consider a few passages in which the "Father" is mentioned in the Gospels.

Matthew, 23:9 gives us, "And call no man your father upon earth: for one is your Father, which is in Heaven." The passage is most contradictory, each of us having an earthly father, but in the sense that the High Self is the Father-Mother on the higher or heavenly level, all becomes reasonable. The word "one," as we have seen, is code for the united male and female selves who make up the High Self "One."

Matthew, 10:37 reads: "He that loveth father or mother more than me is not worthy of me: and he that loveth son or daughter more than me is not worthy of me." In this passage we may wonder why Jesus should be so loved. The usual answer is that he is God and the Savior who will save us from eternal damnation. The inner teaching is simple when we see that here Jesus is speaking as the High Self, not as the man of the lower pair of selves. He is stressing the necessity of coming to know that the High Self "Father" is part of the triune man, and that it is nearer to us than any father, mother, son or daughter in the flesh could possibly be, and more deserving of love, even of worship. It should be noted that the symbols of the code are being used here rather than the words and roots with their multiple meanings. The Huna symbol of the "Father" stands always for the High Self.

In Mark, 13:31–32, we have the coded passages: "Heaven and earth shall pass away: but my words shall not pass away. But of that day and that hour knoweth no man, no, not the angels which are in

71

heaven, neither the Son, but the Father." To understand what is said here, we must know the Huna belief
that only the High Self can see into the future to a
limited extent. The angels are the spirits of the dead,
not High Selves, and Jesus as the Son is the lower
man. These have no ability to see into the future as
does the High Self. The "words" mentioned here as
never "to pass away," may well be the Huna code
words themselves.

The kahuna who placed coded passages in Luke,
or who may have written this account in its entirety,
says, (Luke, 10:22) "All things are delivered to me of
my Father: and no man knoweth who the Son is, but
the Father; and who the Father is, but the Son, and he
to whom the Son will reveal him." This is simply to
say that the lower man knows his High Self when he
becomes an initiate, and that, of course, the High Self
knows the lesser pair of selves far better than anyone
else possibly could. The inner teaching, we see, is one
in which the Son, knowing well his Father, reveals the
secret of the triune man to his chosen followers. All
things (or knowledge and ability to work with the
High Self to produce miraculous results) are said to
be given to the Son by the Father. That is straight
Huna. Each man or woman is a Son, and each has a
Father-Mother High Self with whom to work, once the
way of working is known.

John, 1:14, mentions the "Father." We read: "And
the Word was made flesh, and dwelt among us, and
we beheld his glory, the glory as of the only begotten
of the Father, full of grace and truth." The "Word"
in this case is the High Self in so far as the "glory" is

concerned, as this is a symbolic attribute of the High Self. But, as the triune self is "made flesh," the reference passes to the Son, or lesser man. In saying that he is the "only begotten" we cannot have the human begetting and so know that this must be a symbol of similar creative activity on the level of the High Self.

Jesus did not call himself "the only begotten son of the Father"—a dogma accepted as part of the doctrine of the Church. It was the writer of the Fourth Gospel, whom we know as John, who wrote this as his own statement, and in doing so he revealed the fact that he was an initiate kahuna and that he wanted to pass on a bit of the secret information through the use of the code.

The word for "begotten" in the code language is *hiwa-hiwa*. It means, "much loved." As the word is doubled to increase the meaning or strength of the love so expressed, we look at half the word, *hiwa*, and find that it means "something totally acceptable which is offered as a sacrifice to a god." (This is mana, as we shall soon see.)

Continuing, we read, John 14:7–11, "If ye had known me, ye should have known my Father also: and from henceforth ye know him, and have seen him. (As a very part of the three-self man, Jesus.) Philip, saith unto him, Lord, show us the Father, and it sufficeth us. Jesus saith unto him, have I been so long a time with you, and yet thou hast not known me, Philip? He that hath seen me hath seen the Father; and how sayest thou then, Show us the Father? (It is evident that Philip was not a finished initiate.) Believest thou not that I am in the Father, and the

Father in me? The words I speak unto you I speak not of myself: but the Father that dwelleth in me, he doeth the works. Believe me that I am in the Father; and the Father in me: or else believe me for the very works' sake."

We have examined several passages in which the "Father" is mentioned, and there are a number of others which are significant, but in almost every passage the coded information is so set forth that it covers several of the basic elements in Huna. For this reason we will pause in our study of the nature of Jesus and the "Father" while we familiarize ourselves with something which is constantly being added directly, or by the code words or by Huna symbology in passages which, to all outer appearances may be speaking of a single item or topic.

CHAPTER 7

THE *HA* PRAYER RITE AS THE FIRST
GREAT MYSTERY

Before going further with the general story of the life of Jesus, as given in the Gospels, our study will be made much easier if we bring together in one unit the many coded references to the secret method of making the Huna type of prayer.

This method will be called, for convenience sake, "The *Ha* Rite." In it lies the greatest promise of the First Act of the initiatory drama. In it is offered a workable method of getting the help of the High Self through a special method of prayer.

The Lord's Prayer, which belongs to the outer teachings, contains a few code words, but not enough to explain the method of the inner teaching in full. Only enough is inserted in the prayer model to call attention to the complete Ha Rite which an initiate familiar with the code would have learned as almost the first step in his training.

The Church, not knowing the inner teachings, made the mistake of thinking that when Jesus said (Matt. 6:6) ". . . pray to thy Father which is in secret; and thy Father which seeth in secret shall reward thee openly," he meant pray to Jehovah, the God of the Jews. This mistake was compounded by a passage in John (14:13) which reads, "And whatsoever ye shall ask in my name, that will I do, that the Father may be glorified in the Son." As a result of trying to strike a happy balance between these two passages, the Church promulgated the dogma that Prayers should be addressed to Jehovah, but in the name of the triune God consisting of Jesus as the Son, and the Father and the Holy Spirit. Matthew and Luke mention the Lord's Prayer. Mark made no mention of the prayer form, neither did he speak of "asking it in my name." John also omitted the Lord's Prayer, but put in the "ask in my name" idea.

In the preceding chapter we examined the nature of the "Father," and saw that He was not Jehovah. We also examined the nature of Jesus, and saw that he spoke first as the Man, then as the High Self. When, in John, he promises to do what is asked in prayer addressed to the Father, "in my name," he is using the code idea behind "name," which in this case is a concealed reference to the use of the "word of power" or the Ha Rite in which, when one knows the "name" or High Self and how to pray to it, the magic of the "answer" will be forthcoming. (We have already noted the Egyptian belief that if one knew the name of a god, one could oblige that entity to do one's bidding by speaking the name.)

The Huna method of making the prayer which calls down miracles in response, is based on the use of breathing exercises in which four deeper and slower breaths are taken at a time, and during which exercise the middle self commands the low self to accumulate or create an extra amount of mana. The mana, once created, is held in readiness while the second step is taken by the low self in response to the orders of the middle self, this step being that of reaching out to find the High Self at the far end of the connecting shadowy or aka cord. When this contact is successfully made, the third step is taken, that of sending the surcharge of mana as a "sacrificial gift" to the High Self to give it the strength to form the "answer" to the prayer. The prayer is sent as a mental picture on the flow of mana as it rises to the High Self, and, if all has been properly done, the Ha Rite is well under way. By daily repetition of the act of making the prayer, the mana is supplied to the High Self for as long as it may take to bring about changes needed to give the "answer."

That in brief, is the magical method of prayer as divulged by the code. By keeping this outline in mind, one will be able to follow the explanation of the coded elements which follows.

To begin with, the clever makers of the code concealed in the numbers used in counting up to four (the four long breaths), a quantity of side-light explanations. And for the number "four," they used two names, *ha* and *kau-na*, in this way being able to make use of the many secondary or code meanings of both words. Outwardly, one is instructed by the use of the word *ha* to take four strong breaths. Inwardly, the reasons for doing this are to be found in the several code meanings of the names for the numbers, 1, 2, 3, 4: or *kahi, elua, kolu* and *kauna* or *ha*. Let us examine the numbers and their hidden meanings.

Ka-hi: "one." This word, as the maker of the dictionary explains, was often used in place of one pronounced at times in almost the same way, *ka-he,* both have the meaning of "to cut longitudinally," (split open) which was, with the Huna people, "to circumcise." Behind this strange custom of circumcision, which has spread around half the world and which even the Australian Arunta people practiced, lies the secret meaning of sacrifice—the sacrifice of a part of the creative or life force. The male sex organ was symbolic of this creative force, and with many ancient peoples the circumcision rite was one of great importance. It was accompanied by special acts and, with some tribes was part of the initiation of a boy into the estate of manhood.

It is most interesting to find that there was no defi· nite reason given in the Bible where, in Genesis 17: 10–27, God was said to have spoken to Abram, ordering him to establish a new covenant between his people and their God. In this covenant all males were to be circumcised, but no reason was given for the command. One suspects the reestablishment of an older custom, or the borrowing of one from some other religion. The Huna system would seem to be the most likely source as it was evidently older, and as it gave in its secret word code a reason for the practice.

This reason is to be seen in the code words and their roots. *Oki* is "to cut," and *omaka* is the "fore· skin." That gives the outer meaning. The code meaning comes from the secondary meanings of the words or roots. To cut is also *kahi*, meaning (1) The Number One; (2) A place; and (3) the pronoun, one. As "cut" it has the meaning of "opening," and in the alternate word, *kahe* the secondary meaning is "a flow of blood." The thing to be opened by cutting, and

78

with the accompanying flow of blood, is the *omaka* or foreskin, but this word also means, "the fountain-head of a stream of water" (water symbolized mana), and in this we have the secret. The covenant was one established in Huna with the godlike High Self, and the creative force or mana was to be sent as a gift or sacrifice. The cutting, foreskin and blood flow stand as outer symbols for a pact or pledge to supply the High Self with the mana it needs to perform its part of the work of living—living as part of the three-self man. Perhaps no better example can be found of the mis-understanding of a Huna code teaching, and its blind use in outer form, than that of circumcision. We see clearly that the Ha Rite of prayer, starting with the count of "one" calls for the accumulation and sending of mana to the High Self, certainly not for the actual cutting of the foreskin. (The women kahunas were on a par with the men, and sent mana to the High Selves in the usual way, and they, naturally, were not circumcised.)

That the rite was very ancient, is shown by the traditional use of a flint knife for circumcision. In Egypt the religious aspect of the rite was very clearly outlined in the fact that Horus, son of Osiris and Isis, died and was resurrected as a part of the Mystery of Amenta, and was shown then in his statues and paint-ings as circumcised. The Mohammedans borrowed the rite from the Israelites and used it, but in India and China, if practiced, circumcision had no religious significance. Only in Yoga is there a trace of the belief that the life force is connected in some way with the male sex organs, for "serpent force," or *prana*, was supposed to originate in the genitals, rise along the spine and pass out through the top of the head during the performance of elaborate breathing exercises which were accompanied by mental visualizations. The Yoga practitioners believed that the *prana* (mana) they accumulated was drawn from the air. The kahunas seem only to have known that the heavier breathing made the accumulation of extra mana possible. In modern times we would say that the extra oxygen taken in was used to burn blood sugar already circulating in the blood stream, and thus make of it the vital force. It is evident that in Yoga there was once a knowledge of the Ha Rite, but that as time passed, the reason for accumulating mana was lost. In "arousing the serpent force" it came to be sent from the body through the "Door of Brahm" or top of the head, but after leaving the body its destination became Supreme God, not the "Father" or High Self.

Getting back to the code word, *ka-hi* once more, we find in the root, *hi*, the secondary meaning of (1) "to flow away," and (2) "to be weak." This would tell us little if we did not already know that it was the mana which flowed like its symbol, water, and that the flow was directed at the time of making the Ha Rite prayer to the High Self, which is "weak" if not supplied with the mana. Those initiated into Huna learn that this mana-sending "covenant" between the lower pair of selves and the High Self is to be observed daily, without fail, and its observation marks the initiate as one above the lower ranks.

The code also places in *kahi*, for "one," two other significances for the initiate. The three-self man becomes "one" when the contact with the High Self is made in performing the Ha Rite. The meaning of "a place" is better understood if we look for the "place" to which the flow of mana is directed—the place of the High Self.

E-lua or *A-lua* is "two." The root *alu* also means "weak," and so we have a repetition of one code meaning in the number "one" (it was a common practice in presenting the code to use more than one word to repeat the inner meaning lest it be overlooked). The same root, *alu*, means "to combine"; "to aid or give assistance"; and "to adhere." These meanings point to the combining of the three selves in the prayer work and the "adhere" idea symbolizes the low self, which is described in its name, *unihipili*, as something that adheres to something else, or, in its case, to the middle self. By calling attention to the low self in this way the reminder is given that the low self is the one which, on command, accumulates the extra mana, reaches out along the aka cord to contact the High Self, and sends the flow of mana.

The root, *e* in *elua*, the alternate word for "two," has the meaning of, (1) "to call or invite attention," which codes the low self making contact with the High Self; (2) "something strange or new," and this description fits the High Self, especially when the root, *e*, is doubled to make *ee*, which means "something out of sight."

An odd but important significance is to be found in the meaning of *alu*, "to break or crumble to pieces." This codes the Huna belief that the future is automatically made for us by the High Self out of the shadowy substance, in a "pattern world" on its level. It is made to match our plans and hopes and even fears. When we decide to ask in prayer for quite a different future, the High Self must break up the patterns already formed and begin to build them again to fit the prayer.

The roots *lua* and *lu* give us "seeds" and "to scatter seeds" as in sowing them. The belief here is that when we pray for something, we must make a mental picture of the desired thing or condition, and that this picture is composed of tiny thought-forms or ideas impressed on microscopic bits of the aka substance by the low self. These clusters of thought-forms are the "seeds" which must be sent floating with a flow of mana to the High Self, and if accepted, are then symbolically watered with mana and made to begin to grow into the thing which will be the "answer" to the prayer.

KO-LU is "three." Again we have a repeated root carried from the preceding number, *lu*, for "scattering seeds." But in the root *ko* we have the sign of the possessive case which tells us in code that in making the prayer we must exert faith and believe that what we have asked has been built already in the pattern world by the High Self. We are reminded of the words of Jesus, ". . . believe that ye receive them, and ye shall receive them."

The root *ko* also means "to accomplish; to fulfill; to bring to pass," and this tells us the part played by the High Self in the answering of prayer. There is also the meaning of, "to create; to beget; to obtain what one has sought after." The High Self creates the patterns of the changed future for the man, and gradually brings about the new conditions.

Ha, for "four" means "to breathe strongly," and this gives us the method of accumulating extra mana. It also means, "a trough" for running water, symbolizing the sending of the flow of mana to the High Self.

KAU-NA, the alternate word for "four," gives us the root, *kau*, and this has great value in the code because of its many meanings, one of which is, "to place something in a designated place," and in which we see the idea of placing the mana and thought-form "seeds" of the prayer in the keeping of, or place of, the High Self. The meaning of, "to set before one, as food," points to the offering of mana to the High Self. Another meaning is, "to fall upon; to embrace affectionately," in which we have the code for the love shown the lesser man by the High Self. The 17th meaning listed in the dictionary is, "to rehearse in the hearing of another that he may learn," this giving us the idea of repeating the prayer often and without changing it. The 22nd meaning is, "to place and then to rest," which describes the action taken in making the prayer, the mana and thought-form picture being "placed" with the High Self, and the completed action then stopped or rested.

It is of interest to note that after the elaborate pains taken by the kahunas in placing the special code meanings in the names for the first four numbers used for counting, the following numbers drop the code completely. If we count on to "five" we find in *elima* only the secondary meaning of "a hand" indicating the use of five fingers and the hand in primitive counting. In "six" we have *e ono*, with only the secondary meaning of "something pleasant to eat." Going on to "ten" to conclude the ten-finger count, *umi*, the secondary meaning certainly does not apply to the Ha Rite of prayer. It is "to choke" as in using both hands to choke an enemy.

Keeping in mind the meanings hidden in the numbers from one to four, and the significance of those meanings as applied to the making of the Huna-type prayer, let us take up other Huna angles to get a clearer picture of this important rite.

✿　✿　✿　✿　✿

Admittedly, the *HA* rite is complicated. It involves special work ahead of time to get the man ready to make the contact with the High Self. This is best referred to as "opening the path to the High Self." The contact may be prevented if the low self refuses to obey the command to accumulate the mana, make the contact and then send the mana to the High Self. In this case the path is said to be "blocked."

Three major things prevent the low self from making the contact. (1) A sense of guilt which makes it figuratively hang its head in shame and refuse to face the High Self or reach out to call attention to itself and its lesser man. The sense of "sin" may be caused by hurtful deeds actually done to others, or by illogical and "fixed" beliefs on the part of the low self stemming from religious training. It may feel most sinful and unworthy because its man had not "sold all and given to the poor," if this Gospel command has been deeply impressed on the lesser man in his formative years. Or there may be a deep sense of guilt connected with failure to attend church services, or failure to obey any of the many dogmatic commands formulated by the Church because of the misunderstanding bred from lack of knowledge of the true meaning of the Bible, as revealed by the Huna code. (2) The low self may also be prevented from making the contact by evil spirits if they influence it strongly. These are the "devils" which Jesus cast out, and which we will discuss later. (3) Contact may be prevented by lack of belief. The low self may have been afflicted with fixed beliefs in some form of Materialism, and so may be irrationally convinced that there is no High Self to contact. Or the fixation may be that the only thing which one may contact is Ultimate God, as the Gospel "Father," and that there could not be a High Self in between to whom one might address a prayer. The low self may also have a strong suspicion that the middle self has been deceived by the Huna teachings and that there is no mana, no aka cord and no High Self.

However, even with all the doubts and fears standing in the way of "opening the path," the High Self always makes periodic contact with the low self, usually in sleep, and draws from the body sufficient mana to use for the purpose of creating in pattern form the future of the lesser man. But once the way of making the HA prayer is learned, prayers can be made to have any bad future patterns changed to good ones. In this was thought to lie the greatest advantage of having a working knowledge of Huna.

A further complicating element in the prayer rite is

the need to understand just HOW to formulate and deliver the prayer. Three things enter into this very necessary step. Before one makes a prayer, time must be taken to decide upon what is to be asked. (Of course, if one is planning simply a contact to offer love and worship and the gift of mana so that one may enjoy the blessings of the communion with the High Self, no prayer has to be made ready ahead of time.)

In making the decision concerning what is needed and is to be asked, a prime consideration is the question of whether or not the answering of the prayer would hurt someone else. For instance, one cannot ask help from the High Self in any plan to rob or injure or force one's will on others. All men are allowed to enjoy "free will" and it is hurtful to force them to give up this privilege unless it is for self-protection or the good of the whole community. The only "sin" recognized in Huna is that of hurting another in some way, and this includes "hurting the feelings" as well as hurting in a material way.

The person who is skilled in formulating a prayer will take plenty of time to imagine that the prayer has been answered and to see whether he and his low self are satisfied with the results after they have been attained. If the low self has a deep emotional attachment to something, such as a home, for example, it may not go along with the plan to ask for a different home or for a move to a different place. It is difficult to be sure what reaction may come from the low self, but by imagining oneself in the desired new condition, and "living" in the projected new home or surroundings for a time while watching the emotions that arise, the attitude of the low self may be ascertained. If it wishes to remain in the old home or old conditions, it will produce in one the emotion of reluctance, fear, dislike, etc. On the other hand, it may give the emotion of joy or contentment or may let the matter stand and depend upon the better judgment of the middle self. If the "shoe fits" when tried on it is safe to "wear it" when it comes to deciding what to ask in prayer.

Then comes the making of a clear and unchanging mental picture of the desired condition. This is made as if the condition had already been brought about in answer to prayer. And, once the picture is visualized and is strong and clear, it must be memorized or rehearsed so that it will not later suffer by being changed. This mental picture is a thing which in Huna is believed to be made of the aka substance of the low self. All memories are believed to be microscopic bits of this substance molded in some way to embody the original thought or mental impression. But, as each memory is made up of a train of impressions, the tiny and invisible thought-forms or impressions are tied together by threads of the shadowy substance. In modern psychology we have discovered this fact and speak of "association of ideas" in telling how one remembers names, places and events. One has to find the right aka thread to "pull" to bring up a needed memory chain or string of impressions threaded like beads on an aka thread and stored in the shadowy body of the low self.

As we go on into the study of the coded material we will continually run into the symbol of "seeds." These "seeds" are the clusters of thought-forms which make up the mental picture of the condition for which one plans to pray. The symbology continues with the likening of the High Self to one possessing a garden. It accepts the "seeds" which are sent floating along the aka cord on the flow of proffered mana, and once accepted as worthy, the seeds are planted in the garden so that they can grow into the actual plants.

This brings us to the follow-up step in which the carefully made prayer picture is daily recalled and sent anew to the High Self as a prayer. This is done to make the "seed" picture ever stronger and clearer, and woe betide any one who keeps changing his mind and who makes changes once the prayer has been decided upon and has been offered. Changes of the picture cause the High Self to keep tearing down its patterns of the future and starting all over again to build them, or refusing to build at all. In passing, it may be said that there is a Huna belief that if the old future is a bad one and it is to be replaced by a better new one in answer to prayers, the bad old future must be destroyed. In the process of doing away with it, the symbolic "pieces" of the old future "fall on one's head." With great suddenness the ingredients of the bad future may appear in one's life as they are done away with. Job coded this in part in his words, "The thing which I have feared has come upon me." The sudden rush of trouble, however, is the "storm tempered to the lamb" and if one endures and keeps steadfastly presenting the prayer picture of the desired condition, the old is lived through and the new appears in time. "First the seed, then the plant, then the fruit."

Not less important than the daily sending of the prayer picture to the High Self without the slightest change, is the sending of the daily gift of mana. As the prayer begins to be answered, the giving of thanks is in order, and this is also a very helpful thing to do, for giving thanks that the prayer has been fully answered here and now in the pattern stage is a way of impressing the low self and keeping its faith strong. If the prayer is slow in being answered, a day of doubting may so upset and discourage the low self that it will refuse to continue the repetition of the daily rite and the "fruit will wither on the vine" so that nothing will come of the effort.

When only small changes in the future are needed, the High Self can often bring instant answers to prayer. In cases where things are to be restored to a former condition, as in healing the body, the answer can be in the order of the miracle, but only if enough mana is made available to the High Self to make the immediate changes which are needed to remove a bad physical condition and bring all back to normal. The things which take time and much manipulation behind the scene, such as with many social or business contacts and agreements, may take a long time. Where a major change is needed and needed very soon, the instruction to "pray constantly" is to be obeyed in so far as possible. In the Catholic Church the "Novena" is a series of such prayers frequently made, and as the prayer is usually not changed, and as the emotions are aroused by the pressing need and the hopeful faith in the coming of the "answer," the large amount of mana is supplied unknowingly by the low self of the one making the hourly prayers. Often the answer is swift in coming.

The High Self is part of the three-self man, and as such is loved rather than worshiped. This love is often felt in prayer by the lower man as a great welling up of sudden emotion.

In this respect it is an impressive proof of the truth of the Huna belief in the validity of the Ha Rite, to consider the word used by the kahunas for "worship." It was *hoo-mana*, and meant, literally, "to create mana." When we know the prayer secret, we also know what is done with the extra mana which is created. It is sent as a gift of love to the High Self. The code could hardly have made this basic point more clear to the initiates.

In the pre-Polynesian version of the story of the Garden of Eden, the worship of the Creator was done by offerings of *awa*, a drink similar to the nectar of the gods in the Greek legends. This was, in the code, mana. We know this because *awa* also means "fine rain," which is the symbol of the mana of the High Self after it has been accepted from the low self and given a different potency.

Adam and Eve were told to let the fruit of the sacred tree in the Garden alone. This was fruit or food tabooed and reserved for the Creator or High Self. But they took the fruit and ate it. In this we have the symbol of the lesser man who uses all his mana himself, sending none to his High Self. This leaves the High Self weak and prevents it from playing its normal part as helper and guide of the lesser man, the result being the loss of the ideal conditions of the symbolic Garden. The kahunas had a saying to the effect that, "The life of the kahuna is the god: and the life of the god is the kahuna." It was also a maxim that, "Without worship, the gods die." Without normal contact with the High Self and without sharing with it the mana, the lower man gets but little help and guidance. However, this cannot in any way be twisted around to fit the Pauline idea that the sins of Adam and Eve caused a curse to be placed by God on all mankind—a curse which could only be removed by the blood sacrifice of God's son, Jesus.

CHAPTER 8

THE WAY, LIFE, LIGHT AND PATH

As mana is so important in Huna, it may be well at this point to recall that the early Egyptian symbol for it was the life-giving fluid which the grasshopper brought to the lesser soul in the tomb to keep it alive and strong. The bee also came, and it brought the *sa* or honey which symbolized the nectar of the gods, and which matches the mana when changed by the High Self to the frequency or strength that can dissolve matter, as in the break in a bone, and instantly rebuild it in the aka mold of the broken limb so that the healing is miraculous and complete.

In the Old Testament we have the very code word mana, as manna, put to open use, but the story of its use was not at all open, and the word was not part of the Hebrew vocabulary of the period, for in consulting our Concordance we learn that manna meant simply a question "What is it?," and that when the hungering children of Israel awakened in the morning and saw the manna covering the ground like hoar frost, they named it by crying, "What is it?" or "Manna?" The Huna symbol for mana is, as has been said, "water," but water takes many forms. It is the "fine rain" of the prayer ending, and it is also frost or snow, or mist and cloud.

In this case it was in the "frost" form, and was

"bread from heaven," at least symbolically. (In the Gospels we come across it as "the bread of life.")

In the Old Testament we have the story of the wanderings of the Children of Israel in the wilderness and read that manna fell nightly to feed them. It could not be stored or kept, for it became wormy and stank. When the wilderness had been left behind and food was again obtainable in the ordinary way, Aaron, who was appointed high Priest and keeper of the Ark of the Covenant, was instructed to place in the Ark a pot of manna as a reminder of God's mercy.

The fact that the manna had to be obtained fresh each day gives us the symbolic knowledge that the mana of Huna was something which must also be accumulated fresh each day before being used in the Ha Rite.

There is also Huna symbology in the "water" which had to be provided by Moses lest the tribe wandering in the wilderness perish. In the first case they had come to a bitter lake and he purified the water by throwing a tree into it. In the second case he smote a rock with his staff and water gushed out. In the inner teaching the water of the outer teaching becomes the "Water of life" which Jesus promised that he would give. This "water" is the low mana sent to the High Self and returned by it as high mana to bless and cleanse and help the lesser man.

The ancestors of the Polynesians, when they migrated to the Pacific, carried with them legends which have a striking similarity to some recorded as belonging to early Egypt, as well as Assyria, Chaldea and Israel. It may well be that the original versions of the legends came from Huna. In one legend told in Hawaii, it is related that two Polynesian gods were traveling together, Kane and Kanaloa. Kanaloa complained of thirst, and Kane, like Moses, used his staff to produce water, only instead of striking a rock, he thrust the end of the staff into a cliff and out gushed a stream of pure water. This was part of the "Waters of Kane" legend in which the Polynesian Garden of Eden was blest by Kane—the "god of Light" (as Ra was the Sun god in Egypt)—with a pool of "living water" in which, when one felt age creeping upon one, a bath could be taken and youth restored. In this garden beside the pool grew a tree of great size whose leaves, when cooked, gave any kind of food desired. The Adam who was created, and in some versions was placed in the garden, was made of two kinds of clay, red and white, one color for the head and one for the body, these symbolizing the low and middle selves. A god pair, acting as the High Self Father-Mother, breathed the mana of life into the clay image and thus embued it with "spirit," so that it became a living man. Later, Eve was taken from Adam and given to him as a companion.

A long and beautiful chant which accompanied a religious dance in Polynesia, tells of the lost "Water of Life" of Kane and in one stanza we find the symbols of high mana mentioned as rain, mist and cloud. The stanzas read:

"This question I ask of you:
Where, pray, is the Water of Kane?
Yonder, at sea, on the ocean,
In the driving rain,
In the heavenly bow,
In the piled-up mist-wreath,

In the blood-red rainfall,
In the ghost-pale cloud-form,
There is the Water of Kane."

The chant ends with the plaintive plea:

"A well-spring of water to quaff,
A water of magic power—
The water of life!
Life! Oh, give us this life!"

Going back to the offering of mana as the perfect sacrificial gift, we find in Genesis that several kinds of offerings were mentioned, among them one called a "drink offering." In Hebrew it was called *necak*, and from the prime root of this word we get the meaning of "to flow," which at once points to the code symbol of mana flowing as water to the High Self. The root also has the meaning of "fusion" and of "to interweave," these indicating the contact with the High Self in which the lesser man is, at least temporarily, "one with the Father," as Jesus expressed it.

The outer teaching on this point was that some desirable drink should be poured as a sacrifice to the god either at the altar or wherever such a drink was about to be imbibed. In the legends of the Huna people there is a story which accounts for the tradition of the "fallen angel" who caused the "fall of man." The story is that when the ceremonial drink of *awa* was being poured out as an offering to the great gods of Light, Stability and Sound, (Kane, Ku and Lono), one of the jealous lesser gods, angered because he was not offered the drink by the worshipers (as mana is offered to the High Self) revolted against the higher gods, was beaten, and in revenge set about corrupting the good men whom the High Gods had created.

In Greece the "libation" was a carefully observed

offering to the gods, and was made before taking each drink. The idea survives in Christianity in the saying of Grace before meals—a far cry from the original intention and the frequent sending of mana to the High Self in the Ha Rite. The word "libation," in Latin, has the meaning of "taking a little of a drink to taste." It may be that the small sips of wine in the Communion Service of the Church has come to echo the pouring out of the wine (or blood) on the sacrificed object, as was done by the early Hebrews before the altar. In the Catholic Church of today, the wine is not poured over the wafer, but the wafer dipped into the wine before being placed in the mouth of the worshipers kneeling before the priest.

❀ ❀ ❀ ❀ ❀

Having surveyed the meanings of mana as associated with the making of prayers, we are now ready to go back to our inspection of passages from the Gospels in which the word, "Father" is used. When we paused to take up the Ha Rite, we had just finished the reading of John 14:7-11, and the words, "Believest thou not that I am in the Father, and the Father in me? The words that I speak unto you I speak not of myself: but the Father that dwelleth in me, he doeth the works." In this verse we see Jesus, like Moses, speaking for the High Self as a god, and in the word "works" we have a very good example of the use in the code of the word *ha*, as a significant root in longer words which have quite a different meaning.

"Works" or "work," is *ha-na* in the code language, and the *ha* root at once reminds the initiate that the entire Ha Rite is being indicated. The root *na* has here the meaning of "ing" in English (as a shortening of *ana* to *na*), so we have *Ha*-ing as the way in which the lesser man works as "one with the Father" to get some "work" accomplished—not by the lesser man alone, or by the High Self alone, but with all three selves working as a team to get something done. Jesus advised his hearer, Philip, to believe in the verity of the High Self, or, if he could not, to accept the evidence of the miraculous answers obtained through prayer.

In John, 4:23 we have an excellent example of how the code was used to give more information in condensed form. We read: "But the hour cometh, and now is, when the true worshipers shall worship the Father in spirit and in truth: for the Father seeketh such to worship him."

Here Jesus is speaking as the lesser man while using code words to explain to the "chosen" or "elite" who were gathered around him the fine points of one phase of Huna. The "true worshiper" is the man who knows the Ha Rite of prayer. The time to begin using the Rite is "now." To "worship" it will be recalled, is *hoo-mana*, in the code, which means "to make mana." The informed listeners had to fill in from that point and know that the reason for "making mana" was to have it to send to the High Self when contact was established, then to present the prayer. To give mana is the only "worship" or "sacrifice" desired by the High Self, and it is said to seek those who can worship in this "true" way. This is, indeed, to "worship in truth." The code word for "truth" is *mana-oia*, meaning the "truth, or the thing believed or faith." We know the root word *mana*, also its significance. The root word *oia* also means "truth," but it has secondary meanings which tell us much of how the Ha Rite is to be conducted. The root *oi* means "to project out," and this indicates the activating of the aka cord and the "projecting" or reaching out to make contact with the High Self. It also means, "to approach" as one may be said to do in reaching out to touch the High Self. The root word *ha*, in the Ha Rite is made to have a significant meaning by doubling it, and in *ha-ha*, we have the meaning of, "to reach out and feel around to try to find something, as in the dark or as a blind person." This is a fine symbol of the act which the low self performs for us in making contact with the High Self, as we, of the middle self, are unable to see the Parental Spirit Pair or sense the existence of the aka cord leading to the Father.

The root *oi* also means "more of something" or "excess," and here we have the key to the accumulation of "more" mana to send to the High Self. *Oia*, in addition to meaning "truth," means "to continue," "to endure," to "remain the same," and this points to the need to continue daily to send the mana and the prayer in the Ha Rite and to endure whatever trouble may come when the old future pattern is broken up and time is taken to build the desired new one. It also has, with the causative prefix *hoo*, the important meaning of "affirming the truth," as is done in making the prayer and repeating it often. We must have faith and affirm strongly our belief that the true or real and good new condition has already been made in pattern form as the "seed" or mental picture which is presented daily to the High Self with the mana-water to keep it growing.

To "worship in spirit" gives us again the *ha* symbol of the use of breath to accumulate the excess charge of mana. In the Samoan dialect of the code language this root means not only strong breathing, but a spirit such as any one of the three selves of the man, or of a deceased person. The High Self is worshiped as a "spirit," because it is just that, and by the use of the *ha* breathing to accumulate and send the offering of mana. The word *mana* has for one of its several meanings that of, "to empower," and it is the force that makes the High Self strong and able to work in forming the patterns of the future and making them materialize or become real on the physical level.

Mana, as used in the Ha Rite, has three more meanings which we will do well to consider. They are, "to reverence," "to desire greatly" and "to love." This tells us that if the low self does not feel these things and create a fitting emotional response, it is not working at full capacity in making the prayer. Still another meaning is an odd one which seems to have something to do with the mana as a force resembling an electric current, with a positive and negative polarization. The roots, *ma* and *na* give us "active" and "quiescent," also the idea of a force which accompanies something such as, we may conjecture, the thought-form prayer which is sent on a mana flow to the High Self.

Before leaving the meaning of "spirit" in connection with breath and prayer, it is well to remember that the word as used in Greek, and in English as a borrowing, has the dual meaning of "breath" and of "a spirit." Huna adds to the meaning, that drawn from mana, or "life." The "breath of life" is the *ha* breath and in it one shares one's "life" with the High Self. In Huna, "to become inspired" is literally to have the High Self, as a spirit, come into contact with one for a short time.

✻ ✻ ✻ ✻ ✻

In addition to his cryptic statements concerning the fact that he and the Father were one, and that he was in the Father, and the Father was in him, Jesus gave definite information concerning his nature when he spoke of himself as "The Light of the World." He said, (John 14:6) "I am the way, the truth and the light." And here we have him describing himself, NOT as the lesser man of the middle and low selves, but as the High Self. Here he speaks as "the Father" self.

If the student will consult the little list of code words and their meanings, it will be seen that the root word for "light," *la*, is the key to the inner teaching at this point. (We have already considered the code word for "truth," *mana oia*.)

Notice that *la* is the root in:

La-a: "Holy", the symbol of the High Self, it being symbolized by "Light". This accounts for all sun worship in early Egypt where initiate kahunas were involved.
O-la: "Life", or, literally, "of the light" shows the belief of the kahunas that there can be no light or life without the High Self.
La: "Light, as of day or the sun."
A-la: "Path or way."

In *la-au*, the word for "wood," we have "light" plus "A self," indicating the High Self. The efforts made to

100

give through the use of the code the assurance that Jesus was a kahuna initiate is clear to see in many parts of the Scriptures. It is of interest to note that Jesus was described as a carpenter and the son of a carpenter. In the Samoan dialect of the sacred language, the word kahuna means also a carpenter (*laau*) or a person skilled in the working of wood. In Mark 6:3 we read: "Is this not the carpenter, the son of Mary, and the brother of James, and Joses and of Juda, and Simon? and are his sisters not here with us? And they were offended at him." In this we see a simple outer meaning hiding the one intended for later initiates.

The symbol of the "path" is basic code, but it, also, appears to have moved from inner to outer circle uses in the dim past. It is an especially favored term in India, and in the digest made by Theosophists of the Hindu systems of belief, we read often of the course of life through many incarnations as "the Path." On the other hand it retains a fragrance of the hidden meaning in referring to the path or way to the Higher Beings or great Real Self of Yoga, with whom final union is (mistakenly) believed to take place at the end of the more mystical "Path." In Huna the path has little to do with the course of life in so far as the inner teachings are concerned. It means the contact along the aka cord connecting the lesser man with his High Self.

The code words, "path" and "way" were used in Isaiah and were repeated in Mark, 1:1 as, ". . . Behold, I send my messenger before thy face, which shall prepare thy way before thee." In the outer or non-secret teaching of the Gospels, this has the simple meaning of John the Baptist coming ahead of Jesus to announce his impending arrival and ministry. In verse 2 we have the word "paths" as we read: "the voice of one crying in the wilderness, Prepare ye the way of the Lord, make his paths straight."

The original in Isaiah, 40:3, Fenton's translation, is, "A Voice cries in the Desert, 'Prepare the Lord's path: —And straighten for passage the road of our God! Raise the valleys, and cut down each mountain and hill. Make the crooked path straight, and the rough places smooth. The Lord's glory unveiled, let all see it at once, As the Lord's mouth has said.' "

In the code a small "path" is *a-la* and a larger path or "Way" is *a-la-nui*, or "big path." As the "Lord," as God, does not use a path, we see that it is a symbol, and we ask, then who does use the path that is to be made open and easy to use? The code answer is obvious. It is the path-way along the aka cord to the High Self over which the mana and prayer pictures pass. If the path is closed, then it must be opened wide and the symbolic valleys are raised and mountains of obstruction leveled. Or, reversing the symbolic travel along the path, we have the High Self coming along the path to contact the lesser man. In either case the important thing is the information that the "way" must be opened for the contact with the High Self—and in this part of the Gospel story, Jesus is representing the High Self combined with the lesser two selves.

The *la* root in the words for "light," "path," "way" and "life" is almost as important in some respects as the *ha* root in the prayer rite, and we will find it used frequently as we continue.

Looking back to John, 14:6, we read: ". . . no man

cometh unto the Father, but by me." One person cannot come "through" another to the Father except symbolically, and the early Church decided on the dogma that this "through" was via a belief that Jesus pacified the Father or Ultimate God (who was also Jesus and also the Holy Ghost), by sacrificing his own life in the crucifixion, and that "Salvation" came only through Jesus because of the sacrifice.

This Pauline conclusion, which was accepted eventually by the Church, damned all those who had lived before the time of Jesus and also those who might never have heard of him during his lifetime. To get around this, the belief was promulgated that all who had ever lived would be raised from the dead and judged on The Last Day, and in some vague way might be given a chance to share in the one and only possible chance for Salvation. The salvation was from a hell which automatically swallowed up all of the children of Adam because of the "Fall."

This dogmatic explanation by the Church of the words, ". . . only through me," added complication to complication and contradicted the teaching that "God is love," but it was the best the Church Fathers could manage.

The entire problem is solved so simply by one who knows the code meanings. Jesus had just finished saying that he was the "way, the truth and the life" when he added the coded statement that the only way to the Father was through him—as "the way," or through the aka cord. The code words "truth" and "life" show the mechanism of the Ha Rite by which the aka cord "way" can be put to use, and the "life" des-

103

ignates the mana or life force which is the life of the lesser man as well as the Father-Mother Self.

Let us pause to solve another mystery which has plagued the Church for centuries. This is the mystery of the "Comforter" who was to come, but who never seems to have done so. We read on (John 14:16-18):

"And I will pray the Father, and he shall give you another Comforter, that he may abide with you forever; Even the Spirit of truth; whom the world cannot receive, because it seeth him not, neither knoweth him: but ye know him; for he dwelleth with you, and shall be in you. I will not leave you comfortless: I will come to you."

Jesus is here speaking alternately as the lesser man and as the High Self. If the ancient initiatory drama is ever restored and used again as is the Pilgrimage Play, the actor who takes the part of Jesus will have to have a veil to hold before his face each time he speaks for the High Self, or there could, in these modern times, be special light effects used in which he would glow with white light each time he speaks as the High Self.

The "Comforter" can be none other than the High Self, for it is said to be, "Even the Spirit of truth," and Jesus has hardly finished saying that he, as the High Self was the "truth." As to the word, "spirit," this this takes us back to "breath" and so, once more to the Ha Rite. The Father is said in the code to be "in" one when, in fact, it is never more than in contact with the lesser self for a short time.

A slightly different angle on the code word "truth" which we have just been studying, comes when we replace the word "Truth" with the word in the code for "true," which is not *oia*, but *io*. In English the two words are almost interchangeable, but in the code they differ slightly in symbolic meaning. The "messenger" whom we have seen mentioned as going "before the face of the Lord" in Isaiah and in the opening of Mark's Gospel, is *io*, which means "messenger," but the primary meaning is "true, real and not imaginary."

In the dialects of the code language as used in the Managian, Tahitian and Maori, the meaning is much more complete than in the Hawaiian. The word has the meaning of, "spirit" also "power, energy, force" (check mana), and "God." With these meanings applied to Jesus when he calls himself the "truth," the High Self meaning cannot be mistaken. Also, the variant meanings once more take us back with a reminder of the entire Ha Rite.

John gives a slightly different version of the account compared to that of Mark, and we read: (1:6-8) "There was a man sent from God, whose name was John. The same came for a witness, to bear witness of the Light, that all men through him might believe. (Note again the use of the word "through," and that it does not in this place limit the way to "Salvation," even when the Light is indicated.) He was not that Light, but was sent to bear witness of that Light. That was the true light which "lighteth every man that cometh into the world."

Here we have in the words, "true Light," the assurance that the High Self is "real, not imaginary," thanks to the word *io*. And, in the word *mana-o-io*, the makers of the code gave assurance that the mana used in the Ha Rite also produced things that were very real, even if not visible—such as the aka patterns of the future which are made to "grow" from the "seeds" or mental pictures of the things desired. *Mana-o* is a "thought" or mental image, and the roots show that mana is used in thinking and in making the mental pictures which are part of the prayer. The *io* root added, give us *mana-o-io*, for "faith," or the picture made real. One must, we see in this bit of code, have faith that the new condition is real and is being carried toward full physical materialization from the time the prayer is first delivered, through its frequent repetition, and to the final "answer."

After the prayer is answered, it is in order to give thanks, and in the code *ma-ha-lo* is "thanks." *Ma* is "by means of," and *ha* is the whole process of the Ha Rite, while *lo* is the fore part of the head and symbolizes the middle self who is actively engaged at every step in making a Huna-type prayer, and who is most involved in giving thanks. The "thanks," as we see by the roots of the word, takes the form of sending a gift of mana with love and thanks each day to help the High Self keep strong and able to do its work, whatever that happens to be, on the higher level. The wise initiate never lets a day pass without making contact with his High Self and presenting his gift while expressing his love and trust.

The code words and their meanings interlock in an amazingly perfect way to hide and still reveal the "Secret."

Using the knowledge that John is speaking of the High Self, we begin again with verse 10: "He was in the world, and the world was made by him, and the world knew him not." The code word used for "world" is *ao*: "Light," day as the opposite of *po*, "night." This is a play on words, apparently to make certain that the symbol of "light" for the High Self would not be lost or overlooked. There is also the outer meaning of the "world" as that of "the people," these, when not of the initiates, having no knowledge of the presence or reality of their own High Selves. The High Self, represented as that of Jesus, is the one meant in the cryptic verses, 11 and 12, where we read, "He came unto his own, and his own received him not. But as many as received him, to them he gave power to become the sons of God, even to them that believe on his name."

To become a "son of God" to the Huna initiate, is "to become one with one's own High Self." To the lower man the High Self is a god, not Ultimate God, but a spark of the Supreme Light. The phrase, "Son of man" applies to Jesus as the ordinary man. The phrase, "Son of God," applies to Jesus as the initiated Jesus who was consciously one with his High Self.

In addition to the meaning already given for *a-la*, or "path," there are three other significant meanings which were used in the code:

1. "To rise up," symbolizing the rising of the mana along the connecting aka cord to reach the High Self as the sacrificial gift from the lower man.
2. "To anoint." In this meaning we see the gift of mana as something used to anoint or "make holy and sacred." The initiate who knows the secret of the path and its uses, is an "Anointed One" or a "Christed One."
3. "To awaken." In this we have the symbolical meaning of awakening one to understand the fact that there is a High Self. It is the same as "enlighten," which is to

dispel "darkness" or ignorance of the verity of the High Self.

There are a few more passages in which the inner nature of Jesus and his High Self, the Christ, are touched upon. We can take these up as we come to them in the course of our study. For the moment let us continue to look at the coded meanings found in the account of the baptism of Jesus by John the Baptist.

Of first importance is the statement by John that "He who shall come after me, will baptize you with the Holy Spirit and with fire." Matthew and Luke mention the "fire" element in the baptism to be administered by Jesus, but Mark and John do not.

The coded meaning here centers on the word for fire, *a*: "To burn." Fire creates *light*, and here we have once more the secret information that the High Self, symbolized by the light, and also symbolized by the Holy Spirit, is in some way to be involved in the superior baptism or final cleansing. The lesser man, when he has learned the lessons of life and of love, is cleansed by the endlessly kind and loving High Self, the "Mother" half being stressed in this case because of the great love of mothers for their children the world over. Jesus, who was to "come after me" could administer this final cleansing rite because he could act as a High Self.

There is some disagreement in the accounts of the baptism. John makes no mention of John the Baptist baptizing Jesus, but his account says, "I have beheld the Spirit descending as a dove out of heaven, and it abode on him." Matthew says that after he was baptized, the heavens were opened to Jesus, "and he saw the Spirit of God, descending like a dove and lighting upon him." Luke writes, ". . . Jesus also being baptized, and praying, the heaven was opened, And the Holy Ghost descended in a bodily shape like a dove upon him. . . ." All but John speak of the "voice from heaven" declaring, "This is my beloved Son; in which I am well pleased."

In these accounts we know that the water of the baptism symbolized mana, and as Jesus was immersed, we can guess that an excess amount of water was used, this standing for the Huna practice of accumulating a surcharge of mana to send along the shadowy cord to the High Self to call its attention and to serve as a gift. Luke adds the vital information that Jesus was "praying" in connection with the baptism in water, and so we know that the entire Ha Rite of Huna prayer was being indicated in the code. The contact with the High Self, which is so necessary to the successful sending of the prayer, is dramatically pictured in the assurance that the Spirit descended as a dove and lighted upon him. The Spirit or High Self is symbolized as a bird in Huna (as are all spirits), and whether others saw the dove or heard the voice, is not as important as the fact that Jesus was aware that his path was open and that he had made contact with his High Self. As the "son" in this instance, he represents the lower man made up of the low and middle selves. The cleansing of the baptism symbolizes the clearing away of anything which might have "blocked the path" to the High Self and prevented contact.

With his path to the High Self open for immediate use at any time, Jesus was ready to begin his ministry as a man, or as a High Self who worked with the lower man when the need arose. The teachings could come either from the man or from the High Self, as the code reminds us when the accounts make the Spirit speak and announce that Jesus was the beloved son. However, as the High Self speaks through the mouth of the lesser man, care must always be taken to see which level is providing the teachings.

Luke, 3:16, adds some coded information to the story of John the Baptist. We read, "I indeed baptize you with water; but there cometh he that is mightier than I, the latchet of whose shoes I am not worthy to unloose. . . ." The "latchet" here is a string, in the code, *kau-la*, which means "cord" and indicates the aka cord to the High Self. The word for "unloose" is *kala*, which also means "to cleanse" and indicates the process of unblocking the "path" along the cord to the High Self.

Matthew and Luke both report that John the Baptist compared the expected one to come to one "whose fan is in his hand" to clean the threshing floor and separate the wheat from the chaff. The code for fan is the word, *peahi*, and it has as one of its several meanings, that of "power" or "authority." The High Self has the power to unblock the path and to help the lower man separate the good from the bad in his life.

Although John in his account makes no mention of Jesus going into the wilderness immediately after his baptism, Matthew, Mark and Luke give that story. There is some coded Huna in the account, mostly given as symbols. The "wilderness" is a symbol of the condition in which the sense of guilt prevents the low self of the man from playing its part and making normal contact with the High Self. Adam and Eve sinned and were cast out of the Garden of Eden to live in a land where weeds and briars made planting and harvesting very difficult. Wild animals are mentioned as being with Jesus in the wasteland, and these, like the *moo*, or serpents and lizards of the kahunas, and like the wild beasts in Isaiah, represent the animal or low self of the man and its savage side which must be changed by growth and experience and by the control of the middle self until it becomes tamed and helpful.

The Satan of the story is a personalization of all the darker side of the savage low self and of its angers, hates, greeds and fears—of its unreasoning fixations on such beliefs as it chances to accept. Mark writes, ". . . and he was with the wild beasts; and the angels ministered to him." The High Self ministers to the lesser man even when he knows nothing definite about the Father-Mother, and while his low self is gradually taught gentleness, kindness and obedience.

(The temptation scene will fit better at a later point in the accounts, but for the moment let us say that after his baptism Jesus was in full contact with his High Self and began his ministry).

CHAPTER 9

JESUS, AND THE FULFILLMENT OF PROPHECIES

A study of the code as found in the Old Testament, reveals the handwork of initiate kahunas from the story of the Creation through the adventures of Adam and Eve and their sons, and through the account of Noah and the Flood. Then comes a lapse in which little or no code material appears, and then in the prophecies and Psalms the fine hand of the kahunas reappears. The Old Testament was written almost entirely in Hebrew, and the starting date, beginning with Abraham is thought to be from 2250 to 2000 B.C. By the year 1750 B.C., the Israelites entered Egypt and settled there, but became enslaved. Finally, in 1320 B.C., they escaped in the "Exodus." During the time of association with the early Egyptians, we must suppose that there were kahunas along the Nile and that some of the Israelites were initiated. While there are definite indications that Huna was known by the Egyptians at the time of the earliest use of their system of picture-writing, there is little in THE BOOK OF THE DEAD that will give us back coded information. This seems difficult to explain when we see the Israelities, who borrowed much of their culture from the Egyptians, turning up with the same stories which the kahunas later carried into Polynesia. More than that, we find in Genesis some of the most valuable coded material to be preserved for posterity.

There is a question as to when the language of the Hebrews was first reduced to writing, but, as it was a system in which an alphabetical script was used, it must have been long after the Egyptians learned to write with hieroglyphics. In any event, we must conclude that kahunas were involved in the writing of Genesis either at the very first, or that, at a later period, some of them were able to insert the coded material in the ancient Scriptures during some process of copying.

In the Chaldean we find priests called *kahen* (pronounced kaw-hane), according to STRONG'S CONCORDANCE, page 54 of the Hebrew word section. In Hebrew the word for "priest" is given as *kahan, kohen* and *kahen*, while *kehunnah* (which most nearly matches the Hawaiian word for a priest, *kahuna*) is "priesthood." From this similarity of words we may draw the legitimate conclusion that kahunas were known at the time of the writing of Genesis, and it follows logically that some of the Huna lore or "Secret" must have been known in Hebrew inner circles. The word, *kahuna,* means "Keeper of the Secret."

The Exodus seems to have been followed by a fairly stable period of about 250 years, but at the end of Solomon's reign and the building of the temple, a split came in which the Tribes of Judah separated from those of Ephraim, the latter now designated as the "Israelites." The two branches, beginning in about 938 B.C. fought many battles with neighboring tribes, and the Palestine area was repeatedly invaded by the people of Egypt, Babylon, Assyria and Syria. By

697 B.C. Jerusalem had been captured, and the Ephraimite branch was ended as a special tribe or kingdom. During these times when the Hebrews were battling their powerful neighbors, Isaiah, of the tribe of Judah, date about 736 B.C., (which is more than seven centuries before the birth of Jesus), had his vision and had his prophecies recorded in Hebrew script, or so we may suppose. Whether Isaiah was a kahuna initiate in his own right and whether he wrote down his prophecies, we cannot say, but whoever did the writing, selected words which, when translated back into the language of the code, give information concerning Huna which runs parallel with the writing done much later in Greek in the Gospels.

The Jews, after the time of Isaiah, struggled along with a seesaw series of wars to hold their own against the enemies who pressed them from all sides. Jerusalem was won back and lost again, captivity and release were experienced, then, in about 331 B.C. some of the Jews began to settle at Alexandria, in Egypt, and found favor with the ruler, Ptolemy I, Soter. In 285 B.C., the next Ruler, Ptolemy II, Philadelphus, with the Greek influence by then very strong, ordered the sacred books of the Jews translated into Greek, thus marking a new era in religious thought in the Near East. Meantime, Alexander the Great had invaded the East and left his mark on the thought of the time. By 332 B.C. he had made Greek the official language. Alexandria, a city which he had founded, became a world center of learning, and it was there that most of the Gnostic literature was produced—with Huna often coded into it, and with translations made from the Greek originals into Coptic, from which a part of the Gnosis was recovered centuries later. In addition, there was written in Greek a collection of writings concerning the sayings of Jesus. Later a longer account of his life and work was written, although we cannot say whether this account originated in Alexandria or not. By the time the account was fully written in the Four Gospels, the birth of Jesus had taken place and his short life had been lived. The Romans had replaced the Greeks as rulers and the Christian Church had been slowly taking form. Roughly, from the time of Isaiah to the full establishment of the Gospels as a canon, almost a thousand years elapsed. One can only wonder whether the story of the life of Jesus had already been formulated, or partly so, in the time of Isaiah, but had not been fully elaborated and put into writing.

From an examination of the prophetic material in the early part of Isaiah, which may have been written by someone quite different than the writer of the latter part, it appears that even at the time of the voicing of the prophecies there may have existed a Mystery Drama based on Huna. The code words which were used certainly indicate a knowledge of the basic beliefs of Huna, and it is far easier to set the material in order as part of the Drama than to link it definitely to the life of Jesus as a man who was born in accordance with the prophecies and was crucified, then transfigured.

Had it not been for the insistence of the writers of the Gospels that Jesus lived and died to fit exactly the prophecies, and had Paul not followed suit, there might never have been developed the belief that there was a connection between the Messiah whose advent is dimly forshadowed by Isaiah and the man, Jesus, who first plays the part of the Messiah and then of the spiritual leader who has rejected all earthly rewards and promises.

Following the guidance of what the code tells us, let us treat the prophecies of Isaiah in two parts. The first part fits neatly into the first part of the Mystery Drama as if belonging with the Annunciation section of the Gospel version. This we will consider now, while the prophecies covering the sufferings and exaltation of the Righteous Servant (Chapters 52–53 of Isaiah) will be taken up as part of the climaxing end of Act 1, in which Jesus suffers and dies on the cross. Admittedly, this will be a great simplification of the prophetic materials, for in the Gospels there are quoted parts from forty-seven chapters of Isaiah, to say nothing of occasional reference to other Old Testament writings.

For the prologue of Act 1, let us take up Chapter 6 of Isaiah and see whether the code words which were used indicate a prophecy of the birth and ministry and death of Jesus, or simply serve to state for the benefit of candidates for initiation the fact that there is a High Self.

Isaiah wrote that in a vision the seraphim took a live coal from an altar and laid it upon his lips to "purge" away his sin. The code enters here, for the "coal of fire" is the symbol of fire, which makes light, and light is the symbol of the High Self and of its contact along the aka cord with the lesser man. This cleansing "baptism of fire" made Isaiah ready to hear the Lord, and he reports what was said to him—giving us one of the most baffling passages (of the outer teachings) of the Bible, as it suggests strongly that the Lord did not want people to understand. We read what, to an initiate of Huna, is a clear statement of the fact that there is an inner teaching hidden behind an outer one, and that it is to be so presented that only the initiates can understand. We read, Isaiah, 6:9-10:

"And he (the Lord) said, Go, and tell this people, Hear ye indeed, but understand not; and see ye indeed, but perceive not. Make the heart of this people fat, and make their ears heavy and shut their eyes; lest they see with their eyes, and hear with their ears, and understand with their hearts, and convert (turn) and be healed."

The code key here is the word "convert." It is *huli*, which means, "to turn back," also "to change" and "to seek." From this we can only conclude that under the Huna system there was the belief that until one had lived several incarnations and was far enough evolved to be ready for the inner teachings, one is better off with the simple teaching of Brotherly Love and kindly living—which is something even the least evolved can understand as an ideal, even if living up to it is one of the most difficult of accomplishments. The gist of the passages is that the Huna secret lore should be carefully preserved lest the unready should suspect the inner meaning for which they were not prepared, and waste precious time trying to search out the hidden meanings.

The mysterious writers of the various accounts, from the time of Isaiah to that of Jesus, almost a millenium later, may be seen carefully following the same coded pattern of knowledge and practice in recording the words of Jesus. We find in Matthew, 13:10-15:

"And the disciples came, and said unto him, Why speakest thou unto them in parables? He answered and said unto them, Because it is given unto you to know the mysteries of the kingdom of heaven, but to them it is not given. For whosoever hath (the key of the Huna code), to him shall be given, and he shall have more abundance: but whosoever hath not, from him shall be taken away even that he hath. Therefore speak I to them in parables: because they seeing see not, neither do they understand. And in them is fulfilled the prophecy of Esaias which saith, By hearing ye shall hear, and shall not understand; and seeing ye shall see, and shall not perceive. For this people's heart is waxed gross, and their ears are dull of hearing, and their eyes have closed; lest at any time they should see with their eyes, and hear with their ears, and should understand with their hearts, and should be converted, and I should heal them." Jesus continues, "But blessed are your eyes, for they shall see: and your ears, for they hear. For verily I say unto you, That many prophets and righteous men have desired to see these things which ye see, and have not seen them; and to hear those things which ye hear, and have not heard them."

Whether the prophetic vision of the advent of Jesus was genuine prophecy, or the general outline of such a life was taking form when Isaiah spoke, we do not know, but we can see that the simple and basic Huna of the prophetic passages was greatly expanded in making the later account of the life of Jesus.

The famous Chapter IX of Isaiah is one generally accepted by Christians as predicting the coming of Jesus. The coded passages are in verses 2 and 6. In the first we read, "The people that walked in darkness have seen a great light; . . ." This is pure Huna undisguised, as the "darkness" symbolized the early stages of evolution through which men must pass until they are ready and come to know the "Light" or High Self. In the second part of the passage, ". . . they that dwell in the land of the shadow of death, upon them hath the light shined." In Huna the spirit survives in its shadowy body between incarnations, and in the very end of the cycle of incarnations, the Light will show the way for the individual middle self to graduate to the High Self level of existence.

In verse 3 we have a possible code unit where we read, ". . . they joy before thee according to the joy in harvest, and as men rejoice when they divide the spoil." The "harvest" may stand for the beginning of a prayer action in which a surplus of mana is accumulated. This "harvest" is then happily "divided" and sent to the High Self along the connecting aka cord. The word "divide" is a standard Huna symbol of this sending of a part of one's mana to the High Self.

Verse 6 (Fenton in his translation gives it as 5, and we will use his version): "For a Son has been born, a Gift to us,—On his shoulder the Princedom rests,—The Wonderful Counsellor, call His name, The Great Leader, Time's Father, the Prince of Peace!"

First we note that the past tense is used in this passage, not the future to indicate that the "son" would be born centuries later. He is a "gift" now. He is the

119

"Prince of Peace," now. He is all of the things mentioned as attributes. From this we see that the High Self is meant. It is at all times present and is part of the three-self man made up of the Father-Mother self and of the low and middle self man symbolized as the "Son."

The word "gift" is code (*haawiia*), and has the meaning also of "to commend to one's care"—in which we see that the gift of the "son" is veiled allusion to the fact that the High Self is given the care of the lesser man composed of two selves. The middle self in its turn has the "care" of the low self, so the more evolved selves are obligated to care for the less evolved as the man passes through the school of life.

The "Princedom" (or "Government") is the "Kingdom of Heaven" of the teachings of Jesus. The code word *aupuni* covers all three. As the High Self is symbolized by this word, we see here the same switching back and forth from the standpoint of the Father to that of the Son as in the sayings of Jesus. The "Prince of Peace" is here the High Self, for the word "peace" is *malu* in the code, which also means "to overshadow," or "to protect." The High Self, living in its shadowy or aka body, overshadows and protects the lesser pair of selves. (Note: More meanings will be given in Chapter 14 for "Prince of Peace.")

"Wonderful" (*kupaianaha*) has the code or secondary meaning of, "to send away by water," which points to the sending of the thought-forms on the flow of mana (symbolized by water) to the High Self, in making the prayer. The word also means "to reflect light," and this points to the return or "reflecting back" of the mana by the High Self to bless the lesser selves. In the code word, *kupaianaha*, the roots translate to give us the secret meaning in this way: *ku* "to rise up" (as the mana flowing to the High Self); *pai*, "a bunch or cluster" (the cluster is the symbol in Huna of the thought-forms sent to the High Self on the mana flow); *ana* is our English "ing" ending; and *ha* is the symbol constantly used in the code for the entire Ha Rite.

"Counsellor" is *kaka-olelo*, and the inner meaning duplicates to a degree that of the word "wonderful," in that *kaka* also means "cluster" as a bunch of fruit, and so points to the thought-forms. In addition, this root means "to bail out water," which is the code symbol of sending the surcharge of mana to the High Self. The root, *olelo* means "to counsel or to plan" as in deciding on a way to accomplish something. The sub-root *ole* means "to lack something," and in this we have the High Self helping the lesser pair of selves who need something to plan a prayer, and ask for help in getting what is needed.

"Great Leader" is *keukuamana*, in which we see the inner meaning given in code to the roots: *ke* means "to urge" also "to force," giving us the urging by the lesser man in prayer to the High Self; *akua* means "a god," and the High Self is a lesser "god" in Huna; the last part, *mana*, repeats the fact that mana must be used in all prayers to make the High Self strong enough to act as a "Great Leader" to help bring about the desired conditions.

"Time's Father" is not quite the right translation to fit the code meaning, and "Time Father" is better. The word for the High Self is *Au* ("time" or a "self")plus *makua*, "parent," literally, "The Older Parental Spirit Pair." Another word in the code for "Time Parents" is *ka-makua-mau-loa*, literally, "the parent of great age," and this also fits the older of our three selves precisely.

*   *   *   *   *

Having seen, thanks to the code, that neither Jesus nor a Messiah was what Isaiah had in mind in his prophetic utterances as given in Chapter VI, it is of interest to note how mistaken was the conclusion of the early Church that the advent of Jesus as a Messiah had been accurately predicted. Moreover, we see that little effort was made by the Church Fathers to explain the contradiction that an earthly or Messianic king was to be born and the fact that in the account of the ministry of Jesus he taught first that a physical Day of Judgment would come, then that the "kingdom of heaven" which, likewise was said to be "at hand," was something to be found "within" instead of as an earthly condition outside of men. Nor has the contradiction been explained away even today, as we can see in reading what Rev. A. E. Dunning had to say in the INTERNATIONAL SERIES BIBLE some years back. His summary is still quite inclusive of what is believed today by most branches of the modern Church. He wrote: "Prophecy. This includes institutions and ordinances pointing to Christ and the Christian church; as the sacrifices and the priesthood; prophetic types, as the tabernacle and the temple; the law of the kingdom, since all education is prophetic of the ends aimed at; history leading to a declared end; persons related to the kingdom, as Abraham, Moses, and David; and the distinct utterances, as found in the sayings and books of the prophets.

"Thus we see that the Messianic idea of an everlasting kingdom under the reign of a spiritual and supreme King is the fundamental idea of the Old Testament. This Messianic idea grew with the Jewish kingdom until it reached the height of its prosperity; but as the kingdom declined and crumbled away the idea of the coming Messiah grew brighter and clearer till it was realized in Jesus Christ.

"His (that of Jesus) fundamental doctrine was the kingdom of God, created through the allegiance of the individual souls to himself as supreme Lord, (Mark 1:14, 15: Luke 14:26, 33) maintained by doing the will of God (Matt. 6:10), and certified by the overthrow of the kingdom of Satan in the soul (Luke 11:21,22). It does not come with display, for it is the enthronement of Christ in the individual life (Luke 17:20,21; John 14:23). Its consummation will be the perfect love and perfect obedience of all redeemed souls to God. . . .

"Jesus taught that the way of salvation is the entrance into the kingdom, which is entered through confidence in himself and self-surrender to him (Mark 8:34; 10:15), through repentance and renunciation of sin (Matt. 4:17), and appropriation of himself as the sacrifice for sin (John 3:14, 15; 12:32). He taught that the new birth through the Holy Spirit is the condition of entrance into his kingdom (John 3:3); for in the unrenewed heart is the source from which all evils spring (Matt. 12:35). But whoever renounces his sin

123

and chooses God as the supreme object of his worship, obedience, and love is renewed by the Holy Spirit (John 6:37, 3:16).

"He taught that the law of love is the law of the kingdom (Mark 12:29-31), and that such love centers in himself (John 14:23; Luke 14:26). He presented himself as the King of the kingdom (Matt. 16:28), to whose sway all nations must finally yield (Matt. 25: 31-46), who demanded the same devotion to himself (Luke 14:33) as is demanded by the Father (Luke 10:27, and the same honor (John 5:23).

". . . He taught the resurrection from death for all men, that he had the power to raise himself, and was himself the power that would raise others to life. He taught that there is to be a final judgement, to occur at a definite time (John 11:25), and that he would be the Judge; . . . and that he would come in the majesty of the Son of God, but that he holds the position of Judge because he is the Son of man. . . . Thus the Christian Church is spreading today through all lands, preparing for the perfect society, 'the holy city, new Jerusalem, coming down out of heaven from God.' "

While the majority of Christians are content at this late date to accept the doctrine that Jesus did not mean that a physical form of the Messianic Kingdom would come, there are some who cling to the literal interpretation of his words, and who will have none of the efforts to blend the contradictory teachings concerning the "kingdom." They are willing to believe that the "kingdom" may be within, but they must also have it appear in a quite material form "without."

When we come to a study of the code as it applies

to the Crucifixion, we will return to Isaiah and see how his supposedly prophetic words, in Chapters 52 and 53, apply to the great event which closes Act 1 of the Initiatory Drama of Huna.

It may be well to note here that Isaiah spoke almost openly of the use of the code in his Chapter 33:18–19. We read, "Where is the scribe? Where is the receiver? Where is he that counted the towers? Thou shalt not see a fierce people (but) a people of deeper speech than thou canst perceive; of stammering tongue that thou canst not understand."

The code word for "tower" is *pakui*, which has also the meaning of "to graft onto, or to unite one thing with another", and so we have Isaiah revealing the fact that the scribes were grafting on to other writings something to be had from a "not fierce" people (the ancestors of the Polynesians?) who spoke a different language as signified by "stammering" and who told of such "deep" things that ordinary people could not understand, although the "receiver" undoubtedly know the code—otherwise why should the "scribe" take the trouble to write and graft on the coded passages? The word for "count", in the code is *helu*, which means "to explain, relate or tell about something", and that is exactly what was done by the scribes through the use of the code. They told about the hidden truths of Huna.

CHAPTER 10

JESUS BEGINS HIS MINISTRY
THE MIRACLES

As though stepping out of the prophetic frame constructed around his life by Isaiah over seven centuries
earlier, Jesus appears in the center of the Gospel stage.
There has been no introductory act in the drama to
show what his first thirty years had held in the way of
education, initiation or travel.

As the curtain rises, he has been attracted to John
the Baptist and has been baptized by him. He has
been healing and casting out devils, and has now returned to his boyhood home in the village of Nazareth
to announce himself as the one whom Isaiah had fore-
told, and to begin his ministry.

In Luke, 4:14–21 (Fenton's translation), we read:
"Jesus then returned to Galilee with the power of the
Spirit; and his reputation spread throughout the whole
of the neighborhood. And he taught in their syna-
gogues with the approval of all. He afterwards came
to Nazareth, where he had been brought up; and, as
his custom was, he entered the synagogue on the day
of rest. And standing up to read, there was handed to
him the roll of the prophet Isaiah. And opening out
the roll, he found the place where it is written, 'A
spirit of the Lord is upon me, by which He has appointed me to tell good news to the poor; He has sent

me to heal the broken-hearted; to proclaim freedom to the enslaved, and restoration of sight to the blind; to set at liberty those who are oppressed; to proclaim the year honored by the Lord.'

"And having rolled up the book, he returned it to the attendant, and sat down. And the eyes of all the synagogue were fixed upon him. Then he began to say to them, 'To-day this Scripture is fulfilled in your hearing.'"

From the Huna and secret code point of view, the phrase, "A spirit of the Lord" indicates his own High Self. The "poor" to whom he brings the good news are, (*ili-hune*) those who are the opposite of being rich (*wai-wai*, "much water"), and so have no water, or mana, to send to the High Self. The broken-hearted (*eha-eha*) means in code those who have breaks in their *naau* or intestinal self, in other words, whose low selves are prevented by fixations from being able to open the path to the High Self and make the contact necessary to prayer. The "enslaved" are (*pio*) those held captive by evil spirits who must be exorcised, not those held in civil prisons—and we have no account telling us that Jesus ever tried to empty the prisons. The "blind" (*maka-po*: "eyes darkened") were those living in darkness to whom he would give knowledge of the High Self "Light." The "year honored by the Lord," (or "appointed by the Lord" in other translations) is *maka-hike* in the code and simply means the "beginning of a new year." This is not the year of the coming of the Messiah, but is part of the inner teachings and indicates the secret teaching to be given the "elect." This is the teaching already mentioned, that at the end of the needed number of incarnations, there is a "graduation" or new start on the next higher level of life by each of the three selves of the man. The middle self goes up a level in the school of life and becomes a High Self. This marks the end of the final year of several incarnations.

In the accounts of the beginning of the teaching and ministrations of Jesus, as given by Matthew, Mark and Luke, only the latter contains the story of the reading of the scroll which immediately showed that Jesus continued in his own person the prophetic tradition of the Messiah recorded in Isaiah.

The writer of the Book of John made no mention of the claim that Jesus was fulfilling the prophecy of Isaiah, and leaves out the story of the rejection of Jesus by the people of his home town. However, the tradition is brought to mind in John 4:44 where Jesus is quoted as saying, ". . . a prophet hath no honor in his own country." He might well have said that a teacher of the inner truths could have no hearing from those unable to understand what was being laid before them.

When Matthew wrote his account of the life of Jesus, he did not say that Jesus believed himself to be the Messiah, although he referred constantly to the prophecies and wrote of various events, "This came to pass in order that the prophecies might be fulfilled."

After Luke's little drama in which Jesus announces himself as the one to fulfill the prophecies, we are told that his doubting listeners refused to believe him to be what he claimed. To them he was just the son of Joseph, and a carpenter. But they had heard of the miracles of healing which he had been performing and so demanded that to prove himself he repeat the miraculous performances before them and "show signs." For some reason, usually said to be because the townsmen lacked faith, Jesus could not comply, and, as a result, was about to be stoned and thrown over a cliff, but he managed to escape.

The question of whether Jesus was or was not the expected Messiah had not been settled. The code shows us that Jesus had not the slightest thought of becoming a leader in the military sense or one to lead the Jews to a position of world domination. But the common people failed to understand this. In their eagerness to have the Messiah of earthly power arise, they flocked around Jesus, listened to him when he taught in parables, and marveled at his power to heal and to cast out devils. Meantime, the learned Jews and their religious leaders watched with increasing indignation.

The Good Tidings or message proclaimed by Jesus takes us back once more to Isaiah and the prophecies, then to John the Baptist as the first in line of those coming to fulfill the prophecies. Like John, Jesus also taught, "Repent ye! The Kingdom of heaven is at hand!" And, to try to explain what he meant, Jesus at once began to use parables. These had an outer as well as an inner meaning, and, as the inner meaning was understood only by those of the "chosen," the prophecies were again brought to the fore.

In Isaiah, 28:9–13, we read: "Whom shall he teach knowledge? and whom shall be made to understand doctrine? them that are weaned from the milk and drawn from the breasts. For precept must be upon precept, precept upon precept: line upon line; here a little and there a little: For with stammering lips and another tongue will he speak to his people. To whom he said, This is the rest wherewith ye may cause the weary to rest; and this is the refreshing: yet they would not hear. But the word of the Lord was unto them precept upon precept, precept upon precept; line upon line; here a little, and there a little; that they might go, and fall backward, and be broken, and snared and taken."

The implications in this prophetic passage, when the "weaned from milk" is mentioned, is that the old and mature were the only ones who could understand the Huna secrets. Even these more advanced individuals when "chosen" and instructed, would have to be taught "precept upon precept" and with the use of the words of the code language—this resulting in the teaching "with stammering lips and another tongue. . . ." The ones who were to listen, however, were not all to be able to accept what was offered. Some were to "fall backwards, and be broken, and snared and taken." The Huna symbol of the "snare" stands for all the obstacles which prevent the "path" from being opened to the High Self. Fixations and the influence of evil spirits also come under this symbol.

Perhaps no single doctrine has caused more misunderstanding and controversy than the one centering on the exact nature of the "Kingdom of heaven," so let us see what light the code can throw on the matter.

The Hebrew and Greek words used in the Bible for "heaven," both mean the upper atmosphere or sky. In both languages the word for "kingdom" simply indi-

cates the place over which a king rules. There is no
hint of hidden meaning to be found. But if we take
the word for "kingdom" in the language of the code,
au-puni, the inner teachings given by Jesus become
clear to one initiated into Huna. *Au* means "I," as a
High Self. The *puni* root has the outer meaning of "a
Place," so we can say, "The place of the High Self" or
"Kingdom of heaven." The inner teaching, of course,
revolves around the fact that we each have a High Self
and that it lives above us but is a very definite part of
the three-self man. *Au* also means, "a place" and
puni, "what surrounds a place." The root *pu* has the
significant meaning of "together," and "to inclose," the
idea being that the three selves are "together" as if en-
closed in a single body, thus making a single unit.
Puni also means, "to finish" or "to complete," and in
this respect it points to the High Self as the one which
has completed its evolutionary schooling and who has
reached the high estate from which it acts as the
highest or third part of the man.

We are told in the Gospels that Jesus healed as well
as taught when he began his ministry. In the outer
teachings the healings are said to have been brought
about by Jesus, using his "will" or by calling for the
help of the Father. Quite another set of meanings appears when the code words are inspected and at the
same time the Huna healing philosophy studied. To
the kahunas the usual cause of illness was the "blocking of the path" to the High Self. To bring about
healing, the "blockings" were removed, then the High
Self requested to accept a goodly supply of mana and
use it to do the actual healing. Jesus explained, in

131

John's account, "Not I, but the Father, he doeth the work." In cases where the contact with the High Self had been "blocked" by a sense of guilt or by fixed false ideas held by the low self, there was the need to cleanse away the blocks. Jesus sometimes said, "Your sins are forgiven you." Or he might say, "Be cleansed." This cleansing or forgiveness is ka-la, in the language of the code. It means, "of the light" or "to restore the light," this symbolizing the opening of the shadowy cord "path" to the High Self so that mana can be made available and can be used to bring about healing.

In cases where evil spirits fasten themselves on victims, they prevent the contact with the High Self and so keep the Father-Mother from casting them out. Jesus healed the obsessed by casting out the evil spirits, using the mana in the Mesmeric or Hypnotic form to force out the spirits, after which he instructed the victim to accept the "cleansing" and to give up his own evil ways so that his bodily "house" would remain clean and contact kept with his protecting High Self.

As we will consider the matter of casting out devils in the chapter to follow, let us go on with the regular healing.

The healing of a leper was described in detail. (Mark, 1:40–42.) "There came a leper to him, beseeching him, and kneeling down to him, and saying unto him, If thou wilt, thou canst make me clean. And Jesus, moved with compassion, put forth his hand, and touched him, and saith unto him, I will; be thou cleansed. And as soon as he had spoken, immediately the leprosy departed from him, and he was cleansed."

The code word for cleansing or "make clean" in the

healing sense is *hui-kala*. The root *hui* means "to unite," and so we see that the man had his path opened and was once more united with his High Self as a part of the healing action. The same root has the meaning also of "a cluster or bundle," this being the symbol of the cluster of thought-forms making up the mental picture of the man in the healed condition—this picture being sent to the High Self on a flow of mana to enable it to make the physical changes resulting in the healing. The word "will" is also code, *make-make*, which means "to desire greatly." The single word, *make*, has the meaning of "to be right, fitting and proper," also of "to permit." These meanings all apply directly to the making of the Huna prayer for healing. The patient must be "made fitting or proper," through the cleansing rite that reopens his path to his High Self. The one making the prayer must also have a very strong "desire" for the healing to be brought about, and on this hinges the Huna belief that all emotions, such as desire, are generated in and by the low self in cooperation with the middle self. If the low self does not desire to have a prayer answered, it will not do its part in the work and the effort is useless. The root word *make* also has the meaning of "to die; to perish," and this is a code way of saying that the life force or mana is much used up in enabling the High Self to perform instant healings.

In verses 30 and 31 we read, "But Simon's wife's mother lay sick with a fever; and anon they tell him of her. And he came and took her by the hand, and lifted her up; and immediately the fever left her, and she ministered unto them." The key code words here are "lifted up," which is the usual symbol for "lifting up" the mana and the thought-form picture of the prayer for healing to the High Self.

Mark, 2:3–6, relates the story of the healing of the man suffering from palsy. Jesus said, "Son, thy sins be forgiven thee." This tells us that the "cleansing" was given, and the fact that the man suffered from palsy gives the clue as to what needed to be cleansed away to open his path to the High Self. Palsy is *lolo*, in the code, and the root *lo* indicates the kahunas' belief that the seat of the mind of the low self was in the intestinal tract—and the low self the place where fixations and convictions of unworthiness and guilt must be sought out and removed.

The kahunas, after leaving the Near East to settle in Polynesia, used a baptismal ritual with water as part of the cleansing of a patient, and if the one to be healed could make amends to persons who had been hurt by him, this was demanded before the cleansing rite was performed and the healing was asked for in prayer. In the code in the Gospels, the elaborate details of such rituals were impossible to describe, but the ones who were initiated needed only to be given hints in code words to remind them of the entire process.

Mark, 3:1–4, gives us unmistakable information about the need for the heavy charge of mana to be sent to the High Self in order to bring healing. We read that a man with a "withered hand" was healed. The code word for "withered" is *maloo*, which has also the meaning of "dried out or wilted," which symbolizes the lack of mana, the symbol for which is "water." The man's affliction had, supposedly, come about because he had lost his full contact with his High Self and had let it "dry out" or lack a sufficient amount of mana to protect him, the lesser man. Jesus corrected this and with the mana supplied, the healing was made possible.

The need for mana to empower the High Self to heal is touched upon again in Mark, 5:25-30 in which the woman with the long-standing "issue of blood" touched his garment and was healed. The "virtue had gone out of him" at the touch, so he knew what had happened. The word in the language of the kahunas for "virtue" is mana, and here no code is needed, simply a statement that the mana had been taken from him so that he felt it and so that the healing was accomplished.

In Mark 6:38–42 we have the account of the healing of the damsel of whom he said, "the damsel is not dead, but sleepeth." In healing her he took her by the hand (the hand being *limalima mana*) and symbolizing the accumulating of mana, then dividing it with the High Self,) he raised her up and she was healed. When he commanded her to "arise" the code word was used (*iluna*) symbolizing the rising of the prayer picture and mana to the High Self.

Passing from healing to the control of wind and sea by Jesus, we come to the familiar story of the "rebuking of the winds" and the command to the sea to be still. The later kahunas in Polynesia practiced a similar control over wind and weather as well as over fish and turtles in the sea, so as we go on in the story of Jesus, we also find that he exerted his powers to bring about

the "miraculous draught of fishes." The feat of walking on water was not known to the Polynesian kahunas, but is included in the gospel accounts.

The miracle of walking on the water is related in
Matthew, Mark and John, but not mentioned in Luke.
It is possible that what the writers were telling in the
code had a direct bearing on the large amount of mana
needed to perform a major miracle, and the Disciples
may well have assisted in accumulating and sending
the mana to the High Self of Jesus or of the ones to be
healed. This brings us to the calling of the Disciples
and the code meaning of words used in giving that part
of the story.

To understand the role played in the drama by the
Disciples, we must keep in mind the fact that "many
are called, but few are chosen." The "chosen" or
"elect" were those who had lived a number of lives and
had learned the lessons of loving-kindness sufficiently
well as to be almost ready to "graduate."

There is no mistaking the fact that the Disciples,
perhaps with the exception of Judas, were of the
"elite." This is made very clear by the code in the
account given in Mark: 1:15–20, which begins: "And
saying, The time is fulfilled, and the kingdom of God
is at hand: repent ye, and believe the gospel. Now as
he walked by the sea of Galilee, he saw Simon and
Andrew his brother casting a net into the sea: for they
were fishers. And Jesus said unto them, Come ye after
me, and I will make you fishers of men. And straightway they forsook their nets and followed him."

It will be recalled that we were told through the
code that Jesus was a kahuna when the writers of the

Gospels said that he was a carpenter, this word being "a kahuna" in the code language. In a similar way, very clever use was made of the code in selecting the trade of the Disciples and making them fishermen, for the word for this occupation is *lawaia*, and in it the roots and general meanings allow a most excellent description of the high state of evolution which had been reached by these chosen ones. They were all ready to accept the secret teaching which would allow them, at the end of their present incarnation, to "graduate" to the level of the High Selves.

Mark does not say that Jesus had preached to those he later called, or that they had repented and been baptized. But in the very fact that they were using nets for their fishing and that they "left their nets," tells us that their paths had been unblocked.

A "net," *u-pena*, is the symbol of the "snare" which catches the unwary and "blocks the path" to the High Self. But the roots of the word give the information that the "selves" of the fishermen, (*u*, for *au*, a "self") were "anointed" or made into "Christs." (The root meaning of *pe-na*, short for *pe-ana*, is "anoint" plus "ing"—an "anointing.")

Let us look at the code meaning of "fisher," *lawaia* with its overlapping roots.

La: the symbol of the High Self.
Wai: meaning "water" and symbolizing the mana.
Wa: meaning the space between two things, and symbolizing the space between the High Self and the lesser two selves, this space having to be bridged by the aka cord of the "path."

Lawa: "to take" as fish, or "to hold fast." Redoubled we have, *lawa-lawa*, which has for one of its meanings, "to stretch cords from one place to another to fasten something," and here we have the shadowy cords established between the lower man and the High Self. The Disciples were in contact with their High Selves, if the code is to be believed at this point. And they sent mana (*wai*) to their High Selves (*la*). This mana was accepted as the root *ia*, meaning "fish," tells us in one of its alternate meanings, which is, "to enter in, as something into the mouth." *Lawa* also means, "The full finishing of a work," which tells us that the fishermen disciples had finished their several incarnations and so the work of gaining their evolutionary training. The word also has the symbol meaning of "white or shining," which is the symbol of the High Self, and which tells us here that the Disciples were ready to go on up into the High Self level when the incarnation of the present time was finished and Jesus had instructed them fully.

Returning again to the miracles, we note that only John relates the story of the miracle of turning water into wine. In this there are a few significant meanings hidden in symbols, and, knowing as we do that water was the symbol of mana, and that miracles were done by asking the Father to perform them, the accumulation of a surcharge of mana is seen in the filling of the six water pots "to the brim." The servants who filled the pots were then ordered to "draw out" and "bear unto the governor of the feast," the latter symbolizing the High Self, to whom the surcharge of mana is sent in all Huna prayer actions. The water is then revealed to have become wine, a symbol of the change which the High Self makes in the lower mana to use it to bring about changes in physical matter, these usually resulting in healing, but in this story the water was changed to wine.

John, in 9:1–10, tells of the restoration of sight to a man who had been born blind. An important bit of philosophy was touched upon openly in the question asked by the Disciples, "Master, who did sin, this man, or his parents, that he was born blind?"

The belief in reincarnation is plain here, as the man could not have sinned before his birth unless in a previous life. Jesus replied, "Neither hath this man sinned, nor his parents: but that the works of God should be made manifest in him." The Huna belief was that man, having to incarnate in an animal body, shares with all life on the physical level, the chance that by some accident of circumstances the imperfections may replace the intended and normal course of life. Here, the outer meaning was given in the statement that the man had been allowed to be blind in order that the power of God might be exhibited in the healing.

Jesus spoke of himself as the lesser man of the low and middle self combination in verse 4: "I must work the works of him that sent me, while it is day. . . ." The word, "day" is the symbol of "light," or the High Self, and so we see that this "work" is to be done only when the High Self is united with the lesser selves to perform the miracles.

In verse 5, Jesus speaks as the High Self united with the lesser man, saying, "As long as I am in the world, I am the light of the world."

The account continues in verse 6, telling how Jesus

139

spat upon the ground and made clay of spittle and earth. The code word is that for "spittle," *ku-ha*, in which the root *ku* has for one of its several meanings that of, "to stretch out or reach, as with the hand." This is the symbol in Huna of reaching out to make contact with the High Self. Sometimes it is symbolized by the act of "stretching a cord." The root, *ha*, in the word, is the now familiar symbol of accumulating mana and beginning the regular Huna prayer action. The blind man was ordered to wash the clay from his eyes in the "pool of Siloam," which was noted for its healing powers. The high mana of the High Self is indicated in this washing, because it caused the changes in the physical matter of the eyes to correct the condition of blindness. (The Huna belief appears to have been that the shadowy body of the low self duplicates every part of the physical body and acts as a mold surrounding it. If the blind eye was to be restored, the substance of the eye would be dematerialized for a moment, then materialized once more to fit the shadowy or *aka* mold, the latter always being perfect, even if some "accident" in the physical level has injured the physical counterpart of the mold which forms at birth and survives after death. The man who loses a leg during life, reaches the other side of life in the spirit world after death, clothed in his shadowy bodies—one for each self. As the shadowy body of the man remains perfect, the leg is replaced and is normal in so far as a spirit is concerned.)

The mystery of how the miracles were performed is not explained in the outer teachings of the Gospels. In a similar way, the Old Testament tells of the miracles of Moses, but the explanation is only that God told Moses to do things, such as casting down his rod, and it is taken for granted that God then performed the miracle of changing the rod into a serpent.

In the inner teachings of the Gospels, as revealed by the Huna word code, the mechanics of healing are only partly described. The kahunas of later times in Polynesia were the physicians and healers and used various methods. Some specialized in the use of herbs known to have medicinal value. Some used a form of massage which included manipulation of the joints, much as Chiropractors do today. There were kahunas who specialized in counteracting spirit attacks and spirit influence exerted over the living. Other healers (there were several grades of healing kahunas), laid on hands and sent their mana, with the mental pictures of the normal condition, into the part of a patient which had gone wrong. Instant or nearly instant healing was performed with the help of the High Self of the kahuna (or, in some cases by the help of the High Self of a good spirit who could be called upon for help by the kahuna, much as modern healing is accomplished by the "guides" of some Spiritualists).

A kahuna patient was, in fairly modern times, examined to learn whether or not he had a sense of guilt resulting from hurting others. If such a sense of guilt was found, the patient was sent to make amends for the hurts. If they could not be made to individuals, certain acts such as fasting or making gifts to the needy were prescribed by the healer, the idea being that the patient must come to believe that he had righted the wrongs, and also that physical acts and self-sacrifice would impress the low self that its man was now cleansed of guilts and ready to be healed by the High Self through the agency of the kahuna.

The actual healing by the kahuna often took the form of the preliminary cleansing (*ka-la*) of the patient with a sprinkling or baptism with water while the kahuna affirmed that the last taint of guilt was washed away and the patient was fully cleansed. The invocation was then made to the High Self, and often the kahuna laid his hands on the patient. The mana needed by the High Self for the healing was usually supplied by the kahuna when the prayer for healing was made. The prayer was often repeated three times, word for word. Where instant healing of a broken bone was done, the amount of mana needed was not great. Natural healing was caused to take place with greatly increased speed.

In cases, such as the healing of the eyes of the man who had been blind from birth, as told in the account of John, more mana would be needed to dissolve the eye tissues momentarily and rebuild them in the perfect shadowy mold of the eyes, as normal eyes. In modern Spiritualism, where materialization and apports are being worked for in a seance, it is customary to form a "circle" of several people, these joining by clasping hands, with the medium acting as the focus of the "power" generated. Without knowing it, the sitters can often supply enough mana for a spirit to use to produce the desired phenomena.

It will be noted that Jesus selected the twelve Disciples before beginning his production of major miracles of healing or of physical changes, such as turning water to wine or causing the fig tree to wither, to say nothing of forcing evil spirits to leave those who were afflicted by them. In the Disciples we have the evidence of the code to show that a "circle," somewhat similar to the seance circles, was used so that a large amount of mana could be drawn from them to enable the High Self to do the actual work.

In the code the word for "disciple" is *hau-mana*, and the root *hau* has for one of its meanings that of "to inhale or sniff up, as the wind." This confirms the root *ha*, in *hau*, which stands for the accumulation of mana and the entire rite of sending it and the prayer picture to the High Self. The root *mana*, needs no explanation and conceals no coded meaning. Outwardly, the meaning of "disciples" was that of apprentices, students, or simply followers. The inner or coded meaning was that the Disciples made up a circle to furnish needed mana when major miracles were performed. In making the code, the initiate writers very often used a play on word sounds, cutting up the words into root parts and taking off a letter sound now and then to produce a word with a slightly different code meaning. In this case, if the initial letter is removed from *hau-mana*, we have *au-mana*, and the *au* root means the High Self (as in *au-makua*, for the High Self), this showing where the mana accumulated and furnished by the Disciples was sent to be used.

Individuals differ in the amount of mana or vital force they normally have or can produce. In seance records we find that some mediums can, without a circle to draw from, produce physical phenomena such as "direct voice," apporting, transportation of objects from place to place, (even of themselves) and levitation. The extravagant use of mana, however, often depletes and weakens the medium.

From the coded Huna in the Gospels, we are given to understand that the High Self Father of Jesus performed all the miraculous "works." But it is possible that the High Selves of the Disciples also had a part in major miracles. The kahunas often spoke of "The Great Company of High Selves" and believed that on the higher levels of life there was often a close association of groups of High Selves. In bringing about world or national changes, these groups may work together, drawing mana from the lower men as needed. The code word for "company" is *poe*, which also means "to break up," and this suggests the Huna belief that the future events which have been constructed by the High Selves in the aka substance, to fit the actions of men on the lower level, may be "broken up" when prayers are made and events are to be changed for the better. We can only speculate as to the amount of supervision given by the "Great Company" or the many "Great Companies."

Although the outer teachings in the Gospel are that Jesus was accustomed to forgive sins, there is little to show that the ones he healed were first made to make amends for the sins of hurts done to others—but it is safe to conclude that the healing work, as taught in the inner circles, included the kahuna method of cleansing. The sins of failure to obey the religious instructions of the priests of the Church are not actual sins in terms of Huna. But any act that hurts another was,

144

to the kahunas, a sin of the kind for which amends had to be made directly or in kind. Because the code shows so clearly the elements of Huna belief and practices in the accounts of the life and work of Jesus, it is permissible to conclude that forgiveness for the sins of hurting others was actually given only after amends had been made, even if the details of the steps taken to bring about the cleansed condition of "restored light" were too many and perhaps too complicated to set down in the coded portions of the writings.

The code words for sin are *he-wa* and *ha-la* (also the word *ino*, which means to hurt or injure another in some way, physically or mentally—this being the common idea of sin of the outer teaching). *He-wa* means, literally "the space" and symbolizes the condition in which the lower man is cut off or separated from the High Self, the "space" being the distance between. The word also means to "miss the mark," or leave a space between the thing thrown and the target. The word *ha-la* also means to "miss the mark" or make a mistake or to believe an untruth, but when the two root parts are examined, we find the familiar *ha* indicating the prayer ritual in its entire form, and *la* standing for the "Light" or High Self: so we see that if we fail in an effort to contact the High Self properly in prayer, that falls under the heading of sin in its Huna meaning. It is unfortunate that we have only one word for "sin" in English instead of the three very descriptive ones found in the language of the kahunas.

In Mark 2:4–12, we have Jesus offering an alternate healing command to the man stricken with palsy.

One is, "Son, thy sins are forgiven thee." The other is, "Arise, and take up thy bed, and go thy way into thine house." The forgiveness of sin is "to restore the light." The "arise" is code for sending the mana "up" to the High Self while praying for healing. The outer doctrine of the Church, and the priestly rite of confession and forgiveness, falls far short of the fuller meaning of the inner teaching, but is excellent if the person asking forgiveness is also made to do penance —which is similar to the Huna demand that amends be made for hurts done others.

The miracle of the multiplication of the loaves and fishes is given in all four of the Gospels, and no code words were used. However, the open symbology of the several incarnations needed to perfect the man are pointed up in the account of the "Twelve Baskets" filled with what was left after the multitude had been fed.

Only Luke tells of the miraculous draft of fishes. In this incident there are no new code words used.

The walking on water episode, as related by Matthew, 14:25–26, tells us that the Disciples mistook Jesus for a spirit, and the word used as code for "above" (the sea or "on") is *maluna*, the first part of the word being *malu*, which means "shade" and so gives us the symbol of the shadowy body—a symbol as old as early Egypt, when the "shadow" was listed as part of the man, both when alive and when dead.

The ability of Jesus to change himself into spirit form and appear to others has been counted by some as miraculous, and with this may be classed the ability to vanish in some way. Luke, in 4:28–30, tells how the angered citizens of Nazareth tried, after Jesus failed to heal or "show signs" in his home village, to take him to the brow of a hill outside the town "that they might cast him down headlong. But, he passing through the midst of them, went his way."

The implication is that he was able to make himself invisible, or that he left his body and went with them, as a visible spirit for a time, then vanished, passed through the midst of the crowd and went his way. The code in this passage hinges on the opening words, "But (*aka*) he, passing through etc." The word aka is used for "but," and is, in one secondary meaning, the "shadow" or "dim outline of a thing," which is the symbol of the shadowy body one uses after death, or when out of the body during life, as a spirit or apparition. It may be that the coded suggestion given here and in the account of walking on water were both intended to lay the background for the scenes in which Jesus, after the resurrection, appeared before the Disciples in a fully materialized spirit body.

In Spiritualistic circles there sometimes is to be found a medium who can produce healing of the miraculous kind. In the years beginning with 1962 there were occasional reports of the healing produced by a Spiritualist in the Phillipine Islands some miles in the back country from Manila. His name was Eleuterio Terte, and he was photographed and his work observed as he prayed, laid his hands on his patients, and often performed operations such as the removal of an appendix, with no visible instruments or incisions. The healer attributed the help given him to God, but, as he was known to be a Spiritualist, it is probable that he acted as a medium and furnished the mana while good spirits who were in contact with their own High Selves, actually did the miraculous work.

Similar reports of "Psychic Surgery" and spirit healing have come from various parts of the world in recent years, especially from Brazil, where Spiritualism has attracted many, despite the opposition of the Church, and where there is a hospital given over to spirit healing.

A glance at any of the magazines published for Spiritualists will show that there is a considerable number of mediums who advertise and who attempt to send their spirit friends to any part of the world to answer calls for healing ministrations. The results, of course, are often disappointing, and it may well be that without the path to the High Self of the patient being opened and amends made for hurts done others, the spirits find healing either difficult or impossible.

CHAPTER 11

EVIL SPIRITS OR "DEVILS"

We have considered the nature of Jesus, and have seen him speaking as a man as well as a High Self. We have also examined his teachings concerning the "kingdom of heaven," not as a place but as the High Self and its higher level of evolutionary progress—as the Place of light, and as the Light itself.

We have seen that man is a triune being, made up of three spirits, and that each of these is at a different level or grade in the evolutionary School of Life. The low self is seen to be the cause of most of the "sins" of greed and cruelty, also that it often gets the wrong idea about something and clings to it with stubborn purpose, so that these fixations or complexes may prevent the better-reasoning middle self from setting the low self right on troublesome points. In addition to the fixed and irrational ideas of the low self, to which it reacts too strongly at times for the good of the man, there is another cause of trouble, the influence of the spirits of the dead. These spirits are the "devils" which Jesus cast out, and it is most important that we consider what Huna and the code can tell us of the matter.

The belief that evil spirits can and do obsess, or influence in varying degrees, the living, is as old as history, and together with mediumship, can be traced back to Totemism. There is no need to argue that there has been such a belief down the ages, but on the other hand, there is no escaping the fact that such a belief is accepted by only a few in modern times, even by those Christians who feel that every word of the Bible is divinely inspired and so must be correct.

In my book, the SECRET SCIENCE BEHIND MIRACLES, I have given the details of the Huna beliefs covering spirits of five kinds and their survival after death.

However, it may be worth pausing here to explain again that most spirits are made up of their own normal three selves. These are usually good. But there are also spirits who, because of guilt feelings or fixations in life have a "blocked" path to their High Selves and so, in death, remain evil and predatory. These learn to exert hypnotic control over some living victim and to force upon him their evil emotions and desires. They steal his mana or vital force and so keep themselves hypnotically strong. They vary in degrees of badness and they may influence their victim in different ways. In some cases they obsess the man completely and take over the body, pushing out the rightful middle self. This may result in a complete change in personality in the man, or, if the low self is also thrust out and the spirit's own low self enabled to take almost complete control of the body, the man becomes so changed that he is insane. Obsessional insanity accounts for most of those victims who are so badly bothered that they have to be hospitalized, but there are a great many whose obsession is so slight that they can carry on fairly well. The majority of the slightly obsessed do not know what causes their emotional explosions and strange and unaccountable hates and fears, or strange bodily ills. Many of those who are treated by psychiatrists for the removal of fixations are, in reality, victims of spirit influence.

There are two other kinds of spirits who influence the living. One is the middle self spirit which has in some way been separated from its low self at death. The other is the low self which has been separated in a similar manner from its middle self. Either or both of these can cause trouble and be very difficult to live with, but the presence of either or both types is almost never realized unless a Psychometric Analysis reading is made which discloses the condition.

In our search for the code in the Gospels, we will deal only with such spirits as the normal low and middle selves who are cut off from their High Selves and so are evil and are out of control from the higher level.

Unfortunately, the kahunas who inserted coded passages into the Gospel scripts did not give us many instances of obsession and the casting out of the evil spirits. Had more instances been given, we might have gained through the code a much fuller understanding of the methods to be used to drive away the spirits and heal the victims.

The hypnotic influence exerted on the living by spirits does not affect the victim's middle self, but, like all such force, controls to varying degrees the low self. For this reason the influence works in the "subconscious" or away from the notice or understanding of the middle self. The low self reacts to the spirit's suggestion unless, as in hypnosis administered by the living, the low self has a very strong resistance. In the same way, if the low self is strongly of the opinion that certain acts are bad, it will not respond and try to perform such acts. This is something to be kept well in mind because those influenced by spirits usually have similar ways of acting and willingly accept promptings of hate, plus fear and evil, as well as of hurtful attitudes. A person who is good, and whose low self has been well schooled in the matter of what is right and wrong, will resist spirit suggestion which would otherwise cause a desire in the low self to act wrongly.

We read in Luke 11:14–26: "And he was casting out a devil, and it was dumb. And it came to pass that when the devil was gone out, the dumb spake: and the people wondered." (From the Huna angle this evil spirit was one who had taken complete control of the victim and had prevented him from speaking. The spirit may have been a dumb individual during its earthly life and may have brought this affliction with it so that the victim became dumb when under full control.)

"15. But some of them said, He casteth out devils through Beelzebub the chief of the devils. 16. Then others, tempting him, sought of him a sign from heaven.

"17. But he knowing their thoughts, said unto them, Every Kingdom divided against itself is brought to desolation; and a house divided against a house, falleth. 18. If Satan also be divided against himself, how shall his kingdom stand? because ye say that I cast out devils through Beelzebub. 19. And if I by Beelzebub cast out devils, by whom do your sons cast them out? therefore shall they be your judges.

20. But if I with the finger of God cast out devils, no doubt the kingdom of God is come upon you."

The outer meaning of the above passages is clear, but it is apparent, when we begin to apply the code and translate the words back into the code language, that the writer was giving inner or hidden information on the nature of obsession by evil spirits.

Unfortunately, the Greek tongue in which the coded account was written, contained no definitive words to be used to tell which of the five kinds of evil spirits was being discussed. In the translation the Greek word "demon" is used, and this tells us nothing via the code except that evil spirits in general were being named. Had the code language been used for an evil spirit made up of two selves, its low and middle, but cut off from its High Self, it would have been called *a kino wai lua*, literally, "a body of two waters," but as this is the term applied to a spirit, the "body" would be its shadowy or aka body, and as "water" is the symbol of mana, the name shows that this ghostly spirit used the two kinds of mana, the mesmeric form common to the low self, and the hypnotic form which only the middle self uses. If, in the case of the "dumb spirit" which had been cast out (verse 14), the code word would probably have been *unihipili*, meaning the low self, and we remember that the low self, in common with animals and their indwelling spirits, cannot talk. The middle self and it alone has the ability to talk. If the middle self is not with the obsessing low self, the spirit and its victim are dumb.

The ordinary use of the word "divide" simply means that parts of the person or "kingdom" or "house" are

153

in opposition. But the idea of "to divide or of dividing" is the symbol all through the Huna lore of the dividing of the vital force or mana. The low self, having an animal body and being able to digest food, creates all the basic or low mana as part of its essential job. It divides or shares this mana with the middle self, and the High Self must depend upon it when it wishes to get mana for its work on its own level of consciousness.

The word mana names what is made and used by the low self. When it is divided and part given to the middle self, this becomes the hypnotic power which is used to control the low self. It is then called *mana-mana*, doubling the idea of its power. The mana of the High Self is not usually named, but would be *mana-loa*, or "strongest mana." It can be used to tear down physical substance and to put it together again, a mechanism employed in bringing about instant or miraculous healing. The whole work of making a prayer in Huna fashion centers on having the middle self instruct the low to accumulate extra mana, then contact the High Self via the connecting aka cord, and then send or "divide" the mana with the High Self. The symbol of this division is the hand and its fingers, the fingers being held apart to show the division. The word for "finger" is *mana-mana-lima*, in which we recognize at once the two kinds of mana, in the repetition of the word mana, also the implication of the hypnotic form of the force, and in the word *lima*, we have two meanings, one, "finger or hand, arm or foot and leg," but with the secondary meaning of "power" or "force."

This last meaning enables us to understand the inner meaning of the lines, "If I by the finger of God cast out devils. . . ." The finger in this case is the mana power of the High Self as a god. It is the high mana and it is evident that it was used to "cast out" the dumb Spirit. And, as the passage continues, saying that there is left, ". . . no doubt that the kingdom of God is upon you," we have double proof that the casting out was done by the High Self and that full contact was made with it along the "path" of the aka cord—the High Self being the "Kingdom," symbolically.

In verse 21 and on, we see the idea well presented of the strong or good man or low and middle selves who are able to resist the influence of spirits, but we are told that even the strong may be overcome by one stronger, that is by the superior force of hypnotic (*mana-mana*) power. We read: "When a strong man armed keepeth his place, his goods are in peace. But when a stronger than he shall come upon him, and overcome him, he taketh from him all his armour wherein he trusted, and divideth his spoils."

Here the coded inner meaning lies in the words "divide" and "goods." *Mana-mana* means to divide, as in separating the fingers of the hand, or as a tree dividing into branches. In this form of dividing, there is a basic connection or union of the fingers at the hand and of the limbs at the trunk of the tree. This is a most excellent symbol of the mana that is 'divided' but which still remains in the three-self man.

Another word for "divide" is *moku-aha-na*, and we find this used in the translation of the verses into Hawaiian. The full word means to be divided into opposing parts or parties. The root words give the very significant meaning of breaking the aka cord which connects the lower man with his High Self. (The cord is not actually cut or broken, but is "blocked" and remains unused by either an evil man or an evil spirit obsessing him.) *Moku* is "to break or cut as a cord" as well as "to divide." The second root word, *aha*, repeats the coded information that it is the aka cord which is blocked, cut or divided, its meaning being "a cord." (It has several other meanings, among which is the significant one of "a certain prayer," and the implication being that the prayer is sent over the aka cord to the High Self. It also has the meaning of, "to stretch the cord by which the first posts of a house were lined up to get them straight.") The root *na* is a grammatical unit like our "ing" added to a word. Still another meaning of *aha* is a "company," usually four or more, and this is significant in telling us that while three spirits make up the normal man, the obsessing spirit which attaches itself to the man makes four, or, if several spirits fasten themselves to the victim and join in obsessing him, we have then a larger "company." In another part of the Gospel account such a company is mentioned and it is said, "His name is Legion," or a great many. (The budding science of Psychology, in its branch called "Abnormal Psychology," is given over in part to the study of "dual" and "multiple" personality cases. In these there are seen cases in which only one obsessing spirit takes over the victim at times, or cases in which three or more "personalities" or spirits take over the man, using or influencing him in turn. These personalities are supposed to be parts of the original one of the patient, and the whole as a unit is said to have been "split." Treatment is mostly in the form of using hypnosis to suggest to the patient that the split off parts unite. Needless to say, the treatments are seldom successful in doing more than submerging one of the obsessing spirits so that it works only out of sight and by influencing the resident low self.)

The "strong man" in the passage under examination is overcome by one even stronger despite his arms and resistance, and then his "goods" are taken and "divided" as spoils. The division implies that there is more than one victorious attacker of the vanquished "strong man." We may ask with whom he divides the "goods," and the answer can be that he takes only part of the mana from the victim or that he invites other spirits to come and take a share. We know that the mana of the victim is what is being spoken of in code, for the word for "goods" in the code language is *waiwai*, or "water-water," and as we know, water symbolizes mana in any of its forms. This word equates with *mana-mana*, or the hypnotic grade of basic mana, and so we know that the stolen "goods" of mana become hypnotic force with which the victorious spirit continues to control the despoiled victim.

In verse 23 we read, "He that is not with me is against me; and he that gathereth not with me, scattereth." Here Jesus speaks as the High Self, and we can paraphrase his statement in Huna terms of the inner teaching, as: "The man who is not in contact along the unblocked aka cord with me, is against me and given to evil deeds. He who does not gather mana

157

and send it along the cord to me in prayer, wastes or scatters the very life force." *Ho-ili-ili* is "to gather or collect," also to "inherit." "Goods" which are inherited are spoken of in the code as "treasure," and again the word *wai-wai* is used. We can be sure that it is mana which is collected. "To scatter" is *lu*, which also means "to drip water," indicating a waste of water as from a leaking vessel, so that it does no one good. The implication here is also that the "seeds" or thought-forms of the prayer which should be made by a good man, are scattered and wasted instead of being planted by sending them along the aka cord to the High Self. The mana which should then be sent daily to "water" the "seeds" is not sent, but wasted. This verse seems out of place in the context as it has little to do with obsession except to show what an evil man does not accomplish and why he remains without "Light" and Guidance from the High Self.

Continuing with the discourse on evil spirits, we read, "24. When the unclean spirit is gone out of a man, he walketh through dry places, seeking rest; and finding none, he saith, I will return unto my house whence I came out. 25. And when he cometh, he finds it swept and garnished. 26. Then goeth he, and taketh to him seven other spirits more wicked than himself; and they enter in and dwell there: and the last state of that man is worse than the first."

Here we see the evil spirit, after being forced to leave his victim, having to wander in "dry" places. As "water" is the symbol of mana, the "dry place" is the symbol of the lack of mana. The spirit, unable to steal mana was without rest. The word for "rest" is *maha*, which also means "to steal," so the code tells us the spirit found no place where he could steal mana. But, he returns hopefully to his victim, and there finds him—pictured as a "house"—all swept and garnished. The key word here is "swept," which is *ka-hiliia*. This has several meanings, one of which is "to plait; to twist." (Brushes were braided with feathers at the base by the kahunas and used as dusters.) The symbol of putting to use the aka cord reaching to the High Self is "to braid" and this braiding also suggests the existence of a cord, as does *aha*, met in earlier parts of the discourse. To sweep with a plaited or braided brush has a special meaning of "to scatter" and applied to particles of dust, these being hard to see and so like the thought-forms of prayers which we have just seen mentioned as being "scattered" and so wasted. Here we have the coded information that when a spirit has been cast out, and when the victim continues to fail to recognize his High Self and to begin asking it in prayer to take its rightful part in living the three-fold life, the "house" is left open and unguarded. The word, "garnished" repeats the idea of the "braided aka cord" because the kahuna people, in making ready for a guest, garnished their houses by braiding wreaths of decorative greenery and flowers to hang here and there and to place around the necks of guests. The word, *hoo-lakolakoia*, for "garnished" has also the meaning of providing a goodly supply of everything a guest might need. This points to the victim, still filled with mana, and with no protection, so the evil spirit goes to find his evil friends, and they play the part of the guests, taking over again, but in greater numbers.

The moral is not drawn openly in the passage, but it is apparent in the code teaching. If one is set free from an evil spirit, one is safe against its return only if contact is at once established with the High Self and the proper and prayerful life is lived. Jesus often said to those whom he healed, "Go, and sin no more." This especially applies to one freed from obsession. The old evil ways and thoughts and impulses must be given up. The symbol of a house all made ready and inviting for guests, has another significance. The person who loves evil to some degree, automatically tends to invite the friendship of spirits of equally evil leanings. In most cases, the victims of obsession do not wish to give up their evil spirit companions and will resist all efforts to get them to turn to better living and thinking.

In the account found in Matthew 8:28–32, of the violently insane man whose obsessing spirits recognized Jesus as the "Son of God" or High Self, and begged to be allowed to enter the swine when cast out, we have little else by way of inner teachings than the intimation that it is the High Self who casts out evil spirits, as, in this account, even the spirits recognize Jesus as the High Self. The exorcism was complete and permanent in this account because the swine, once taken over by the spirits, rushed into the water and were killed. This water may have had some significance as the symbol of the high mana, but it is not apparent. The fact that the evil spirits were of human origin is given in the words telling that they came out of the tombs. The code word for "tomb," *kupapau,* means the dead body, the tomb in which it is placed and something that has belonged to the dead body, that is, its spirits.

Mark gives us a valuable code word when he tells of the casting out of an unclean spirit obsessing a man in a synagogue. In 1:25, we read, "and Jesus rebuked him, saying, Hold thy peace and come out of him. The code word here is "rebuke," *papa*, which also means "to shine, or create light and heat," symbolizing the opening of the path of the man so that the "Light" or High Self could help in removing the evil spirit.

CHAPTER 12

THE PARABLES AND RESULTING
CHURCH DOGMAS

In his sayings, as well as direct teaching, Jesus continually spoke of "my, our, or your Father which is in heaven." The root *au* for "I" or "self" appears in each word. These, in the language of the code are, *"ko'u* (my), *kakau,* (our), *oukau* (your) *Makua* (parent). *Lani* is "heaven." It is of importance that we keep in mind the code fact that it takes both the father and the mother to make the parent, and that, in the word for "heaven," *la-ni,* we have the root *la* for Light, as the symbol of the High Self which is made up of a male and female self, and the obscure root *ni,* which is found as *ni-ni* in the word meaning "to heal," or in the word *ni-ni-ni,* meaning "to pour out, as a liquid": the healing given by the High Self in answer to prayer is accomplished by the use of the mana which is usually supplied by the one who makes the Huna-type prayer for healing.

In his teachings Jesus is made to attribute many powers, besides those of healing, to the High Self Parental Spirit Pair. Whether we have the original story accurately preserved for us in the Gospels, we do not know, and in some cases the scholars who have made long studies of the teachings are often forced to decide that different items were added by revisionists and redactors as well as by the Church Fathers during the long period in which conflicting dogmas and beliefs were being fought over. Some of the passages have been seen as additions to the original writings, their purpose being to give the appearance of authority for some claim made by the Church.

Now and again we can solve the problem by looking for a coded meaning in some passage which is either obscure, contradictory, or nearly meaningless in the context of the discourse in which it is found. In many cases the men responsible for the King James version of the Bible in English (which was used by the Hawaiian Missionaries in making the translation from English into Hawaiian), had difficulty in deciding which passages belonged to which discourses and which stood by themselves as sayings or teachings embodied in a single passage and not related to what had gone before or what was to follow.

An example of this problem of the relationship of passages is to be found in Matthew 18:13–21, in which is given the parable of the lost sheep and the value of the sinner in the scheme of things. We read, ". . . it is not the will of your Father which is in heaven that one of these little ones should perish." In this we have the love of the High Self for the lesser pair of selves, and the "will" to preserve them through their sinful growth upward from one incarnation to the next rather than to destroy them for being slow to learn.

Students of the Gospel have long tried to find a way to cover the contradictory and inconsistent teaching that the wicked are to be cast into hell by a God of Fatherly love such as we find described in the parable

163

of the lost sheep, in which the main herd of sheep is left to shift for itself while the shepherd ranges afar to find and bring back the one sheep which had gone astray. In a similar way the loving father of the prodigal son left the good son to carry on as usual but made a feast for the prodigal.

There follow passages directing the manner in which a single man or a congregation of his fellows, should try to judge a sinner and cause him to right his ways. The sinner, if he refuses to be set right, is to be considered an outsider in so far as the congregation is concerned. This presupposes a form of church congregation already organized during the ministry of Jesus—a point open to question. Then follows the passage (set off slightly by double spacing in the King James Bible), which is supposed to give authority to the congregation to "bind" or in some way force the sinner to obey. We read, (18) "Verily I say unto you, Whatsoever ye bind on earth shall be bound in heaven and whatsoever ye shall loose on earth shall be loosed in heaven." The angry men who have assailed the Church of Rome, point to this passage as the only authority for giving priests the power to forgive sinners here or in heaven. In the later Protestant churches, where the priests were repudiated, this passage has been rejected or given some other meaning.

The very old conflict between the opposed sections of the Church, is easily settled when we examine the passage in the light of the code. It is seen at once that the passage was one which must be considered apart from the preceding discourse, for it contains only code meanings which relate to the Ha Rite of prayer—not in any way being related to men judging fellow men as sinners and putting a form of "binding" curse on them if they fail to conform to the wishes of the judging majority. The code meaning is in no way related to the Church practice in which the sinner who insisted upon remaining a "lost sheep" was cursed from here to eternity by a priest reciting the ritual of excommunication—a flagrant contradiction of the teaching of Jesus that one should live under the law of love and love one's enemies, even the sinners who refused to accept the salvation offered by the Church (and denied to all others until the year 1964).

The code key to verse 18 is to be found in the word for "bind." It is *paa*, a word which has a dozen different meanings and which is ideal for use in this saying. It means "to bind," but also, from the root *pa*, "to divide." It means to "touch" or to make contact and to "hit the mark" as in shooting an arrow, this being the Huna symbol of making successful contact for prayer with the High Self. The thing to be "divided" is the mana which is accumulated before the making of a Huna-type prayer, and the division is with the High Self as the contact is made and the mana is sent flowing over the connecting shadowy cord. The making of the mental picture to be sent with the mana flow is specifically indicated in the *paa* verbal meaning of "to retain in memory," as one must remember the words which are used in the prayer to describe the pictured thing asked for and desired.

Another verbal meaning of *paa* is, "to affirm, confirm, establish, to affirm positively." In this the code tells us that we must hold the prayer picture firm, once it is given to the High Self, and be positive in our faith in its effectiveness. The prayer is to be repeated often and the mana frequently sent to make possible the creating of the desired condition by the High Self. Difficult changes may take a long time to bring about.

The "binding" or "tying" or "making fast on earth" is all related to the necessity of making a firm decision about what is to be asked in prayer, then holding to that decision and holding the picture of the desired condition without change. The "binding" in heaven relates to the prayer picture when accepted by the High Self to be "watered" daily with the sacrificial gift of mana, until made to "grow" to full maturity, at which time it will "materialize" or become a reality on the earth level.

The passage says "whatsoever," not "whosoever" and has nothing to do with the mistaken meaning attached to it later by the uninitiated priests who claimed the privilege of making people on earth "bound" as by rituals of christening or baptism or marriage, even of exorcism and, finally, of "extreme unction" in dying. The claim that these earthly rituals, when used on people, were binding on their souls in heaven, if they reached it, are all dogmatic additions to the simple outer teachings found in the Gospels.

The opposite of "to bind" was given in the code as "to loose," and again nothing is said of people in the word, "whatsoever." The code word for "loose" is *kala*, "to restore the light." The outward meaning was taken to be "to forgive one's sins," but we know that this was used in the passage under discussion as part of the coded explanation of the correct way to make a prayer. The "loosening" was a matter of opening the "path," or way of contact with the High Self, so that the aka cord could be put into action and the working contact made before sending the mana and prayer picture. The "stumbling blocks" symbolized in Huna any of the several things which might "block the path" and prevent one from making proper contact via the low self with the High Self. We have already considered the hurts done others and the resulting sense of guilt which makes the low self refuse to face the High Self expectantly and with a sense of being deserving. The obsessing and evil spirits who fasten themselves on people who will share their evil impulses, also "block the path,' as do doubt and fear and ignorance of the fact that there is a High Self.

The "loosening" on earth is the opening of the "path" whose other and far end is in heaven or touching the High Self. This is the secret of the earth and heaven angle of the passage, and has nothing to do with the priestly assumption of authority to forgive sins or to withhold forgiveness. Another claim of priestly authority is based upon the passages in which Jesus says, (Matt. 16:19), "And I say also unto thee, That thou art Peter, and upon this rock I will build my church; and the gates of hell shall not prevail against it. And I will give unto thee the keys of the kingdom of heaven: and whatsoever thou shalt bind on earth shall be bound in heaven; and whatsoever thou shalt loose on earth shall be loosened in heaven." The passages which we have just been examining for code meanings (Matt. 18:13–21) duplicate the part about binding and loosening, but with no mention at all made of

Peter. The other Gospels make no mention of binding and loosening authority or of a church to be founded on Peter. The expectation was that the promised Parousia would come even during the life span of the listeners, with the heavens "opening" and the Kingdom established. The idea of "church" strikes a strange note in the story, and certainly Jesus did not seem to be looking forward beyond the "Coming of the Kingdom" to a time when a church with priests would be established and men given the very keys to heaven.

The code further straightens out the matter, for the name "Peter" is that of "a rock," and in the code the "rock" was the very epitome of a thing "fixed, fast, secure" firm and unchanging, as described in the word *paa*. Peter, in this piece of the code, simply becomes the symbol of the initiate who is given the "keys" or understanding of the secret methods of performing the Ha Rite. Not only Peter, but all Huna initiates, were given the "keys" to the method of contacting and working with the High Self, the latter being the embodiment of the "Kingdom of heaven."

The code symbol of the "rock" is found in Matthew, 8:24–28 and also in Luke, 7:47–49, in the parable in which Jesus explains that those who hear his teachings and act in accordance with them are like a man who builds his house on a rock foundation where it will be enduring; but those who do not follow his teachings, build on sand and their houses are swept away. In terms of the code, the house is the thing which the High Self builds in answer to the prayer, and if the prayer is *"paa"* or rock-firm and unchanging, it is rightly made. If the prayer is not firmly made and if

168

it is changed with each passing day, it is built on sand and the resulting "house" cannot stand. There is little chance to mistake this meaning, for, when the code is applied, we find "house" is *ha-le*, with the familiar *ha* root to indicate that the prayer rite is being referred to, and the secondary root *le*, as found in *le-le*, meaning to "leap or fly upward," this symbolizing the movement of the mana and thought-forms of the prayer upward to the High Self.

Another isolated passage follows the one on binding and loosening in Matthew 18, and we read on, verses 19 and 20, "Again I say unto you, That if two of you agree on earth as touching anything that they shall ask, it shall be done for them of my Father which is in heaven. For where two or three are gathered together in my name, there am I in the midst of them."

These passages have been misunderstood in outer circles and have appeared to be a false promise in as much as experience has taught that a prayer made by two people who agree on what is to be asked, is not more frequently answered than when made by one person. Moreover, the promise that the prayer should certainly be answered by the Father, has seldom been fulfilled. Something was seen to be amiss, but what?

Here we have Huna symbology to explain for us without the use of code words. The two who are to agree on what is to be asked are the low and middle selves of the man. Often the low self does not agree and will not do its part in making the prayer. One may wish to give up a habit, or to leave a job and be helped to find a different one. If the low self clings to the habit or to the old job, it will refuse to "agree."

Going on to the next passage, Jesus speaks as the High Self when he says that when "three are gathered together in my name," he, as the High Self is in their midst. In Huna terms, when the three selves are in full agreement and work together on the making and answering of the prayer, all will be well.

✿ ✿ ✿ ✿ ✴

In Matthew 13 we have several parables. In the three which deal with the sowing of seeds, as in verses 4 through 8, the outer teaching is that Jesus gave the good teachings, as a sower sows good grain, but that if those who hear the teachings are not ready to accept them for one reason or another, no benefit comes to them. The inner teachings are seen through the code and symbol words. The seeds which were sown are *ano-ano* in the language of the code, and seeds symbolize the prayer picture which is likened to a seed sent to the High Self to plant, and which is to be watered with the water of mana and made to grow, mature and bear good fruit "after its kind," or to conform to the original prayer picture. *Ano-ano* not only means "seeds," but has the meanings of "a solemn stillness," and of a "sacred or hallowed place." In making the Huna prayer one composes oneself for the work, becoming still in a solemn way, and the prayer-seed is sent to the High Self as the "sacred place."

The root *ano*, of the full word has a number of distinct meanings and a few which overlap. (See the word list for these). It shows in the root, the seed as the "likeness, resemblance or image of a thing," and this gives us the mental picture which we make of the desired thing or condition before the picture is presented as the "seed" to the High Self. The verbal meaning is surprisingly to the point when applied to the "seed" in connection with a prayer. It gives us, "To transform, to change the external appearance." (With *hou*: "to make new.") "To change the state of things"; "to transform" etc. These are items, all of which describe the prayer and its answer.

An odd meaning of this root word is that of "to fear," and in this we may have the origin of the ancient expression, "Fear of the Lord" as a term signifying a worthy condition on the part of the worshiper—who is the "God-fearing man." In its adverbial sense the root word *ano* means, "now, at the present time," and here we have the Huna belief that the answer to the prayer is real and is "now" given in the acceptance of the seed by the High Self. The reality of the answer is not yet a fact on the physical level, but is considered a veritable fact in terms of the "seed" or pattern or mental picture of the coming condition. Faith is to be held that the answer is "now" given and will be materialized on earth in due time.

In the parable the birds of the air may eat some of the seeds, and in Huna the symbol for a "spirit" is a bird. The birds which eat the seeds are bad ones, and symbolize the obsessing spirits who often prevent the low self from doing its proper part in making the prayer. The seeds which fell on stony or shallow ground were said to begin to grow, only to wither and die for lack of moisture. This is the Huna symbol of the prayer "seeds" which do not grow with the High Self for lack of the regular sending of the mana to

171

"water" them. Some seeds were choked out by thorns, and in the thorns we have the symbol of the fixations or irrational beliefs embedded in the consciousness of the low self. If there is a fixed belief that the man is guilty of some bad thing, the low self may be ashamed and refuse to try to make the contact with the High Self. Fixed disbelief is also a "block" in the "Path." But says the parable, the seeds which fell on good soil grew and rewarded the sower with a goodly return.

❖ ❖ ❖ ❖ ❖

The parable of the mustard seed is simply a variation of the one of the sower. The point here is that the mustard seed is so small that it is almost as nebulous as the mental picture of the prayer, but when it is grown into the answer, it is large and strong to the point of being almost a tree.

In a similar way, the very tiny thing which stands for the "seed" of the prayer, is likened to the leaven which the woman hid in three measures of meal, but which soon grew to leaven the whole. The growth from a mental picture to a materialized or earthly condition, situation or object, is a similar progression from the immaterial to the material. . . . In this case the "meal" that rises or increases in size represents the "seed" watered by mana and made to grow.

Reading farther in this chapter which is as famous for its parables, (Matt. 13) we come, in verse 34, to the section in which Jesus explained the parable meanings as, "things which have been kept secret from the foundation of the world."

The actual explanation begins with verse 37 in which

he says, "He that soweth the good seed is the Son of man." From the Huna lore we draw the inference that the lesser pair of selves, as the "Son of man" must sow the seeds, that is, make the prayer and use "good seeds" or carefully selected prayer goals.

Jesus continues, "The field is the world. . . ." In the code the word (as we have seen) for "world" is *ao*, which also means "light," so we see here the double meaning in which the High Self becomes the "field" in which the good seed is planted. Continuing, ". . . the good seed are the children of the kingdom. . . ." This repeats the fact that the seeds are to be planted with the High Self, for it is "the kingdom" in the inner symbology. The idea of "children" suggests growth to maturity, as growth of seeds to fruition. ". . . but the tares are the children of the wicked one." The poorly made prayer or the one in which a person prays for something harmful to others to come to pass, comes under the heading of the "tares." The High Self will have no part in bringing about a condition which hurts others or which may deprive someone of the use of his free will, even if he is a wayward son whose drunkenness may cause him to learn life's lessons the hard way.

Verse 39 is a rather obscure part of the explanation of the secret processes of Huna. It speaks of "the devil" as the one who planted the tares. In Huna there is no "devil," only "darkness (*po*) which is the opposite of light (*ao* "light and the world, and enlightenment"). Only through ignorance will one plant tares for himself by praying for conditions which will hurt others if brought about. ". . . The harvest is the end of the world, and the reapers are the angels."

Here the "harvest" *ohi* is simply "to glean," but the "reapers" in the code are *oki-oki,* which not only means to "reap" but "to be left destitute," so we see that the man who makes the prayer with the wrong goals becomes the reaper or one who gets nothing at all from his prayers. The "angels" give a backward glance at the High Self who has seen to it that the hurtful prayer is rejected.

These Gospel passages, which on the face of them seem to tell of the "end of the world," when taken with passages describing the Parousia as something to happen very soon, or at least during the lifetime of the listeners, have caused much misunderstanding, with some Christian sects still basing their claim of correct information on the forlorn expectations which for almost 2,000 years have been unfulfilled.

Continuing our reading with verse 40, the writer repeats in slightly different words what he has just presented. However, in verse 42 another code word is inserted and we read, "there shall be wailing and gnashing of teeth." The outer meaning seems to be that human beings who are evil will be cast into the fires at the end of the world, but the code words are *uwe* (to wail, weep and cry with tears—the tears being water and symbolizing mana) and *uwi* ("to gnash the teeth or to wring water out of something to dry it.") In both of these words we have the coded information that the "tares" or evil prayer pictures will have the water or mana taken from them so that the "seeds" will dry out and not grow.

Verse 43 gives a triumphant ending to the secret teachings, "Then shall the righteous (*po-no*, "good," or

174

those without darkness—the good seeds) shine forth as the sun in the kingdom of their Father." The good seeds will flourish as the answer to the prayer takes more and more material form. "Who hath ears to hear, let him hear." The last phrase indicates that what has been said above is part of the secret lore and is to be understood only by the initiates who have learned to hear the code words and know their secondary meanings.

In verse 45 we have another parable started. "Again, the kingdom of heaven is like unto a merchant-man, seeking goodly pearls: Who, when he had found one pearl of great price, went and sold all he had and bought it." In the preceding verse a man finds a treasure buried in a field and sells all in order to buy the field. There are no particular code words here, but as the kingdom is being described, we see that the "good seed" or prayer for something which is really good for the growth and well-being of the lesser man, is treasured highly by the High Self and all possible efforts are made to exchange the present unwanted conditions for the good and desirable conditions. Buying and selling, is, in the code, *kuai*, "to exchange one thing for another," or here, the bad old conditions for good new ones.

In many religions the problem of the good and the bad men has been dealt with in various ways. In Huna the bad men appear to have been looked upon as those still darkened and low in the evolutionary scale. They are not condemned to a hell, but are thought to be under the loving care of their own High Selves who bear with them with endless patience and help in every possible way to guide them into the light.

Only a few religions have presented the belief that part of humanity is of the devil and can never be saved. In the Gospels the "elect" and the "chosen" are mentioned, and the outer circle teaching has seemed to be that only these favored ones can be saved, but that the rest are naturally evil and are not worth saving, the final Judgment being looked upon as the time when the tares will be separated from the good grain and burned in the everlasting fire by an impatient God.

Christianity, set against the Jewish background, inherited to some extent in its outer doctrines the vengeful God of the prophets. This unloving and impatient attitude appears in the parable of the rich man who forgave the money debts of a man who came before him unable to pay. The same man then went to find one who owed him a small amount, and showed no mercy, taking him by the throat to force payment. When the rich and generous man, standing in the place of God in the parable, was told of the complete selfishness of the man he had so helped, he angrily revoked the earlier forgiveness and demanded the payment of the entire debt. (Matt. 18:34–35) "And his lord was wroth, and delivered him to the tormentors until he should pay all that was due unto him."

CHAPTER 13

REINCARNATION IN THE CODE

Before we continue with the inspection of coded meanings in the Gospels, it will be well to pause to look at the question of whether we live but one life, or come back several times to continue our evolutionary schooling.

For those readers who are familiar with my earlier books on Huna, this may be a surprise. When the code was first broken and the work of assembling the recovered parts of Huna was begun, a careful search was made for a code word for "reincarnation."

It seemed that there certainly should be one in the language used by the initiates of a system which was so complete in comparison to any other known system. But no word was found and it was thought possible that the kahunas did not believe in more than one life.

This vacant spot in the coded Secret, however, was eventually filled when it was discovered that the theory of reincarnation was considered such a commonplace truth by the makers of the code that they made no effort to conceal it with a code word. They simply called it, "living again," or "a new life" or "to repeat a life." Their phrase was *hou ola*, and it covered the various facets because *hou* means "new" and also "to repeat," as to repeat a life, or "to do over again as before."

The nearest to a code word in this respect was the phrase *ala hou ana* which can have several alternate meanings because of the root word, *a-la*, which can mean "to awaken," "to rise," or "a path." The writers of the Gospel of Luke chose to use this phrase as code, for it also means "resurrection" in the Biblical sense. In Luke 20:27–36, Jesus is asked about a problematical case in which a woman had been married and widowed seven times. Upon the event of her resurrection at the "Great Day," which of the seven husbands would be the rightful and permanent one? In verses 34–36 we see the code still intact after all the copying of years:

"And Jesus answering said unto them, The children of this world marry and are given in marriage: But they which shall be accounted worthy to obtain the world, and the resurrection from the dead, neither marry, nor are given in marriage: Neither can they die any more: for they shall be equal to the angels; and are the children of God, being the children of the resurrection."

The word "world" is used twice in this bit of coded information, and in English or in Greek (the probable original) there is no difference between the world as first mentioned or as mentioned the second time as one "they shall be accounted worthy to obtain. . . ." The hidden meaning can only be found when we return the lines to the code language and see that the word *ao*, for "world" has enough alternate meanings to satisfy any initiate attempting to tell in code of the end point of several incarnations.

Ao means also "light" and enlightenment and instruction, and "to have learned to do a thing" or, "to have learned a lesson." So, it follows, via the code, that those who have reincarnated often enough and have learned their life lesson so that they are ready to have the possession of the "world" or of that precious thing "enlightenment," which will be given, so they will become "equal unto the angels"—or High Selves into which the middle self will "graduate." Having at last "obtained that world," they will no more need to reincarnate and be resurrected. Nor will they longer be married or given in marriage in terms of the lower earth lives, for they are now to be allowed the reunion of the Adam and the Eve parts of themselves to make them a High Self. In this they are the equals of the angel High Selves who are already on that level of life, and they are, indeed, the "children of God, being the children of the resurrection"—or "Sons of God" as was Jesus himself when speaking as the High Self.

The words *ola honua* translate, "a preceding life," also, "naturally, without cause." In the latter meaning we see that the kahunas believed it natural and to be expected that all men live through several incarnations to evolve to the proper state of enlightenment.

There has been much puzzlement over the words of Jesus, "Suffer the little children . . . to come unto me for of such is the kingdom of heaven." It is usually said that this passage means that we must become innocent like little children in order to enter the Kingdom, but once we understand that reincarnation is being discussed in code, we can see that when the cycle is finished and the lessons are learned, the next life will find us at the point of graduation. And there, after the low self becomes a middle self, the middle self becomes a High Self, and, just as little children being born to start a new life, the new cycle of incarnations begins.

John gives us a statement in which the code is hardly used. We read, 3:3 (Jesus said) "Except a man be born again, he cannot see the kingdom of God." We may paraphrase this line and say, "Unless a man live and grow through a sufficient number of incarnations, and then be born as a triune being, into the next higher level, he cannot, as a middle self, see (or enter) the kingdom of the High Self."

Jesus is made to say in John, 3:5, "Except a man be born of water and the Spirit, he cannot enter the kingdom of God." This tells us that the High Self uses mana (water) and helps the lesser pair of selves to move up a level at graduation time when cycles of learning end. One is helped rather than "born" by the High Self as the "Spirit." There is a code meaning in the word "born." In the code this is *hanau*, which can be broken into *hana* for "to make or to work," and *au*, a "self." In other words, we have here the information that the High Self "Spirit" makes the middle (*au*) self into a new High Self, and the low self into a new middle self, all with the use of mana and its superior powers and wisdom.

Reincarnation is mentioned clearly in the code word for "resurrection," (*ala hou ana*) which means "to live or rise again." In John 11:25, ". . . I am the resurrection, and the life: he that believeth in me, though he were dead, yet shall he live." The code for "yet shall he live" is "*ola hau*" or to have "a new life" or to "repeat life." (Repeat a living.)

Jesus speaks as the High Self in these utterances

180

because it, and only it, is symbolized by "light" and by the code words for "life" and for "reincarnation." We might paraphrase by saying in code terms, "I, the High Self Father-Mother, am the Light of the World, and only I can lead men out of darkness or give them fresh incarnations—more lives—so that they may grow out of darkness and to the Light."

One may well ask why, if the Secret of Huna was of such great value, it was kept from the masses. The answer seems to be that in olden times, even as today, the masses were unable to understand and accept the abstract ideas of the inner teachings. Only when a person has gone through a number of lives and has evolved to a fairly high degree of mental ability, can the Secret be of value. Moreover, it may have seemed to the ancient kahunas that the knowledge that we live several lives and have the opportunity to correct our mistakes might make people less anxious to live up to their best moral and ethical standards in any one incarnation. In the Church much pressure was used to force the laymen to live the right life according to its lights. It was taught that man lived but once and that then he gained heaven and eternal salvation or descended into hell to suffer eternal punishment. In purgatory, if not too sinful, he might eventually be purged and get on up to heaven. For life under a "God of Love" this was a most unloving state of affairs.

On the other hand, in India, where reincarnation had been known and taught openly from the most ancient days, the people profited little by knowing that they could come back to try to correct their faults in fresh incarnations. The great trouble was that in India the idea of a dozen or so incarnations was stretched out to an almost endless series of lives, and with the added dogma of a law of cause and effect (*karma*) which made balancing out the bad old deeds all but impossible, the people fell into a form of spiritual lethargy. They mouthed the rituals and performed the rites in the manner in which they were taught by the priests, but they were, for the most part, all but hopeless.

Jesus taught a very simple outer way of life which the masses could easily understand and follow, if they would. It was the "Golden Rule" of "Do unto others as you would have them do unto you." The same Golden Rule was current at that time (and in even earlier times in parts of Asia). The kahunas taught the simple doctrine of non-hurt. They taught that the only sin was that of hurting others. Jesus injected a little of the higher teachings into the outer when he added the positive instead of the negative. One not only abstained from hurting others, but learned to love and serve others. We have found to our sorrow that to love all men, especially when they are very evil, is next to impossible, and to live we must look out first for ourselves and families, then turn to serving others. Only in the Kingdom where the command to love and serve is easy to obey, is love found in its full flower. To try to love impersonally and to serve is a splendid training for those who are nearing the graduation point, and even with the masses, where the effort is more than difficult to make, some good may be accomplished. Perfect love is possible only to the High Selves.

In the Gospels it is apparent that a cetain amount of

knowledge concerning reincarnation was part of the outer teachings. The Jewish religion goes back very largely to Egyptian beginnings, and so includes little covering such a thing as a series of lives. However, by the time of Jesus there had been much trading back and forth with India, and a very considerable exchange of ideas. In John, 1:21 we read, "And they asked him, What then? Art thou Elias? and he saith, I am not." Even the idea of the Second Coming of Jesus may have been a reflex in outer beliefs based on a scant knowledge of reincarnation.

CHAPTER 14

THE MYSTERY OF THE CROSS AND THE CRUCIFIXION

There are two distinct stories given in the Four Gospels which cover the life and ministry of Jesus. The first story tells of the expectation of Jesus that the "Last Day" was near and would come even during the lifetime of those who heard him tell of the opening of the heavens and the setting of the stage for the Last Judgment—with himself seated on the right hand of God-the-Father to act as judge.

In this version of the Life, the coming of the "kingdom of Heaven" is a material event, not a spiritual accomplishment. The followers of Jesus were encouraged to expect the advent of the Messiah, but without having him conquer with armies and take over the earth as it then stood. The heavens would open and there would be no need for armies or worldly leadership—in fact, no time for such things. The end of the world would have come with divine intervention and the wicked would be sorted out from the good and destroyed in the fires of hell. The loving Father of the second version of the story was not to be there to search for the lost sheep and bring it into the fold.

In the second version of the story, Jesus expected only a spiritual kingdom of heaven to be gained, and then only by a few—the "elect" or "chosen." He expected to be made perfect, himself, after completing his ministry, and to be allowed to enter the kingdom. He failed the test at the end of the first life—the crucifixion marking the failure. He was resurrected and in the new life succeeded in gaining the necessary perfection and in being "transfigured"—symbolically entering the "kingdom" or graduating to become a High Self.

In the first materialistic version of the story, Jesus confidently expects the Great Day to arrive. When it is delayed, he sends the "Seventy" to preach the Gospel far and wide in Israel, but even then nothing happens. At this point he changes his belief that the end is at hand, and goes a step farther in fitting himself into the picture of the "Righteous Servant" of Isaiah. He tells his Disciples that he will suffer the final and utter degradation, even being crucified, but rising from the dead after three days—after which his prediction breaks off abruptly with nothing said of the Last Day. (In this section, Matt. 20:18-19, Jesus says that he will "be delivered to the Gentiles to mock, and to scourge and to crucify him: and the third day he shall rise again.")

In John we are told that Jesus knew all that was to happen to him, but no definite prediction was made as in Matthew. Again, nothing is said of the arrival of the Last Day and the Judgment.

In much the same way, we have the story of the Life made to fall into three teachings, the outer, the inner and the inner-final. Or, we could call these divisions, the outer salvation, the second salvation and the third and final salvation.

185

The mixing of the various versions and elements resulted in a tangle that even the code does not completely resolve. For instance, it is still not at all clear just why the command should be placed in the story as it was when Jesus is made to say, ". . . take up thy cross daily, and follow me." At that point in his life he had not yet predicted his own death on the cross.

In beginning our study of the crucifixion through the code, our first problem is to try to decide just why Jesus died on the cross, and whether or not his death had anything to do with the saving of mankind from the Adamic curse, as claimed by Paul.

In the Old Testament account, Satan, as the evil serpent, worked through Eve to tempt Adam to disobey the command of the Lord to stay away from the Tree of Life located in the garden.

In one of the legends preserved centuries later in Polynesia, a powerful and evil spirit, who equates well with Satan, revolted because he was denied the ritual *awa* (drink) of worship by humans, and as a result, made it his business to corrupt mankind, beginning with the first man, Adam (Kumu-honua).

The code symbology tells us that what happened in both legends was that evil spirits came to exert an undue influence on living men. They were the "devils" who had to be cast out by Jesus and the Disciples. And, as we shall soon see, they were the cause of the failure of Jesus to pass his first tests and enter the "kingdom of heaven," as a new High Self, this failure resulting in the crucifixion, although in a later incarnation the "transfiguration" marked his successful graduation into the next higher level of being. In the matter of evil spirit influence, it was basic Huna belief that no evil spirit could influence or live with or partly obsess a living person unless that person already had a taint of similar evil in him.

Adam and Eve, having been slightly evil, allowed themselves to be tempted to disobey God's commands, and as a result they were driven from the Garden of Eden and they, with all their descendants were made to suffer physical death. In addition, they were made to earn their bread by the sweat of their brows and to be plagued by tares and thorns in their crops.

The idea that Jesus was sacrificed by God to save humanity from the curse of Adam could have offered only salvation from the necessity of dying, and so symbolize some form of "eternal life"—a form which all agreed must be spiritual life in heaven, not in bodies made everlasting on earth. By the time Christianity began to take form, the sin of Adam had become one of disobedience. As disobedience is a human failing, it was not counted a major or Adamic sin in Genesis, for right upon the heels of the story of Adam and his children, follows the story of a drastic punishment for sin by the sending of the Flood.

A curious element enters with the Flood legend and a very ancient tradition is refurbished and used. It is one that may have originated when men were trying to explain in some way how the animal, man, came to have with and in him the human (middle self) spirit or intelligence. The theory of upward-evolving from the animal self to the state of the middle self was either unknown or was rejected, and in its place was substituted the belief that lesser gods had been created by

God and that these came down to inhabit the bodies of the animal men and share their lives with them. (Many still cling to this belief, and Venus is favored as the place from which the gods came.)

We read in Genesis, 6:1–4, that men multiplied on earth and then, "That the sons of God saw the daughters of men were fair; and they took them wives of all they chose." But the offspring of the gods and human women became more and more wicked in some way not specified in the account. Eventually God decided to destroy mankind for its sins—whatever they may have been. He saved Noah and his children and enough of the earth's creatures to allow a fresh beginning, but wiped out the wicked ones by sending a "flood."

In Hawaii a century ago there were four versions of the Flood, the word *Kai-aka-hinalii* being the one for the deluge, and the roots of the word giving the inner meaning in this fashion:

Kai: water or mana; aka: here expressing "opposition"; *hina*: "to fall from an upright position, symbolically to fall morally"; *lii*: "anguish." Putting these together in the code sense we have the mana of the High Self as the "sea" and so the most powerful of the three manas, opposing the sinful state of the lesser pair of selves and punishing them by visiting upon them conditions which created "auguish." The Flood is an excellent symbol of the overpowering force used by the High Self when necessary to correct the lesser man, cleanse him and set him back on his evolutionary course. (This is not the "karma" of India, which is impersonal and is the working out of a vaguely defined

188

"law." It is a very definite action on the part of the High Self to assist the growth of the lesser selves over which it has charge.) (The Flood legend, as well as the Creation legend, was well known to the ancient kahunas, so the use of the code symbology here to try to identify the pre-Noah type of sin is justified.)

Whatever the sin may have been, God made a covenant of forgiveness with Noah and set the rainbow in the heavens as a reminder of it.

Ten generations after Noah came Abram and the covenant of circumcision, which in the code is a pledge not to neglect sending mana to the High Self. To neglect to do so would be a sin, but not one which could be atoned for on a world scale by the death of Jesus. Abram became Abraham and would have sacrificed his own son as the necessary offering to Jehovah, but at the last moment was given something else just as satisfactory—and in terms of the code, this was mana to offer—a part of his very own life force.

Not much was developed from the early traditions and the early Hebrews had no rite in which they sought forgiveness for the taint of sin left upon them because they had descended from Adam. They made a large annual sacrifice and asked forgiveness for the current sins of the entire tribe, but not, it is to be supposed, for the Adamic sin.

The idea of heaping the sins of the people on a scapegoat and driving it into the wilderness came later. In Leviticus 16:8–22, we have the account of what the Lord commanded Moses to instruct Aaron to do as a special rite to gain forgiveness for the sins of the people and himself, as High Priest. The blood of a bullock and of one of a pair of kid goats was to be sprinkled seven times upon the mercy seat of the Ark of the Covenant, and the second kid served as the scapegoat. In this recital there is no mention made of Adamic sin, and we may conclude that for them any such basic sin as that was cancelled out by the covenants which had been established earlier by Noah and Abraham.

When we inquire what the attitude of Jesus was concerning the necessity for a blood sacrifice to win forgiveness for sin, we find in the Gospels that he was entirely against the ancient beliefs concerning such sacrifice. He took it upon himself to forgive the sins of those whom he healed, or, without a show of authority simply stated, "Thy sins be forgiven thee." In Luke 6:37 we find him saying: "Forgive that ye shall be forgiven." This indicated the discarding of all the old Jewish rites of sacrifice. He said openly that he was giving a new teaching to replace all the old ones, and this command was, "Love ye one another." His chief quarrel with the orthodox Jews centered on his rejection of the old, bloody and savage sacrificial system and the ignoring of the equally savage Jehovah.

The belief that Isaiah had prophesied a "righteous servant," who would have to be killed and offered in the Jewish fashion as a blood sacrifice to Jehovah for the redemption of the sins of all the world, is in no way justified by the prophecies themselves when examined in the light of the code.

Note: In my book, THE SECRET SCIENCE AT WORK, when the first report was made after the discovery of the code, I presented in detail the secret meanings behind the accounts of the Last Supper, the Foot Washing Rite, and especially, of the Crucifixion, but at that time the code significance of the accounts had not yet been fully uncovered. This was especially true in the matter of the reason for the Crucifixion and the Transfiguration. At that time only a beginning had been made of unraveling the code and seeing in it a great Mystery Drama of initiation and progress through to graduation into the High Self state. For this reason, and at the risk of repeating material already familiar to some readers, an expanded report is being made, and in it the things learned only later are being incorporated.

Let us take up the matter of the command of Jesus to take up one's cross daily, which has been mentioned as one of the prime objections to accepting the dogma of salvation through crucifixion. This command or admonition to the willing followers simply cannot be interpreted logically as a reference to the cross upon which Jesus was later to be crucified. We cannot escape the conclusion that behind the word "cross" is a hidden and a very different meaning.

Let us ask just what it was in terms of the code that was to be "taken up" each day as a preliminary to following Jesus. In the code we have the word *kea* used most often for "cross." In addition to having the meaning of two crossed timbers such as make the cross of the crucifixion, there is also meant the older form of X cross, but while we know that men were crucified on the X form of cross, we also know that it stood as the sign that something was taboo. A wooden X cross standing on the path leading to a Polynesian temple warned against any approach. In ancient magic an

X mark was used to prevent the approach of any evil being or influence, and in later Christianity the same custom survived, with the other type of cross put to use. In the games of children we have "King's X" used to stop the action of an opponent player. Amulets which were worn around the neck or on the person for protection from evil forces, usually had an X ingredient in their designs. In the language of the code we have the main meaning of *kea* that of "to obstruct," and this obstruction is usually one of movement along a path. As the "path" is the symbol of the shadowy cord running from the lesser man to the High Self, we must inquire what it is that moves over this "path" which is obstructed. There is but one answer: a flow of mana. Perhaps the flow is intended to carry the thought-form prayer picture to the High Self. In any case, the basic idea is that of something that prevents normal interchange between the lesser man and his High Self. Huna symbolizes this type of obstruction also as "a stumbling block in the path." Another symbol is a "knot" in the aka cord leading to the High Self, the knot stopping the mana flow.

A second code word for cross is *a-mana*, and in this case the Y cross is usually indicated, the example being the Y branching of two tree limbs. This is the symbol of division. The fingers of the hand may be held in a V to denote the same thing, and the secret meaning of this kind of division is the dividing of the mana between the lesser man and the High Self. The root *mana* in the word also tells us what is being divided, and the root *ama* means "to feed" or "satisfy with food" as in offerings made to the gods. "Food" symbolizes mana as a sacrificial offering made to the High Self.

The answer to the question of what is to be taken up as a cross, is unquestionably mana. And, as the "cross" is to be taken up or lifted up daily, we have the Ha Rite and the sending of mana to the High Self.

This meaning is reinforced in the code word for "take up," which is *kaikai*, the secondary meaning of which is "to lift up on the hands and carry something along," this points to the "lifting up" of the mana along the aka cord. The root, *kai*, means sea water, and as water symbolizes mana, we have the meaning repeated obliquely.

"To follow" was a very adroit way of repeating the meanings already given. *Ha-hai* means, "to follow," and in the *ha* root we have the symbol of the entire Ha Rite of prayer. The second root *hai*, means "sacrifice," and this symbolizes the one and only "sacrifice" acceptable to the High Self—that of mana. (In calling his Disciples, Jesus said, "come and follow me." Here the meaning is the same.)

Thus, the code shows that the entire phrase, ". . . take up thy cross daily and follow," can be paraphrased in the secret admonition "to keep the path to the High Self open and send along it daily the gift of mana."

Luke adds to this admonition a mysterious command, "to deny" oneself, and the only thing which could be denied or given up in this case is part of one's mana, as we see in *hoo-le-mana*, which is the word for "deny" and which, in the root *le*, gives us something made "to fly upward," the "something" being specified in the following root, *mana*. Again, we see stressed the necessity of opening the path and sending the mana to the High Self.

The Church saw only the outer meaning and set about deciding what a man should "deny" himself. Sex gratification was placed at the top of the list, and following that came practically everything which a man could possibly do without. An accompanying dogma for "follow me" drove all the faithful to preach the Gospel, and to become missionaries, hermits and zealots. Those who resisted "the call" and continued to live normal lives with their families were usually tinged with a deep sense of guilt because they had not "answered the call."

Continuing, in verse 24, Luke's account reads, "For whosoever will save his life shall lose it: but whosoever will lose it for my sake, the same shall save it." We know that mana is the life force, and here we find Jesus speaking as the High Self. The statement, opened by the use of the code symbology, tells us that when we give part of our life force to the High Self, and in turn the High Self sends back a return flow to bless and cleanse and help the lesser man, "life" is regained in full and normal form.

Matthew and Mark (20:28 and 11:45) give a word-for-word series of passages which seem to show that Jesus, by his own words, described himself as a saviour. We read, "Even as the Son of man came not to be ministered unto, but to minister, and to give his life a ransom for the many."

If in this saying, Jesus meant that he would save the world by his death, nothing in his teaching could have been more important. But neither Luke nor John thought the passage of sufficient importance to record it. However, the code gives the inner meaning.

The "Son of man" is here the lesser self or man and is the symbol of the lower pairs of selves in all men. "Son" is *keiki* in the code and has the meaning of a "little one," boy or girl. The man of a middle and low self is, indeed, "a little one" compared with the High Self Father.

The word for "minister" in the code is *lawe-lawe*, which means to "serve another," but the root word, *lawe* holds the key to the inner meaning of such service. It is "to transfer from one place to another," and one may well ask what it was that could be so transferred as an act of service, if not mana sent to the High Self.

We have already seen that mana is the life force—the very life of man—and so need not pause to inspect *ola*, (of the light) for "life." We go on to the word "give" as in "give his life." It is *ha-awi*, in which the root, *ha*, is our familiar symbol of gathering a surcharge of mana while breathing heavily and sending it as a gift to the High Self, (the root *awi*, we are told in the dictionary, was not found, but it may well have been *awe*, which has the meaning of a "thread or strand," which would at once give us the shadowy thread along which the mana gift flows to the High Self.)

The last key word is "ransom," and in the Hawaiian translation of the Gospels from English, the early missionaries and their helpers must have been uncertain just which of two words should be used, for in Matthew they used *lawe-lawe* which we have just seen to mean "transfer from one place to another," and in

Mark they used *hoo-kau-waia,* which means "to serve," but in which the root *kau* has, as one of its many meanings, that of "placing something in a designated high place or setting food before someone." The mana is sent to the "high place" symbolizing always the High Self, and it is often spoken of as "food" in the Huna lore where sending mana was called "feeding the god." The root *wa* means "the space between two things," indicating the separation by space of the lesser man and the Father—the space across which the mana flows along the shadowy cord. Here there is also a neat play on words to give the code further meaning in the passages. The passive form of the full word is made by adding *ia* at the end, and so we have the root *wai* in *waia,* and once again, mana as symbolized by water.

In the outer teachings of the Gospels the words "ransom" and "redeem" have long since become confused. Jesus is said to have been sacrificed by God in the Crucifixion as a "ransom" paid to "redeem" all those who could not possibly have escaped Hell's fires because they still were under the curse of the Fall of Adam and Eve.

We have just seen that the coded inner teaching concerning a "ransom" dealt only with the sacrifice or gift of mana made to the Father-Mother High Self so that the properly made prayer could be duly answered.

The answer to the prayer was "redemption," or *hoola,* to "restore light or life" (*ho* or *hoo* can be used as the causative "to make" or "to bring about.") *La* is light and *ola,* "life." Healing and all of the help in living given by the Father comes under the heading of "restore life" or "redeem." Jesus taught the sacrifice of mana as the "ransom" and the High Self as the "redeemer."

The early Christians mistakenly came to look upon certain passages in Isaiah as prophecies of the coming of Jesus, as the Christ who would be the ransom paid for the salvation of the people as well as, in himself, the redeemer. By the time the King James Bible was being put together, the belief had become so unquestioned that it appears in the chapter headings. For example, the heading for Isaiah, Chapter 49 reads, "Christ being sent to the Jews, complains of them: he is sent to the Gentiles. God's love to the church perpetual." Of course, the "church" came much later as the Christian Church.

There was much coded Huna in the various prophecies of Isaiah, but the idea that the coming of Jesus was being predicted has little support except that in the Gospels the same ideas of "ransom" and "redemption" and of a "redeemer" were used. The code shows us with certainty that the High Self Father-Mother was the "redeemer." Where the word "Lord" is used, it stands in the Old Testament for Jehovah, although Christians often think that Isaiah was speaking already of Jesus as "the Lord."

In Isaiah, 49:26, the prophet is telling the people what Jehovah has said to him, and we read, "And I will feed them that oppress thee with their own flesh; and they shall be drunken with their own blood, as with sweet wine: and all flesh shall know that I the Lord am thy Saviour and thy Redeemer, the Mighty One of Jacob."

Fenton, in his careful translation of the above pas-

197

sage gives us . . ."And all men know your Saviour, The Life, and the Redeemer, The Mighty of Jacob." We know that Jesus certainly was not "The Mighty of Jacob," and in the code the word for "saviour" is *hoo-ola* or *hoo-la*, the "giver of life" or "the giver of light." The code gives exactly the same meaning for "redeemer" and in the translation of the passage into the Hawaiian, the early missionaries used, "I, Jehovah, and the Life (*Ola*) and the ransom-redeemer," (*Hoo-la-panai:* which translates "to cause light and to give one thing in exchange for another"—the latter root word, *panai* covering the sending of mana to the High Self in prayer in exchange for the answer to prayer. This root also has the meaning of "to stitch together, splice" and "sewing or stitching" is a Huna symbol of making contact along the shadowy thread with the High Self— the "thread" being behind the idea of the uniting by stitching.)

In an earlier chapter we considered the prophecies supposedly pointing to the birth of Jesus as the "Prince of Peace," and through the code we saw that the High Self was being described in the Huna manner. At this point we are ready to take up the later prophecies found in Isaiah, Chapters 52 and 53.

In orthodox Christianity the belief remains that in these chapters, as in Chapter 6, the prophecies concerned Jesus and his life and work. In the King James version of the Bible the heading for Chapter 52 shows the belief well. It is, "The church roused with God's promise of free redemption. Tidings of the gospel. Prophecy of the glory of Christ after his sufferings." The heading on Chapter 53 reads, "The prophet com-

198

plains of the want of faith. Sufferings of Christ, etc."

If the reader will pause to take up his Bible and read these two chapters, it will be seen that starting with 52:13, and running through 53:12, we have what may be regarded as a single prophetic unit covering the same general material. Primarily, we have here alternating descriptions or facets of the experience of the "servant" who is the central figure of the action. First he is presented as prudent and wise, then as one so marred by his sufferings that he astonishes those who see him. This continues, with the sufferings alternating more or less with the listing of his rewards and accomplishments. The mixture in the presentation becomes confusing, and one is justified in suspecting the prophet of mixing the elements in order to make the understanding of the coded meaning more difficult.

For our purpose, in trying to reconstruct the Mystery Drama, let us put the sufferings together, then group the ultimate outcomes, accomplishments and rewards of the "servant." We need to order the material so that we can see whether the High Self as the "Prince of Peace" is again indicated as the actor. or whether we have the whole man, consisting of low, middle and High selves. Especially we must see what indication there might be that Jesus is being mentioned.

THE SUFFERINGS:

52:14. "As many were astonished at thee (the servant?); his visage was so marred more than any man, and his form more than the sons of men.

53:29. "For he shall grow up before him as a tender plant, and as a root out of a dry ground: he hath no form nor comeliness; and when we shall see him, there is no beauty that we should desire him. He is despised and rejected of men, a man of sorrows, and acquainted with grief: and we hid as it were our faces from him; he was despised, and we esteemed him not. Surely he hath borne our griefs, and carried our sorrows: yet we did esteem him stricken, smitten of God, and afflicted. But he was wounded for our transgressions, he was bruised for our iniquities: the chastisement of our peace was upon him; and with his stripes we are healed. All we like sheep have gone astray; we have turned every one to his own way: and the Lord hath laid on him the iniquity of us all.

7. "He was oppressed, and he was afflicted, yet he opened not his mouth: he was brought as a lamb to the slaughter, and as a sheep before his shearers is dumb, so he opened not his mouth. He was taken from prison and from judgment: and who shall declare his generation? for he was cut off out of the land of the living: for the transgressions of my people was he stricken.

9. "And he made his grave with the wicked, and with the rich in his death; because he had done no violence, neither was any deceit in his mouth. Yet it pleased the Lord to bruise him; he hath put him to grief: when thou shalt make his soul an offering for sin, . . ."

THE REWARDS: Accomplishments and successes.

52:15. "So shall he sprinkle many nations; the kings shall shut their mouths at him: for that which had not been told them shall they see; and that which they had not heard shall they consider.

53:11–12. "He shall see the travail of his soul, and shall be satisfied: by his knowledge shall my righteous servant justify many; for he shall bear their iniquities. Therefore will I divide him a portion with the great, and he shall divide the spoil with the strong; because he hath poured out his soul unto death; and he was numbered with the transgressors; and he bare the sins of many, and made intercession for the transgressors."

(The end of verse 10.) ". . . he shall see his seed, he shall prolong his days, and the pleasures of the Lord shall prosper in his hand."

52:13. "Behold, my servant shall deal prudently, he shall be exalted and extolled, and be very high." (This verse opens the presentation unit which is regarded as a prophecy of the advent of Jesus and his life.)

With the opening verse we are at once told by the word "servant" that the entire three-self man is being indicated. Again we note that the code for "servant" is *kau-wa*, which means from the roots, *kau:* to carry and present, as food, and from *wa*, across a space. This is familiar Huna symbology. The "food" which the servant presents is the mana, and it is presented by the low and middle selves across the intervening space to the High Self by means of the aka cord. The word *lawe-lawe*, also means "servant" and means more especially a servant who serves food or otherwise ministers to someone.

So we see that Isaiah is setting down in code for the guidance of the initiated, the fact that there is a three-self man and that the lower selves have the duty to supply mana to the High Self. If this is done, the High Self, as seen in the next verse (52:15), ". . . shall sprinkle many nations." The return flow of mana from the High Self, as we have seen, is symbolized by fine rain, and is the "blessing" or help of the High Self as given to the lesser man. The two verses, along with later verses telling of the successful ending of the cycle and the rewards, give us the successful or end condition in which the lesser selves, after a number of incarnations, become "prudent" and are "exalted" and "extolled." And in 53:11–12, we see the lesser man satisfied after the "travail" or birth into the High Self level, and having reached this state, the "righteous servant" will take up his duties as a High Self and "justify many," also bear with them their troubles and "iniquities," for the High Self must suffer as a parent does when watching a wayward child learn by hard experience the lessons of life.

He will have divided with him a portion "with the great" or share in the life and privileges of other High Selves who form the "Great Company of Aumakuas." He will be able to share with the "great" because "he hath poured out his soul unto death," or died as a middle self to reincarnate as a High Self, and because, as a middle self, he has suffered (along with the low self) for "his transgressions" through many lives. The "sins of the many" which he is said to have had to bear, were not those sins of all other men of all ages and places in the world (a preposterous idea in itself) but the sins of the "many" incarnations of his own triune self.

The several verses which recite the sufferings of the "servant," never once mention death until the last of the presentation where the line reads, "hath poured out his soul unto death," which does not give us any of the deaths during the several incarnations except the final one which ends the cycle and leads to graduation. Not once is death by crucifixion mentioned, as one would legitimately expect it to be had the prophecy actually pointed to the life and death of Jesus.

All through the listing of the sufferings we have code words. The mention of "dumbness" on the part of the sufferer points via the code symbol to the low self, which cannot talk, but which suffers with the middle self. "Stripes" code the obsessions or obstacles met by the lesser man. We will take these up as we go on to consider the account of the events which led up to the crucifixion and the crucifixion itself. Suffice it to say here that the prophecies, when interpreted through the code, have nothing to say about an actual man such as Jesus, but instead, describe in cryptic lines the path each of us must take through several incarnations to reach the point of graduation.

It is odd that the tradition of a coming Messiah should be so poorly described in the Old Testament, providing its importance was as great as it would seem to be when we read Matthew in the New Testament. The actual word, "Messiah" is only to be found in Daniel 9:6 and in the Gospels in John, and in the account of John, we find only that people who hear of Jesus and his miracles are reporting to others their belief that he must be the Messiah.

The "Prince of Peace" does not fit a Messiah who acts as a worldly king and great leader to wage wars and make the Jewish people masters of earth and heaven. The word, "anointed" has been applied to the Messiah (it is given as the real meaning of the title by

Strong), and also to Jesus as the "Christ"—the latter term being, as we have noted, the Greek for anointing with oil as a sign of cleansing and spiritual elevation. The "Prince of Peace," in the code is *Kealiiokamalu*, as used in Isaiah 9:6, and the roots of the word translate, "The Chief of the Peace." *Malu* is of great importance here in the code for its secondary meaning is "secret," and so we have the alternate title, "The Prince or Leader of the Secret, or Huna." Huna means "secret," and so the great leader who is predicted by Isaiah is not a Messiah who will bring about a restoration of the lands and authority of his people, but who will instruct them in the secret knowledge of Huna. The root *oka* has a peculiar significance also as a code unit, as it can mean, "to move the lips, as in speaking, but without sound," this pointing obliquely to the fact that even if one hears Huna being described, the sounds remain meaningless unless one has been initiated. The root *kea*, which uses a letter from *alii* (chief) means "cross" and *oka* gives as one of its several meanings, that of "a snare, such as is used to snare birds," this being the standard Huna symbol of the obsession of the living by evil spirits, and something which we shall soon find playing a large part in the cause of the crucifixion. In the one code title, "Prince of Peace," Isaiah was able to cover the main events in the life of the hero of the Mystery Drama up to the point of the great failure. Little wonder that Luke, in his version of the Drama was at pains to connect his account with the Huna found so much earlier in Isaiah. They were writing in code about the same initiatory process. Both introduced the key figure in the drama as they knew it: Isaiah giving us the "righteous servant," and Luke giving us Jesus as he stood up in the synagogue and read a passage first voiced by the prophet.

Taking up the events which led to the crucifixion, we need to keep watch for the coded units which tell us why Jesus failed in his initiation and died on the cross at the end of the great First Act of the Drama. We must ask ourselves what it was that prevented Jesus from passing the initiatory tests, and if we conclude that it was some form of "sin," we must ask what this sin could have been.

To begin with, we are told that Jesus was "betrayed," and here we have the code word, *hoo-ku-maka-ia*, which is, literally, to have "an eye set on one," and equated with "the evil eye" of black magic, and the placing of a curse on one. The root, *kuma*, indicates that one is made "to stand with a company of others," and as curses are placed by the sending of evil spirits to mislead or injure the one cursed, we have here the intimation that Jesus became the victim of the very "devils" whom he had so often cast out of others. One must watch to see what had happened that laid him open to this spirit invasion or interference. In Huna we learn that we attract evil spirits to us only in and to the degree of our own evil.

Helpless in the hands of his enemies, he was tried, scourged, crowned with thorns and made to carry a cross which was so heavy that it was beyond his strength and he could not. He fell, and another man had to be pressed into service. This inability to "take up" his cross gives us the symbol of inability to remove the blocking of his path.

Thorns are one of the symbols of blockings, and compare with snare and tare and net . The compelling influence of evil spirits is a greater disaster than suffering from a misconception or a fixation. To be caught in a net, to be snared, or to be entangled in a thorny bramble hedge, all symbolize spirit interference.

We have already considered the code words for "cross" and know it to be the major symbol of the blocked path. *Kau-la* is the code word for the scourging, this being done with a whip made up of several heavy cords. The word means "a stripe" and we recall the prophecies of Isaiah, in which the righteous servant was made to suffer with "stripes." The root *kau* means "to hang up; to crucify;" also "to light down on one, as a bird," and here we have the evil spirits symbolized by birds. There is still another meaning of the root which may well apply here, it being, "to come upon one unexpectedly," and from this we may guess that the evil spirits which gained control of Jesus and blocked his path had taken him completely by surprise and had found him off guard. The root *la* is the familiar symbol of "light" and it tells us that the High Self was involved in some way in this code meaning. The meaning of the full word is "a rope or cord," and so we find that we are being told once more that the aka cord to the High Self had been blocked and that this was the cause of the trouble.

The word for "cup" as in the "cup of bitterness" which was to be drained by Jesus, we have the code word *pai*, which also means to "scourge"; to "speak evil of one, slander, accuse falsely"; "to mingle water and blood," (as when Jesus was speared in the side as he hung on the cross and blood and water gushed out,

206

showing that he was losing his mana and life force.)

The word "hang" as to hang on the cross, is *li*, in which the root, *li* (as *lili*) means "to hate, to abhor, to be filled with wrath, to be jealous." This repeats the things which make the low self evil and which may also contaminate the middle self which is strongly influenced by any low self emotion. Also described are the evil things which obsessing spirits force upon the lesser man when they gain power over him.

The mention of the crown of thorns is found only in John 19:1–5. "Thorn" is *kaka-laioa*, in which the root *kaka* means "to whip," this duplicating the idea of "scourge," which is *ha-hau*, and which has a peculiar code meaning hidden in the roots, for we know that *ha* stands for the entire process of accumulating mana, sending it to the High Self and presenting the prayer for the thing desired. The root *hau* means "snow or ice" and here the mana, as symbolized by "water" is shown to be "frozen" so that it will not flow along the shadowy cord to the High Self—a very graphic statement of the completely blocked path of Jesus as related in the story. The root *lai* in the word given above for "thorn" means "to be silent," and this reinforces the idea that the prayer was impossible to make effectively. (It also points to the obsession of the "dumb" low self, as we have seen in our study of Isaiah, 53:7.)

Jesus died on the cross between two thieves. In the code *ai-hue* is "thief," and the literal meaning is "to steal food." This is the symbol of the evil spirits who fasten themselves on the victim and live by stealing part of the mana made in the body. Their presence in the drama indicates the reason for the blocking of

207

the path which caused the disaster for Jesus. One thief or spirit repented, and in this we have the information that evil spirits can sometimes be reformed and made to leave. (In modern times much work has been done to try to find a way to talk through mediums with the obsessing spirits—as the kahunas often did—to show them the error of their ways and to get them to go on with good spirits to be helped and instructed in the spirit level of life. In medical circles the possibility of spirit obsession is not admitted, but "shock treatments" are used to try to get rid of whatever it is that causes the trouble. Unfortunately, no reliable remedy has been developed although obsession increases steadily and helps fill the mental hospitals to bursting.)

The word for "death" is *make*, and one of its secondary meanings is "to desire," while another is "to be made right, fitting and proper." From this we see that death was not the end of everything for Jesus, but simply a delay in his evolutionary growth—this being the inborn desire or urge of humanity, no matter where in the evolutionary growth scale an individual may stand.

Jesus was laid in a "new tomb" or *hou ilina*, the "new" part having the code meaning of getting ready to start a new incarnation, after having met death. The word for "tomb," *i-lina*, has also the meaning of "to tighten or stretch, as a cord or rope." This tightening is the Huna symbol of opening the shadowy cord and making it ready for use, in this case in the following life. The great stone which was rolled away from the tomb can be thought of as the total of the "stumbling blocks" which could not be removed on the cross, but which were cleared away before the next in-carnation so that a clean slate might be provided for the next life. The evil spirits would leave at the death of their victim to find a new place to steal mana and have their evil urges shared by a living person.

The "resurrection" is *ala hou ana*, meaning from the root words, "to open the path anew."

In order to understand better the dramatic lesson of the crucifixion, and to try to determine why Jesus be-came open to obsession, let us go back to the scene of the Passion. In John 17:1-5, we find a most significant piece of information. Jesus had been speaking to his disciples, and standing before them, he lifted his eyes unto the heavens and made this prayer: (The Fenton translation is used again.) "Father, the time has come! Perfect your Son, so that your son may magnify You; for You have invested Him with authority over all mankind in order that he may give eternal life to all whom You have intrusted to Him. And the eternal life is this: to obtain a knowledge of You the only true God, and the Messiah Whom You have sent. I have exalted You upon the earth by completing the work which You entrusted me to do. So now, Father, you restore Me to the honour which I had along with your-self before the world existed."

The opening line, "Father, the time has come! Perfect Your Son . . ." is the code key. In a later chapter we will see that the word "perfect" indicates the last step or "graduation" from the level of the middle self to that of the High Self. In the drama, it marks the time of the final tests and the gaining of complete initiation.

Not only do we see that Jesus, as the lesser man, was asking to be helped to take the final upward step, but he was counting his accomplishments boastfully before the listening disciples. This boastful attitude may be seen also in the following prayer made for the good of the disciples, and then in the prayer made for all believers, and finally, the prayer for the future of the believers.

As shocking as it is to consider his attitude boastful, when we have for so long been made by the outer teachings and the Church to believe that Jesus was God as a part of the Trinity, and so was perfect in every way from the beginning, the words of the prayers, if placed in the mouth of a modern religious leader, would at once identify him as a zealot and one afflicted with the arrogance of the smug, "better than thou" attitude. In the mouth of Jesus, the words are tolerable only if we accept him as an already perfect man and as a god and part of the Trinity—a part which has been with the Father "from the foundations of the earth."

In the drama of his failure and crucifixion, which fills the long preliminary series of scenes, we see Jesus building up to the climax which will see the "heavens opening as a scroll" and himself elevated to a seat on the right hand of the Father. When the drama opened, Jesus showed humility and gave the Father credit for all the "works" which he performed. Later he is made to identify himself more and more with the "Righteous Servant" of Isaiah, and so sure of himself did he become near the end that he dared to antagonize openly both the religious and political authorities of the day. It appears that only at the very end, after his betrayal, he began to doubt that the Last Day would arrive to save him and place him in the seat of honor.

If we understand the code of the betrayal correctly, it was at that time that his spiritual pride laid him open to obsession by certain spirits who were evil because they forced on him the emotions of pride which were their own besetting sins in life.

In his early ministry, Jesus taught that "the kingdom of heaven is within." Nearing the end of his life, he sent the "seventy" out to preach the gospel with the promise that if they did so, the "Last Day" would arrive and all would reap a shining reward.

In Mark 14:61–62 we see the trend in this direction as we read, ". . . Again the high priest asked him, and said unto him, Art thou the Christ, the son of the Blessed? And Jesus said, I am: and ye shall see the Son of man sitting on the right hand of power, and coming in the clouds of heaven."

Jesus, early in his ministry, had roundly condemned the Jews who gave alms too openly and who made a pretense of righteousness when they voiced long prayers in public. At the end he had no alms to give, but his pride and the making of his prayer before his disciples was the very thing he had formerly condemned.

If we turn to India, where Huna was known and left its imprint on the Yoga system, we find the sin of spiritual pride very clearly recognized and its opposite, "selflessness," continually advocated.

In the YOGA SUTRAS OF PATANJALI, Johnson translation and commentary, page 141, Book III, Sutra No. 51, we have a good example of the need to rise above pride and selfseeking. We read, "There should be complete overcoming of all allurement or pride on the invitations of the different realms of life, lest attachment to things evil arise once more."

The idea of attaining that "selflessness" which is needed for the "graduation" step of Huna, was beautifully expressed in a book written some years ago by Talbut Munday, OM, THE SECRET OF ARBOR VALLEY, in which a Tibetan master of Yoga who had elected to instruct the English hero of the tale, was often quoted. One of the *guru's* sayings illustrates the matter under discussion when what would be called "graduation" in Huna is touched upon. The lines run like this:

"Oh ye who look to enter in, through discipline to bliss,
Ye shall not stray from out the way, if ye remember this,
Ye shall not hope with hope that's vain, or waste a weary hour,
If ye persist with will until, self-righteousness is slain."

In this passage the "discipline" is that needed to bring one to the state of desirelessness or selflessness in which all egotism has been overcome and the individual is ready to leave behind the world and all that belongs to it—to enter Nirvana as the state of "bliss."

As the curtain falls on the last scenes of the drama of the crucifixion, all seems to be lost. The man who had learned to make himself "one with the Father," had been rendered impotent by evil spirits who had been able to obsess him and block his path. His weakness had been self-righteousness, the cardinal sin of the highest spiritual level. He had been held back by his desire to enjoy the fruits of his labors. He had not been content to have as his goal the "graduation" in which he would have given up all thought of "me and mine."

He still desired to sit in glory on the right hand of the Father—at least that is what the drama and the code tell us.

But there is the epilogue which followed. In it Jesus is symbolically "raised from the dead," but the code tells us that this is a return in a fresh incarnation. He rose from the tomb in "three" days, and his return was in "three" selves as a three-self man. His appearance before his disciples in the actual flesh symbolizes the reincarnation in the flesh. He said to one of his friends, "Touch me not, for I have not yet ascended to the Father." The code symbol given here is embodied in the statement that he has not yet "ascended," and we know that he will continue his effort to "go up," or to reach the stage at which he can become a full initiate and "graduate" to the High Self level.

The Temptation in the wilderness, which we found out of place in the first part of the Drama, comes in the second part, and in its final stage when Jesus has rejected the offer of worldly riches, and has refused even to save his earthly life by exerting the power which he could have called down from the Father, Satan and his "devils" can no longer obsess or influence him, even on the most exalted spiritual level. He has passed that phase and is ready to move on up.

The code word for "temptation" is *wale-wale*, and the root, *wale*, means, "to exist; to exist without qualifications." Jesus had resisted temptation so completely that he had no "qualifications" clinging to him to hold him back. No longer did he ask to be honored or given a place of authority beside the Father. He was, at last, free from every desire but one—this one being the proper and natural desire to evolve and move on from the level of the middle self to that of the High Self. In this there was no taint. He was progressing "under the law," and this final desire was not such that it invited disaster by being over-stimulated by evil spirits, as in the sequence which led to his betrayal and crucifixion.

We will continue the story of Jesus as told in the second part of the initiatory drama a little later. Paul entered the picture at the end of the first act, not knowing that there was a mystery teaching behind the outer meanings, and hardly guessing that there was to be a second, final and climactic act. From his writings we see that he was not an initiate into Huna, nor did the Disciples propose to enlighten him when he made his one visit to them in Jerusalem and quarreled with Peter, departing after a few fruitless days to go into the Arabian desert for three years, there to work out his theories and theology. When he came out of the desert and began to preach his version of the Gospel, it was not at all the "good news" of Jesus. It was a conglomeration of claims and theories to which he tried to give authority by making everything fit the prophecies or the Scriptures, and often with the items he cited as proof having not the slightest bearing on the topic which he was covering.

It was Paul, certainly not Jesus, who evolved the

doctrine that a savage and vengeful God had demanded the sacrifice of his only begotten son as a necessary "blood sacrifice" to atone for the Adamic or "Original" sin. We may summarize his teachings, and fabrications as: (1) The idea that all mankind was still cursed because of the sins of Adam. (2) The idea that only by the blood sacrifice of Jesus, who was the divine son of God, could that curse be removed by a "paying back" that would buy "redemption," and (3) The most surprising idea of all, that only certain select people could benefit by the scheme of redemption, all depending upon whether or not God had chosen them—for all depended upon God's "election," NOT upon man's deeds or will, his fate depended on "mercy," and was determined by "predestination."

The Disciples did not form a church organization. We know this because the writings in the Epistles which were supposed to be from their hands, especially the hand of Peter—upon whom the Church of Rome was based—contain not a single passage to show that the writers had ever been initiated into the inner cycle by Jesus. (Read the few short epistles supposed to have been written by the Disciples, keeping in mind what they must have known of the inner teachings, and see how impossible it would be for them to write what is attributed to them in those documents.)

Had the Disciples wished to organize a church, the outer teachings offered almost nothing upon which to construct a set of dogmas which would draw members. The Messiah of the materialistic first part of the story had failed to appear, and the god-man, Jesus, had failed in all his promises and died in disgrace. His

215

resurrection offered very little to build on, although it provided an invaluable section of the final drama for the few who could understand the hidden meaning.

Jesus had not said that he was a "savior" and the Disciples, who were initiates, knew very well that he was not. He had given them the knowledge that the High Self was the one and only source of salvation. Baptism and repentance of past sins had been advocated, but this was nothing new. The Jews had long since had cleansing rituals of this kind, and the people were familiar with them. The crucifixion had branded the teachings with utter failure, and the coming of the Comforter was a vague thing which belonged to the world of spirits and the dead rather than the realm of the living.

If things had been left as they were, the mystery teachings might have continued secretly. But, if we are to judge from what took place from beginning to end, what happened originally was that the mystery drama was stolen from some initiate or group of initiates. Four versions of the drama fell into the wrong hands, and, perhaps after a short time were passed from hand to hand and mistaken for an actual history of a living man-god, Jesus.

If there was only the Jesus of the mystery play, we are forced to conclude that the Disciples and all other characters involved in the drama were fictitious. If they actually were fictitious, we can only decide that Paul, after becoming acquainted with the Four Gospels or Four Versions of the Drama, and after deciding that the accounts were historically correct, must have drawn a very long bow in claiming that he was able to visit the Disciples in Jerusalem, and to add that they had not agreed with his version of what happened and had quarrelled with him. Unfortunately, the Disciples left no account of what happened after the death of Jesus. All we have to go on is the Pauline story and the "acts," which certainly may have been as spurious as Paul's account of visiting the Disciples. The suspicion of fraud and misinformation and pure invention is strengthened by the incredible fact that the writers of the Pauline section of the New Testament did not know or use the code, and knew nothing of the inner teachings.

The organization of a church always needs a basic set of beliefs and practices. The Disciples furnished nothing of this nature, but Paul invented a complete Theology and started building a church replete with dogmas of salvation, heaven and hell. The Church Fathers, being his followers and not those of the Disciples, could not have avoided the acceptance of the system as invented by Paul and made to sound valid by the claims that events in the life of Jesus fitted prophecies, and that the Old Testament proved conclusively that Paul's doctrines were correct. Having nothing else, the Church Fathers used what Paul had provided. True, they quarreled over points in the Gospels, but were not stopped.

From the purely historical point of view, we have very little to go on other than speculation. We find students generally agreed that the Gospels were not written until almost a hundred years after the time of

Jesus, although there were "Sayings of Jesus" in circulation and perhaps more complete accounts of the Life passed around by word of mouth.

We have no certain knowledge of Paul and his life and work, most, if not all, of the information being derived from what he is supposed to have written. The genuineness of the Acts and Epistles has been strongly challenged on the ground that the events of the life of Jesus run parallel to the story of the life and work of a contemporary, Apollonius of Tyana, whose story was preserved in the writings of Pausanias in his DESCRIPTION OF GREECE. In this account the hero (similar to the Gospel Jesus) was also miraculously conceived, performed miracles, and, at the end, was transported physically to heaven.

The only hint to be found in the Pauline writings to suggest that Paul knew that there were mystery teachings in the Gospels, comes in Hebrews, 9:28, where we read, "Christ was once offered to bear the sins of many; and unto them that look for him shall he appear a second time without sin unto salvation." This causes us to wonder what sin it may have been that Paul thought Jesus had carried with him in being crucified, and how he expected him to rid himself of that taint upon his second coming. Knowing the code, we see that in this respect Paul may have guessed right. The first part of the drama of initiation showed Jesus being crucified because he could not rid himself of that last taint. The second part of the drama, in the Transfiguration, shows Jesus completely cleansed and ready to take the full initiatory step of "graduation" into the High Self level.

(Again, see the later chapter on the Transfiguration.)

If Paul had in his possession a copy of the Four Gospels, his confusion when trying to evaluate the meanings could easily be explained, for the accounts are not only filled with code, but the different accounts vary in detail, especially on the very points upon which the later dogmas were based.

What can be made of all this in terms of Huna? Certainly not that Jesus, as a low middle self man, or as a triune man including his own High Self, was forced by Ultimate God to lay down his life as a sacrifice or "ransom" for humanity. Only the lesser man is indicated in the "Son," and he clearly serves by generating and sending mana to the High Self. In terms of the code this is all—no other possible meaning. This allows the belated correction of one of the worst and most outstanding misconceptions to be found in Christianity. It turns us away from the angry and blood-thirsty Jehovah of the early Jews and gives us back the loving Father who, of course, is not Ultimate God, but always the High Self Father-Mother of Huna, whose love never fails or falters.

To the initiate or one simply familiar with the meaning of the code, the use of the cross as the symbol of all possible salvation by the Church contains an element of shuddering horror. The savagery of the constant worshipful contemplation of the images of the suffering and dying man in the very throes of utter failure, becomes more and more repulsive when it is realized that the drama did not end there—only paused.

Perhaps some day the cross will go and in its stead

219

the emblem of the High Self will be used and venerated. This could be, as in ancient times in Egypt, the Sun, or it could be a single candle burning on a simple altar, representing the Light.

CHAPTER 15

THE TRANSFIGURATION MYSTERY

If Jesus is to be considered historically real and we are to accept the Life from the evidence of the Four Gospels, we are justified in asking whether or not the four accounts have come down to us as correct reports. From the contradictions and variations which are encountered in trying to match the accounts and the sequence given in them, we may wonder whether various incidents in the life of Jesus had not been told as recalled, and with the sequence lost so that the writers of the Gospels were obliged to try to guess just where some of the incidents should be placed. The Transfiguration as found in Matthew, Mark and Luke, breaks sharply into a running story in which Jesus is moving rapidly to the climax of the crucifixion.

As Jesus is almost at once to announce his impending death to the Disciples, it may well be that the writers decided that the Transfiguration scene should be inserted and that it should be stated that in this contact with Moses and Elias as spirits, they had in some way made him aware of his impending doom.

In Matt. 16 comes a part of the story which should logically have come after the Transfiguration, for Jesus in verse 16–28, asks Peter who he thinks he is, and Peter says, "Thou art the Christ, the Son of the Living God." Jesus then says that the Father had undoubtedly revealed this identity to Peter, after which his listeners are pledged to secrecy. "From that time forth began Jesus to shew unto his disciples, how he must go unto Jerusalem, and suffer many things of the elders and chief priests and scribes, and be killed, and raised again on the third day." He rebukes Peter for questioning the need for such disastrous happenings, saying, "Get thee behind me Satan: thou art an offence to me. . . ." Turning to the Disciples he then makes the famous pronouncement, "If any man will come after me, let him deny himself, and take up his cross, and follow me." In a few moments he ends his discourse with words which show that he expected the anticipated death to be followed by the Great Day. We read, "Verily I say unto you, There be some standing here, which shall not taste of death, till they see the Son of man coming in his kingdom."

The Transfiguration is inserted here (Matt. 17) and then follow six long chapters in which the predicted death seems to have been forgotten. These chapters, if one were writing fiction in modern times, would certainly be lifted and placed before the important event of the indentification of himself as a Christ and the prediction of his end. Mark and Luke follow much the same sequence. John overlooks the Transfiguration entirely for some reason.

After the strange break to insert the Transfiguration, Matthew (17:14) picks up the regular story and Jesus and his three companions come down from the mount to be met by a man whose son had a devil which the Disciples had been unable to cast out.

Here we see the necessity for separating the life

events of the gentle Jesus who taught tolerance, love and the complete forgiveness of one's enemies, from the events in which the proud and angrily impatient Jesus drives out the money changers from the temple, curses the fig tree and makes dark threats against the priests and scribes and Pharisees. Testily, Jesus says, (17:17) "O faithless and perverse generation, how long shall I be with you? how long shall I suffer you? bring him hither to me."

❖   ❖   ❖   ❖   ❖

If, on the other hand, we consider the Transfiguration in the light of the code and place it in the sequence of the mystery drama of initiation, we must place the crucifixion at the end of the first long act, and the Transfiguration in the second act. We must either have Jesus rise from the dead in the flesh or reincarnate. In the Huna of the code, the Jesus who fills the second act is the man who has failed in one incarnation because of his spiritual pride and his inability to give up the physical rewards of participation in the Last Days and the Judgment. He has come back in the flesh, and this time if the act is lengthened, it will include all the things done with humility and love. The Sermon on the Mount will come in here for in it is stressed the blessedness of detachment from material things.

This renewed Jesus is suggested in the Gospel accounts of the activities of the risen Jesus, either as fully materialized in the flesh or as a spirit—in this part of the story he blames no one. He scolds not at all. He is lovingly tolerant when Thomas doubts his identity and asks to be allowed to put his fingers into the nail holes in his hands and his hand into the wound in his side. He shows only the greatest love and sympathy for those left leaderless by his passing, and promises that he will send them a "Comforter."

Here we see focused the meaning of the life of poverty led by Jesus, and of his withdrawal from the normal way of life in which one marries and rears a family, working to make a living for himself and his dependents, and doing his full part in promoting the good of the community. Only when we understand the code significance of the withdrawal from material things and ambitions can we see the trend of the action in this part of the drama.

The temptation in the wilderness scene belongs here just before the ascent of the mount and the successful Transfiguration or graduation into the "kingdom of heaven" which is the state of being a High Self.

Wale-wale is the code word meaning "temptation." The root *wale* gives us the description of the condition of an initiate who has successfully passed the final tests.

The root meaning is "to exist" and also, "to exist without qualifications." In this we have the selfless state which Jesus was able to attain and in which he had risen above all pride and desire for the things of the life of the middle self on earth. His eyes had become fixed upon the things of graduation and of the High Self level.

The code, as we shall soon see, tells us that at the end of a sufficient number of incarnations one dies. Instead of reincarnating in a fresh body of flesh, one is helped through the "grace" of the High Self to become "perfect," and a graduation then takes place. In this graduation all three of the selves of the triune man are promoted a grade in the School of Life. The low self becomes a middle self and will incarnate in a body with a new low self brought up from the lower levels. The middle self will be brought together with the other half of itself which was separated from it in the past. The mystery of the legend of Adam and Eve was one in which the male and female selves were separated so that they might better learn the lessons of their grade in the school. Now, the rib is replaced in Adam, and the two are made one again. They are united and become a new being on the High Self level. The Father-Mother self which has so long supervised the lesser pair of selves, also graduates. It steps up to a still higher level in which it is called an *"Akua Aumakua"* or "god High Self." (This sublime state is so high that the middle self mind cannot do more than imagine it vaguely. The kahunas did not try to describe the state, but contented themselves by counting it very real.)

We have put the "cart before the horse" in presenting at the beginning of this piece of the story what would naturally be placed at the end if one were following the standard presentation in a drama or a fictional tale. But for our purposes it will make a complicated section of our investigation much less difficult to handle, once we know where we are going and what is to be the goal.

To continue the Gospel account as we have transposed events and placed them in the drama, we return to the time when all is in readiness for the graduation attempt. Jesus enters the "wilderness" in which there is the lack of all things. The "world and the Devil," in the form of Satan, comes to tempt Jesus with food when he hungers, and then with offers of worldly power and authority. At last Satan takes him to the pinnacle of the temple and challenges him to show his power to call down the miraculous help of the Father to save himself when he falls from the height. But by this time Jesus has come to value nothing, to desire nothing, to be free from pride and the slightest wish for recognition. He cares not even to save his own life. He has become selfless and unattached. Satan leaves him and he has passed the great test.

The saying, "Seek ye first the kingdom of heaven, and all things will be added to you," comes in here as we ask what keeps Jesus striving after passing the test? We go a step beyond the sages of Yoga. Where the Yoga "union" had to be completed without the slightest trace of desire to attain it (which is as foolish as it is illogical in the writings we have from that source), the Huna position made it not only normal but imperative at that stage of progress that Jesus should replace all former desires by the all-embracing one of wishing to progress to graduate, to become one with the mate, and to step into the shining estate of a new High Self.

In the story of the Transfiguration as we find it in the Synoptics, Matthew and Mark say that "after six days" Jesus took his three companions with him and ascended the mount. Luke says, "after eight days." Presumably these days had been spent in the usual

226

ministry, but we do not need a code word in either case to tell us that several incarnations are symbolized as ending and that the time has come for the graduation or symbolic Transfiguration.

There is an interesting tradition that Jesus had in Didimus Thomas a twin, and in the watered down version of the Synoptics, he is given only a brother, James, who went with him up the mount. In the drama, if the Huna meaning were faithfully followed, the "twin" would be represented by the female mate with whom Jesus was to be united to make a new High Self. It would be romantic to speculate on where she had spent her similar number of incarnations to become ready at precisely the same time for the transition into union, but the code tells us little. We must content ourselves with the knowledge that the kahunas believed that when one of the middle self pair was ready, the other would be, and that from the ends of the earth they would be brought together, not in bodies of flesh, but in spirit, for the great event.

In the drama, Moses and Elias represent members of the "Great Company of High Selves" who have come to witness the graduation. But the High Self, who has watched over both the male and female halves of Jesus through many incarnations, is the one who actually officiates and brings about the change.

The curtain falls as Jesus passes into the new life and higher level, made perfect through grace and no longer visible to the eyes of men except as a white light.

In the Synoptics, however, the story could not end with the final and glorious fadeout. It had to go on, and so Jesus is made to revert to his usual form and to return from the mount with his friends to continue his ministry.

❀   ❀   ❀   ❀   ❀

Knowing now what the users of the code in the Gospels were at pains to try to pass on to future candidates for initiation through the code, let us see how they went about their task and with what success.

Perhaps the most important thing was to find words in the language of the code to fit their needs in undertaking this part of their task. In English the words they selected have only the outer meanings, but in the code the meanings are multiple and weighted with the greatest significance—as if, there being so few words to use, they must be of the finest and fullest.

"Transfiguration" is the first thing to inspect for hidden meanings. We must inquire into the nature of the Huna concept of this stage of man's progression and see how one set of meanings may interlock with others to complete the picture.

Hoo-pa-hao-hao is, "to be transfigured" or "to cause a change in appearance or to another form." This fits the lines in Mark (3), "And was transfigured before them. And his raiment became shining, exceeding white as snow, so as no fuller on earth can whiten them." (The first interlocking of meaning comes with the mention of "raiment" which also means "robe," *kapa* and *lole lue-lue*, to which we will return later to see that the shadowy body was changed and glowed with white light.) The symbol of the High Self is "light" and it is sometimes seen in the physical sense as an intense white light which comes from no known source and which has in it no heat. We know from the

228

mention of shining white light that the transfiguration must be a change in more than "appearance" or "form." The whole man has been changed, and into the only thing which shines with the amazingly white light, the High Self, housed in its robe or shadowy (aka) body.

The root word *pa* means "to be barren or childless," and this interlocks with the idea that when the female half of the candidate is ready to graduate, she gives up bearing children and, figuratively, leaves the material world. (Later on we will come to discuss this point when we read what Salome had to say in a Gnostic passage.)

The roots *pahao-hao* give the secondary meaning of, "That which cannot be laid hold of; not material; as a ghost." This is a most important meaning as it tells us that the man has been changed to something "not material" in the physical sense. This is the High Self, which does not incarnate in the flesh. One cannot lay hold of it and it is "as a ghost." This also applies to the shadowy body of the High Self, as all ghosts live in their shadowy bodies.

The root *hao* has a very important part to play in the code at this point. It has several meanings, but most important are those of "to put two lesser things together to make a greater," and "to wonder at; to be astonished." This unmistakably gives us the wonder of having the two lesser things, the middle selves of the male and female, put or joined together to make the greater and more wonderful new High Self. There is a strange and provocative pointer in the direction of the twin of Jesus, Thomas, whom we know as "Doubting Thomas." *Hao-hao* means, "to doubt," and if

Thomas, as the symbolic twin soul was the female half of Jesus hiding behind the code symbol, this would throw light in that direction. It would also tend to explain why none of the Disciples was pictured as a woman in the story. In Huna men and women stand equal in every respect. Still another meaning for this doubled root is, "to seek or hunt for," and this may be a code reminder of the endless search for "the beloved" which reaches its absolute and complete fulfillment when the mates at last find each other and are united.

Having seen what happens in "transfiguration," the next question is HOW to go about becoming ready and getting on with this step which is of such great importance in the drama. Looking back through the Gospels we search for any instructions given by Jesus which might tell the method of gaining transfiguration.

Eventually we see that behind the word "perfect" lies the coded secret. This word appears but a few times in the Gospels, but is used most effectively. In the second act of the drama we recall that Jesus gave up all material things and ambitions, and in the strange and completely impractical and anti-social Beatitudes found in the "Sermon on the Mount," ends by giving a commandment so entirely beyond the power of earthy men to fulfill, that it has caused endless trouble in the outer teachings adopted blindly by the Church. We read, Matt. 5:48, "Be ye therefore perfect, even as your Father which is in heaven is perfect."

Knowing ahead of time what temptation Jesus had to overcome and how selfless he had to become before going up for his transfiguration, we can see that the final step before graduation is indeed an onerous one.

In Matthew 19:21–30 we have the story of the "Rich

young man," to whom Jesus said, "If thou wilt be perfect, go and sell all thou hast and give to the poor, and thou shalt have treasure in heaven: and come and follow me." When the young man had gone sorrowfully away, Jesus said to the disciples, "Verily, I say unto you, That a rich man shall hardly enter into the kingdom of heaven." The disciples were amazed, for they had seen the Master on the best terms with rich men as well as publicans and sinners. They exclaimed, "Who, then can be saved?" Jesus answered, "With men this is impossible; but with God all things are possible." This statement may well have been one which came to the ears of Paul when he studied the problem and later decided that men could not work out their own salvation but that to be saved was "an election" or pure gift on the part of God.

In order to find a clue to the secret method to be used to get God to exert his power to help make a man perfect, we continue to "search the Scriptures" to find the word "perfect" used in other passages. Although John has not mentioned the Transfiguration in his account, he has given all of Chapter 17 to the prayers delivered by Jesus before the day of the crucifixion, and we read in the Fenton translation, 17:1,

"Father, the time has come! Perfect Your Son, etc." Again, we must remember that his prayer was delivered before the crucifixion, and before Jesus had learned the lesson of complete selflessness. However, he is made by John to ask, even if with too little humility, that he be made "perfect," and in some mystical way made completely ready for the great promotion or Last Day.

As men cannot perfect themselves, we may now inspect the code to see if it will tell us what God must do when and if He will.

Hemo-lele is "perfect" in the code. The roots, fortunately, tell us just what makes for perfection in the Huna sense. Hemo has two meanings which run together or which follow one on the other as would a cause giving a result. The first is "to loosen" and when this is accomplished, there comes "to separate" or a "separation" from what has been loosened. All through our study we have seen that "stumbling blocks" need to be cleared from the "path" of contact with the High Self, so we are safe in concluding that the things which are to be loosened are these blockages. This is confirmed at once by the second root, *lele*, which means, "to rise or fly upward." Again we know that it is the mana and the prayer pictures which rise along the aka cord to the High Self, so we see that we have chanced upon what seems to be a perfection which is brought about by the Father and which must be a cleansing so complete that it is beyond the ability of the low self to bring it about. This seems odd when we remember that Jesus was pictured as in full contact with the Father and was at times speaking as if he were the Father.

For the moment we will leave the question of the nature of a perfection which is of a superior kind— "without restrictions"—and go on with our searching.

The complete perfecting is seen to be an act of kindness or mercy on the part of the Father, and we at once recall the use of the word "grace," and go on to see what it may offer in the code.

"GRACE" is mentioned in the code sense only in

Luke 2:40 and John 1:14–17. The two mentions in the Old Testament which may have code meanings are found in Zechariah, 12:10 and Psalms 84:11. Let us look first at Zechariah, who has much the same approach as Isaiah and may have the same connection with the knowledge of the code. We read:

"And I will pour upon the house of David, and upon the inhabitants of Jerusalem, the spirit of grace and of supplications; and they shall look upon me whom they have pierced, and they shall mourn him, as one mourneth for his only son, and shall be in bitterness for him, as one that is in bitterness for his first born."

This has been taken by some as a prediction of the coming of Jesus and his crucifixion, as have similar passages in Isaiah. The "sprit of grace" might well be the High Self as the one to help the lesser man at the time of "graduation," although the words which follow would point to the mourning of the High Self over the lesser man during the periods when contact was cut off and the symbolic crucifixion resulted.

Psalms 84:11 is more open in its code meaning. We read, "For the Lord God is a sun and a shield: the Lord will give grace and glory: no good thing will he withhold from them that walk uprightly."

The word "lord" when used in the code has the meaning of the High Self. It is *ha-ku*, the first root part giving us the familiar code word for the prayer method, and the second (in one of its many meanings) "to extend or reach from one place to another," indicating the shadowy cord connecting the lesser man with the "lord" High Self. The "sun" as applied to "Lord God" in the passage confirms the code meaning, for Light and the Sun were the High Self symbols first and last. The "glory" is the symbol of the halo or shadowy body in which a High Self is clothed. Here is given the promise that "no good thing" will be withheld from the one who is to become a High Self through the exercise of "grace" and who then will be able himself, after "graduation" to use the same "grace" to help his own low-middle self "son" or "only begotten."

Coming to the Gospels and Luke 2:40, we have a passage which may foreshadow the later adult Jesus. "The child grew, and waxed strong in spirit, filled with wisdom; and the grace of God was upon him." Fenton translated it, ". . . and the favor of God rested upon him." If the writer of Luke was inserting the word "grace" here to carry the code meaning, it would be pointing to the High Self of the boy, Jesus, having a very good natural contact with him and helping him with inspiration and general guidance. The word for "wisdom" is *ike*, which has for one of its secondary meanings that of "To receive, as a visitor or messenger," and from this we may conclude that the writer had in mind the High Self coming close to the child.

In John 1:17 we have a verse which seems to have been inserted well out of the general context. In the King James Bible the translators noted this and set the passage off from the rest of the preamble with spaces. We read,

"For the law was given by Moses, but grace and truth came by Jesus Christ."

We see at once that the outer rules or "laws" of life are being superseded by something else, presumably of a much higher order. When we know the code meaning of "grace" we shall see at once that its use in the final salvation through "grace" is being called to the attention of the initiated reader.

Loko-mai-kai, is the code word for "grace," it also means, "favor, good will, kind, and mercy." These are the meanings of the word in Greek or English, and they give us only the outer meaning—the same thing found in the Acts and Epistles. But when we look at the roots, we find something very different.

Lo-ko gives us a word with two basic meanings. 1. "The inner part; that which is within," as the inner organs of a person or his moral nature. 2. "A pond; a lake; a small collection of water."

The "inner part" in this piece of code is the lesser man—his middle and low self pair. These are up for "graduation" and are to be given the final cleansing which is symbolized by baptism. The pond or lake is the baptismal font, and the water of cleansing is the mana used by the High Self.

Lo: "The fore part of the head," or the center of consciousness of the middle self. This tells us that the middle self is to graduate.

Ko: 1. "To accomplish; to fulfill; to bring to pass, as a promise. 2. "To draw or drag with a rope." This root has to do with the code symbol of "a sufficient supply of mana," and reminds the initiate at once that the lesser man must accumulate a good supply of mana sent through the aka cord to the High Self to empower it to act on the physical and mental levels to help the lesser selves. In this symbology it repeats that of the water and cleansing by baptism. All is necessary in order that the High Self may accomplish the "work of Grace" and bring to pass the promised graduation." The second meaning, of "to drag with a rope" is symbolic of the effort made by the High Self to bring the middle self up to its higher level. The rope is the symbol of the aka cord of connection. The middle self is helped at this point to "ascend" "up" to the higher level symbolized as "heaven" in outer circles, but not understood for what it really is—not a place but a condition beyond the physical level.

Ko also has the meaning of "to proceed from, as a child from a parent; to beget, as a father." Here we have the code intimation in symbol that the low self and the new sub-human self which will be brought up to join it, will become as a "son" to the High Self Mother-Father. The phrase, "only begotten son of the Father" applies to both the male and female units over which the High Self presides. Each High Self has one son and one daughter middle self to bring along (also their low selves, of course), and as the pair eventually unite, they are symbolized in the code simply as "the son."

Mai-kai: "To be good" (with the causative *hoo,* as in *hoo-mai-kai*), "to be repaired; to be made beautiful (or glorified), and excellent in all ways; to be made kind." This is a very good general description of the state reached by the help of the grace of the High Self. But to get more details concerning the things done in the process, we need to examine the two roots of the word.

Mai: 1. Fade. 2. Sick. 3. Almost; nearly. 4. To prohibit.

Selecting different meanings from the list above, we

come first to the meaning of "fade," which is the code symbol for lack of mana, and here the lesser man symbolically gives all of his mana to the High Self to make it able to help him with "grace." After "graduation" the new High Self must depend on drawing mana from the new man and woman over whom it will be set, but while this is done for many incarnations, there finally will come a time when the lesser man and woman will come to know the presence of the High Self, and when mana is happily accumulated and sent as an empowering gift along the aka cord to the High Self.

The work of "grace" which makes "good," corrects and heals and removes the abnormal conditions which appear in early incarnations as sickness, but which in the final incarnation before graduation is the sickness of the soul, so to speak. All guilts and all blockings of the "Path" of contact with the High Self are lifted, as unnecessary "burdens" and removed. This is a stage at which the graduating middle self and the companion low self are "nearly" ready for the upward step, and are "almost" ready to be "separated or parted asunder" from their state of association.

Let us digress for a moment to go back to the word for "perfect," *hemo-lele*, and recall the meaning of the actions which follow one on the heels of the other: those of "to loosen" then "to separate." This applies to clearing the path, but also gives us the process of loosening the bond that has held the low and middle selves together through the whole series of lives. This intimate relationship is now to be broken and the bond "loosened" after which, the middle self is separated from its old companion so that it can become a "solitary," standing all alone as it enters the symbolic "bridal chamber" to meet the mate and be united to her in a bond infinitely closer than that which held it to the low self. (We will come back later to consider this in Gnostic references.)

The second root of *mai-kai* is *kai:* 1. To lift up on the hands and carry, as a child. 2. To transfer, as a person from one place or another; (with *hoo*) to separate or part asunder (as in loosening and separating). 3. The sea; sea water (mana), a current or flow in the sea; a fishing net or bird snare. 4. The state of a person having no desire for food. 5. A long period of time. As *kai-kai*, "To take off, as a burden; to promote; to exalt." We get in these many variations of meaning the duplications which make certain that the inner meaning of the "perfection through grace" will be preserved for the candidates for initiation through the times to come.

To round out our study we have only to return to John 17:23 and consider his phrase, ". . . that they may be made perfect in one. . . ." From this we have a second meaning to add to that of the lesser man being "made one" or placed in contact with his High Self via the aka cord. In this meaning the "perfecting" includes the making ONE of the male and female middle selves who then become the new High Self.

CHAPTER 16

THE UNION IN THE "SAYINGS" AND IN GNOSTIC WRITINGS

The knowledge of the union of the male and female to make a new High Self is clearly presented in code in the early Christian writings which were not included when the canon was made up by the Church Fathers. More coded material is to be found in the literature which we have come to call "Gnostic."

One of the best sources of additional information is to be found in "The Gospel of Thomas," of which there have been a number of copies discovered in modern times. This book is very short and contains the sayings of Jesus rather than an account of his life and ministry. The author is said to have been the twin brother of Jesus and to have passed on to Matthias the sayings. The original was composed in Greek, and was translated later into the Egyptian language of the period, either Coptic or Sahadic.

In the same general period, with Alexandria in lower Egypt the center of such activities following a still earlier development of similar thought in Greece, the literature of the "Gnosis" was written with many veiled meanings and used in the Mysteries of the time, probably as initiatory dramas. In the "Sayings" and in some of the gnostic writings we find almost identical passages dealing with the great secret of "graduation."

Again the secret lore is found in sources farther afield, as in the writings belonging to the Mythraic Mysteries.

A good source book of this material is FRAGMENTS OF A FAITH FORGOTTEN, by G. R. S. Mead, an English scholar of great learning and strong Theosophical leanings who wrote at the close of the last century.

From the Gospel of Thomas we have the passage, "When the Lord was asked by a certain man, When should his Kingdom come, He saith to him: When two shall be one, and the without be as the within, and the male with the female, neither male nor female."

A woman named Salome appears in some of this literature, either as a questioner or as one passing on information concerning the secret teachings. Here is a passage in which we have the one above more or less duplicated:

"When Salome asked how long should death hold sway, the Lord said unto her: So long as ye women bring forth; for I came to end the works of the female. And Salome said unto him: I have then done well in not bringing forth. And the Lord answered and said: Eat of every pasture, but of that which hath bitterness of death eat not. And when Salome asked when should these things of which she enquires be known, the Lord said: When ye shall tread upon the vesture of shame, and when two shall be one, the male with the female, neither male nor female."

In one translation a passage in the Gospel of Thomas reads, "Simon Peter says to them: Let Mary go out from our midst, for women are not worthy of life. Jesus says: See, I will draw her so as to make her male so that she may also become a living spirit like you

240

males. For every woman who has become male will enter the Kingdom of heaven."

We also find a significant passage which reads, "Jesus said: Many stand outside at the door, but it is only the solitaries who enter into the bridal chamber."

These passages touch upon several things connected with the graduation. Salome is told that the time has come to stop bearing children and stop reincarnating or suffering physical death. This is, of course, the condition to be realized when one has evolved to the point of being ready to be united, as in Salome's case, with her male half, to make a new High Self which is no longer subject to physical death.

In the passage where Simon Peter wishes to have Mary put out of the group, we have what may have been the first sign of mistaken ideas in the outer version of the teachings. Much later, in the writings attributed to Paul, we have him taking much the same attitude. The Church, however, could not follow Paul in this putting away of women. The race has to be preserved through them. What Paul and others who abhorred marriage and intercourse with women missed entirely was the inner teaching that in the final incarnation the candidate for graduation draws away from all earthly ties of marriage and family, valuing the promised state of the High Self and desiring it greatly instead of the things of the physical and mental level which will be left behind.

One can only speculate as to the number of hermits who have become "solitaries" in the past because of their mistaken belief that this had something to do with winning salvation. "A little knowledge is a dangerous thing" says an old saw, and when we see the absurdities and misdirected efforts of the centuries, we can hardly avoid feeling that it was a very bad thing that the inner teaching of the code ever leaked out in the form which gave the outer teachings so many false directions.

Another separation is to be experienced when the middle and low selves are separated before graduation. Their two shadowy bodies must also be separated. During life and through the cycle of incarnations, the two shadowy bodies which house the two selves are connected and interblended, especially when in the physical body during the living periods. But as two garments are removed and one taken from the other, the *aka* bodies are separated. When the middle self, as a candidate, is ready to graduate, there is provided by the High Self a new garment which will clothe the united male and female selves as one unit, not as two.

This shadowy-substance garment is called in some texts the "Robe of Glory," in others the "Robe of Light," and when it houses the High Self it gives out white light which is seen on rare occasions by lesser men on the physical level.

The "seamless" robe or garment is the symbol of the single shadowy body of a High Self, also of the united male and female selves living in it. In the crucifixion scene, the code is used to show that the man, Jesus, on the cross was not a High Self. He was stripped of his robe, and we read, John 19:23–24,

"Then the soldiers, when they had crucified Jesus, took his garments, and made four parts, to every soldier a part; and also his coat. Now the coat was without a

242

seam, woven from the top throughout. They therefore said among themselves, Let us not rend it, but cast lots for it, whose it shall be."

The changing of the shadowy bodies or garments ties in closely with the idea of transfiguration in the code word for "garment," this being *lole*, which also means, "to alter from one thing to another" and "to rectify." Thus we see that the final "making perfect" includes the correcting of any faults and the changing from one self level to the next, the shadowy body also being changed in some way. That the low self also steps up a level is indicated in the roots *lo* and *le*, the first meaning "the brain of a person or animal" and referring in the older usage of the language to the seat of intelligence in the intestines, this being a sure indication that the low self was meant. The second root has the meaning of "to leap or fly upward," and so gives us the upward progression to the next level at the time of graduation, when all three of the selves of the man play their parts.

The idea of going up a step is found in the coded phrase, "to tread upon the garment of shame." "Tread is *hele*, which has the same *le* root and which also means "to pass on," or in this case, "pass on a step higher." "Shame" is *hila-hila*, which gives in the root *hi*, "to droop; to be weak," and *la*, "light." As the shadowy bodies are worn out they may be said to become "weak," and to lack "light," which we know is also "life" in terms of the code. From another angle we may say that with the low and middle selves, during their cycle of incarnations, they become tired and weak in contrast with the High Self which remains ever the same. The "garment of shame" can only refer to the lower selves and the animal nature which must be cleansed and made ready for the upward step. Adam and Eve may be said to have put on the first "garment of shame" when they were placed in bodies and came to know that they were naked. Not until they could, after many incarnations, put off those bodies of flesh and reunite as a High Self could they rise above the level of the lesser man who knows shame.

In one of the Sayings we have the word "mingled" used instead of "shame." We read, "There is a mingling that leadeth to death, and there is a mingling which leadeth to life." Here we have the sex union on the lower levels where death follows each incarnation and the mingling or uniting effort is left incomplete. But at the time of graduation the mingling of the male and female results in a continuing life beyond physical death. The code word for "mingle" is *kaa-wili*, in which the root *kaa* has a secondary meaning of "a cross." *Wili* is "to writhe in pain." The code intimation seems to be that all efforts to complete the lesser union on the level of the incarnating selves results in pain because of the lack of "perfection."

One of the gnostic fragments dealing with the union of the male and female selves is to be found starting on page 74 of Mead's small book, titled, THE WEDDING SONG OF WISDOM.

From the translation of the ritual we read, "For this is the Mystery of the gate of Heaven, and this is the house of God, where the Good God dwells alone; into which house no impure man shall come—but it is kept under watch for the Spiritual alone; where, when they come, they must cast away their garments, and all become Bridegrooms, obtaining their true Manhood through the Virginal Spirit."

The "Virginal Spirit" is the female half of the pair about to graduate. She is "virginal" in the sense of being purified of all earthly things which do not belong on the high level where physical generation has ended. The male completes his "manhood" only by adding to himself her "womanhood." Together they reap the promised reward of the hundred times greater mental and mana powers belonging to the High Selves. (See THRICE GREATEST HERMES, i. 180, 181.)

Sophia represents the "Virginal Spirit" in some of the gnostic literature. After graduation, or the "marriage made in heaven," she becomes the Holy Ghost or Mother half of the Father-Mother High Self.

Mead tells us on pages 75 through 78 of the ritual of the "Sacred Marriage," as given on page 50 of THE HYMN OF JESUS, in which Sophia, as the candidate for initiation says:

(1) "I would be wounded (or pierced)." In an alternate Latin translation it reads, "I would be dissolved" (that is) "by consuming love."

(2) "I would be begotten."

(3) "I would be adorned."

(4) "I would be at-oned."

These four statements of desire and intention cover the ground of graduation, and in the first we meet again the need to suffer in order to be cleansed. There is still something veiled in this matter, however. Jesus, when crucified, was pierced in the side by a spear to bring about his death. That is the outer meaning, and

245

death seems to be presented by the writers as the final disaster when one is cut off from one's High Self. But the word *hou*, for "pierce," also means "new; repeat; do again," and is the code symbol for being born again in a fresh incarnation. In the case of the candidate for graduation, the death of the middle self, so to speak, is to make possible the rebirth into the Kingdom of Heaven or the High Self state.

Also, in the matter of the desire to be "pierced" we note that the word "side" is *ao-ao* in the code, with a secondary meaning of "to enlighten, to escape, and a new way or course of life." All of these meanings apply well to the things desired by the candidate, perhaps as a result of the suffering of the cleansing to make him "perfect." Certainly, the rebirth into the High Self level ushers the middle self into an entirely new way of life, and a way of vastly greater enlightenment.

The Latin translation of "be dissolved" fits well the idea of the doing away with the shadowy body and the separation from the low self to make possible what is to come. "By consuming love" would suggest that in the love of the mates in the new union the very power of the love consumes the unwanted things left behind. The old middle selves, male and female, are "consumed" and their substance and very being enters into the formation of the new High Self.

The second desire, "I would be begotten," repeats the idea of rebirth into the level of the High Self. "To beget" is the code symbol of bringing about a birth or a rebirth. "Beget" is *hoo-hua* in the language of the code, and means "to bring forth, as a female" or to be born.

The desire to "be adorned" is simple to understand,

now that we have learned the meaning of the "robe of light," which is the shadowy body of the newly united pair—this union being plainly stated as the great desire in, "I would be at-oned."

Mead comments on the desire for "at-one-ment," saying, "We now approach the Mystery of Union, when the soul abandons with joy its separateness and frees itself from the limitations of its 'possessions'—of that which is 'mine' as apart from the rest. Enough has now been given to assure the reader that the Sacred Marriage was a fundamental mystery with the Christian Gnostics."

A slightly longer, and very similar invocation or expression of desire is given by Mead in his booklet, MYTHRAIC RITUAL, page 33. We read:

"Hail Lord, Thou Master of the Water!

"O Lord, being born again, I pass away in being made Great, and having been made Great, I die.

"Being born from out the state of birth-and-death that giveth birth to mortal lives, I now, set free, pass to the state transcending birth as Thou hast stablished it, according as Thou hast ordained and made the Mystery."

This covers well the matter of the death of the old middle self as it is helped to perfection by the use of the grace and power of the High Self. The title, "Master of the Water" is Huna in that the High Self is the master of the high mana which can be used to produce miracles and to bring about the union of graduation.

❈　❈　❈　❈　❈

The world is filled with people of different degrees of progression in the evolutionary school of life. We might say, figuratively, that there are twelve grades in the school, and that the inner teachings are not given until one has been through about ten grades and is well along in the work of learning to live the kindly and hurtless life, which is the goal as one nears graduation and makes ready to pass through the twelfth grade.

The discovery of the Huna code and its meanings has given us the first new light on the Christian mystery teachings in all the intervening centuries. But while the inner teachings concerning the High Self and prayer are in themselves marvelous additions to our knowledge, the most splendid and exciting part of the teachings has to do with what we have called "graduation." In this lies the promise of all the many things for which we have striven in our several incarnations and which we have always failed to realize in more than a partial fashion.

Through incarnation after incarnation we have tried to find the perfect love and the perfect mate, even as we have tried to be in ourselves the perfect mate, but have failed inevitably. As long as the middle self, who is the one who will graduate, is living in the flesh and is forced to share the life and emotions of the low self, there is no chance to reach perfection. Only after passing through the last incarnation and learning sufficiently well the lesson of hurtless and helpful living, can one come to the point at which application to the High Self can be made for help in reaching the full perfection. This help is given after the end of the last incarnation through the grace of the loving Father-Mother, and we are helped to make the step upward, there to meet and blend with, in perfect love, the perfected mate, and then go on to live and serve as a new High Self.

All of the frustrations and imperfections of love which have haunted us in our several incarnations will have served their purpose in teaching us to love more perfectly. The old dream of the "true love" which has been held through thick and thin, and which utter failure in one's love life has never been able to put down, can at last come into full realization. Here is the very heart of romance and beauty. Here is the mystery of the great fulfillment in which the sundered halves, male and female, of the Adamic man are put back together.

In the new state, there is also the vastly greater mental ability to be enjoyed. And, with the greater reach of mind, there comes the greater mana-power to use to accomplish the things which are seen to be good to do. The new High Self becomes the Father-Mother of the old low self, which in its turn steps up to the level of a middle self, and there will be a new low self coming up from the level just below the human to form the third member of the new triune man.

The test which will tell one roughly whether or not he or she is ready to graduate is outlined in the Gospels. If one has come to desire above all else the state of being perfect in love and in hurtless living, one may be ready.

A test which one can make for oneself is to pause for self-examination and to ask whether one is attached strongly to the things of the world and prefers them to the promised love and wondrous beauty and greater mental power of the High Self. One should ask whether one would be willing to give up the home and friends and close ties of the present in exchange for the privilege of gaining the more abstract values of the next level. Many of us, even when we find life almost intolerable, cling to things as they are and shudder at the prospect of going on. Many back away from the thought of being made one with someone of the opposite sex, or of giving up the individual or personal sense of "self" in order to blend with the true mate and have the greatly enlarged sense of being.

Even if one is well along in the school of life and is almost ready to graduate, it will be natural for one to feel reluctance at the thought of leaving forever the beauty of fields and mountains, seas and deserts, or the tender love of dear ones. It will be a natural reluctance because these are the things dearest to the heart of the low self with whom we middle selves reside. We are always sharing with the low self its pleasure in the beauty of the physical world and the loveliness of the loves that are based on the physical as well as the mental levels in which we presently exist.

On the other hand, life may be so difficult for some that any way of escape seems welcome, even if it is nothing but the promise of oblivion. One caught in such a difficult life experience may be unable to judge accurately whether or not the willingness to give up earthly things is the mark of nearing the graduation point or whether it is simply a vast weariness which calls for the blessed rest which is provided for all between incarnations if they can and will accept it. (Some cannot accept rest and try to stay on the physical level, fastening themselves as evil spirits to the living and stealing their mana to live upon and to work with as hypnotic force.)

For the circumspect individual who sees clearly how lovely the earthly things can be, but who prefers to leave these to the enjoyment of the low self while he moves on up to greater beauties and wisdom and creative power, the time has come to ask that the High Self begin the perfecting action through grace.

It must be kept in mind at all times that there is no hurry. Each of us has all the time that is needed to grow and to learn the lessons of life. It is as right and proper and enjoyable to be living through one's first or third or seventh incarnation as it is to be near the end of the twelfth and to be ready to ask for help to graduate. Everything in its time, everything in its necessary place. The High Self watches with loving care to direct and assist at every step upward along the road— a path that should be normal and pleasant. It also stands by to watch and wait when the normal progress is held back by association with evil spirits or by fixations, or by the natural evil in the low and middle selves of the man. At such times the needed lessons have to be learned by bitter experience while the High Self patiently looks on, knowing that in time the lesson will be learned. By being hurt himself, the man eventually learns not to hurt others.

One "takes up his cross daily" and life is normal and therefore good and pleasant on the whole as long as one is following the teachings of Jesus. These ways are simple enough for even the youngest in the school of life to understand. They are, first, to refrain from hurting others, and second, to come in good time to realize that the High Self is part of oneself and to start to learn to contact it and invite its help each day in the work of living the hurtless and helpful life.

Jesus said, "My yoke is easy, my burden is light," and this is the cross taken up daily and made light by the love and help of the Father-Mother.

CHAPTER 17

THE PROBLEM OF A DRAMA

Owing to the many contradictions in the Four Gospels, it is much simpler to reconstruct the Life as a Mystery Drama than as a history of a man who was both man and God. In a single incarnation of Jesus it is almost impossible to get around the teaching that the kingdom of heaven is within, and the contrary teaching that it was a physical kingdom which lay outside and above the man so that it could take a material form on the Day of Judgment and provide thrones for the Father and also the Son.

In treating the material as it is made clear to us through the code, and accepting the postulated drama as basic in the presentation, there is an advantage which is enjoyed by the dramatist but which is entirely denied the historian. The former can juggle the time elements, while the latter must stay with the supposed sequence of events.

Another great advantage enjoyed by the dramatist is that he can employ someone who comes out upon the stage when needed, to explain what has been going on or to predict what is about to take place. He is the hierophant or expositor of the sacred mysteries in the Greek mode of the Eleusinian mysteries. If the time sequence is to be turned even end-for-end to bring out some important point, he has only to speak a few words to warn the audience that a flash-back is in order, or that for a few moments an excursion into the future is to be made.

Such an excursion was neatly made by Matthew when he took the living woman, Mary, who was to be the mother of Jesus, and allowed her to be projected into the future two full incarnations, at the end of which time she appears resplendent as the Virgin, utterly pure, no longer making ready to give physical birth to Jesus, but ready now to become his heavenly bride in the "marriage made in heaven." No longer is she to "bring forth." That task lies behind her. She is the Eve returning to meet her Adam. The rib is to be replaced, and the man made wonderfully whole and One. She is the Salome of the Gnosis, and the Mary whom Peter wished sent away, but whom Jesus said he would "draw" (to him in union) so that she should also be male. She is the wife, daughter, mother, sister and friend of many incarnations—the "Beloved" under all guises and in all stages of progression, despite all misadventures.

As dramatists, the writers of the Gospels differ widely in the materials which they selected. Mark opens the First Act with the appearance of John the Baptist. Matthew makes short work of the events leading up to the birth of Jesus, but Luke makes much of them and of the virginity of Mary. John, who followed more closely the Greek way of treating his material, has the curtain rise on the profound statements of the hierophant beginning with, "In the beginning was the Word, and the Word was with God, and the Word was God."

In looking over the code information inserted by only one of the writers at a time in their opening, one wonders whether they planned to depend upon future initiates to pick up points from the different versions and combine them to get the complete picture.

If we take the fine presentation of Mary as the "Virgin" in Luke, then the Three Wise men and the Star from Matthew, and ignore Mark while going on to John for his elaborate exposition of the "Word," we can compose an impressive opening unit in terms of the code.

We have already seen the meaning of Mary as the Virgin. Next we can go on to the Star which led the Three Wise Men to the place where the infant Jesus lay, and connect the Star and the "Word," for in the code, *ho-ku* is star, but also "word." And, thanks to John's roundabout statements, we know that the "Word" is the High Self.

So, we may say that The High Self was the leading actor who announced the impending advent of Jesus, selected Mary for the virgin mother (who was at the time of her selection symbolizing the Bride of Christ who was still to come), and acted as the Star-Word to lead the Three Wise Men. The "Magi," or wise magicians, were, of course, kahunas, and as masters of the inner secrets, would be the proper ones to be led to the place of the birth of Jesus at the right time.

This may point to the three selves or the number three in the prayer steps.

Just why there should be three Wise men, is not clear, it may be that there would have been four of them specified had Mark also opened the first act in the earlier part of the story. He may have been purposely left out of the group by the others in their first approach. On the other hand, the number "three" was used in the code at various places with telling effect—as in the scene in which Peter thrice denies his allegiance to Jesus before the crucifixion, and is reminded of his failure by the crowing of a cock. To "crow" is *ooo*, in the code, and its secondary meaning is "a small cup containing water to drink." So, we learn that Peter's failure was that he did not send the "water" or mana to the High Self, as represented by Jesus. A "cock" is *moa*, and the secondary or code meaning here is "to dry out," which repeats the fact symbolically that the mana was denied by Peter.

The "drying out" or denying of mana to the High Self is emphasized in the story of Peter and the predicted crowing of the cock by the further fact that Peter was huddled over a fire at the time of this episode. The word for "cock," *moa*, has still a third meaning, which is "to roast," and as roasting is done over a fire, the denying of mana to the High Self appears certainly to have a deeper meaning to offer for the event which led to the crucifixion. On the other hand, the dramatists may have seen fit to toss in the detail scene just to restate the fact that disaster can follow the failure of the lesser man to supply mana to his High Self. Noting how scenes were placed quite out of time sequence, this interchange may have had, in actuality, little or nothing to do with the predicament of Jesus that dark night before the trial. Or, the scene may have been placed there to show that Jesus was left helpless by spirits who had stolen his mana and cut him off from the saving contact with his own Father.

Leading up to the crucifixion, there are several things carefully coded to tell the dreary fact that the cause of the loss of contact by Jesus with his High Self Father was spirit interference in which his low self was snared and its mana taken. Before Peter denied Jesus, he and his companions had been instructed to keep watch while Jesus prayed, but all had fallen asleep. Left unguarded in fact and in symbol, Jesus prayed in anguish, ". . . if it be possible, let this cup pass from me. . . ." and then, ". . . if this cup may not pass away from me, except I drink it, thy will be done. (Matt. 26:39 and 42).

The "cup" is the usual poison cup of bitter fluid, in the outer meaning, but in the code *kiaha*, or "cup" also has two roots which overlap. The first is *kia*, which means, "One who snares or catches birds," and here we have the snare as the symbol of the obsessing spirits and in "birds," the symbol of the spirit of the man when snared or caught. The root, *aha* is "a cup," also "a company," here a company of evil spirits.

In verse 41 this coded information is repeated when Jesus uses the occasion of finding Peter and his companions asleep to say, "Watch and pray, that ye enter not into temptation: the spirit indeed is willing, but the flesh is weak." Here the "spirit" is *uhane*, or the middle self and the "flesh" is the low self in the body. We hardly need the hierophant to whisper an aside from the wings to tell us that Jesus is speaking of his own great temptation as a middle self—the irrestible "bait" being intellectual or personal pride in his own spiritual status. He had been snared by evil spirits and his low self taken over. After more prayer, and no rescue, we read (verse 45) "Then cometh he to his disciples, and saith unto them, Sleep on now, and take your rest: behold the hour is at hand, and the Son of man is betrayed into the hands of sinners." The "sinners" represent here the evil spirits which had conquered him and who were most evil.

In John and Matthew the tale is told of how one of the followers of Jesus, at the time of his betrayal by Judas, took his sword and cut off the ear of one of the servants of the high priest. Jesus rebuked his follower and told him to put up his sword, but he did not heal the servant's ear. This oversight on the part of the healer who could perform such miracles of healing, can only be explained as a coded way of saying that for the time being, owing to his loss of mana and of contact with his High Self, he stood a helpless captive in the hypnotic grip of the evil spirits as well as in the hands of the men who had taken him captive. (Luke is out-voted, two to one, when he says Jesus healed the servant's ear—a statement which is out of keeping with the situation).

In that part of the drama which leads up to the crucifixion, there should be, if the proper sequence of events is to be kept, all the incidents in which Jesus looks forward confidently to the material triumph of the Coming of the Kingdom with his own glorification as the Last Judgment begins. In the long first act he should be seen enjoying food and wine and the good things of life, eating with publicans and associating with sinners despite the criticism of the officials of the

Jewish church. His Disciples also share the good things, and one of them carries a purse containing money to meet their expenses when they are not being entertained by converts and friendly followers.

In the Second Act of the drama there should be found the austerities in which Jesus and the Disciples have given up all desire for the things of earth and have set their faces toward the goal of graduation and transfiguration.

Judas and the betrayal for a price of thirty pieces of silver furnishes a symbolic ending to the first part of the action. In the story as told by Matthew, he repents of his actions even before Jesus is brought to trial, casts away the poor bribe, and goes out to hang himself. This final renunciation of the wordly goods should, properly, come at the beginning of the second act to show that all desire for wordly goods and standing had been given up. Also at this point should come the story of the rich young man who asked what he should do to inherit eternal life, and who was instructed to sell all and give to the poor.

Far along in the second act should be placed the admonitions of Jesus, as given in Matthew 6:19–34, beginning, "Lay not up for yourselves treasures upon earth. . . ." Then giving us, "Ye cannot serve God and mammon." And finally in verse 34, "Take therefore no thought of the morrow. . . ." The whole philosophy of the discourse is found in the lines, "For where your treasure is, there will your heart be also." All is to be given up except the goal of graduation into the High Self level. Here the drama should move steadily toward the climax of the Transfiguration.

If the writers of the Gospels actually did shuffle the time sequences in their accounts of the Life as a way of further complicating the code to prevent it from being broken, they indeed used a clever and effective subterfuge. And, if we who have come so lately to unraveling the tangle, try to place everything into orderly time sequences, we may never arrive at a completed picture of the corpus of initiate knowledge.

There is a strong indication that certain units of the account were used in such a way that each provided a "degree" in the initiation of the candidates. Such degree units do not depend so much upon the main story and its progress as upon the fact that in each there is divulged some single facet of the secret teachings.

An example of such a degree unit is to be found in the parable of the Wise and Foolish Virgins, Matt. 25:1–13: "Then shall the kingdom of heaven be likened unto ten virgins who took their lamps, and went forth to meet the bridegroom. And five of them were wise and five were foolish. They that were foolish took their lamps, and took no oil with them. But the wise took oil in their vessels with their lamps. While the bridegroom tarried, they all slumbered and slept. And at midnight there was a cry made, Behold, the bridegroom cometh; go ye out to meet him. Then all the virgins arose, and trimmed their lamps. And the foolish said unto the wise, Give us of your oil; for our lamps have gone out. But the wise answered, saying, Not so; lest there be not enough for us and you: but go ye rather to them that sell, and buy for yourselves. And while they went to buy, the bridegroom came;

and they that were ready went in with him to the marriage: and the door was shut. Afterward came also the other virgins, saying, Lord, Lord, open to us. But he answered and said, Verily I say unto you, I know you not."

After the little drama had been played out in this degree, we can imagine the candidates being instructed in the hidden meanings by the Master of the degree, using questions and answers after this fashion.

What is the kingdom of heaven? It is the level or state of being of the High Self.

How does one enter into this kingdom? When one is ready as a middle self, one is perfected by an act of grace by one's High Self and then helped to evolve into the state of a High Self, this entailing the meeting with the mate and the union of the two in the "marriage which is made in heaven," with the result that the pair become ONE and are a new High Self or member of the kingdom.

What does the bridegroom represent? And what the virgins? The bridegroom is the male middle self who is ready for the "union." The virgins represent the female mates, one of whom will be selected and united with the bridegroom. The number ten is symbolic of the many who become almost ready to take the final upward step.

What is the significance of the lamps and the oil? The lamps represent the final stage of perfecting on the parts of the virgins. Each virgin must be ready, as she enters into the house—which is here the kingdom. Her preparation is complete only when she has her lamp and oil for it—only when she is ready to become a High Self in union with the male, and so light her lamp and radiate the Light.

The injunction, "Watch therefore; for ye know neither the day nor the hour wherein the Son of man cometh," warns all candidates to be ready at any time for the final upward step, for the time may come unexpectedly, life being as uncertain as it is. One "prays always" and strives to remain ever ready to be made perfect and helped through the graduation process. The selected virgin is, in reality, the bride, and she brings extra oil so that the groom may also be able to light his flame and join in radiating the Light.

It may be that the woman, as the virgin, will arrive at a state of readiness before her male mate. Her capacity for love is greater, and her task is to learn to love unselfishly, completely, and not in any way possessively. His love for her, after he "has overcome the world and the devil" of spiritual pride, will lead him to her as to a light burning in darkness. Her light will kindle his, and together they will burn as a single and enduring flame.

❉   ❉   ❉   ❉   ❉

There are several passages in the Gospels which repeat the work of the initiatory degree of the "marriage made in heaven," and some of these furnish short scenes which lead up to the final scenes in which the Union is shown as completed.

In Matthew, Chapter 19, we have a passage already mentioned as having caused much misunderstanding in outer circles, so that men became hermits and castrates in the hope of gaining entrance into the Kingdom of Heaven. In verses 11 and 12 we read, "But he said unto them, All men cannot receive (understand the inner meaning of) this saying, save those to whom it is given. For there are some eunuchs, which were so born from their mother's womb: and there are some eunuchs, which were made eunuchs of men: and there be eunuchs, which have made themselves eunuchs for the kingdom of heaven's sake. He that is able to receive it, let him receive it."

The translators of the New Testament in yesterday's Hawaii, may have felt that the Hawaiian word for "eunuch" was not sufficiently descriptive to be used, so they worked over the English word and used it in the text as "eunuha," which lost for it the whole of the code significance. The word *ma-hu* contained the code, but did not mean a castrate. The root *ma* means "to accompany" or may be used as a "formative" root, and in this case with the root *hu*, which means "to rise up," we have "to accompany someone and cause a rising up." This is most obscure except to the ones able to "receive" it.

We have just watched a degree scene acted out in which the woman is depicted as the "virgin" and as the mate ready for the "marriage." Here we have the male, also in a state of progression in which he has left the world and the work of procreation to become a symbolic eunuch. The barren female and the sterile male have become free from all lesser desires and wish only for the final Union.

This sterile condition is beautifully presented in the drama by having the little children brought into the scene for Jesus to bless and he says, ". . . for of such is the kingdom of heaven." He was not speaking of the children as the "little angels" we have with us when fond parents present to visitors most unlikely offspring. He was speaking in veiled terms of their lack of reproductive powers and activities.

There is an obscure word familiar to the kahunas, but which does not have the meaning of "eunuch," but which applies precisely to the Union of the mates. It is *ko-ko-hu*, which means "to have a form; to take the garb or assume the manners of another." This word is used to describe the *ma-hu* who is an individual imitating the opposite sex. The code meaning of "to have a form" covers the full range of the Union in so far as the new shadowy body is concerned—this being the new "garb" or "body of light" to be put on by the new High Self. The "to assume the manners of another" touches on the very depths of the secret concerning the state in which the mates become One.

We cannot have this state of splendid love and Light explained to us too often. The candidate must be helped to understand that in this blending and union of the mates, nothing is given up—nothing. Nothing is lost: all is gained. The male retains all of his treasures of maleness, and so does the female her treasures. But each is blessedly permitted to annex a whole world of sensibilities and powers owned by the other and developed through the toils of several lives. There is nothing to lose, and ALL to gain—with the magnificent bonus of the perfect love that no longer has "the naked sword that lies between thee and me" of the physical low self and the opinionated middle self.

In the new state of oneness there is no longer the

necessity to form opinions from possibly faulty information. The new High Self identifies itself with the thing to be known, and is able to know the exact truth about it. At last there is the realization of the meaning of the cryptic saying, "Ye shall know the truth, and the truth shall make you free." The code word for "free" is *kuu-wale*, which also means from the two roots "to be released" and enabled "to enter a state of being without qualifications" or the usual limitations belonging to the mental limitations of the two lesser selves.

While the Book of Revelations is not too clear in its ,ode implications, there are parts of it which fit in simple symbology the Union which is the goal and end of the great drama. In 21:2–5, we read, "And I John saw the holy city, the new Jerusalem, coming down from God out of heaven, prepared as a bride adorned for her husband. (The pair ready for the marriage which is made in heaven may be symbolized here.) . . . And God shall wipe away all tears from their eyes; and there shall be no more death, neither sorrow, nor crying, neither shall there be any more pain: for the former things are passed away. (The new High Self is to be set free of the things which trouble the lesser pair of selves, even of the need for physical death.) And he that sat upon the throne said, Behold, I make all things new. . . ."

Continuing with this provocative comparison of the "bride" and the new Jerusalem, in verse 9, we select bits to apply to the central thesis of Union. ". . . Come hither, I will shew thee the bride, the Lamb's wife. . . . And had a wall great and high, and had twelve gates

265

(perhaps the needed number of incarnations to reach the time of Union . . . and three gates. . . ." (Perhaps standing for the three selves and their progression through the series of incarnations until all three graduate to the next higher level.)

One can but wonder whether the writer of the Revelations had in mind the same "grace" as had the kahunas who believed that only by the "grace" of the High Self can the middle self be made "perfect" and ready for Union. At any rate, the writer ends his book with the lines, "The grace of our Lord Jesus Christ be with you all." And we know that in the code version of the Gospels, Jesus became a Christ, but only after taking the great upward step into the Kingdom.

❖　❖　❖　❖　❖

A degree might well have been centered on the coded information that only a part of humanity is ready at any one time to graduate to higher levels. In Revelations, 14:1 we read, "And I looked and lo, a Lamb stood on the mount Sion, and with him a hundred forty and four thousand having the Father's name written in their foreheads."

The "forehead" symbolizes the middle self in contrast to the "heart" of the low self, so we may conclude that the ones described as standing with a "lamb," emblem of the High Self, were the "elite" or "chosen" of the gospels and were those ready for graduation.

The number given is symbolic, meaning simply a large number. With the kahunas the number "forty" was used to indicate "many." If we consider the number of men and women on earth at any one time, and divide that number roughly into twelve parts, each part standing for one of the needed incarnations necessary for graduation, we may then say that about one-twelfth of those living at any time should be ready for the evolutionary upward step into the Kingdom.

While it seems so difficult for us to become sufficiently perfect to be ready for graduation, we have but to look about us to see that there are many who have learned to be gentle, kind and helpful. They are, of course, not entirely free from the petty things or even minor evils, living as they do in the flesh and with the far-from-perfect low self. But, given the priceless boon of "grace," and helped by the High Self to become "perfect," these can move on and up to become One.

Paul's dictum that only those favored ones selected by God could be "saved" is not at all in keeping with the Huna lore in which each of us earns his reward, and in which none is denied it when the proper time has come. One thinks once more of Revelations, and may read with renewed interest 3:11, "Behold I come quickly: hold that fast which thou hast, that no man take thy crown. Him that overcometh will I make a pillar in the temple of my God, and he shall go no more out: (into fresh incarnations) . . . and I will write upon him my new name. . . ."

The code word for "name" is *i-noa*, from the roots of which we get the secondary meaning of "Being released by a command." The "release" is from the many things which have hindered the lesser man. One enters the realm where all is light, and where time and the limitations of space are no longer the great burden that they are on the lower levels of life. Each graduate middle self becomes in turn "the Light of the world" in so far as those who come under his-her charge are concerned, and the new name is the one which will eventually be spoken in prayer by the newly invested low self with its middle self when the lesser man learns that he has a High Self Father-Mother upon whose name he may call for help and guidance.

✿   ✿   ✿   ✿   ✿

The Sermon on the Mount is placed in Matthew immediately after the temptation in the wilderness, and for the Drama this is correct, providing we lift both from the context and place them one after the other in the Second Act. If this is done, we find Jesus risen from the dead and his progress marked by successfully passing the tests of the temptation to show that he has given up the desire for wordly things, even position and power, and is ready soon to go on to the final triumphant scene of the Transfiguration.

In the Sermon on the Mount scene, he teaches the way of life which he and his Disciples came to follow after ceasing to expect an earthly Kingdom to be established. Jesus is not preaching to the ordinary people who were far from ready to try to follow instructions which would lead them to try for graduation. We read (Matt. 5–1), "And seeing the multitudes, he went up into a mountain: and when he was set, his disciples came unto him: (2) And he opened his mouth and taught them."

There followed the Beatitudes, and in these instructions for living, such a high standard of loving and forgiving kindliness is set that Christians have been unable to meet them in daily living. No mention is made of families or family obligations. The evil persons who impose on one are not to be fought off in the normal manner, but one is to offer no resistance to the harm or injustice imposed on one. The "other cheek" is to be turned. This was not to be passive resistance. If one were to be forced to walk a mile with the enemy, one was to walk another mile of one's own accord.

As impractical as these teachings were for the masses, they were right for those seeking to free themselves of all hates, fears and desires so that they could have deep peace of mind and keep their thoughts centered on the preparation for graduation.

One can almost imagine Gautama, the Buddha, replacing Jesus in the scene and beginning to prepare his followers for the yellow robe and begging bowl of his "Sanga" and for the great and final effort to graduate into Nirvana.

Gautama and Jesus, alike, taught quite a different way of life for the masses, the former advocating his Middle Way and Eightfold Path in which one lived normally but tried always to become more kindly and harmless. Jesus taught a very similar way of life to be lived in conformance with the moral laws of the Jews, and, if Buddhists and Christians could have understood and have avoided the mistake of thinking that the path for the "elite" was for the masses, they could have saved themselves from endless heartaches and the suffering of having to repent the sin of failing to live in the abnormal way. They would have saved themselves from martyrdom and the life of the hermit, or the renunciation of the monastery or nunnery.

In sharp contrast we have the lives lived by the Brahmans in India. Their life goal was that of coming to know the Real Self and to become merged with it. This is similar, in so far as it goes, to the Huna goal of graduation. In India the spiritually advanced individual rears a family and cares for all the mundane obligations of society, then, after middle age, retires into a life of study and meditation in which preparation is made for the highest possible inner attainment.

The Buddhist ideal is not to marry or enter the world, but to retire at the earliest possible moment to a monastery and don the yellow robe. No obligation to society is recognized.

In Hawaii, where the early kahuna beliefs and practices survived down to modern times in a surprisingly good state of preservation, the kahunas reared families and at the same time acted as healers or leaders in various fields of endeavor. Judging from their attitude toward life and inner growth, we may safely conclude that anyone who wishes to try for graduation at the end of the present incarnation can do no better than to live as normally as possible while making every effort to learn to live the hurtless, kindly and unselfish life which is the mark of the candidate who has become ready to move on and up.

The secret of secrets, that of the "soul mates" who will eventually be united, need not worry the candidate for graduation. Wherever he or she may be in the world, makes little difference. The High Self will take care of the work of finding the mate and bringing about the Union at the proper time. For the candidate, the real and pressing task and necessity is to learn to love as greatly and as unselfishly as possible. The mate may be in the home or the vicinity, or may be in some other land, or even waiting as a spirit. We have no way to know the mate even should we meet him or her, or even if married to one who seems less than perfect because still a middle and low self on the physical level where the lovely perfections are not yet to be realized.

But love is the bridge, and only when we learn to love despite all the obstacles which are met on the lower levels, and to make ourselves as nearly lovable as is humanly possible can we become ready.

CHAPTER 18

THE CODE IN THE RELIGIONS OF INDIA

After the writing of the Gospel and Gnostic accounts of the life of Jesus, the early Church borrowed from other religions to add to the growing dogmas of Christianity. The Mystery Cults of the time, like that of the Mithraic, in which some Huna beliefs were to be found, were drawn upon, and various ideas were borrowed from the Zoroastrianism of Persia.

We know that there had been for some time a considerable contact between Egypt and the countries of the valleys of the Euphrates and Tigris. Trade was carried on with India, and after the conquests of Alexander the Great, there was a building exchange of assorted information, including information covering religions.

Evidence accumulates to prove that Huna had been known in India well before the beginning of the Christian era, but that in those parts there had never been an effort on the part of an intitate kahuna to use the language code to insert elements of the ancient "Secret" into the sacred writings of India.

However, some of the symbol words of Huna were retained and are still to be recognized in Yoga and Vedic literature. Buddhism developed a few centuries before the beginnings of Christianity, but not until about four hundred years after the death of its founder,

Prince Gautama, were his teachings put into writing. Up to that time they had been passed on by word of mouth, and it is probable that many changes in the original teachings were made. When at last reduced to writing, in Ceylon, the original language used by the founder was put aside in favor of the Pali tongue. Had there been code words in the early teachings, however, they would have appeared, just as in the Gospels, no matter what language had been used in the writing. It is safe to say that while at least some of the Huna beliefs had been known in India as late as the time of the Buddha, the inner teachings had been as completely lost as in Christianity.

At the time that the early Egyptians were using their picture writing and THE BOOK OF THE DEAD was taking form, the men of India who had come in from other parts as Aryan invaders and conquerors, had worked out a system of writing based on an alphabet. They wrote in Sanskrit and produced the Vedas which were accounts of the gods and of Creation, also listings of laws. There were many tales and parables, and morals and customs were dealt with in detail. Following the Vedas came the sacred writings of a religious sect whose main teaching revolved around "yoga" or the means of attaining union with a postulated divine, eternal and "real" Self. Buddhism came still later and included elements of the other systems of religious thought.

In the Vedas there was an Ultimate God which was beyond the power of man to imagine, and under Him came a descending chain of lesser gods, all of whom, like the High Self of Huna, were male and female.

The Huna word *mana* and the Sanskrit word *manas* are so similar in pronunciation that this may account for the use of the word *prana* to stand for what *mana* represented in the "Secret." *Manas* means "mind," but *prana* which means "breath," served very well for the vital force which can be accumulated by an act of mind and by breathing more heavily. In Yoga the breath control was used to accumulate prana, and is so used today, but while this seems to be the retention of a former knowledge of the Huna *ha* prayer method, there is now no knowledge of the way to send the mana or prana to the High Self along the aka cord.

The literature of Yoga and of later Hinduism, based on the Vedic beginnings, give ample evidence of a former knowledge of the three selves which make up the triune man, but in later times the low and middle selves of Huna became represented by a single "lower self" while the High Self became a vague entity which endured eternally while the lower self died and vanished. The major effort in Yoga became one of uniting the lower self with the Higher Self, and in this way getting rid of the lower self and escaping forever from the things of its level of life.

The sages of India became entangled in a mass of speculative doctrines which revolved around the idea that nothing was "real" unless it was able to withstand the changes wrought by time. The man and his body were, patently, subject to the change of time, but the High Self was supposed not to be. It stood apart unchanging and not in any way involved in the moving spectacle of the lower man who constantly changed and aged.

As the High Self was "real," all pertaining to the lower man and his realm had to be considered "unreal," transient, and therefore bad. The apparent reality of the physical world of the low self was dismissed as entirely made up of "illusion," or "*maya*."

The belief in reincarnation is very old and has been an important factor in Indian religion down the centuries. The Aryan sages were the world's greatest speculators and hair-splitters when it came to religion. They carried every train of thought to its "logical extreme." From a practical series of reincarnations they stretched the series out until there were as many incarnations as there are "grains of sand beside the seas." A concurrent belief was that of the working of the law of cause and effect. This was called "Karma," and it was taught that any act in the world of unreality in which we live, creates more "karma" which in turn causes more effects. It was practically impossible to escape Karmic influences and therefore almost impossible ever to finish with having to reincarnate. It became a most disheartening and hopeless prospect— a constantly turning "wheel."

Yoga may have come as a revolt based on a promise of escape from the "wheel" of rebirth and the sufferings of life in the flesh. In any event, it offered at last a way of escape, although it was a very difficult one. By means of a severe discipline one was supposed to be able to cease to desire anything connected with the world of illusion, even existence itself. One was to become purified and completely moral. In the end, one could succeed in uniting the lower self with the "real" and eternal High Self, at which time the low self would vanish into the world of illusion from which it had sprung, and the High Self would be the vehicle of all that was true consciousness. In this way the "wheel" could be broken. But the life and austerities demanded of the Yogin were such that the average man or woman despaired of ever escaping from the world.

Buddhism was a reform movement, just as Christianity was a contradiction of the old ideas of the Jews. Prince Gautama, who later was given the title of "Buddha," or "An Enlightened One," accepted the belief in the endless succession of incarnations and the burdensome Law of Karma. He also accepted the belief of Yoga that there was a way to escape "being broken on the wheel." But he refused to be deeply involved in the endless speculations concerning the real and the unreal.

From the great similarity of the system which he evolved, in comparison to that embodied in the coded Christian teachings, we can only conclude that he, also, had some access to Huna.

It is impossible at this late date to learn from the Buddhist scriptures what inner doctrines might have been known and taught to the "elect" of Gautama's day. The tradition of an inner or "esoteric" doctrine is accepted by a great many students, much as has the tradition of a mystery teaching in Christianity.

Whatever knowledge Gautama came to have, he used it in making his new religious system. In the outer teaching he held that men and women should follow the "Middle Path" or way of life, doing the things necessary to normal living but taking care to hurt no one. The Golden Rule was preached, and the promise held out that in due time such kindly living would help one to "escape the wheel."

Shortly before the writing of the "Sayings" of Jesus or the enlarged account of his life—to say nothing of the Mystery writings, Gnosis and initiatory dramas current at the beginning of the Christian era—Gautama was teaching his version of "graduation." As it has come down to us in the surviving outer teachings of Buddhism, he taught that one could leave the illusionary lower world and enter a special state which was called, "Nirvana." This is a Sanskrit word which means "to stop blowing." It suggests the ceasing of physical breathing and so the extinction of physical life. The escape was likened to the "blowing out of a candle"—leaving nothing—an extinction.

This was a very strange doctrine in that it failed to provide the needed motives for trying to enter Nirvana. All that it offered was relief from the much emphasized pain of living and dying. At least that is all that has come down to us in the Buddhist Scriptures. On the other hand, judging from what Gautama actually did during his ministry, we cannot avoid the conclusion that to the ones near him he must have taught something very similar to the Huna theory of graduation.

Gautama gathered around him a band of disciples who may well be compared with the "elect" of Jesus. He formed them into a brotherhood or "Sanga," and taught them that in order to attain the Nirvanic state they should give up all desire for the things of ordinary life. They were to give up all possessions and all attachments to family and friends. They were to get rid of all obligations and put on the yellow robe of the outcasts. Thus identifying themselves as pilgrims bent on wending their holy way to Nirvana, they became homeless vagabonds, begging daily for food to sustain them.

In this respect, the disciples of Jesus were almost as extreme. They did not put on distinctive garb, but they stopped working and lived on charity.

In the beginning, both Buddhist and Christian systems were confined to a certain "chosen" few. But in both, the inner teaching soon became lost and the masses invaded the ranks of the "elect." In Christianity the hermits flourished and monasteries and nunneries grew with great rapidity. In India a mass movement seems to have crushed out the inner teachings, for men and women broke all caste restrictions and, rich and poor, including a king or two, took the yellow robe. Rich men gave their fine homes and grounds to the Sanga, and princes their palaces and gold. It became a very easy way of life and very attractive. The trouble was that it was contrary to all the rules of social progress. Men and women refused to bring up families or to produce things for the support of communal life. It was inevitable that the strange structure should be forced to change or fall. In India the ruling Brahman caste made war on the new religion so energetically that many of the faithful were driven out, but did missionary work in far places. Changes took place. The call to try to enter Nirvana became mingled with the more practical call to work and to meet obligations. But the good and kindly way of life of the "Noble Eight Fold Path" or "Middle Way" was preserved, just as the more practical side of Christianity was later preserved.

The older beliefs of India,* which antedated Buddhism, had far less influence on Christianity than the monasticism of the "Sanga" organized by Gautama. But in time the older Hinduism, especially the Brahmanistic priesthood and its powers, came to furnish an example upon which the Papal structure of the early Church was fashioned.

While Christianity became dogmatized and contaminated by borrowings from other beliefs, it was saved from the caste system and the folly of too much karma and too endless a series of reincarnations. This was due to the fact that in the Gospels those items, against which Gautama had revolted, had never been markedly present.

Christianity, once its basic patterns had been rather completely set, by about the year 400 A.D., became fixed, and, in a static condition, droned on and on through the Dark Ages. In India, during this long period, Buddhism was stamped out by the Brahmans and the cruel caste system was enforced, with the priests at the top and the outcasts at the bottom of the religio-social scale.

❂　　❂　　❂　　❂　　❂

In the Huna system of belief, the vast complications of comparable Hindu systems are condensed and simplified. All the endless speculation concerning the Absolute and Ultimate, the Manifest and Unmanifest, is put aside in favor of a collection of folk tales which

---

* For an excellent account of the religions of India, see Philosophies of India, by Heinrich Zimmer, in English translation, edited by Joseph Campbell, Meridian Books, the publisher, at 17 Union Square West, New York 3, N. Y.

deal with the gods and their activities in a manner sufficiently childish to be grasped by the most unevolved minds. However, if the kahunas believed that the Beings higher in the evolutionary scale than the High Selves were beyond the intellectual grasp of even the most advanced, they did not go as far as Gautama, who advised, "Sink not the string of thought into the unfathomable: who does, errs."

To the Huna initiates the invisible and intangible High Self was quite within the power of man to understand, at least it was when the man was well advanced in his evolutionary progress. One can almost hear, in imagination, some ancient kahuna proclaiming at the opening of the first act of the Great Drama of Initiation, "The High Selves exist! This is the great truth. They are REAL!"

One can also imagine this statement being heard in ancient India, and, as time passed, being misunderstood and the real significance almost lost. The sages of Vedic, Brahman, Yogic or other persuasions came to agree that there was something of the greatest importance, and that its identifying feature was that it was REAL. It followed, as the misconceptions were compounded by speculation, that if IT was real, and only IT, then all else must be UNREAL. With that profound result of their reasoning, the sages rested. . . . and still rest.

To get to the original Huna concept of what was REAL, in terms of our study, we need only to turn again to the code for assistance. *Io*, is "real" in the code. It is also, "truth, verity, a part of something, and a forerunner who goes ahead to announce something to come, as the approach of a chief." If we apply these meanings to the High Self we see that it is REAL, and that this fact is TRUE. We also see that the High Self, as a forerunner, is the older one of the three selves of man and one which has gone on ahead. (In the dialect used in Tahiti, *Io* also means, God as Jehovah, but carries the additional meanings of "power, energy and soul." These variations point us to the mana of the High Self, and to its being a "self" or one of the "souls" of the man).

Another code word reinforces the meanings of *io*, and also means "truth" or verity." It is *oia*, and it has a very important secondary meaning which may well have been part of the reason why the men of India mistook the idea of the REAL for one of ETERNAL, this being "to continue, to remain the same." Here we see that the High Self, as the one who is real, true and farther advanced, REMAINS UNCHANG-ING in its nature so that it is always to be depended upon under all circumstances. This does not, however, fit the idea of being "eternal" and unchanging in terms of time, as the REAL was thought to be in India when the misconceptions had crystallized into dogma. The High Self remains unchanging in that it is "utterly reliable"—that being its most important characteristic in so far as the lesser man is concerned. The High Self "endures" (a meaning of *oia*), when the lesser man "sins," and does not vary or become a jealous God, such as is met in the Old Testament Jehovah.

As an expression of the greatest possible truth and reality, the kahunas used the combined words to make *oia-io*, the "absolutely true and real truth" (as we would say, not as given in the dictionary, where the definition remains simply, "truth.")

A "thought" was, in the code, *mana-o* (something thought with the use of mana), and a correct thought or BELIEF was manao-ia, while to have FAITH and to believe something, as, for instance, the fact of the existence of the High Self, was *manaio,* giving us both *ia* and *io* as endings to be used at this important point where correct understanding is so necessary. (As we see when recalling the misunderstandings in India when "unchanging" in character became "unchanging in terms of time.")

In the Vedic lore of India there was developed the concept of a major "Spirit," *brahman,* who was the one and only timeless reality and the Self of the Universe. A spark of this all-inclusive Self was said to animate every man as his individual Self—the *atman.* These were one and the same in essence, and the goal of the system is contact with and absorption into the individual Self. The lesser Self was, like the greater Self, pure spirit, pure perfection, timeless, all powerful, and once the shadowy and illusionary man was able to become absorbed into the Self, it once more became a part of the Cosmic Self. "The dewdrop slips into the shining sea," and the little self again becomes a part of the greater self. The man who must be absorbed into his Self, is neatly got rid of by making him unreal and an illusion from first to last. When he is discarded, nothing is lost—only a hampering delusion is tossed back into the lap of the Goddess Maya, mother of all the unreal things which are material only in the imagination.

It has become customary in modern times to group under the heading of "Brahmanism" the religious writing of the Vedas, Brahmanas and Upanisads, while the sacred literature of the post-Buddhic period includes the Vedantic, Puranic and Tantric literature as well as the Bhagavad Gita, these being classed as "Hinduism."

The Bhagavad Gita is a mixture in its ideas of the Vedic beliefs of the Aryan invaders of India and of the beliefs preserved by the people who lived in India before the Aryan invasion. The blending of the two sets of beliefs is surprising, as the non-Aryan systems which were represented included Jainism, Gosala's teachings and those of Sankhya as well as Yoga. While there were many contradictions of thought in the mixture, the people of India came to value the book as the most satisfactory and inclusive. Today it remains the most widely accepted sacred writing in India, and wherever Hinduism has become known in the West, it is the foremost text. For this reason it will be of value to our study to examine passages from the Gita and see how much Huna has been retained—always providing there was an early knowledge of Huna in India.

The Gita comes the closest to being a Mystery Drama of Initiation, similar to the Gospels, to be found in India. On page 130 of the Judge translation we find the character Krishna, who stands for the divine Self, instructing the lesser man represented by Arjuna. We read:

"Thus have I made known unto thee this knowledge which is a mystery more secret than secrecy itself;

ponder it fully in thy mind, act as seemeth best unto thee."

In reading the Gita, one will find it necessary to try to distinguish between the Supreme Self or Universal Spirit, and the spark of it in man, the lesser Self. On page 24 we see this necessity as we read:

"Beings are nourished by food, food is produced by rain, rain comes from sacrifice, and sacrifice is performed by action. Know that action comes from the Supreme Spirit who is one; wherefore the all-pervading Spirit is at all times present in the sacrifice. . . . But the man who only taketh delight in the Self within, is satisfied with that and content with that alone, hath no selfish interest in action."

We also read on the same page, ". . . nourish the Gods, that the Gods may nourish you; thus mutually nourishing ye shall obtain the highest felicity."

It will be noted that we are finding items that remind us strongly of Huna and the coded parts of the Gospels. Turning now to the translation made by Atkinson, page 28, let us continue to watch for similarities of concept.

"As the soul, wearing the material body, experienceth the stages of infancy, youth, manhood, and old age, even so shall it, in due time, pass on to another body, and in other incarnations shall it again live, and move and play its part. Those who have attained the Inner Doctrine, know these things, and fail to be moved by aught that cometh to pass in this world of change; to such Life and Death are but words, and both are but surface aspects of the deeper Being.

"For verily I say unto you, that the man whom these

things (pleasures and pains) have ceased to further torment—he stands steadfast, undisturbed by pleasure and pain—he to whom all things seem alike—such an one, say I, hath acquired the road to immortality.

"That which is unreal hath no shadow of Real Being, notwithstanding the illusion of appearance and false knowledge. And that which hath Real Being hath never ceased to be—can never cease to be, in spite of all appearances to the contrary. The wise have inquired into these things, O Arjuna, and have discovered the real Essence, and Inner Meaning of things.

"Know that The Absolute, which pervades all things, is indestructible. No one can work the destruction of the Imperishable One.

"These bodies, which act as enveloping coverings for the souls occupying them, are but finite things of the moment—and not the Real Man at all. They perish as all finite things perish."

(Going on to page 31). "Or if, perchance, thou believeth not these things, and liveth in the illusion of belief in birth and death as realities—even so, asketh thee, why shouldst thou lament and grieve? . . .

"Some wonder greatly regarding the soul, while others hear of and speak of it with credulity and lack of comprehension. And no one, by mortal mind, really understandeth the mystery, or knoweth it in its true and essential nature, in spite of all that has been said, taught and thought concerning it.

(Page 37). "When thou shalt rise beyond the plane of illusion, then shalt thou cease to disturb thyself regarding doctrines, theology, disputations concerning rites or ceremonies, and other useless trimmings upon the cloth of spiritual thought. Thou shalt be liberated from attachments to sacred books, to writings of the learned theologians, or to those who would interpret that which they fail themselves to understand; but instead, shalt thou fix thy mind in earnest contemplation of the Spirit, and thus reach the harmony with the Real Self, which underlies all."

(Going back to Judge, page 18). "A man is said to be confirmed in spiritual knowledge when he forsaketh every desire which entereth into his heart, and of himself is happy and content in the Self through the Self." (Atkinson gives this as, ". . . in the Real Self within himself.") "His mind is undisturbed in adversity; he is happy and contented in prosperity, and he is a stranger to anxiety, fear and anger. . . ."

(Page 41 of Atkinson). ". . . He, who hath left behind him Pride, Vainglory, and Selfishness, goeth straight to Happiness. Yea, so goeth he!

"This, O Prince of Pandu, is the state of Union with the Real Self—the Blissful state—the state of Spiritual Consciousness. And he who hath attained it no longer is bewildered or led astray by Illusion. If, having attained it, he dwelleth therein unto the hour of death he passeth straight to the Bosom of the Father." (Judge gives us: "This, O son of Pritha, is dependence upon the Supreme Spirit, and he who possesseth it goeth no more astray; having obtained it, if therein established at the hour of death, he passeth on to Nirvana in the Supreme.")

In one passage we find the word "grace" used in a way reminiscent of the code used in the Gospels. We read, "In Him alone then take refuge with all thy being, and by His Grace shalt thou attain Supreme Peace and the Everlasting Abode."

The Yoga teaching that one can attain Union with the Real Self, is cut off abruptly in the Gita and the Yoga Aphorisms of Patanjali, as if there had never been a knowledge of the Huna secret that there are two "unions" to be made, the first the simple contact with the High Self, and the second, the final union of the male and female middle selves as they graduate into the High Self level. If this uniting of the mates was known by some of the Initiates of India, it may well be that when it came to writing about such matters, the female was consigned to the Vastness of Silence, if for no other reason than that she was looked upon as a temptation to the male and the cause of his failure, all too often, to keep his mind on the work of contemplating steadily the Self.

Despite the lack of the element of the union of the mates, the Gita repeatedly gives passages which seem beyond question to resemble Huna in symbology. We read, (Atkinson, Page 92). "I would tell thee, O Prince, of that time of death, in which men, passing out, shall never return; and of that time of death, in which they, passing out, shalt again return to earth. He who departeth in the Light returneth not to this plane of pain. But he who departeth in the Darkness, returneth he to mortal re-birth, again and again, until he findeth the Light. The true Yogi understandeth this saying, O Prince! . . . The Yogi, learned in the knowledge of the Truth, passeth beyond these (the outer forms of worship), and taketh precedence to those who follow them; he reacheth the Supreme Goal."

In the last century the idea of the "Real," as opposed to the "unreal," began to become known in the West. With this pattern, which was cut bodily from the holy cloth of Hinduism, should have come the belief in karma and reincarnation, but in some strange way these were filtered out before reaching a few of their several destinations. As a result, there arose in New England the teachings of Christian Science and New Thought, both affirming that God is the only possible "reality," and that, because God can be only good, no possible reality could attach itself to anything which is evil.

In India one was warned to take great care to avoid making fresh "evil karma," and was urged to perform all possible good deeds to pay off bad karma which already had accumulated. Behind this lay the ever present threat of unending reincarnations for those who failed to become hurtless and helpful.

After New Thought came the "Science of . . ." teachings, and, as in New Thought, the magic formula for correct and prosperous living was, "Think right, and all will be right." The necessity of making amends for misdeeds was vanquished with a flourish of phrases. So, also, was the need to believe in a Savior who had made a vicarious atonement for sins and who would save all who were willing to accept that salvation.

The new "Reality" cults had one very important thing in common with Hinduism, this being the conviction that if one suffered illness or poverty, it "served him right." In India he was pitied, but nothing could be done about the trouble because the victim must be allowed to "pay off bad karma." In the West,

nothing could be done about similar conditions because the sufferer was "in error" and should know
enough to get out of it by beginning to think right—
"right" in terms of the unreality of all which was not
good. The West had inherited the kite without its tail.

* * * * *

In Huna the idea is very clear that the prayer made
in the Ha Rite is first to be pictured in the mind as a
set of conditions which the High Self is to be asked
to bring about as the "answer" to the prayers. The
picturing causes the low self to make "memories" or
"thought-form" structures out of the shadowy substance—these to be sent on a flow of mana to the High
Self, and to be accepted and USED AS SEEDS from
which, symbolically, the answer to the prayers is made
to "grow." We have seen the parables in the Gospels
in which this matter of the SEEDS of the Huna-type
prayer were explained in the terms of the code.

The secret of the "seeds" has been misunderstood
in the outer circles from the very beginning of the
leaking of the Secret to the uninitiated. The cause of
this trouble was simple. In most languages, including
the one used by the kahunas, the word "seed" can
mean the seed of a plant or of a man, and as the
human "seed" the concept has caused religionists century after century to conclude that the male seminal
fluid was in some way connected with "creative force"
and so was to be conserved and in some way or other
offered to the gods or used by the man to help him
perform religious magic of sorts.

Paul seems to have had an inkling of the importance

of "seeds" in the teachings of Jesus, but it is evident that he accepted some current religious belief in which the conservation of the male seed was very important. Because women tempted men to falter in their attempts to live the completely chaste life, they were classed as unfortunate necessities and sinful "Daughters of Eve," to be avoided in so far as possible by the men. Paul mourns because "all men cannot be as I am . . ." And we have seen the same tendency to discount women in the Gnostic and early Christian writings.

This general mistake resulted in a slow and regrettable contamination of the original system of Yoga in India. Once knowledge of the true Huna lore had been lost, guessing and experimentation were resorted to, but the Secret was never recovered, and when it came to be written down in the contaminated form in Sanskrit, and passed from hand to hand, a strange and unnatural set of beliefs and practices resulted. These, as the end product, became the system called "tantric Yoga," and the very fact that the texts survive in Sanskrit shows their antiquity.

In modern times the texts have been translated by Sir John Woodroffe in his large book, THE SERPENT POWER, which he wrote under the pen name of Arthur Avalon. The basic idea in this form of Yoga is that at the base of the spine lie forces having a definite male and female polarity if this can be brought out and put to use. Accumulating *prana* (our mana) and directing it to act upon the "Serpent Force" is advocated. The result is said to be that the force, once set into action, can be caused to rise in a double spiral like two serpents, one rotating in an opposite direction from the other, and both moving upward along the outside of the spinal column until six main centers have been touched and awakened. At the head, the forces are supposed to unite and a third force rise along the center of the spine. Then comes the great and magical miracle of enlightenment and the union with the "Real" is accomplished—the result being a vastness of "bliss" which can only be compared to the continuing and endless bliss which in sexual intercourse is experienced for only a few seconds.

The sexual nature of the dual forces and the climax of "bliss" indicate that there had been at one time the initiate knowledge of the union of the male and female middle selves at graduation—this being the fulfillment of love on the very highest level of consciousness in so far as mankind may imagine it.

The preliminary "union' was also included in a mixed form, here taking the shape of the "union with the Real Self," which in Huna is the first upward step in which the initiate learns that there is a High Self and succeeds in making contact with it. This contact, however, is only a temporary union, not a complete and permanent blending and intermixing as between the mates in the UNION of graduation.

Occult students in the West have long been puzzled by this confusion of the idea of the lesser union with that of the greater UNION. They have searched in India for the experts in the use of the several systems of Yoga, especially for users of the tantric system—always looking for individuals who can show the results in their own persons of the "union" or related accomplishment. But, like the search for the "Masters" who were so prominent in Theosophical circles when that organization was in first flower, the "adepts" of all the systems seem to have vanished. Moreover, in the matter of trying to arouse the sleeping "serpent forces," the student has long since been warned that this practice is not for him. Any attempt to use the art is said to lay one open to the risk of being killed should the force rise high enough.

That there was a knowledge of the interblending or "mingling" of male and female at the time of graduation, is to be seen if one inspects the carvings on old temples. Some of these show a male and female figure, both representing gods, locked in the tightest possible sex embrace, this symbolizing not the physical or low self union but that of the god-like pair making up a High Self.

In missionary circles such carvings were pointed out to show the depravity of the religions of the heathens of India, but in late years the old symbology has been studied and in at least one German book on occult practices which have originated in India, the charts give unashamedly the picture of the male and female in close sex-interblending in the heart of the opened lotus flower. (See the English translation title INITIATION INTO HERMETICS, by Fr. Bardon, published by Osiris-Verlag, kettig Uber Koblenz, Western Germany. The illustration or chart, in full color, is to be found on page 17, and although the author does not see that there is a union and a Union, as in Huna, he is certain that the "Real" self is hermaphroditic in so far as it is made up of both male and female forces and principles.)

In the next chapter we will inspect the Chinese version of the process by which one may accomplish much the same things as have been hoped for by the users of the Yoga systems in India.

CHAPTER 19

HUNA IN CHINA

By far the most open presentation of the Huna system is to be found in China. There it had been written out in the form of a small book and while a slight effort had been made to conceal the real meanings in the ideographs used in the writing, the symbol words were often used openly and in such a way that their secret meanings were all but impossible for the uninitiated reader to decipher.

The little book was called THE SECRET OF THE GOLDEN FLOWER, and a second or secret title was written down by so placing the ideographs used in the writing that the bottom of one could be moved down to touch the one below it and instead of giving the meaning of *Chin hua*, or "golden flower," the word for "light" was given. As in the original Huna, "Light" is the symbol of the High Self, and indirectly names the high mana and the shadowy body owned by the High Self.

By further clever manipulation the "Light" as High Mana, was made to appear as "water," and, as in the Gospel version of Huna, as the "water of life," or a magic "elixir" which would give renewed and continuing life. This was also mentioned as a "golden ball or pill," and in covering up the secret meanings in the book, it was sometimes called, as by one Chinese printer of the book, THE ART OF PROLONGING HUMAN LIFE.

The most clever piece of work done in the organization of the hidden Huna information was accomplished in making a single symbol word or idea double its duty so that it could be used interchangeably. For instance, one could point at the same time to the low and middle self pair, or at the male and female pair who join to make the High Self. "Light" and "darkness" was the symbol, and it was alternated with the "Sun and Moon' in standing for the male and female parts of either the lesser man or the High Self Father-Mother.

The book had originally been written down only after long circulation by word of mouth. In this it was similar to the "Sayings of Jesus" which were orally transmitted before the Gospels were produced. In China these "sayings" were attributed to a certain Lu Tung-pin, who was said to have been a guest in the cave of a wise old initiate who lived in "the pass," and who obliged his guest by answering questions and giving general information about the secret lore.

The "pass" in the mountains where the cave was supposed to be located, was also a mystical "pass" something like the "path" of Huna, but having more of the meaning of the final passing from the middle self level into the High Self state in graduation.

The book is thought to have appeared in the earlier centuries, but the first actual evidence of its existence dates back to the eighteenth century. At first it was printed from wooden slabs on which the writing was carved. In the year 1920 a thousand copies were printed in Peking and soon after that it was translated into German by Richard Wilhelm, with his version to be translated and published in English in 1929.*

As the GOLDEN ELIXIR OF LIFE, the author places the book in the Tang period of the eighth century. How long the material had been passed on orally before that, is difficult to say, but at some points in its progress from initiate to initiate, changes were made to include ideas borrowed from the Chinese Taoism, Buddhism and Nestorian Christianity. Buddhist missionaries had introduced the Mahayana version of the religion into China, and the Nestorians, who had flourished for a time in the West, were exerting a marked influence in China well before 781, at which time a Nestorian monument was built in Sianfu and inscribed both in Chinese and Syrian. Undoubtedly the Gospels in some form accompanied the Christian missionaries, but we have no way of knowing whether some of them were initiated into the Huna secrets which they contained. All that is certain is that in the mixture of several religions in the little book, the Huna code words found in the Gospels are easily identified, but entirely without mention of Jesus, a vicarious atonement, a crucifixion or a resurrection. In his comments on the materials of the book, Wilhelm (page 9 of the English translation), points out the similarity of things to be found both in the Gospel Parables and the Chinese book. The mystical marriage and the needed oil for the lamps, even

---

* The entire book, along with comments by Wilhelm and Carl G. Jung, should be studied by the earnest student. The publisher: Wehmen Bros., 712 Broadway, New York 3, N. Y. The price for the 1955 edition was $3.75.

the bridegroom, are common to both as well as the baptism or "bath" in which one is cleansed by symbolic "water and fire." Jesus was "the Light of the world," and he offered "the water of life," while in the Chinese version the "elixir" and the "light" give the same code meanings.

In addition to the ideas borrowed from Christian, Buddhist and Taoistic sources, there are bits from other books which were classics in China, among these the BOOK OF CHANGES (I CHING).

The book proper begins with a short and veiled statement to the effect that the Tao, Great ONE, Essence or primordial Spirit is the upper section of life, the creative source and embodiment of all that exists. There is nothing above it.

But, as one reads on, it is to be seen that the Great One is a term also used to stand for the High Self. It is said to have two eyes, and later these are identified as the Sun and Moon, giving the Father-Mother ingredients of the High Self who is "ONE."

It is then stated that the Golden Flower is Light, and that Light is the true power of the Great One, so that the Flower, Light, and life force or mana are all contained in the word image. The comment seems to have been made by some initiate other than the writer of the main body of statements, and he breaks in to explain that if one guards the Light power, makes it "circulate" and puts it to use properly, one's life span can be prolonged and a new and immortal body created by "melting and mixing." This idea of "mixing" is the one from Huna with which we are familiar, the "mixing" or uniting of the male and female middle selves to make the "almost-immortal" High Self in the graduation process. Here "melting" is *hee-hee* in the Huna code and has the general meaning of "to flow," which is the sense utilized outwardly in the Chinese presentation where much stress is laid on the necessity for making the "light" (mana) "circulate or flow." In the code the secondary meaning as given in the root *hee*, is "a rope" especially one used to hold up the mast of a boat, and in this we are told in unmistakable terms that the aka cord, whose symbol is "a rope" was part of the mechanism put to use to circulate the "light-mana-power."

After a little philosophical discussion we are told that the "Light" is first to be accumulated in a process of quiet meditation, then made to circulate or flow upward to the higher Consciousness or "Heavenly Heart" (in contrast to the lesser man as the lower "heart"). The High Self, "Heavenly Heart" is said to lie between the two eyes or Sun and moon (which gives us again the place or location of the High Self or "Light," matching well the "kingdom of heaven").

The statement is made that the deepest and most wonderful part of the Secret is that one must make the Light circulate, and cause a "backward or return flow." The "backward flow," when brought about, is something that sets the house of the sender in order. It is pictured as a gift made to a ruler, which gift causes the ruler to make the men-servants and maids perform their duties well, and who produces a condition of calm and order. This is excellent Huna.

It is next stated that if the circulation of the Light process if continued long enough it, the flowing "light," crystallizes into a "natural spirit-body" which takes form "beyond the nine Heavens." Here we have the Huna concept of the formation of the new shadowy body and the use of it after graduation by the new High Self. The "nine Heavens" idea is said later to equate with the "nine paths" of Buddhism, and here we appear to have the number of necessary incarnations cut from the Gospel twelve to nine in the School of Life to be worked through.

We in the West who call ourselves "occult students," for want of a better name, have been long familiar with the idea of the creation of a new "body" to be used to house the "real self," but it is mistakenly believed to be something of a physical nature that is gestated for a period of eighteen months by the person who knows and uses the magical methods of "occultism."

A similar muddled conception of an "occult" process is that of which the student reads in the text on Yoga. Here the idea of circulating the "Light" as *prana* is to the fore. The prana is drawn from the air by proper breathing exercises, and then is confused with the "life force" or sex-creative force, which is supposed to lie coiled up and asleep at the lower end of the spine or in the gonads. It is not clear in this system whether mana-prana flows and "circulates up and down the spine" or is accumulated and sent upward through the top of the head to some vague version of the "Real Self."

The prana accumulated for the beginning, however, is thought by some to be the tool used to awaken the sleeping "serpent force" and send it circling up and around the spine, "awakening" as it rises, the several "chakra centers." It, also, is supposed to go up and outward through the "Door of Brahm" or "soft spot" at the top of the head. Where it goes, or what it is supposed to do, is a matter upon which there is little agreement. In Theosophy (from which most of us find such information as is available) we are repeatedly warned that the serpent force is very dangerous, once aroused, and that unless one is guided by a well qualified *guru*, one runs the risk of being killed.

The Huna concept is very simple. Mana is the creative or life force. It is light and life, but acts only under the direction of a conscious "self." It is something that is accumulated by breathing more heavily and by its production in extra amounts in the body— the low self doing the work upon the request of the middle self. The "circulation" then is started by making contact along the shadowy cord with the High Self and once the mana flow has been started flowing properly to the High Self, it is returned as a "backward" flow of changed force which heals and harmonizes and helps the lesser man. The customary prayer ending used by the kahunas was, "the prayer is released: let the rain of blessings fall." High Mana is symbolized by fine rain, white mist or clouds or ice and snow. In the text in question, the white cloud and snow are the symbols chosen for use.

The Chinese initiate explains that there is needed much intelligence on the part of one who essays to use the "golden ball" or "pill" (which is also the Golden Flower and the Elixir of Life) to bring about, "All changes of spiritual consciousness . . ." In this we find the equivalent of the Huna belief that one must be well advanced in the school of life to be ready to graduate. This condition is the mark of the "chosen" in the Gospels, and in its perfection, as in Yoga, the devotee must be able to reach what the text refers to as, having "the utmost capacity for concentration and calm. . . ." This is the state of desirelessness which in the code is a state "without qualifications." But where other systems allow no desire of any kind to remain, Huna demands that the desire and determination to graduate and to be joined to the mate be retained.

In our "Golden Flower" text, the philosophical (in its veiled and coded symbology) gives place soon to the instructions which "double in brass" or cover both the process of making the *HA* rite prayer of Huna and of graduating. The double use of the symbols is in itself a monument to Chinese ingenuity. It covers the inner meanings so deeply that the uninitiated are thrown completely off the trail.

The idea of making a "seed" or mental picture to be used as a "prayer" and to be sent along the aka cord to the High Self on a flow of mana, is beautifully illustrated in one of three pictures in the text. In the first picture the Chinese sage is to be seen seated on a large cushion, legs and arms in the usual posture, and meditating while he accumulates the "Light" and circulates it so that it goes up and down as on a wheel.

In the second picture the sage is seen to have the body of a tiny child formed in the region of his solar plexus. This represents the beginning of the graduation and the formation of the new shadowy body for the new High Self. It also represents the mental picture of any condition for which one is making ready to pray in the Huna fashion. The child is the "seed" in the prayer sense and will grow into maturity in the hands of the High Self, but still remain on the physical level as the actualization or materialization of the prayer picture.

There is no mistaking the "seed" meaning in the text, for the ideographs for "seed" and "water" were combined to give "seed-water" and this was given as part of the "supreme magic." The "water," as we know from Huna, is the low mana which is figuratively accumulated and sent daily in the prayer rite to "water" the "seeds" once planted or placed in the keeping of the High Self. The text includes in the elements listed in the "supreme magic" the one of "thought-earth," this being the High Self as the "earth" in which the prayer picture or "thought" grows. This growing seed symbolically produced the perfect or "golden" flower, completing the symbolized process in its happy outcome.

The third of the series of pictures shows the meditating sage with the tiny child sitting on a cushion above his head and connected to the top of his head by a twisting shadowy cord. This is an intermediate stage in the successful making of the HA rite Prayer, showing the "seed" as the baby, gowing in the care of the High Self. The caption under this picture is properly misleading. It is, "Separation of the spirit-body for independent existence." To the uninitiated this seems to show that a body for the "Real" Self has been born and now exists on some higher or "spiritual" plane, and that in time it will mature and the lesser man can cast off the physical body and rise to live as an immortal in Nirvana in the new spirit-body.

The fourth picture in the text shows the meditating sage with flames creating light around his head, and rising from the circle of fire are five twisting cords which thicken into cushions. On each cushion stands a sage from whose head rises five similar cords, each in turn supporting a cushion and sage. The caption is, "The centre in the midst of the conditions."

The symbology in this picture is not clear in terms of Huna or the code, and the text is cluttered with Buddhistic and Taoistic metaphysical concepts of "emptiness" and of "centers" in and out of states of "emptiness." Only the idea of "five" things can be made to fit, possibly, with Huna. If we count the three selves of the man and add to them the idea of the "two" of the mates who will become one in graduation, we can count the units as five, and see again the double-meaning idea worked out after a fashion.

On page 66 of our text there is what seems to be a summing up of sorts. We read: "Buddha speaks of the transient, the creator of consciousness, as being the fundamental truth of religion. And in our Taoism, the expression 'to produce emptiness' contains the whole work of completing life and essence. All three religions agree in the one proposition, the finding of the spiritual Elixir in order to pass from death to life. (This is the graduation in which one escapes the need of physical death.) In what does this spiritual Elixir consist? It means forever tarrying in purposelessness. The deepest secret in our teaching, the secret of the bath, (*Kala* or cleansing), is confined to the work of making the heart empty. (To overcome all desire except that of graduating.) Therewith the heart is set at rest. What I have revealed here in a word is the fruit of decades of effort."

The accomplishing of the graduation is spoken of as completing the "Far Journey" in the text, and the instructions aimed at giving the methods of contacting the High Self and of making the Huna-type prayer are only stages leading up to the end of the Journey.

The student is advised to study the text for himself, and to consider the comments made by both Wilhelm and the famous psychologist, Carl Jung. But it must be kept in mind that neither of these learned gentlemen knew of Huna and that, because of this lack, their tendency was to force the material to fit the forms of their own conclusions concerning the field of religion and psychism. While they throw light on many aspects of the lore of India and explain much in the Chinese systems of belief, the complete picture is to be obtained only when viewed in the light of Huna and its code and symbology.

❖　❖　❖　❖　❖

There is something nostalgic and deeply pitiful in the spectacle of men searching blindly and endlessly for truth in religion. So many have sacrificed so much in the efforts to find the Truth and to make it workable. Their needs and aims have been endlessly different, ranging all the way from the pressing need for a healing answer to prayer to that of a rationally sufficient concept of God.

Year by year the probes become sharper as we delve into the nature and origins and utilities of religious beliefs. We see the old beliefs cut open and dissected ruthlessly, only to observe that the things which we were taught to venerate in our childhood were tangles of misconception. We are forced to turn away for our reason's sake, but sometimes the old homesickness comes back and we find ourselves longing for the days when Heaven was real and unquestioned, and our Salvation was certain.

Pity is aroused as we see the otherwise good and sane people around the world caught in the iron grip of some dogmatic belief or other and willing to suffer any martyrdom to remain in that grip. In India we look at men living on beds of spikes, or with arms held aloft so long that they have grown fast in that position. Viewing the nations we see those of one religious persuasion swarming out in mobs to murder those of another persuasion.

When we begin to see with eyes opened wider, we began to pity the unsuspecting who are incapable of thinking for themselves and are being led into blind alleys of faith by the blind leaders of the blind—who are all too often rascals preying on the unarmed who can be commanded through emotional appeals and made to accept and defend doctrines which to the thoughtful person are shot through with falsity and fraud.

The most deserving of sympathy we find in those who seek sanely and quietly to find beliefs which satisfy their need for something rational and at the same time morally good and helpful in terms of their own lives and of the lives of the communities and nations of which they find themselves a part. These are the good, well meaning and kindly people. They deserve the boon of a set of beliefs which they can accept and put to use. But on all sides we see these seekers beset with pitfalls and traps. They turn from book to book, finding one false prophet always shouting down the next. The spirits who speak through mediums and dictate endless books of conflicting opinions, often block the paths of the searchers.

But the prospect begins to brighten, at least for a few. By our process of comparison, testing, discarding and adding together, we are arriving at ever more reasonable collections of conclusions in the field of religion and psychology. For some of us, Huna is a great common denominator, for others a deep source of inspiration. With time it may again become something magically and miraculously practical for daily use. Gradually there comes fresh understanding.

A

DICTIONARY

OF THE

HAWAIIAN LANGUAGE,

TO WHICH IS APPENDED AN

ENGLISH-HAWAIIAN VOCABULARY

AND A

CHRONOLOGICAL TABLE OF REMARKABLE EVENTS.

BY LORRIN ANDREWS.

———————

HONOLULU, H. I.
PRINTED BY HENRY M. WHITNEY.
1865.

NOTICES TO THE READER.

The Reader will notice that the *Order* of words in the Dictionary does not follow the order of letters in the English Alphabet, but they follow the order in which they stand in the Hawaiian *first books* for children, viz. : 1st, the vowels; 2d, the Hawaiian consonants, and 3d, such foreign consonants as have been introduced in connection with foreign words. (See the Alphabet below.)

In arranging the definitions, where there are several attached to a word, the Author has endeavored first to ascertain, if possible, the radical idea of the word in its simplest form, and from that he has used his best judgment in arranging in the order of their sequence the various derived significations. How far he has succeeded must be left to the judgment of the Reader.

The Reader of Hawaiian will notice that many words begin with the letters *hoo.* In looking in the Dictionary for such words, he may not find them; thus, *hoonaauao* will not be found under the letter *H.* Throw off then the *hoo* and look for *naauao*, *v.*, and there it will appear, and so of many others.

The sounds of the vowels will appear in the Alphabet below, and in the same order as they stand in the Dictionary.

Hawaiian Vowels.
A as heard in *arch, ask,* &c.
E as in *hate, late,* &c.
I as in *ee* in English, or as *i* in *pique.*
O as long in *note.*
U as *oo* in *coo.*

Hawaiian Consonants
H
K
L
M
N
P
W
as in English.

Foreign Consonants pronounced as in English.
B.
D.
F.
G.
R.
S.
T.
V.
Z.

L. A.

A DICTIONARY

HAWAIIAN LANGUAGE.

A

A in Hawaiian, as in most other languages, is the first letter of the alphabet; "because, if pronounced open as *a* in *father*, it is the simplest and easiest of all sounds." *Encyc. Amer.* Its sound, in Hawaiian, is generally that of *a* in *father*, *ask*, *part*, &c.; but it has, sometimes, when standing before the consonants *k*, *l*, *m*, *n*, and *p*, a short sound, somewhat resembling the short *u*, as in *mutter*, but not so short. Thus *paka*, *malimali*, *lama*, *mana*, *napenape*, are pronounced somewhat as we should pronounce *pukka*, *mullymully*, *lumma*, *munna*, *nuppynuppy*, &c.; reference being had only to the first vowel of each word. It has also in a few words, a sound nearly resembling (but not so strong) that of *au* or *aw* in English; as *iwaho*, *mawaho*, pronounced somewhat as *iwauho*, *mawauho*. To foreigners who merely *read* the language, the common pronunciation of *a* as in *father* is near enough for all practical purposes; but to those who wish to speak it, the mouth of a Hawaiian is the best directory.

A is used for various parts of speech, and, of course, has various significations.

A, *adv.* When; then; there; until. With verbs in a narrative tense, it signifies when, and when, &c.; as, *a hiki mai ia*, when he arrived. With *nei* it signifies a designation of place, as *mai a nei aku*, from here (this place) onward. Until, as *noho oia malaila a make*, he lived there *until* he died. NOTE.—*A nei* is often written as one word, and then it signifies *here*, present place. *A* when pronounced with a protracted sound, signifies a protracted period of time, or distance, or a long continued action; as. *holo ae la ia a—a hiki i ka aina kahiki*, he sailed a long time (or a long distance) *until* he reached a foreign country.

A, *conj.* And; and then; and when. When it connects verbs, it usually stands by itself; as, *holo ka waa, a komo iho*, the canoe sailed *and* sank. When it con-

nects nouns, it is usually joined with *me*; as, *haawi mai oia i ka ai a me ke kapa*, he furnished food *and* clothing. *A* with *me* signifies and, and also, besides, together with, &c. When emphatic, it is merely a disjunctive. *Lunk.* 6:39. NOTE.—In narration, it frequently stands at the beginning of sentences or paragraphs, and merely refers to what has been said, without any very close connection with it. In many cases, it is apparently euphonic, or seems to answer no purpose, except as a preparatory sound to something that may follow; as. *akahi no oukon a hele i keia ala*, never before have you passed this road. *Gram.* § 166.

A, *prep.* Of; to; in connection with motion, e hoi oe *a* ka hale, return *to* the house, (*hiki i*) understood. *Laieik.* 12. Unto; at; belonging. It designates the properties of relation, possession and place; and is often synonymous with *o*, but more generally distinct, giving another shade of meaning and implying a more close connection. *Gram.* § 69, 3.

A, *int.* Lo; behold. It is expressive of surprise, disappointment, astonishment or admiration. It is similar in meaning to *aia hoi, eia hoi, aia ka*.

A, *v.* To burn, as a fire; ua *a* mai ke ahi, the fire *burns*; ua *a* mai ke ahi ma ka waha, the fire *burned* in their mouths.
  2. To burn, as a lamp; to blaze, as a flame.
  3. FIG. To burn, as jealousy. *Hal.* 79:5. As anger. *Nah.* 11:1.
  4. *Hoo* or *ho*. To cause to burn, i. e., to kindle; to light, as a lamp; to kindle, as a fire. Also with *ho* doubled, as *hohoa*. to dry; na hua i *hohoa ia*, dried fruits. *Oihk.* 2:14. See the reduplicate form **AA** and Hoo. *Gram.* § 212.

A, *adj.* Fiery; burning; he lua *a*, a fiery pit.

A, *s.* The jawbone; the cheek bone. *Hal.* 3:7. *A luna*, upper jaw; *a lalo*. lower jaw.

A, *s.* The name of an instrument made of smooth bone, and used formerly for piercing or killing an unborn child. It was called the *a* oo, the piercing *a;* also *a* koholua. See KOHOLUA.

A, *s.* Name of broken lava from the volcano; probably so called from being burnt. See A, *v.* Ke *a* o Kaniku a me Napuuapele.

A, *s.* Name of the white spots that appear in poi when pounding.

A, *s.* Name of a large sea bird often caught by natives; also called aaianuheakane, feathers white.

A, *s.* Name of a small fish that bites at a hook; called also aakimakau.

A, *s.* Name of the Hawaiian alphabet; also the first sheet on which it was printed.

A-A, *v.* *A* doubled. See A, verb, before. To burn fiercely or furiously, as a fire; to burn constantly. *Oihk.* 6:9.
2. FIG. To kindle; to burn furiously, as anger. *Nah.* 11:33.
3. *Hoo.* To cause to kindle; to burn, as a fire; to light, as a lamp.
4. FIG. To burn, as anger. *Kin.* 30:2.
5. To rage; to be angry.

A-A, *adj.* Burning; raging, as a fire, he ahi *aa* loa; also *as* anger.

A-A, *s.* A burning; a lighted fire, &c. *Laieik.* 78.

A-A, *v.* To be bold; to dare. *Nah.* 14:44.
2. To tempt; to challenge. *Puk.* 17:2. To defy. 1 *Sam.* 17:10.
3. To venture, ua *aa* anei oe e hele i ke kaua? Ua *aa* anei oe e hele i ke alii?
4. To accept a challenge; to act presumptuously. *Kanl.* 1:43. He *aa* ka manao; he wiwo ole.

A-A, *s.* A daring; tempting. *Nah.* 14:22.

A-A, *adj.* Spiteful; quick angry; also rogulah: mischievous.

A-A, *v.* To gird; tie around, as a loose garment.

A-A, *s.* A belt; a girdle.

A-A, *v.* To make a noise, as in trying to speak, as a dumb person; hence,
2. To be dumb, ua *aa* ka leo.

A-A, *adj.* Silent; still; lonely, as a house uninhabited; he *aa* ko ka hale, the people of the house are *silent.*

A-A, *s.* Dumbness; inability to speak intelligibly; also a dumb person. *Puk.* 4:11. I loheia e na *aa* lololohe; i mau *aa* lolo kuli.

A-A, *s.* The small roots of trees or plants. *Iob.* 8:17. Also called well.
2. The veins or arteries for blood, from their resemblance to the fine roots of trees, aole lakou i ike ke koko maloko o na *aa.* *Anat.* 1.

3. FIG. The lower part of the neck.
4. Offspring.

A-A, *s.* A pocket; a bag. *Iob.* 14:17. SYN. with *eke.* *Aa* moni, a purse; a scrip; a bag to carry provisions for a journey; aole kanaka *aa* ole, no man without his scrip; a bag for weights (of money.) *Kanl.* 25:13. The name of the envelop for a fœtus. *Laieik.* 190. Kuu kaikaina i ka *aa* hookahi.

A-A, *s.* A dwarf; a small person. *Oihk.* 21:20. Kanaka poupou *aa;* ua ike au i kahi keiki i komoiii, *aa* no hoi ke kino.

A-A, *s.* See A above. Broken lava, i. e., sand, earth, stones and melted lava, cooled and broken up; hence

A-A, *adj.* Stony; abounding with lava; rough with broken lava, as ground to walk over, or to work in. See A, broken lava, above.

A-A, *s.* A covering for the eyes.

A-A, *s.* See A above. Name of a bird that hunts fish during the day, but flies back to the mountains in the evening.

A-A, *s.* The caul of animals; *aa* maluna o ke eke, the *caul* above the liver. *Puk.* 29:13. The midriff. *Oihk.* 3:4.

A-A, *s.* Name of a sea breeze at Lahaina and some other places on the islands.

A-A, *s.* Name of the cloth-like covering near the roots of cocoanut leaves, *aa* niu. Hence,
2. The name of a coarse kind of cloth, he *aa* haole.
3. The outer husk of the cocoanut; the skin of the banana, same as *paaa.*

A-A, *s.* Chaff; hulls; the outside of seeds or fruit. *Ier.* 23:28.

A-A, *s.* Name of a reddish fish. See A above.

A-A, *v.* To send love in compliment; as, e *aa* mai ana o mea *ma* ia oe; the answer would be. Anoai wale laua, er welina wale laua, or aloha wale laua.

A-A-A, *adj.* Hospitable; friendly; kind to strangers, he makamaka aloha; SYN. with *haaa.*

A-A-A, *adj.* Uninhabited, as a house or village; lonely.

A-A-A, *s.* A house without inhabitants; also a low or humble dwelling, he hale *aaa,* aole kiekie.

A-A-A-KI, *v.* To bite often. See AKI, to bite.

A-A-E, *s.* See AA, fine roots. A kalo patch where the kalo is pulled.
2. The young shoots of kalo remaining in the ground after the old is pulled. SYN. with *oha,* as, pau ke kalo i ka hukiia, o ka *oha* wale no koe, oia ka *aae.*

3

A-A-NO, *v.* The 7th conj. of *ano. Hoo.*
To change one's form ; to become another
in appearance ; ua *hooano* no oukou he poe
akamai ; to feign ; to pretend to be something one is not.

A-E, *v.* To pass, physically or mentally, from one state, condition, or place,
to another.
1. *Specifically,* to break a kapu, ua *ae*
lakou iluna o kahi laa ; to violate a law or
agreement, i. e., to transgress, as a law. to
break a covenant. *Ios.* 7.11 ; *Hal.* 89:34.
2. To pass over, as the mind, i. e., to
yield assent to the thought or opinion of
another ; to assent to the request of another ; to say yes to a request or to an affirmation.
3. To permit, grant permission for a thing
to be done ; he mea *ae ia,* a thing permitted or allowed.
4. To pass physically from one place to
another, from one situation to another, as
from land on board a ship ; ua *ae* aku lakou
iluna o ka moku, iluna o ka lio, to *embark,*
to *mount* a horse. *Hoo.,* conj. 3. To cause
to pass from one place to another, from one
person to another ; to transfer.
5. To raise or lift up, as the head, with
joy, e *ae* ko oukou poo no ka olioli.

A-E, *s.* The water or liquid as wrung
from the leaves of vegetables, as kalo, &c. ;
he *ae* kalo. he *ae* wauki, he ohi.

A-E, *adv.* See verb 2. Yes ; the expression of affirmation, approbation or consent ; opposed to *aole,* or *aohe.* With *paha,*
as *ae paha,* a polite way of assenting when
full belief is withheld ; *ae ka paha,* even
so, be it so.

AE-AE, *v.* Conj. 13 of *ae,* 4. To be a
frequent transgressor. he *aeae* oe maluna o
kahi kapu.
2. To step over a thing often.
3. To work over and over, as in pounding poi, until very fine.
4. To be or become very small or fine.
as dust. 2 *Nal.* 23:6.
5. To interrupt one in his speech.

AE-AE, *adj.* Comminuted ; small or fine,
as dust ; fine, as poi well pounded ; he poi
aeae, he poi uouo, he wali.
2. Dark, obscure, as a vision, indistinctly
seen ; po *aeae,* a night of indistinct vision,
not totally dark, i. e., light and darkness
mixed.

A-E-A, *adj.* Wandering ; unstable ; shift-
ing a place ; he one *aea* ke one o Hoo-
hila ; unsettled, as kanaka *aea ;* a vaga-
bond ; wandering about. *Kin.* 4:12.

A-E-A, *adj.* Wanderingly, in a loose
unstable manner.

AE-NEI, *v.* To be here ; to be present ;
to be in existence. *Mat.* 2:18. NOTE.—
This word seems to be compounded of *ae,*
No. 4, expressive of a passing or transfer,
and *nei,* which refers to present time or
present place ; something not fixed or exactly defined, but near by, either in time
or place, as *at this present.*

AE-NEI, *adv.* Now, i. e., about this time,
just now, within a short time past or future.
2. Here ; hereabouts ; near by ; not far
off ; ua holo *aenei,* he has just now sailed ;
ua olelo *aenei,* he has lately spoken ; ua
make *aenei* no ke alii, the king died a
short time ago ; ua hele *aenei* no kahi i
noho ai. he is gone a little ways to his place
of residence.

AI, *v.* To eat ; to consume food, as
persons or animals.
2. To devour, as animals.
3. To destroy, consume, as fire. *Nah.*
16:35.
4. To consume ; spoken of the sword, 2
Sam. 2:26.
5. To eat. consume, as a sore ; aole *ai* ka
mai, the disease has made no advance.
Oihk. 13:5.
6. To taste, eat, enjoy the benefits of, have
the profits of, as land ; e *ai* i ka aina. *Nah.*
32 ; 19th conj., 3d hoo.
7. To cause to eat, i. e., compel or induce
to eat ; huhu loa ia (Kekuokalani) i ka *hoai*
noa ana a lakou i ke alii (Liholiho,) he was
very angry at them for causing the king
to eat freely, i. e., contrary to kapu.
8. To have sexual intercourse ; applied
to both sexes ; also to animals. *Kin.* 30:41.

AI, *adv.,* for *aia.* There ; near by, but
not in contact ; *ai* no iloko o ka hale, *there*
in the house.
2. There, at another place, however dis-
tant ; there ; when ; as, Auhea o Kekuaokalani ? *Ai ae* no mauka mai. Where is
Kekuaokalani ? *There he is* coming by
land.

AI. *verbal directive. Gram.* § 242. It
has reference, generally, to a preceding
noun, verb or adverb, expressive of time,
place, cause, manner or instrument ; often
contracted. thus, hana'i, for hana ai.

A-I, *s.* The neck ; he *a-i* ko ke kanaka,
oia kahi e hui ai ke poo me ke kino, man
has a *neck,* it is that which unites the head
with the body. *A-i* oolea. a stiff neck.
2. *Figuratively,* perverseness ; disobedience. *Puk.* 33:3.

A-I-A, *v.* To be or show one's self contrary to the gods.
2. To disregard the will of the gods ; to
be ungodly in practice.
3. To have the character of an ungodly
person. *Ier.* 23:11. See HAIHAIA.

AI-AU, *v.* To pray or poison to death, as was formerly practiced.

2. To show covetousness in asking; as. ua *aiau* aku i ka hai, he coveted what was another's. Similar to *aluna* and *makee.*

AI-A-HU-A, *v.* To break secretly the kapus of the gods, but to observe them openly; to act hypocritically.

2. To conspire secretly against one.

3. To defraud one's landlord by withholding the tax and using it himself.

4. To pray to death. Similar to *anaana.*

AI-HA-MU, *v. Ai,* to eat, and *hamu,* refuse food.

1. To eat refuse food.

2. To eat up clean; ua *aihamuia* kau mula uala.

3. Applied as an epithet of reproach to the poe kahuna anaana, the priests who practiced sorcery.

Ao, *v.* To be or become light or day, as in the morning; ua *ao* ka po, the night has become light. *Oih.* 12:18.

2. To awake, as from a vision or dream.

3. To come to one's right mind or self-possession.

4. To teach; instruct. *Luk.* 11:1.

5. To enlighten; instruct in one's duty or conduct. *Oihk.* 10:11.

6. To reprove; take heed; beware; to warn. *Kin.* 31:24.

7. To regard with reverence; to obey.

8. To charge strictly.

9. To learn to do a thing; to learn, to study, as a language; e na kumu e, e *ao* oukou i ka olelo Hawaii, O teachers, study the Hawaiian language.

10. To copy the example of others. *Kanl.* 18:9. In the imperative. e *ao,* look out; watch; be on your guard; take heed. *Ios.* 22:5.

Ao, *v.* Found only in hoo., conj. 3. To tempt; to try; to prove. *Dan.* 12:10.

2. To try one's conduct or fitness for a duty. *Lunk.* 7:4.

3. To try; assay. *Kanl.* 4:34.

4. To try to do a thing to ascertain whether it can be done; e *hoao* e ae oe mamua a maopopo, a ina maopopo, alaila hana, try first whether the thing is feasible, if feasible, then do it.

5. To try; taste of. i. e., suffer, as pain or death. *Mat.* 16:18. To tempt, as the Holy Spirit. *Oih.* 5:9.

Ao, *s.* Light; day, in distinction from *po,* night. *Kin.* 1:5. For the different periods of time through the night, see *Laieik.* 30.

2. The world. *Hal.* 89:11. O ke *ao* nei, o keia *ao,* this world; o kela *ao,* the future

world; na wahi *ao,* heavenly places. *Epes.* 1:3.

A-O-LE (ole), *adv.* An adverb of denying. refusing; no: not; a universal negative; for euphony's sake, it takes different forms; as, *aohe, aole, ohe, ole,* and *aoe.* The form *ole* is privative in its meaning. and may be added to almost any adjective, noun (proper names excepted,) or verb in the language. It is equivalent to the English inseparable negative particles, *less, in, un,* &c. See OLE.

A-O-LE, *v.* To not; not to do; *aole* oia i hana, he did it not.

2. To deny; refuse to do a thing; *aole* ae la ia i hoopono ia ia, ia manawa, he refused (he did not) reform himself at that time.

3. Not to be; no existence. *Hal.* 37:36. *Aole e ole.* a phrase signifying the strongest affirmation, as, it cannot but be, it cannot be otherwise, it will not fail of being so, there is no *not* in the case, &c. NOTE.— the sense 2, to deny. is more generally found under the form *ole, v.,* 3d conj. hoo., which see.

Au, *pers. pron.,* 1st per. sing. I; when prefixed or preceded by the emphatic *o,* as *o au.* the compound sound resembles that of *w:* hence it has the forms *au, o au, wau,* and *o wau:* the *o* is no part of the word, and should be written separately.

A'U, *pron.* So written for *aau,* one *a* dropped and the apostrophe supplied. It is the *auipili.* one of the oblique cases of *au,* I. See *Gram.* § 124. Of me; mine.

There is a sensible break in the pronunciation, to distinguish it from *au,* the 1st person, and from *au,* of the 2d person next below.

Au, *pron.* With a more protracted, smooth pronunciation than the foregoing, one of the auipili cases of the 2d per. sing. of *oe.* *Gram.* § 132. Thine; of thee.

Au, *s.* The handle or helve of an axe. *Kanl.* 19:5. The staff of a spear. 1 *Sam.* 17:7. The handle of a sword. *Lunk.* 3:22. The handle of an auger, &c.; au koi, au pahi.

Au, *s.* The current in the ocean; *au* maloko o ka moana; o kahi o ke kai e wili ana, he *au* ia; he *wili au* kahi inoa.

2. The grain in wood.

3. The motion of the hand in mixing poi.

4. An action of the mind; as, ke *au* wale nei no ko'u manao e ake e pulelo iki ae, my mind is exercising, &c. See Au, *v.,* below.

Au, *s.* Time; a period of time, more or

less definitely designated, as the reign of a king. *Ier.* 28:1.

2. The time of one's life; i ke *au* la Kalaniopuu ; i ke *au* o Liholiho, in the time of Kalaniopuu, &c.

3. A season. *Oih.* 11:28. A portion of time.

Au, *s.* A territory ; district of country ; generally compounded with other qualifying words ; as, *auakua*, a desert, a place of gods, ghosts, &c. See AUAKUA. *Au*kanaka, an inhabited country ; *aupuni*, a large region, &c. NOTE.—*Au* is the term representing all places where food grows ; as *kaha* represents such places as are on or near the shore where food does not grow. This applies mostly to the leeward side of the islands.

Au, *v.* To swim ; ua *au* na kanaka i ka moana, a pakele i ka make, the people swam the ocean and escaped death.

2. To float on the surface of water ; to turn, as the eyes to look at something ; i na ua ike oe e *au* ana kona maka. *Laieik.* 145. SYN. with nana ia.

3. *Hoo.*, 3d conj. To cause to swim, to float ; *hooau* hele aku la i na pahu o lakou, they floated along their (water) casks.

4. To convey, as on a raft. 2 *Oihl.* 2:16.

5. To swim through the water by the exertions of the arms and other limbs ; poho ka uhane o ka poe make i ka moana, aole paha e hiki ke *au* iuka, the souls of those who sink in the ocean are lost, they are not able to swim ashore. Used imperatively, to quicken, to hasten ; more generally doubled, as *auau*, which see.

Au, *v.* To long after, or be wholly bent on ; to be fully engaged in a course of conduct ; alaila, *au* loa wau i na ino o ke ao nei, then I was wholly engrossed in the vileness of the world ; makemake, puni, lilo loa. See AU, current, above.

Au-au, *v.* Conj. 6 of *au*, to swim. To bathe in water, as a person. *Puk.* 2:5.

2. To wash ; cleanse with water. *Oihk.* 15:5.

3. To take out wrinkles from a piece of cloth. *Hoo.*, conj. 3. To wash ; cleanse, &c.

4. Used imperatively, to excite ; hasten ; e *auau* aku kakou, e wikiwiki ; e *auau* mai oe, come quickly, e wikiwiki mai oe ; used also with *ho*. See HOAUAU.

Au-ma-ku-a, *s.* Name of a class of ancient gods who were considered able and trustworthy ; na akua i ka po. o na *aumakua* i ke ao, gods of the night, gods of the day ; o Kiha i ka po, o Liloa i ka po, o Umi i ka po, o Mea i ke ao.

Au-ma-ku-a, *adj.* He akua *aumakua*,

able, that may be trusted as a child trusts to a parent ; ua ola ke akua *aumakua*. Kukuluia ka hale no ko Kamehameha mau iwi, i mea e hoolilo ai ia ia i akua *aumakua*, a house was built for Kamehameha's bones that he might become a *substantial* god.

Au-ma-ku-a, *s.* A person so called who provided for a chief or for chiefs ; a trusty, steadfast servant ; one who is not easily provoked to leave his place.

Au-pu-ni, *s.* *Au*, a place, and *puni*, around.

1. A region of country governed by a chief or king. NOTE.—Originally the word did not imply a large country, as there were formerly several *aupunis* on one island. At present, the word is used to signify,

2. A kingdom ; the dominion and jurisdiction of a king.

Au-pu-ni, *v.* To be in an undisturbed state ; to be in a state of peace and quietness, as a kingdom.

Au-wai, *s.* *Au*, furrow, and *wai*, water. A brook ; a small water course. *Sol.* 21:1. The outlet of a pool. *Isa.* 7:3. The general name for streams used in artificial irrigation.

A-ha, *num. adj.* See HA. Four ; the number four ; also *eha*.

A-ha, *s.* A company or assembly of people for any purpose. *Puk.* 35:1. Often compounded with some qualifying word ; as, *aha*aina, *aha*olelo, *aha*kanaka, *aha*hookolokolo, *aha*mokomoko, &c. See these compounds, which are sometimes written in one word, and sometimes divided. *Aha*akohipa, a company for shearing sheep. 2 *Sam.* 13:23.

A-ha, *s.* Name of a certain prayer connected with a kapu ; ina walaau ke kanaka i ka *aha*, make no ia, if a man should make a noise during the *prayer*, he would die, i. e., he would be guilty of an offense for which he would forfeit his life. The name originated in the fact that cocoanut fibre (see AHA, below) is very strong when braided into strings ; so this prayer, with its rigid kapus, was supposed to be very efficacious in holding the kingdom together in times of danger.

2. The success or answer of a prayer, or such a proper performance of prayer as to insure success ; loaa ka kakou *aha*, we have received our *prayer*, i. e., *the answer* ; ua lilo ka *aha*, alaila, e pule hou, the *prayer* is lost, (of no avail,) then pray again.

A-ha, *s.* A cord braided from the husk of the cocoanut.

2. A cord braided from human hair.

3. Strings made from the intestines of animals; ka naau i mea *aha* moa, the intestines for strings to tie the fowls with; he *aha* pulu niu; he *aha* waa a me ka *aha* hoa waa, a cord for tying and strengthening a canoe in a storm; he *aha* palaba, he lauoho i hili nilo ia.

A-HA, *s.* Name of a small piece of wood, around which was wound a piece of kapa, and held in the hand of the priest while offering sacrifices.

2. Name of a kind of kapa made on Molokai.

2. The name of a species of long fish swimming near the surface of the water.

A-HA, *inter. pron.* Declinable with the definite article; indeclinable with the indefinite. *Gram.* § 159. *Heaha*, what? often united with the article; why? for what reason? *Hal.* 68:16. No *keaha?* i *keaha?* It is also used as an interrogative adverb, why?

A-HA, *v.* To what; to do, &c.; e *aha ana* oia? what shall he do? Of course it is used only in the interrogative. *Ioh.* 20:21.

A-HA. An interjection of surprise, wonder, &c. Ua heluhelu lakou, *aha;* ua loaa lakou e moe ana, *aha.*

A-HA, *v.* To stretch the cord by which the first posts of a house were put down or set straight; e kii i ke kaula e *aha* ai, fetch the rope to make straight with.

2. FIG. *Aha*, oia ka ana a me ka *aha* pololei no ke aupuni, *aha*, that is, to measure and direct *straightly* the government.

A-HA, *s.* Used in the expressions, ua like na *aha*, the sides are equal; *aha* like, meaning side—*measure* perhaps.

A-HA-HA, *v.* See HA, to breathe. To pant; to breathe hard on account of heat, as a hog or a dog from a chase; ua *ahaha* keiki e ku imua; *ahea* ka inoa o ke alii; *ahea* no la nalo ka moe ke aahi la i ka pili o ka houpo.

A-HA-MA-KA, *s.* An assembly for prayers.

A-HO, *v.* To be patient, submissive, humble; to be merciful, kind; to be ready to do a kind act. See the compounds AHONUI and AHOLOA.

A-HO, *s. Art.*, ke. The natural breathing of a person; the breath; hence,

2. Patience; i nui ke *aho*, let the breath be long, i. e., be patient.

3. MET. Spirit; courage. *Ios.* 2:11. Resolution; also kindness.

A-HO, *s. Art.*, ke. A line; a cord, as a fish line; ke *aho* lawaia; a kite string; ke kakaiapola a me ke *aho;* alaila, hoolele aku i ka lupe i ka lewa, a paa aku ma ke *aho*, (prepare) the kite tail and the string, then send off the kite into the air, but hold fast by the string.

A-HO-LOA, *s. Aho*, a cord, and *loa*, long. A long string for fishing or sounding in deep water; he *aholoa* loa i ka mio; he *aholoa* i ka luu ilalo o ka moana.

A-HU, *v.* To gather or collect together. *Kin.* 43:11. *Ahu* iho la i kahakai, hu ae la ka lolo, they gathered them together (dead bodies) on the sea shore, the brains flowed; to collect one's food where there is little.

To collect but gain little; *ahu* wale iho no, aole wahi kapa; *ahu* wale iho, aole ai; *ahu* wale iho no i ka oneanea.

2. To lay up, as in a store-house; to lay up for future use, as goods. *Mat.* 6:19. To store in the memory.

3. To lie strewed over the ground. *Puk.* 16:3.

4. To cover one with a cloak; to be merely covered. *Iob.* 26:6. To clothe.

5. *Hoo.* To collect what is scattered.

6. To fall together, as men slain in battle.

7. To keep; treasure up, as anger; *hooahu* iho la i ka huhu maluna o kela poe, he kept in reserve his anger for that company.

8. To pile up, as stones. *Ios.* 8:29. To gather up; glean, as a field. *Rut.* 2:7.

9. To bring condemnation upon.

10. To reply to; to object to something said. *Rom.* 9:20.

A-HU, *s.* See AHA. An assemblage or collection of things; *ahu* ai, a place for storing food; a collection of provisions. 2 *Oihl.* 11:11. Wahi-*ahu*, a place for something. *Iob.* 28:1. *Ahu* pohaku, a pavement; a heap, as of stones. *Kin.* 31:46.

2. A heap of stones as a way mark. *Ier.* 31:21.

3. As a memorial. *Ios.* 7:26.

A-HU, *adj.* Storing; collecting; hale *ahu*, a store-house. *Iob.* 38:22.

A-HU, *s.* A fine mat; a coarse one is *moena*; a mat for covering a canoe; o ka uhi ana i ka *ahu*, ea, oia ka mea e pale aku i kekahi ale, the spreading over a mat, that is what will keep off some of the waves; *ahuao, ahu* mokoloa.

A-HU-A, *s.* See AHU, collection. Any place elevated in the manner of a high path.

2. A bank in the sea; a bank formed by the sand at a mouth of a river; hence,

3. A ford; a place for passing a stream or river. *Ios.* 2:7; *Lunk.* 3:28. He puu; a hillock; he kiekie ma kekahi aoao.

A-HU-A, *v.* To be raised up on a platform ; ua *ahua,* ua *ahawa.*

A-ka. A particle set before verbs to express carefulness, regularity of proceeding, &c.; as, *aka* hele, go carefully ; *aka* holo, sail or run slowly ; *aka* hana, work carefully ; *aka* noho, sit quietly.

A-ka, *conj.* But ; if not ; on the other hand. The word is generally used to express strong opposition of idea.

A-ka, *s.* The shadow of a person ; the figure or outline of a thing ; a similitude or likeness. *Nah.* 12:8. Note.—The shade of a tree or house is *malu.*
2. The dawn or light of the moon before rising.
3. The knuckle joints; the protuberances of the ankle joints ; the joints of the backbone.
4. Fig. A shadow ; frailty ; impotence. *Isa.* 30:2.

A-ka, *v.* To light up, as the moon before rising ; ua aha ka mahina? kokoke puka, ua *aka* mai la, how is the moon? it is near rising, it lights up.
2. To go up and down, as on a hilly road. (See No. 2 above, joints of the backbone.)
3. To be split or peeled up, as the bark of a tree.
4. To be torn off, as the kaupaku of a house ; ua aka ke kaupaku o ka hale.

A-ka, *v.* To laugh ; to deride ; i ko'u noonoo ana i keia kumu manao, ua *aka* iki mai no ka pono, in thinking of this composition, I smiled at its correctness. (The 13th conj., *akaaka,* is more generally used.)

A-kaa, *v.* To break open, as a seal. *Hoik.* 5:2. To tear or take up, as a mat.

A-kaa, *adj.* Anything broken up ; not cohering ; he *akaa* wale, he pipili ole.

A-ka-a-ka, *v.* See Aka, to laugh. To laugh; to laugh at. *Sol.* 4:9. *Hoo.* To cause to laugh ; to have joy. *Kin.* 21:6.

A-ka-a-ka, *s.* Laughter ; exhilaration of spirits. *Hal.* 126:2.

A-ka-oo, *s.* Aka, shadow, and *oo,* ripe. A full grown shadow: applied to a person who is close, hard or stingy.

A-ka-ka, *v.* To be plain ; to be clear, as a thought or the expression of an idea ; to be distinct, intelligible, as language.
2. To be clear, transparent, as glass. *Hoik.* 22:1 ; *Anat.* 2. Clear, as a liquid.
3. *Hoo.* To make plain ; to expound, demonstrate ; to bring to light.
4. To set up boundary lines.

A-ka-ka, *adj.* Clear, as water.

2. Lucid ; bright, as the moon.
3. Certain ; distinct ; transparent ; he *akaka,* kokoke like me ke aniani kona *akaka* ana, clear, almost like glass.

A-ka-ka, *adv.* *Akaka* loa, very plainly; very clearly. *Ioan.* 10:24.

A-ka-ku, *s.* A subsiding of a storm, wind, &c.
2. A delirium ; a trance. *Oih.* 10:10. An ecstasy ; vision. 2 *Oihl.* 26:5. He moe uhane. *Hoo.* A vision. *Oih.* 26:19.

A-ka-lau. See Kinoakalau and Wailua. A ghost that appears to some people. but not to others.

A-ka-mai, *v.* To be wise ; makemake au e *akamai* oukou a pau, I wish that you may all become wise ; mostly used in the causative. *Hoo.* To be or become wise ; to make wise ; skillful. *Sol.* 3:7. To think one's self wise.

A-ka-mai, *s.* Wisdom ; skill ; ingenuity. *Hoo.* Exhibiting wisdom. 1 *Kor.* 2:1.

A-ka-mai, *adj.* Wise ; skillful ; ingenious ; expert ; sagacious ; learned ; *akamai* ma ka naau. *Puk.* 28:3.

A-ku, *v.* To follow.

A-ku. A verbal directive. See *Gram.* § 233, 2, and § 236. In Hawaiian, the motion or action of verbs is supposed to be towards one (*mai,*) or from one (*aku,*) or upwards (*ae,*) or downwards (*iho,*) or sideways, which is also *ae.* *Aku* is mostly connected with verbs, sometimes with nouns and adverbs ; it implies motion or tendency *from* one, *onward,* &c.; as, e hele *aku,* to go *off,* go *from* one ; the opposite of e hele *mai,* to come *towards* one. In narrative tenses the verbal directives are generally followed by the syllable *la* ; as, hele *aku la* oia, he went *off;* noho *iho la* ia, he sat *down,* or he dwelt.

A-ku, *adj.* Clear ; unclouded ; spoken of the moon when fully up ; he *aku* ka mahina, the moon is clear.

A-ku-a, *s.* Among Hawaiians, formerly, the name of any supernatural being, the object of fear or worship ; a god. The term, on the visit of foreigners, was applied to artificial objects, the nature or properties of which Hawaiians did not understand, as the movement of a watch, a compass, the self-striking of a clock, &c. At present, the word *Akua* is used for the true God, the Deity, the object of love and obedience as well as fear.
2. The name of the night when the moon was perfectly full ; a akaka loa o in poepoe ana, o *Akua* ia po ; hence it would seem that the ancient idea of an *Akua* em-

braced something incomprehensible, powerful, and yet complete, full orbed. The names of the four principal gods of the Hawaiians were Ku, Lono, Kane, and Kanaloa.

A-KU-A-AU-MA-KU-A, *s. Akua, au,* time, and *makua,* parent. The ancestors of those who died long ago, and who have become gods; the spirits of former heroes.

A-KU-A-U-LU, *s. Akua,* god, and *ulu,* to inspire. The god which came upon one and inspired him to speak; the god of inspiration.

A-KU-A-HAI-A-MIO, *s. Akua,* god, *hai,* to speak, and *amio,* to be silent. A god speaking silently.

A-KU-A-HA-NAI, *s. Akua,* god, and *hanai,* to feed.
1. The god that fed poison to people; the god of poison; hence,
2. Poison itself; he *akuahanai* ka rama, rum is a poisonous god, a he moonihoawa ka aie, and a poison toothed lizard (serpent) is going into debt.

A-KU-A-HOO-U-NA-U-NA, *s. Akua,* god, and *hoouna,* to send. A class of gods who were sent on errands like Mercury of the Greeks; the names of some of them were Keawenuikauohilo, Kapo, Kapua, Kamakukou, and many others.

A-KU-A-KII, *s. Akua,* god, and *kii,* an image.
1. The god represented by an image; hence,
2. An idol; a god made. *Oihk.* 26:1; *Isa.* 31:7.

A-KU-A-LA-PU, *s. Akua,* god, and *lapu,* a ghost. A ghost; a spectre: an apparition; an evil spirit. NOTE.—According to the old people, the poe *akuahipu* were the spirits of deceased persons seen in the night about burying and other places for the purpose of frightening people.

A-KU-A-NO-HO, *s.* Name of a class of gods supposed to be the spirits of men deceased; they were supposed to dwell with, or be over men as guardians.

A-LA, *v.* To wake from sleep; to watch, i. e., to keep from sleep.
2. To rise up, as from a sleeping posture; e hikilele oia ma ka hiamoe ana. *Puk.* 10:23. *Ala* ku e, to rise up against one. *Puk.* 15:7.
3. To rise up, as a new generation of people; to come forward. *Lunk.* 2:10.
4. *Hoo.* To cause one to rise; to lift up; to rise from the dead.
5. To raise up; excite to action; to stir up, as the mind. 2 *Pet.* 3:1.
6. To stir up; excite to evil. *Puk.* 23:1.

7. To raise up, as a deliverer or benefactor. *Lunk.* 3:9.
8. To repair, as a broken down wall. *Neh.* 3:4.

A-LA, *v.* To anoint; to dress a sore or a limb. 2 *Sim.* 19:24.

A-LA, *v.* A round, smooth stone; a pebble, such as has been worn by the water; he pohaku maloko o ka muliwai. 1 *Sam.* 17:40 and 49. *Ala* o ka maa, a sling stone. *Zek.* 9:15.

A-LA, *s.* A path; way; road; often *alanui,* great road; it is used in some places as synonymous with *kvamoo;* he kahi e hele ai; kuu aku ana keia i ke *ala;* po oloko i ke *ala. Laieik.* 62.

A-LA, *adj.* Round or oval, as a smooth stone or bullet; hence, heavy; kaumaha, e like me ka *ala* o kahawai, heavy, as a smooth stone in a water course. See ALA, a round, smooth stone.

A-LA-EA, *adj.* Relating to the practice of the priest offering the yearly sacrifice; hele mai ke kahuna *alaea* me ke kanaka, nana e lawe ka ipu *alaea.*

A-LAI, *v.* To obstruct; to hinder one in any way; ua alai ia e ka hilabila a hiki ole ke pane aku, he or she was hindered by shame and could not answer. *Laieik.*

A-LA-HOU-AN-A, *s. Ala,* to rise, and *hou,* again, and the participial termination *ana.* A rising again; a rising from the dead. *Oih.* 24:15. A resurrection.

A-LA-LA, *s.* A specie of potato with fruit on the leaves. See ALAALA.

A-LA-LAI, *v. Ala,* road, and *lai.*
1. To hinder one from doing a thing.
2. To obstruct one's road. *Iob.* 19:8.
3. To be in the way of another; ua *alalai* mai oia i ko'u hele ana, he hindered me in my passage; he keakea.

A-LA-LAI, *v.* To consecrate; to render sacred by coming in contact with some sacred object.

A-LE-HE, *s.* A snare; a noose; he abele, he pahele.

A-LO-HA, *v.* To love; to regard with affection; to desire.
2. To have pity or compassion upon.
3. To show mercy; to be merciful as a habit. *Mat.* 5:7. To spare; to pity. *Ezek.* 7:9.
4. To salute at meeting or parting. 1 *Sam.* 10:4.
5. To salute contemptuously; aloha ino kaua, alas for us two. NOTE.—*Aloha,* as a word of salutation, is modern; the ancient forms were anoai, welina, &c.
6. *Hoo.* To give thanks as an act of wor-

ship. 1 *Oihl.* 25:3.

A-LO-HA, *s.* A word expressing different feelings; as, love; affection; gratitude; kindness; pity; compassion; grief; the modern common salutation at meeting and parting.

A-LO-HA, *adj.* Loving; beloved; favored.

A-LO-HA-IA. A verbal from the verb *aloha* above used as a noun. Favor; kindness; loaa ia ia ke *alohaia* mai. he obtained favor: favor; good will. *Kin.* 33:10.

A-LO-HA-I-NO, *int. Aloha* and *ino.* An intensive; it expresses great love, pity or compassion for a person in a suffering condition. It is also used by way of contempt, as poor fellow! good enough for you!

A-LO-HA-LO-HA, *v.* To love much.

2. *Hoo.* To give thanks; to express affection for; to bless in worship. 2 *Sam.* 22:50.

3. To salute. 2 *Sam.* 8:10.

4. To speak kindly to; to entreat gently. *Luk.* 15:28.

A-LU, *adj.* Combined; acting together; he mau ilio *alu* i ka hakaka.

A-LU-A (e-lu-a), *num. adj.* The number two; two. See LUA.

A-MA-MA, *v.* Conj. 9th of *ama*, to offer, &c. To give over to the gods in sacrifice.

2. To offer sacrifice as an act of worship. *Hoik.* 8:3. O ke kino uhane ole e waiho ana, *amama* ae la ke alii, the body lying without life the king offered in sacrifice; ua *amamaia* aku la i kona akua ia Kaili. he was sacrificed to his god Kaili: to offer prayers; *amama*, ua noa, like our term *Amen* to a prayer. *Laieik.* 104.

A-MA-MA, *s.* The offering of a sacrifice; ka *amama* ana i ke kanaka i ke akua.

A-MA-NA, *s.* Two sticks crossing each other at oblique angles.

2. The branches of a tree in the form of the letter Y.

A-MA-NA, *adj.* Crossing; put together in the form of a cross or gallows; ua laau *amana* i kauia'i o Kuhaina; he aleo kahi hale, he *amana* kekahi hale.

A-MA-NA, *v. Amana* mau ke kani ana o ka pu; *amana* mau ke kani o ka pu a ka anelu.

A-NA, *pron.* The oblique case of the pronoun. third person sing.; of him; of her; of it; his; hers. *Gram.* § 139. *Autpili.*

A-NA. The participial termination of verbs answering to the Eng. *ing*; as, lawe *ana*, carrying; hana *ana*, working; but it has some peculiarities.

1. The *ana* is not united with the verb as *ing* is in Eng.

2. The *ana* may be separated from the verb, and any qualifying word or words, and also the verbal directives may come between. *Gram.* § 233. As, e kukulu hale *ana* ia, he is build house *ing*; e hopu bipi *ana*. he is catch cattle *ing*, &c. In many cases the participial termination *ana* becomes united with a noun and becomes a participial noun; in which case the first *a* of the *ana* is dropped. or coalesces with the last letter of the preceding word, and they both become one word: as *hopena* for *hope ana; hanao'na* for *haauoi ana.* &c.

A-NA-A-NA, *v.* To practice divination or sorcery by prayer: e *anaana* ana ia kakou. they were practicing sorcery upon us.

A-NA-A-NA, *s.* A kind of sorcery or prayer used to procure the death or a curse upon one. *Nah.* 22:7.

A-NA, *adj.* Satisfied, as with food, having eaten sufficiently; maona.

A-NA, *v.* To praise much and covet another's wealth.

A-NA, *s.* Grief; sadness; sorrow; trouble from the conduct of others.

2. The feelings of a parent towards a child that refuses his instructions; a mixed feeling of weariness, anger and love. *Oih.* 16:18.

3. Fatigue from hard labor or toil.

A-NA, *s.* A measure, as for cloth. *Puk.* 26:2. A measure of any kind. *Kanl.* 25:14. *Ana* ohe, a measuring rod. *Ezek.* 40:3.

A-NA, *v.* To suffer; to undergo, as an experiment of healing in sickness.

2. To be grieved; troubled. *Oih.* 16:18.

3. To be affected at contempt or vile treatment. *Hal.* 123:3. 4.

A-NA, *v.* To measure. *Hoik.* 21:16.

2. To measure in any way; e hiki ia'u ke *ana* i ka loa. a me ka laulu, a me ka hohonu. a me ke kiekie o keia mea; *mel.*

3. *Ana* wau i kou pono a me kou hewa. I measured your good and your evil; no ke *ana* ana. in measuring. *Oihk.* 19:35. Mea *ana* hora. a dial. *Isa.* 38:8. *Hoo.* To set apart; to set aside. *Puk.* 16:33. To restrain; keep back. *Oih.* 5:2.

A-NA, *v.* To be satiated; satisfied, as the eye with seeing. *Kekuh.* 1:8.

A-NA, *s.* A cave; a den formed by rocks. *Kin.* 19:30; *Ios.* 10:16.

A-NA-A-NA, *adj.* Divining; consulting divinations; kahuna *anaana*, a diviner. *Kanl.* 18:10. Pule *anaana*. a praying one to death.

A-NA-A-NA, *adj.* In small balls, as the

dung of sheep or goats; he *anauna* ka lepo o ke kao a me ka hipa; *anaana* ka lepo i ka ai liilii.

A-NO, s. Likeness; resemblance; image of a thing.
2. The meaning of a word or phrase.
3. The moral quality of an action, as good or evil. or the moral state of the heart.
4. The character of a person, as to his life and manners; the explanation of a thing obscure. *Kin.* 41:8.

A-NO, v. To have a form or appearance.
2. With *hou*, to change the form or appearance of a person or thing; e *ano* ae, to become new. *Oihk.* 13:16. To change the state of things.
3. With *hoo*, to boast; to glory; to hallow; to consecrate. *Kin.* 2:3.
4. To transform; to change the external appearance.
5. With *e*, to set apart to another purpose; to consecrate. *Hal.* 4:3.
6. With *hou*, to change; to transform. 2 *Kor.* 11:13.
7. With *e*, to change, as the countenance, from mirth to sadness and fear. *Dan.* 5:10.

A-NO, s. Fear; dread; ua kau mai ke *ano* la'u la, fear fell upon me; ke kau mai la ke *ano* hewa ia oe.

A-NO, v. To be in fear; *ano* wale mai la no au. See ANO or ANOANO. To be silent; solitary, as a deserted village; ua pau i ke kaua, hauaia na kanaka a pau i ka hana.

A-NO, adv. Now; at the present time; *ano* nei, *ano* la. 1 *Sam.* 2:16. Soon.
2. Often used more as an expression of earnestness or certainty of something doing, or to be done, than of anything literally doing *now*. *Puk.* 6:1.
3. It is used after some other event has been spoken of as a consequence. *Ios.* 1:2. Ina no *ano*, even now. 1 *Nal.* 14:14.

A-NO-A, adv. Same as *ano* above. Now; at this time; immediately; *anoa* no hele; ahea hele? *anoa* no.

A-NO-AI, adv. But; except; lest; perhaps; malia paha.

A-NO-AI, adv. A warm salutation; as, aloha, welina; a salutation; a bow; a courtesy.

A-NO-A-NO, s. Seeds; the seeds of fruit, as apple, onion, melon, &c. *Nah.* 20:5.
2. The semen of males. *Oihk.* 15:16.
3. Descendants; children of men. *Ezek.* 44:22. NOTE.—The fruit itself is *hua*; also, the seeds incased in pods or husks are called *hua*; *anoano* oili, seeds destitute of meat.

A-NO-A-NO, s. A solemn stillness.
2. A sacred, hallowed place. See ANO, s., fear; dread.

A-NO-A-NO, adj. Solitary; still; retired. *Hal.* 17:12. He wahi *anoano*, mehameha loa no ka makau i ka make; aohe lua o ka noho ana i ua kula *anoano* kanaka ole nei.

E, the second letter of the Hawaiian alphabet. It represents the sound of the long slender *a* in English. or its sound is like that of *e* in *obey*. It is sometimes commuted for *a*, as in the numericals from *ehua*, alua, to *eiwa*, aiwa; also in *alelo*, the tongue, *elelo*; *mahana*, warm, *mehana*. In an unaccented syllable at the end of a word. its sound is similar to that of the English *y*, as *ope*, opy; *mahope*, mahopy, &c.

E, adv. Synonymous with and a contraction for *ae*; yes. *E*, yes. is more familiar, and not so dignified and respectful as *ae*. See AE.

E, adv. Other; another; strange; new; mea *e*, a stranger, a strange thing; kanaka *e*, a stranger; often SYN. with malihini. *Nah.* 15:15.

E, adv. From; away; e holo *e* lakou, they will flee *from*; e puhi *e*. blow *away*; i kai lilo *e*. at sea afar *off*.

E, prep. By. As a preposition, it is mostly used after passive verbs to express the agent; as, ua *ahewaia* oia *e* ke alii, he *was condemned by* the chief. Many verbs have no sign of a passive voice, the construction of the sentence alone determines it. and the *e* thus situated helps determine the point as much as anything; nui loa hoi ka poe daimonio i mahiki aku *e* ia. *Gram.* § 105, 11.

E standing before nouns marks the auihea or *vocative* case; it also often follows the same case; as, *e* ka lani *e*, O chief. *Gram.* § 105, 8.

E is used also to call or invite attention to what one is about to say; a contraction, perhaps of *ea*. NOTE.—*E* is mostly used at the beginning of an address. and *ea* in the middle, or if a single sentence, only at the end.

E following either active, passive or neuter verbs signifies *before hand*, and serves to mark a kind of second future tense of the verb; as, lohe *e* au. I heard *before*; hiki *e* mai oia, he had arrived *first*. *Gram.* § 190, 2d.

E is the sign of the imperative mood, and generally of the infinitive also, though after *hiki* and *pono* the *e* of the infinitive is changed into *ke*. *Gram.* § 191 and 193. *E* is also the sign of the future tense. *Gram.* § 190, 1.

'E. After a word ending in *a*, *'e* is a

contraction for *ae.*

E, *v.* To enter, as into a country or city.

2. To dash upon, as waves upon the deck of a ship; aohe o kana mai o ka nui o na ale i *e* maluna o ka moku. See EE.

E-A, *v.* To raise up, as a person bowed down.

2. To lift or throw up.
3. To raise up, as from the grave. *Iob.* 7:9.
4. To mount or go up upon, as an ancient bed. *Hal.* 132:3.
5. To rise up, as water. *Puk.* 15:8.
6. *Hoo.* To be thrown or raised up, as land out of the ocean; ua *hoea* mai na aina mai loko mai o ka moana, the land was thrown up out of the ocean.
7. To rise in sight, as a cloud. 1 *Nal.* 18:44. To heave in sight, as a ship; a *hoea* mai makai aku o Hilo, she *hove in sight off* Hilo.
8. To rise up, as out of the water. *Kin.* 41:2, 3.
9. To stir up, excite, as the affections; ia manawa ka *hoea* ana mai o ka hai, at that time was the exciting of other's love.

E-A, *s.* Takes *ke* for its article. Spirit; vital breath; the breath of life.

2. Life itself; oiai ke *ea,* while life lasts.
3. The natural breath of life. 1 *Tes.* 2:8. E kaili aku ke *ea,* to die. *Kin.* 25:8.
4. The breath of man or beast. *Kekah.* 3:21. Nani ka lokomaikai o ke Akua i kona haawi ana mai i ke *ea* o ke kanaka. *Hal.* 78:39. SYN. with hanu. *Isa.* 42:5.
5. He makani ku malie, oia ka makani e hanu ai kakou, the breathable air.

E-HA, *v.* To be hurt; to be sore; to be painful; to suffer; *eha* ka naau, the heart is pained. *Hoo.* To suffer in any way, as in sickness or pain, or by punishment according to law, justly or unjustly. 1 *Pet.* 4:15, 16. FIG. To cause hurt; to grieve one. *Epes.* 4:30.

E-HA, *s.* Pain; soreness of any kind; sorrow; suffering of punishment; a hurt; affliction. 1 *Sam.* 1:11.

E-HA, *adj.* Sore; painful; hurtful.

E-HO, *s.* A stone idol; he akua o Lono-kaeha.

2. A collection of stone gods.
3. A monument; a stone pillar set up as a memorial. *Kin.* 28:18; also *Kin.* 35:14. Name of a pile of stones set up to attract the attention of fishermen.

E-LE, *v.* To be dark; black; to be dark colored; not clear.

E-LE. An intensive added to many words; very; much; greatly. &c.

I the third letter of the Hawaiian alphabet. Its sound is that of *ee* in English. or that of the French *i.*

I is the medium of communication between an active transitive verb or a verb of motion and its object. See *Gram.* § 105, p. 49. *d* and *e;* also. *Gram.* Syntax. Rule 19. Before proper names of persons and pronouns, the *i* becomes *ia.* See note *Gram.* p. 49.

I has a variety of significations, and is used for a variety of purposes.

I, *prep.* To; towards; in; at; unto; by; for; in respect of; above; more than; on account of, &c.

I, *adj.* Stingy.

I, *adv.* When; while; if.

I, *conj.* If; that; a contraction perhaps of *ina.*

I. A sign. 1st. Of the imperfect tense of verbs.

2. A sign of the subjunctive mood; a contraction of *ina.*

3. As a sign of a tense, it often has the meaning of a potential; that; as, ua hai aku au *i* lohe oukou, I have spoken, *that* you might hear. See *Gram.* § 209, subj. mood, 4th form.

4. The sign of the imperative mood, passive in certain cases; as, i kukui, i wai, i noho, bring a lamp, water, &c.

'I with an apostrophe before it, is a contraction after *a* of the preceding word, for *ai;* as, malaila kahi i waihoia'i ka waiwai, for waihoia *ai.*

I, *v.* To speak; to say, in connection with the thing spoken or said. *Kin.* 1:3 and 20.

2. To address one; to make a speech to one; often SYN. with olelo. *Kin.* 3:1. *I* mai la ia i ka wahine, he *said* to the woman (after this follows what was said.)

3. To say within one's self. *Kanl.* 18:21.
4. To pronounce a single word, as a signal. *Lunk.* 12:6.
5. To give an appellation, and SYN. with kapa. *Isa.* 32:5. To designate the name of a person. *Oih.* 9:36.

I, *v.* To beget, as a father.

I, *s.* Name of the papaia fruit and tree. See II.

IA, *v. Hoo.* To enter; to be received, as into the mouth.

IA, *v.* To beat or pound, as in making kapa.

IA, *s.* The name of the mallet used in beating kapa.

IA, *prep.* Used before proper names of

persons, and before pronouns, as *i* is before common nouns. See I, *prep.* It signifies, to ; of ; for ; by ; with ; on account of ; in respect of, &c. See *Gram.* § 126, 6.

IA, *adv.* In the beginning of a sentence, and before a pronoun, it refers to time; when ; at that time, &c.; as, *ia* lakou i noho ai ilaila, *while* they lived there ; *ia* manawa. make iho la ke alii, at *that* time the chief died.

IA, *pers. pron.*, third pers. sing. He ; she ; it ; more rarely in the sense of *it*, for which Hawaiians use a periphrasis ; thus : *ia* kanaka, *ia* wahine, *ia* mea, kela, keia, &c. *Gram.* § 137, 140, 3d.

IA, *pron. adj.* This ; that ; according as the thing referred to is present or absent.

IA annexed to verbs, forms the passive voice of all the conjugations ; as, ua *alohaia* mai kakou, we *are beloved.* This sign of the passive voice may be annexed to the verb and form one word. or it may be separated, one or more words intervening ; as, na *lawe* malu *ia* ke dala, the money *was taken* secretly. *Gram.* § 211. NOTE.— Sometimes letters are inserted before the *ia* ; as, *awahia*, it is bitter, for *awaia*.

IA'-U, *pron. pers.*, 1st pers. A contraction of *ia au;* the auialo (accusative or objective case) of *au;* me ; to me ; for me ; by me. &c. *Gram.* § 126, 6th auialo.

I-A-HA, *adv. int.* See AHA. For what ? to what ? *iaha* la ka makemake? for what is the desire ?

IA-LO-KO, *s. Ia*, prep., and *loko*, internal. That which is inside ; what belongs inside.

I-O, *s.* Part ; portion ; reality ; truth ; verity. *Ezek.* 12:23.

I-O, *s.* A forerunner; one who announces the approach of a chief.

I-O, *adj.* True ; real ; not imaginary ; ua paa ka mauao o kanaka he akua *io* no o Lono, the minds of the people were firm that Lono (Captain Cook) was a *real* god.

I-O, *adv.* Truly ; really ; verily ; certainly ; *oiaio*, truth. *Io* is a strong intensive. Pela *io* no ka hana ana a lakou ; aohe *io* o ka hewa, the wickedness is great.

I-O, *adv. I*, prep., and *o*, there. Yonder; aia no ia *io*, there he is yonder. See O. *Io* ia nei, adverbial phrase, hither and thither.

I-O, *prep.* Nearly SYN. with *ia;* used before proper names and pronouns. To ; towards. *Iob.* 5:1. But implying motion.

I-U, *adj.* Prohibited ; sacred ; tabooed ; applied to everything within the reach of the kapu : *iu kahi* o ke alii, ano, makau, *sacred* is the place of the chief, it is conse-

crated. it is to be feared.

I-U, *s.* A consecrated place ; he kapu ke alii, noho i ka *iu* la, the king is kapu, he sits in the *sacred place.*

I-U, *v. Hoo.* To lay a kapu for a particular time; e *hoofu* aku i kekahi manawa.

I-U-I-U, *v.* To be afar off; high up; to live in some sacred. kapu ,place. NOTE.— The ideas of *far off* or *high up* seem to be connected with sacredness. or separation from everything common. See HEMOLELE.

I-U-I-U, *s.* A place supposed to be afat off or high up above the earth or beneath the ocean, sacred to the dwelling place of God ; ke Akua noho i ka *iuiu*, the God

I-HA, *v.* To be intent upon; persevering at ; to desire greedily ; ua *iha* wale no, he gives his whole attention.

I-HA-I-HA, *adj.* Firmly drawn, as a rope; ua *ihaiha* ke kaula, na maloeloe, strained.

I-HA-I-HA, *adj.* Ua *ihaiha* ka puukole i ka mimi, ua iheihe ; ua hele a *ihaiha* wale ka poe hana hewa, e hana mau ma ka hewa; to draw in, restrain, as one desiring to fulfill a call of nature. and is restrained by the presence of some one ; so also having a desire to lasciviousness.

I-HE, *s.* A spear. *Ios.* 8:18. *Ihe* hulali, a glittering spear; a javelin. *Nah.* 25:7. He *ihe* pakelo ; *ihe* pahee a me na *ihe* o, the hand staves and the spears.

I-HE-A, *adv. int. I* and *hea*, where ? To what place ? whither ? *ihea* oukou? where are you going ?

I-HO, *v.* To go down ; to descend, as from a higher to a lower place. *Nah.* 12:5. To go down from an eminence. *Puk.* 19:24. E *iho* ana i ka pall. descending a precipice.

2. *Hoo.* To cause to descend ; to bring down, as a punishment. 1 *Nal.* 2:9.

3. To cause to fall. *Ezek.* 26:20.

I-HO, following nouns or pronouns, is equivalent to *self* or *selves;* as, e malama ia oukou *iho*, take care of your *selves ;* eia ko'u manao no'u *iho*, here is my opinion of *myself.* It is equivalent to *own* after a possessive ; as, kona *iho*, his *own.*

I-KE, *v.* To see, perceive by the eye.

2. To see, perceive mentally, i. e., to know ; understand.

3. A form of sending love to an absent one ; as, e *ike* aku oe iā mea, do you salute such a one.

4. To receive, as a visitor or a messenger.

5. To know ; to have carnal knowledge of. *Kin.* 4:1 and 19:5.

6. *Hoo.* To exhibit ; to show ; to point out ; to cause to know : to give testimony in a court concerning one.

I-ke, *s.* Knowledge; instruction; ka *ike*, the person having knowledge. *Puk.* 4:11. Understanding. *Kanl.* 4:6. A parting salutation ; as, e *ike.*

I-ke-a, *v.* Used for *ikeia*, the passive of *ike. Gram.* § 211. It has also the regular passive *ikeia.* To be seen; to be known; to appear. *Puk.* 16:10.

2. *Hoo.* To be exhibited ; manifested.

I-ke-a-ka, *v. Ike*, to know, and *aka*, clear. To know clearly; to perceive distinctly. Syn. with ikepaka, ikelea.

I-ke-i-ke, *v.* See Ike. To see; to know, &c. *Hoo.* To explain ; to exhibit; to show ; to bear witness. *Sol.* 10:32.

I-lo-ko, *prep. I* and *loko*, internal. In ; inside of; within. *Gram.* § 161.

I-lu-na, *prep. I* and *luna*, above. Up ; upward ; upon ; above. *Gram.* § 161.

I-nai-na, *v.* To shake; to move; to stir ; paonioni.

I-nai-na, *s.* Anger; hatred. *Kin.* 3:15. Malice ; wrath.

I-no, *v.* To hurt; to injure ; to render uncomfortable ; oia ka mea e *ino* ai ke kino, that is what *injures* the body.

2. To be or become worthless. *Jer.* 18:4.
3. *Hoo.* To disfigure. *Oihk.* 19:27. To trouble with evil. *Puk.* 7:27.
4. To punish ; to afflict ; to suffer evil.
5. To reproach ; to vex ; to tease ; to harass.
6. To curse.

I-no, *s.* Iniquity. *Puk.* 37:7. Depravity ; anything which is contrary to the general good.

2. The poor quality of a thing ; eia kekahi, o ke *ino* o ka pepa a me ka inika, the poor quality of the paper and ink.
3. The substance in the intestines ; bonowa.
4. *Hoo.* Violence ; iniquity ; cursing.
5. A gale ; a storm of wind and rain ; he *ino* huhu, a horrible tempest.

I-no, *adj.* Bad ; wicked ; vile ; sinful ; mea *ino*, an abomination ; an evil thing. *Mat.* 24:15.

I-no, *adv.* Badly ; wickedly.

I-no. A strong intensive, used in both a good and bad sense ; it expresses very great feeling of affection or hatred ; aloha *ino*, very great love, or with a peculiar tone of voice, very great contempt ; he mea minamina *ino* ka waa, a thing of *very great* loss is the canoe.

I-no-i-no, *v.* See Ino above. To make sad ; to be grieved ; no ke aha la i *inoino* ai kou maka? why is your countenance sad? *Neh.* 2:2.

2. To be very tempestuous, as the sea. *Iona.* 1:13.
3. *Hoo.* To defile ; to deface ; to pollute.

I-no-i-no, *s.* Badness ; worthlessness ; indecency ; ua like ka *inoino* me ka pupuka, a me ka pelapela, a me ke alauka.

2. A bad disposition ; a mind for doing harm. *Laieik.* 101.

I-no-i-no, *adj.* Very poor; lean; miserable ; despicable.

I-no-a. *s.* A name : name of a person.

I-pu, *s.* A general name for all kinds of gourds. calabashes, melons, pumpkins, &c.

2. A general name for small containers, as dish, cup, mug, tumbler, &c. *Kanl.* 23:25. Each kind is designated by some additional word expressive of its quality or use, which see under their own names.

O, the fourth letter of the Hawaiian alphabet. It is the easiest sounded, next to *a*, of all the letters. Its sound is mostly that of the long English o in *note*, *bone*, &c. There is a difference in some words among Hawaiians as to the quantity ; some say *mahope*, others say *mahoppy*. The first is the more correct.

O. This letter is prefixed to nouns, both common and proper, as well as to pronouns, to render them emphatic or definite. This *o* should be carefully distinguished from *o* the preposition. It may be called the *o emphatic*. It is used in particularizing one or more persons or things from others. The *o* emphatic stands only before the auikumu or *nominative* case. *Gram.* § 53.

O, *prep.* Of; belonging to ; ka hale *o* ke alii, the house *of* the chief ; it is synonymous with ko ; as, *ko* ke alii hale, the chief's house ; but the words require to be differently disposed. In a few words it is interchangeable with *a*. See A *prep.* As, ka pane ana *o* ka waha, and ka pane ana *a* ka waha, the opening *of* the mouth.

O, *s.* A place, but indefinitely ; mai *o* a *o*, from there to there ; throughout. *Puk.* 27:18. From one side to the other ; *io* a *io* ae, this way or that way ; here or there. More generally used adverbially ; as,

O, *adv.* Yonder; there; ma *o* aku, beyond ; mai *o* a *o*, from here to there, or from yonder to yonder, i. e., *everywhere*. It takes the several prepositions *no, ko, i, ma, mai. Gram.* § 165, 2d.

O is sometimes prefixed to the imperative mood instead of *e ;* as. *o* hele oe, go thou, instead of *e* hele oe ; *o* hoi oukou i na la, ekolu, return ye for three days. In this case, for the sake of euphony, the *o* may take an *u* after it ; as, *ou* hoi olua, return ye two.

O, *conj.* Lest. This is one form of the subjunctive mood; as, mai ai onkou o make. eat not *lest* ye die; also. *Nah.* 14:42.

O, *v.* To pierce, as with a sharp instrument; to dot into; to prick; to stab. SYN. with hou and ou. See Ou.

2. To thrust; to thrust through; to gore, as a bullock. *Puk.* 21:28. A o iho la kekahi i ka polulu, some one *pierced* him with a long spear. See Oo. PASS. To be pierced, stabbed; hence, to be killed; to be pierced with a spear; mai oia ke kanaka i ka ihe. *Oia,* passive of *o,* to plunge under water, as a canoe or surf-board.

3. To extend or reach out, as the hand or finger; o ka mea e ae mai, e o mai lakou i ko lakou lima, those who assent, let them *stretch out* their hands; to stretch out the hand to take a thing. *Kin.* 8:9.

4. To stretch out the hand to trouble or afflict. *Puk.* 8:2.

5. To dip, as the fingers in a fluid. *Oihk.* 4:6. Hoo, for *hoo-o.* To stretch out, as the hand. *Puk.* 14:27. To thrust in the hand or finger into an orifice. *Anat.* 45.

O, *v.* To call for a thing desired. *Sol.* 2:3.

2. To answer to a call. *Ier.* 7:13. To answer to one's name when called; aohe i o mai, he *answered* not.

O, *s. Art.,* ke. An instrument to pierce with; any sharp pointed instrument; a fork; a sharp stick; ke o bipi, an ox goad. *Lunk.* 3:30. Ke o manamana kolu, a three-pronged fork. 1 *Sam.* 2:13.

2. The effect for the cause; a sharp pain in the body; a stitch in the side. as if pierced by a sharp instrument; a keen darting pain in the side of the chest.

O, *s.* Provision for a journey; travel-ing food. *Puk.* 12:39. E hoomakaukau oukou i o no oukou, prepare *food* for yourselves (for your journey); provision for a voyage; ke kalua iho la no ia o ke o holo i ka moana, that was the preparing the *provision* to go on the ocean.

O, *s.* The sprit of a sail.

O, *s.* The sound of a small bell; a tinkling sound. See OE.

O-A, *v.* To burst over, as a swollen stream.

2. To exceed; to go beyond; to pass over the point intended.

3. To shout, as a multitude of voices.

4. To roll, as a stone over a hill, or toss it over.

5. To change conversation.

O-AU, *pers. pron.,* 1st pers. sing. See AU. I; the o is emphatic, and sounded quickly with the following a, it becomes

o,. as *wau;* when the o is a little more heard, it becomes *owau;* hence the several forms:
1. *Au,* I, simple form.
2. *Oau,* I. with o emphatic.
3. *Wau,* I, the o and a sounded quickly together—*w.*
4. *Owau,* I, the third form again emphatic—*owau.* See these several forms in their places.

O-E, *pers. pron.,* second pers. sing. Thou; you; like *au,* it often takes o emphatic, as *ooe;* no kau i manao ai, *you* thought of yourself; e noho oe me ka makaukau, do *you* sit ready.

O-I, *v.* To project out or over; to go beyond: exceed; generally with *mamua. Ioan.* 13:16.

2. To be more in any way; to be more excellent; to be greater naturally or morally; to be better. *Puk.* 1:9. To be excessive in some condition; as, ua oi paa loa, aole e hemo, it is very firmly fixed, it will not be moved.

O-I, *adj.* First; most excellent; greater; the best.

2. Sharp; full of sharp points; sharp. as a knife; ka hoana oi. the sharp hone; ke apuapu oi, the sharp file.

3. Poor; thin in flesh, that is, having sharp features.

O-I, O-I-AI, *adv.* While; whilst; during some time when a thing was doing; e hele i ka malamalama, oi kau ke ea i ke kino; oi huli wale lakou ia ia, *while* they sought for him in vain; while yet. 2 *Sam.* 3:35.

O-IA, *pers. pron.,* third pers. sing. He, she, or it; the o is emphatic. See IA. *Gram.* § 53 and 54, 3. Oia no wau, I am *he;* o ka laau hua ole, oia kana e oki aku, the branch not fruitful, *that* he cuts off; it is not so often used for things as for persons; oia iho no, he by himself. 1 *Nal.* 18:6.

O-I-A, *v.* To continue; to endure; to remain the same; oia mau no ia. it is always the same; he oia ka mea hawawa i ka heenalu. hai ka papa. the awkward person *always* breaks the board in riding on the surf. *Hoo.* To consent; to affirm; to assent; to confess; to admit a truth or fact; to profess. *Kanl.* 26:3. To avouch. *Kanl.* 26:17, 18. NOTE.—The ideas of being, existence, continuance. firmness and truth are from the same root, and has the same form as the third pers. sing. of the pronoun, and supply in some measure the place of the substantive verb. See *Gram.* § 136, 1st.

O-I-A, *adv.* Yes; it is so; a strong affirmative.

O-I-AI, *adv.* While; whilst, &c. See OI. *Oiai e ola ana kakou i keia manawa, while* we are living at the present time.

O-IA-I-O, *s. Oia,* truth, and *io,* real.
1. Truth; verity; what is true; uprightness.
2. *Hoo.* A pledge; a thing given in pledge for another; a pawn. *Kin.* 38:20.

OI-A-I-O, *v. Hoo.* To declare to be true; to affirm; to verify; to prove. 1 *Nal.* 8:26.
2. To confess as an article of belief; to acknowledge; to trust in. *Kanl.* 1:32.

OI-A-I-O, *adv.* Truly; verily; of a truth. *Ioan.* 3:3. A strong asseveration of truth.

O-IO, *s.* A company or troop of ghosts; he huakai uhane; the same in respect of ghosts as *huakai* is in respect of men.

O-O-E, *pers. pron.,* second pers. sing., *o* emphatic. See *Gram.* § 131. Thou; you. See OE. In the following cases it seems to be used in the auipili; *ooe ke kukulu ana o keia hale*; *ooe ka humu ana a keia pea. Ooe* is used often in *Laieikawai* for *ou,* of thee; *nawai ke kama ooe. Laieik.* 176.

OU, *pers. pron.,* second pers. sing., gen. of *oe.* Thine; yours; belonging to you. Sometimes it is used for *kou,* thy; thine; as, *me ou poe kanaka,*instead of me *kou* poe, &c.; *ou mau kamalii,* thy children. *Gram.* § 132, 1.

OU is sometimes used for *o* in the imperative; as, *ou hele oukou. Mat.* 2:8; *Neh.* 8:5. See *Gram.* § 192, last sentence. The *o* of this imperative is often written *ou.*

O'U, *pers. pron.,* first pers. sing., genitive of *au.* My; mine; of me; belonging to me. *Gram.* § 124, 1.

OU-KOU, *pers. pron.,* second pers. plural. Ye; you.

O-U-LI, *s.* A change in the appearance of a thing.
2. Character; kind; description; applied to many things; *he ouli okoa*; *ua maopopo ka ouli o ka poe hana hewa,* ma ka lakou hana ana.
3. A sign; a token of the approach of a storm or calamity; an omen; a sign in the heavens.
4. Form; change; meaning of a word.
5. A sign of something expected; an earnest or pledge; *e lawe i ka ouli ao,* me ka *ouli* hana i pono ai oe i ka maka o kau poe haumana.

6. A sign or signal of divine authority. *Puk.* 4:28.
7. A wonder, i. e., a thing wondered at.

O-LA, *s.* A recovery from sickness; a state of health after sickness; an escape from any danger or threatened calamity.
2. A living, that is, the means of life, food; e pii ana au i ke *ola,* I am going up (the hill) for life, i. e., to procure food.
3. Life; the period of one's life; living; while one lives. '
4. Life; salvation; deliverance from spiritual death. NOTE.—This last (4) definition is a modern one introduced with the Christian system, and is often used in the Hawaiian Bible along with definitions 1st, 2d and 3d.

O-LA, *v.* To be saved from danger; to live after being in danger of death; to recover from sickness; to get well; i mai la o Kamehameha, ina e *ola* keia mai ana o'u; to enjoy an escape from any evil.
2. To live upon, or by means of a thing without which one would die; *ola* no hoi na iwi, proverbial expression: poverty (bones) shall be supplied, prosperity shall flourish. *Laieik.* 124. See IWI 7.
3. *Hoo.* To cause to live, i. e., to save one, or to save alive. *Ios.* 6:25. To cause to escape, as one in danger; to deliver from. *Puk.* 14:30. To heal, as a disease.
4. To save, i. e., cause to escape from future misery. See note under the noun for the new modern idea of the word.

O-LA, *adj.* Alive; escaped; living in opposition to *dead;* o kou alii make no, a me kou alii *ola.*

O-LA, } *v.* The sense from the
O-LA-O-LA, } sound.
1. To gaggle; to gargle water in the throat.

O-LA-HO-NU-A, *adv.* Thoroughly; entirely; altogether; o ka hoomaka ana, ua like no la me ke ao ana i *olahonua* i ka palapala; i *olahonua,* i pau ka noho hemahema ana. See HONUA, *adv.*

O-LE, *v.* To be not; to cease to exist. 1 *Sam.* 2:31. To pass away. *Iob.* 24:24. A e *ole* loa hoi, and to be no more. *Hal.* 39:14. Aole e *ole. Luk.* 21:9. A ua *ole* ia, and it is gone. *Hal.* 103:16.
2. To not, or not to do a thing, with an Infinitive. *Rom.* 8:32.
3. *Hoo.* To deny; refuse; make void; abrogate.
4. To answer, or plead *not guilty* to a charge.
5. To refuse; forbid; rebuke. NOTE.— *Ole* often has the form of a verb, when it serves only to express negation.

O-LE, *s.* Nothingness; vanity; in vain. *Oihk.* 26:20. Aole ka *ole,* without fail; the not; the negative; ka *ole,* no existence.

Ezek. 12:19.

2. The want; the lack; the destitution of a thing; make ia no ka *ole* o ka ai, he died for the *not* (want) of food. *Iob.* 4:11.

3. *Hoo.* A denial; a want of truth; inability; nothingness.

O-LE, *adv.* A negative; no; not; nor; a particle of deprivation like *un* and *less* in English. See AOLE. *Aole* is used *before* a noun or verb, and *ole* after it.

O-LE, *v.* To speak through the throat

O-LE-LO, *v.* See LEO, voice, and LELO, the tongue. To speak; to say; (it implies a more formal or longer speech than *i* or *hai*); to converse.

2. To teach; to call; to invite, as to a feast. *Ioan.* 2:12.

3. To give a name. *Isa.* 56:7. E *olelo* hooweliweli, to threaten. *Oih.* 4:17. E *olelo* hooino, to curse. *Nal.* 22:17. E *olelo* hoomaikai, to bless; e *olelo* hoonani, to glorify; e *olelo* pohihi, to speak mystically, darkly. *Ioan.* 16:25. Opposite to *olelo akaka. Ioan.* 16:20.

O-LU-A, *pers. pron.*, second pers. dual. You two. *Gram.* § 132, 2d.

U, the fifth letter of the Hawaiian alphabet. It represents generally the sound of the English *oo*, as in *too, coo, fool*, &c.; but when preceded by *i*, it sometimes has the sound of the English *u* or *yu*; as, *waiu, waiyu*; iuka, *yuka*.

U, *v.* To protrude; to rise on the toes; to prepare to stand up; to draw out, as a pencil from a case.

2. To weep. *Mat.* 5:4. To grieve; to mourn. *Hal.* 38:6. E u hele, to go about mourning; to mourn for, i. e., desire earnestly; i kekahi manao o'u e u nei, e ao kakou i ka leo o ka himeni.

3. To drip or drizzle, as water; to ooze or leak slowly, as water from a kalo patch or from the crevices of a rock; e kahe ae.

U, *v.* To be tinctured or impregnated with anything; as, ua u ka pipi i ka paakai; ua u ke kapa i ka mea hooluu; u ke kapa i ka ua.

U, *s.* The breast of a female. *Ezek.* 23:8.

U, *s.* Grief; sorrow; expression of affection; like me ke aloha, ame ka u, ame ka uwe ana.

2. The breast. *Luk.* 23:29. The pap; the udder; hence, with *wai*, milk, i. e., *waiu.* LIT. Breast water.

3. Unwillingness; not disposed to do.

U-A, *v.* See Gr. *uo*, Malay *ujan*, to wet; to rain. To rain; ua iho la ka *ua*, he *ua* nui loa. LIT. The rain *rained*, it was a very great rain.

2. *Hoo.* To send or give rain; to cause to rain. *Kin.* 7:4.

U-A, *s.* Rain; water falling from the clouds. 1 *Sam.* 12:17, 18. Rains were divided by Hawaiians into ua *loa*, long rains; ua *poko*, short rains; ua *hea*.

U-A, *adj.* Vain; useless; to no profit.

U-A, *adv.* In vain; to no purpose; manao no ka poe kahiko ua luhi ua ka lakou hana ana.

U-A, *pron. dem. adj. Ua* before a noun, and *la* or *nei* after it, forms a strong demonstrative adjective pronoun; this; that; as *la* or *nei* is used. It refers to some noun that has just been mentioned. *Ua* kanaka *nei, this* man (just spoken of); hiolo *ua* mau hale *la, those* houses (just mentioned) have fallen down. *Gram.* § 152.

U-A-LO, *v.* To cry; to call out; to complain; to call for help. *Hal.* 4:1. See UOLO.

U-A-LO, *s.* A complaining; a crying to one for help.

U-A-NA, *adv. Ua*, sign of the perfect tense, and *na*, quiet, enough, &c. See NA, *v.* It is enough; it is sufficient; a plenty.

U-HA, *adj.* Slipping away; not easily held, as a cunning rogue.

2. Greedy; craving; eating often.

U-HA, *v.* To belch up wind.

2. To hawk up mucus; to hawk, as a means of raising phlegm from the throat or lungs. See PUHA.

3. To swell; to distend, as the stomach.

4. To squander; to misspend; to waste; to misuse property. See UHAUHA.

U-HA, *s.* The thigh; the thigh of a person. *Lunk.* 3:16.

2. The ham of a hog.

U-HAU, *s.* A whip to strike with. *Nahum.* 3:2.

U-HAU-A, *s.* The stones; the testicles of the male. *Iob.* 40:17.

U-HA-U-HA, *v.* See UHA 4. To live in a wasteful manner; to squander property.

2. To live in every indulgence of passion; a noho *uhauha* ke alii me ka inu rama ame ka aie, the king lived in a *reveling manner*, drinking rum and going into debt.

U-HA-U-HA, *adj.* Riotous; gluttonous; reveling.

U-HA-NE, *s.* See HANE and HANEHANE in the meles. The soul; the spirit of a person. *Oihk.* 5:1. He mea ninau i na *uhane* ino, a consulter of evil *spirits. Kanl.* 18:11. He kino wailua.

2. The ghost or spirit of a deceased person.

3. The Spirit; applied to the third person of the Trinity. *Ioan.* 1:32. *Uhane* Hemolele, the Holy Spirit. NOTE.—Hawaiians supposed that men had two souls each; that one died with the body, the other lived on either visible or invisible as might be, but had no more connection with the person deceased than his shadow. These ghosts could talk, cry, complain, whisper, &c. There were those who were supposed to be skillful in entrapping or catching them.

U-HA-NE, *adj.* Spiritual. 1 *Kor.* 15:44. Partaking of the spirit or soul.

U-HA-NE, *adv.* Me ka hoi *uhane* aku hoi i Kauai. *Laieik.* 95. Their flesh eaten by the birds, they would return as to their souls only to Kauai.

U-HE-NE, } *v.* See HENEHENE, to
U-HE-NE-HE-NE, } mock. To use vile and lascivious language between the sexes.

U-HI, *v.* To cover over a thing so as to hide it; to cover or hide, as the water covers what is in the bottom of the sea. *Puk.* 15:10.

2. To cover. i. e., spread over the country, as an army. *Nah.* 22:5. To cover; to hide, as a sin, i. e., to forgive it. *Neh.* 4:5.

3. *Hoo.* To veil; to cover with a veil, as the face. *Kin.* 24:65.

4. To spread over a cover; to conceal, as a cloud. *Kin.* 9:14. *Uhi* uha mai ka pelo o ka lua ahi, *uhi* mai ka leo o ke ahi o ka pele.

5. To be smothered, as the voice of one by the voices of many; ua *uhiia* kona leo e ka haukamumu. *Laieik.* 22.

U-HI, *s.* A covering; a veil. *Puk.* 26:14.
2. A fence; a protection.

U-HI-KI-NO, *s. Uhi,* to cover, and *kino,* the body. A covering for the body; a shield. *Hal.* 35:2.

U-HI-NA, *s.* A net for taking fish.

U-HI-NI, *s.* An insect something like a grasshopper; the word has been used in the Bible for grasshopper. *Nah.* 13:33. For locust. *Puk.* 10:14. Mai ai oe i ka *uhini;* by a change of letters. See UNIHI. *Uhini* huluhulu, a canker worm. *Nahum.* 3:15. *Uhini* hulu ole, the palmer worm. *Ioel.* 1:4. *Uhini* opio hulu ole. *Ioel.* 2:25.

U-HI-NI, *adj.* Thin; slender; small; almost broken; puahilo.

U-HI-NI-PI-LI, *s.* The leg and arm bones bound up together; he akua *uhinipili;* they were worshipped in that condition. See UNIHIPILI.

U-HI-NU, *v.* To take advantage of a man's ignorance in a bargain; to deceive in that way.

U-HI-PAA, *v. Uhi,* to cover, and *paa,* fast. To cover up entirely so as to be out of sight, as a cloud or fog. *Laieik.* 16.

U-HOI, *v.* See HOI, to return. To return from following one; to turn back. 2 *Sam.* 2:26.

2. To unite together; to live and sleep together, as a man and wife once separated.

U-HO-LA, *v.* See HOLA. To unfold; to spread out, as the wings of a bird.
2. To spread down, as a mat.

U-LA-LA, *s.* Insanity; madness. *Kekah.* 9:13.
2. A crazy person.

U-LA-LA, *adj.* Crazy; demented; out of one's senses.

U-LA-NA, *v.* To weave; to plait; to braid; to intertwine, as vines. *Puk.* 28:32. To wreathe; to weave. 2 *Nal.* 25:17. E *ulana* moena, to braid or weave a mat.

U-LA-NA, *adj.* Lying still or calm, as the surface of water unruffled by wind.
2. Idle; unemployed; lulana, heha, molowa.

U-LA-NA, *adj.* Iwi *ulana. Kam.,* B. 2, p. 7, 3. The prophecy or expression of the kilokilo when looking upon a person in good health, meaning he will soon die.

U-LU, *v.* To grow, as a plant. *Isa.* 53:2.
2. To increase in any way; to grow, as a disease in the skin. *Oihk.* 13:39.
3. To become strong or excessive, as in anger, with *puni. Puk.* 32:22. To grow or increase, as good or evil in a community.
4. To grow up, as men. *Iob.* 31:18.
5. To grow in size and strength, as an infant. 1 *Pet.* 2:2.
6. To be extensively known, as a report.
7. To have spiritual possession, either good or bad; to be inspired; in this sense, mostly in the passive; as, *uluia* or *uluhia. Mat.* 8:16. To influence the affections.

U-LU-IA, *v.* See ULU. *Uluia* is the passive. To be possessed by a spirit; to be inspired; more often written with *h* inserted, *uluhia.* See ULUHIA below.

U-LU-HI-A, *v.* See ULU and ULUIA above. *Uluhia, h* inserted, to be possessed by a spirit; to be influenced or under the direction of some spirit without the person. *Mat.* 4:24.

U-NI-HI, *s.* A species of grasshopper. See UHINI. He mea ebeu liilii me he pinao

la, a little winged thing like the dragon-fly; he mea lele.

U-NI-HI, *adj.* Small; thin; spindle legged; hence,

2. Weak; without strength.

U-NI-HI-PI-LI, *s.* The leg and arm bones of a person. See UHINIPILI. He kanaka mai loa a hiki ole ke hele mawaho; ua unihipili leo, aole hiki ke pane mai, having a feeble voice, not able to speak; ua uuku ka leo. Unihipili was one name of the class of gods called akuanoho; aumakua was another; they were the departed spirits of deceased persons.

U-NI-HI-PI-LI, *adj.* The qualities of some gods; na akua unihipili. ame na akua mano.

U-PE-NA, *s.* A net for taking fish; a snare for catching birds; e malama i ka upena nanana, take heed to the spider's web; upena papale oho, net work. *Isa.* 3:18. *FIG.* Anything for entrapping one in evil; ua makau au i ka upena o ka make, I am afraid of the snares of death.

2. The cord of which fish nets were made; ke aho i hooliloia i upena.

U-PE-NA-NA-NA-NA, *s. Upena* and *nanana,* spider. The web of the nanana, a certain kind of spider. See NANANA.

U-WE, *v.* See UE. To weep; to mourn; to cry for help for one's self or others. *Nah.* 11:18. To mourn. *Kin.* 32:2.

2. To cry in behalf of one, i. e., to pray for him. *Puk.* 8:8.

3. To bewail; to lament for. *Oihk.* 10:16.

4. To cry out for pain; pepehi iho la na kanaka, a uwe ae la ua mau haole la no ka eha, the men (natives) struck them, and those foreigners cried out for pain.

5. To salute, as friends. *Mat.* 5:47. To bid good-by at parting. *Oih.* 18:18.

H, the sixth letter of the Hawaiian alphabet. It represents, as in English, the sound of an aspirate. It is frequently euphonic. particularly between the verb and its passive termination *ia;* as. *maluhia* instead of *maluia.* In this case it is sometimes changed for *l;* as, *kaulia* for *kauia.* See *Gram.* § 48.

HA. A particle expressing strong affirmation, stronger than *no;* as, oia hoi *ha,* so it is *indeed;* truly; certainly; indeed; i mai ia, ua hewa *ha* oe, he said you are *indeed* guilty; e hele hoi *ha* wau, I will *surely* go. *Puk.* 2:7.

HA is often prefixed to the original root of a word, or inserted when it takes the causative *hoo;* as, *inu,* to drink; *hoohainu,* to give drink; *like,* to be like; *hoohalike,* to resemble. It is also often prefixed to

the roots of words without any apparent modification of the sense; in other words, the sense is variously modified: as. *hauli,* a dark color. See ULI, blue. &c. *Lalo,* down; *halalo,* to turn the eyes and head down, to think, reflect.

HA is also used in reciting meles in the middle of a line as *a, o, e,* &c., are at the end for the voice to rest upon while cantillating, as he ana *ha* nui keia no ke auhee

la, where *ha* has no meaning except as the voice protracts the syllable.

HA, *num. adj.* The number four; generally prefixed by *a* or *e.* See AHA and EHA. *Ha* seems to be the original word for the numeral four; as, wawae *ha,* four feet. It becomes an ordinal by prefixing the article; as. *ka ha,* 'the fourth. *Mat.* 14:25. I ka *ha* o ka la, the fourth day; i ka *ha* o ka makahiki. *Oihk.* 19:25.

HA, *s.* See the foregoing. On fours; by fours; e hele ana ma na *ha,* going on four (feet.) *Oihk.* 11:20. 21.

HA, *v.* To breathe; to breathe with some exertion; to utter a strong breath; different from *hanu,* to breathe naturally. *Iob.* 15:30. It is connected with *hanu* in *Kin.* 7:15.

2. *FIG.* To breathe revenge. *Oih.* 9:1.

3. To breathe upon; *ha* ke Akua i ka lewa, God breathed into the open space. *Mele of Kekupuohi.* To breathe out; to expire.

HA, *s.* A breathing; a strong breathing.

2. A strong forced breath, as of anger. *Iob.* 4:9.

3. The expression of anger. 2 *Tes.* 2:8.

4. *FIG.* Light; transitory, as a breath or breathing. *Hal.* 62:9.

HA, *s.* A trough for water to run through; a water pipe; in modern times, a lead or iron pipe through which water flows. See HAWAI.

HA, *v.* To dance; *ha* ana, a dancing; more generally written *haa,* which see.

HA, *s.* A species of wood; ohia *ha* or *hau.*

HAA, *v.* To dance; connected among Hawaiians with singing. 1 *Sam.* 18:6. As an act of worship formerly among the Jews. 2 *Sam.* 6:14.

HA-AE, *v.* To drizzle; to drip; to slabber at the mouth.

HAA-WE, *v. Ha* for *haa,* and *awe,* to carry. To carry on the back; to put upon the back or shoulders for carrying. SYN. with *waha.* See AWE and LAWE.

HAA-WE, *s.* A burden. *Isa.* 58:6. A pack carried on the back. *Lunk.* 11:46.

HAA-WI, *v. Ha* for *ho* or *hoo*. See HOAWI and Awi, a root which has not yet been found.
1. To give; to grant to another.
2. To help; to assist.
3. To offer or propose for a thing.
4. To commend to one's care; *haawi* aie, usury. *Kanl.* 23:20. *Haawi* lilo ole, to lend. *Kanl.* 24:10. To give; with *nani*, to ascribe praise. *Isa.* 42:8.

HAA-WI-NA, *s. Haawi* and *ana*, a participial termination.
1. A giving; a giving out; hence,
2. A portion; something given; a gift; a part assigned to one. *Rom.* 11:29.
3. In *school*, a lesson appointed to be learned.
4. A present from one. SYN. with makana.
5. A gift, that is, ability to do a thing. 1 *Kor.* 12:4.

HAE, *adv.* A word expressive of deep affection for another; as, aloha hoi *hae,* from the deep yearning, breaking or tearing of the heart. See HAEHAE below.

HAE-HAE, *v.* See HAE. To tear or rend, as cloth or a garment. *Kin.* 44:13. With *aahu. Ios.* 7:6.
2. To tear in pieces, as a savage beast does a person. *Kin.* 37:33. To tear, as a garment, through grief or indignation. *Nah.* 14:6.
3. To rend, as the mountains in a hurricane. 1 *Nal.* 19:11, 4. See HAE, *adv.*, above.
4. To be moved with compassion; to sympathize with one. *Kanl.* 28:32. *Haehae* na maka, *haehae* ke aloha.

HA-E-LE, *v.* To go or come as *mai* or *aku* is used. SYN. with hele. See HELE. But requires a dual or plural subject. *Nah.* 4:5; *Nah.* 9:17.

HAI, *v.* Often SYN. with hae. See above. To break, as a bargain or covenant. 2 *Nal.* 18:12.
2. To break open; separate, as the lips that are about to speak.
3. To speak of; to mention. *Puk.* 23:13.
4. To tell; declare; confess; relate. *Puk.* 18:8. Ke *hai* ole, not to tell; to keep secret. *Ios.* 2:14.
5. To break off; to stop doing a thing; as, aole *hai* ke hoihoi aku, he does not *cease* (begging) though sent away. NOTE.—The *ha* of this word is sometimes doubled, then it has the form of hahai, to follow, but its signification is to break away or tear away; as. *hahaiia* ka lepa a ua poe kahuna la, the ensign of those priests *was broken* away.

HAI, *pron.* or *adj. Gram.* § 15, 14:3. Another; another person; no *hai,* for another; ia *hai,* to another. *Neh.* 5:5. Hookahi no makamaka, o oe no, aole o *hai,* one only friend, thou art he, there is no *other.*

HAI, *s.* A broken place; hence,
2. A joint of a limb; ka *hai* a mawe, the elbow joint.

HA-I, *v.* To be vain; proud.

HAI, *s.* Name of the god of the poe kuku kapa.
2. A sacrifice at the altar.

HAI, *s.* Name of a particular form of gathering dead bodies slain in war.

HAI-A, *s.* An assemblage; a number, especially of persons; it is used as a prefix to other words.

HAI-NA, *s. Hai,* to speak, and *ana.* A speaking; a declaration.

HAI-AI, *v.* To do over again.
2. To tie up a bundle of food anew; to tie up, as fagots.
3. To cook over again.

HAI-AO, *s. Hai,* sacrifice, and *ao,* day. A sacrifice offered in the daytime in distinction from *haipo,* a night sacrifice.

HAI-O-U-LI, *v. Hai,* to declare, and *ouli,* the sky. To prognosticate; to declare future events from observing the heavens.

HAI-O-LA, *s. Hai,* to declare, and *ola,* life; salvation.
1. One who preaches or declares there is salvation for men.
2. The declaration of such a fact.

HA-I-LI, *s. Ha* and *ili,* skin; surface.
1. A spirit; a ghost.
2. The impression of something fondly remembered; halialia wale mai no ke aloha, hoanoano wale mai no me he *haili* la e kau iho ana maluna, love brought the fond remembrance, it brought solemnity as if a *spirit* rested on him; lele ke aka o ka manao, leleiaka i ka lani; lele ae la ka *haili* o ka ia nui iluna.

HA-I-LI, *v.* To cry out suddenly; to give an alarm.
2. To gasp; to pant for breath. See AILI.

HA-I-LI, *s.* A temple.

HAI-LI-A, *v.* To be frightened; to start suddenly from fear.

HA-I-LI-A-KA, *s.* See HAILI and AKA, shadow. A ghost; a spirit. See HAILI.

HA-I-LI-I-LI, *v.* Root probably *hai,* to speak, and *ili* (see ILI, hoo 7), to use profane language.
1. To revile the gods; to swear profanely; to curse.
2. To speak disrespectfully of one. *Puk.* 21:17.
3. To reproach; to blackguard; to revile. *Ier.* 15:10.

HAI-LO-NA, *v.* To cast or draw lots.

Oih. 1:28. To distribute by lot.
2. To certify by actions that something will be done.
3. To make a signal for some purpose.

HAI-LO-NO, *v. Hai* and *lono,* the news. To tell the news; to spread a report; aohe

HAI-PU-LE, *v. Hai,* to speak, and *pule,* to pray.
1. To speak or say a prayer to the gods.
2. To worship visibly.

HAI-PU-LE, *s.* A devotee; one addicted to worship; a pious person; a saint. *Epes.* 1:1.
2. Piety; profession of religion; outward worship. *Iak.* 1:26.

HAI-PU-LE, *adj.* Pious; devout; religious; religiously disposed; a ike mai o Vanekouva he alii *haipule* o Kamehameha, &c., when Vancouver saw that Kamehameha was religiously disposed, &c.

HA-O, *v.* To rob; to despoil. *Mat.* 12:29. To strip one of property; to plunder. *Lunk.* 2:14.
2. To kill and plunder. 1 *Sam.* 27:10.

HAO-HAO, *v.* To doubt; to discredit; to distrust a statement.
2. To be troubled in accounting for an event; to be restless; sleepless at night; *haohao* hoi keia po o'u, aole wau i moe iki. *Laieik.* 198.
3. To marvel; to wonder. *Isa.* 63:5. To be astonished. *Isa.* 52:14.
4. To be in doubt respecting one's character. *Gal.* 4:20. *Haohao* hewa, to think or design evil.
5. To seek for; to hunt after; to search.

HAO-HAO, *v.* To distribute; to give equally to many; e haawi like me ka puunawe.

HAO-HAO, *v.* To dip up with the hands; to measure by handfuls.

HAO-HAO, *s.* Disappointment; doubt;

HAU, *s.* The general name of snow, ice, frost, cold dew, &c.; i hoomanawanui ai hoi kaua i ka *hau* huihui o ke kakahiaka, when we two also persevered in the cold *frost* of the morning; *hau* paa, hoar frost. *Puk.* 16:14. In the same verse hau is rendered dew; snow. *Nah.* 12:10.
2. The rough bristles of a hog when angry; huhu ka puaa, ku ka *hau;* hence,
3. Anger; applied figuratively to men.
4. Name of a species of soft porous stone.

HAU-HI-LI, *s.* Carelessness in doing a thing; no ka mikioi o ka hana, aole no ka *hauhili,* for the niceness of the work, not for the slovenliness.

HAU-HI-LI, *adj.* Diverging from the

straight path; blundering; false; not to be depended on for truth.

HAU-MA-NA, *v.* To be or act, as a scholar.
2. *Hoo.* To teach, as one teaches scholars; to make scholars or learners of persons.
3. To teach them some art, or convey to them some knowledge they had not before.
4. To instruct, as a scholar or apprentice in any art or handicraft.

HAU-MA-NA, *s.* A scholar; an apprentice: a disciple. *Mat.* 10:1.

HA-U-PU, *v.* To excite; to stir up, as the affections or passions.
2. To suffer with anxiety; to be much excited or moved; ua *haupu* honua ae la ka makaula, the prophet was much *excited. Laieik.* 157.
3. To rise up suddenly in the mind, as a thought.
4. To stir up one to recollection; alaila, e *haupu* la lakou me ka homanao.

HA-U-PU, *s.* The sudden excitement of the passions. NOTE.—This word was used in a moral philosophy for conscience, or the internal monitor; o ka mea i nanea palaka ka *haupu,* alaila aole e ole kona hewa. Afterwards *lunamanao* was used.

HA-HAO, *v.* See HAO. To put or thrust in. *Oihk.* 10:1. To cram down.
2. To put into, as a person into prison. *Oih.* 16:24.
3. To throw or cast wood into a fire.
4. To put into a particular place; to put, as money into a purse; to put, as into a basket. *Mat.* 13:48.
5. To put into one's head; to suggest to the mind; to put words into one's mouth. 2 *Sam.* 14:19.

HA-HAU, *v.* See HAUA. To whip; to strike with a cane, stick, rod, or sword.
2. To scourge; to chasten. *Puk.* 5:14. *Hahauia* kona kua i ke kaula e ka haole, his back was *whipped* with a rope by a foreigner.

HA-HA-HA-NA, *v.* See the root HANA, and *Gram.* § 225. To cause to work; to do; to do frequently; pela laua i *hahahana* ai.

HA-KE, *s.* See Hoo. To resist; stand against. See KE and HOOKEE. To displace; put aside; put away.

HA-KE-A, *adj.* See KEA, white. Pale, as one sick.

HA-KA, *v.* To stare at. FIG. *Hal.* 22:17.
2. To look earnestly at a person or thing for evil. *Hal.* 10:8.
3. To set one's eyes upon a thing with desire. *Dan.* 10:15. Often connected with

pono as an intensive. *Oih.* 1:10. Syn. with nana, and sometimes with maka.

4. A *huka* mai na moa ma ka lani.

Ha-hi, *v.* To tread upon; to trample down; to tread out, as grain. 1 *Tim.* 5:18. To stamp with the feet. *Ezek.* 6:11. To tread or trample upon. See Ehi and Hehi.

Ha-ku, *v.* To dispose of things in order; to put in order.

2. To arrange or tie the feathers in a kahili; to make a wreath or lei; e *haku* i ka lei; e *haku* oe i lehua. *Laieik.* 146.

3. To put words in order, as in poetry; to compose a song.

4. To rule over people, i. e., to put and keep them in order; to act, as a lord over men.

5. By a change of letters, *haku* for *kahu*, to bake fish with hot stones.

6. Fig. The forming of a new affection in the mind; ka manawa i *haku* ai ke aloha ma ka naau.

7. *Hoo.* To rule over; to direct others. *Oihk.* 25:43. *Haku* mele, a composer of songs, i. e., a poet; nana ia i *haku*, he composed it.

Ha-ku, *s.* A lord; a master; an overseer; a ruler. *Oihk.* 21:4.

2. A hard lump of anything; the tongue of a bell; a padlock; a hard bunch in the flesh; the ball of the eye; *haku* onohi; the name of several species of hard stones formerly used in working stone adzes; ua kapaia kela mau pohaku, he *haku* ka koi ka inoa.

Ha-koi-koi, *v.* To rise or swell up, as water.

2. Fig. Ma ka haale o ka manao e pii iluna me he wai la e *hakoikoi* iloko o ka manawa, through the overflow of thoughts rising up like water, the affections flow within.

Ha-la, *v.* To miss the object aimed at. *Lunk.* 20:16. Nou mai la ia, a *hala* ka pohaku; nou hou mai la ia a *hala* hou no; a i ke kolu o ka nou ana, pa aku la; he threw and the stone *missed*; he threw again and *missed* again; the third time he threw he hit.

2. To be gone; to pass away; to pass over.

3. To proceed; to pass onward; to go beyond. *Nah.* 22:18. To pass away, as time.

4. *Hoo.* To miss the object; to cause to err; to be guilty or blame-worthy.

5. To depart from a command, or act in opposition. *Kanl.* 1:43. To err in opinion; to disobey; to object to a request or command; to refuse obedience. *Eset.* 3:3. To

transgress. *Nah.* 14:4.

Ha-la, *s.* A trespass; a sin; an offense; a transgression.

2. A matter of offense. *Kanl.* 9:21.

3. A law case; e imi *hala*, to seek occasion against. *Lunk.* 14:4. Lawe *hala*, a sinner; *hala* ole, without sin; without cause. *Puk.* 34:7.

Ha-la, *adj.* Sinful; wicked; kanaka *hala*, a sinner; one often breaking some law.

Ha-la, *adv.* Sinfully; in a state of sin; hanau *hala*, born a sinner.

Ha-la, *adv.* (Referring to space past over) onward; throughout; even to; up to; he pa pohaku a *hala* i ka lani, a stone wall (reaching) *clear up* to heaven. *Kanl.* 1:28. Also *a hala*, clear up to. *Kanl.* 9:1.

Ha-la-oa, *v.* To project; to stretch out; to extend upwards, as the mast of a ship; to project, as the horns of the sea-egg.

Ha-la-ha-la, *v.* See Hala. To turn aside; to go astray; mostly used in the causative *hoo*.

2. To object to one; to decline a proposition; to find fault with one's words or conduct; aole *hoohalahala* kekahi o lakou, not one of them found fault.

Ha-la-lo, *v.* *Ha* and *lalo*, downward.

1. To take hold of with the arms under, as in taking up a child or anything else.

2. To drop the head downward, as in deep thought.

3. To begin to think. 2 *Oihl.* 20:3. To think within one's self; pela kuu *halalo* ana ia'u iho, so I *thought* within myself.

4. To think or reflect on the moral actions of others. *Kekah.* 8:9.

5. To look earnestly at a thing near or far off; to think closely.

6. To look internally; *halalo* iho la no au a loaa no.

7. To search closely or look for a thing with effort.

Ha-la-na, *v.* *Ha* and *lana*, to float.

1. To overflow, as water over the banks

Ha-la-pa, *v.* In a *prayer*, to bring to pass; to pray that a thing hoped for may be granted; *halapa* i ke mauli kukala ia hale hau.

Ha-la-wai, *v.* To meet, as two persons; to meet, as two lines in an angle.

2. To assemble, as persons for business or for public worship.

3. *Hoo.* To cause to meet with, i. e., to find. *Kin.* 27:20.

4. To come to one for assistance. *Hal.* 59:4.

HA-LE, *s.* A house; a habitation; a dwelling place; mostly for men.
2. A sheltered and inclosed place for any purpose. NOTE.—In ancient times every man was supposed to have six different houses of some size.
1. The *heiau*, house of worship where the idols were kept.
2. The *mua*, the eating house for the husband, and distinct from the eating house of the woman. Husband and wife never ate together. The *mua* was kapu to the wife.
3. The *noa*, the separate house of the wife, but was free for her husband to enter. The woman ate in the hale *noa*.
4. Hale *aina*, the eating house of the wife.
5. The *kua*, the house where the wife beat out kapa.
6. Hale *pea*, the house of separation for the wife during the periods of her infirmity. They had other houses and for other purposes, but these were considered necessary fixtures for every person in respectable standing. See the above words in their places.

HA-LI-A-LI-A, *s.* The rising of a fond recollection of a person or friend in the mind; ke kau mai nei ka *halialia* aloha ia lakou; malaila no ka *halialia* aloha ana, there was the beloved recollection. *Laieik.*

HA-LI-A-LI-A, *v.* To have a recollection of a friend; e *halialia* ana no nae ke aloha ia'u ma na wahi a kaua i ao ai.
2. To become intent, as the mind, or fixed, as thoughts which keep one wakeful.
3. To spring up, as thoughts or affections in the mind; *halialia* ke aloha. See LIA.

HA-LI-A, *s.* A symptom; a premonition; the first beginning of a feeling; ke kau e mai nei ia'u ka *halia* o ka makau, ame ka weliweli. *Laieik.* 180.

HA-MA-MA, *adj.* See HAMA. Open; disclosed.

HA-MA-MA, *adv.* Openly; standing open, as a door. *Ios.* 8:17.

HA-MO, *v.* To stroke over with the hand; to wash the face; to rub or brush, as in cleaning clothes.
2. To besmear with blood; to plaster with lime; to anoint with oil. *Puk.* 29:2. Or ointment. 2 *Sam.* 12:20.
3. To bend or crook the arm, as in doing the foregoing things; to crook round; to bend round, as an oval surface.
4. To be exactly circular, as a good calabash; ua *hamo* ka ipu. See *Ana. Hon.* 10.

HA-NA, *s.* Work; labor; duty; office; calling; trade, &c.; *hana* mana, a miracle;

hana a ka lani, the doing or the work of the chief.

HA-NAI, *v.* From *hana* and *ai.* To feed; to nourish, as the young.

HA-NAI, *s.* Name of the strings that surround a calabash.
2. Kite strings.

HA-NAU, *s.* Child-birth.

HA-NAU, *adv. Hoo.* Ka holoi *hoohanau* hou ana, the washing of regeneration. *Tit.* 3:5.

HA-NA-MA-NA, *s. Hana* and *mana*, supernatural power. The words are often separated; as, *hana mana.*
1. Something done above or beyond human ability; a work of the gods; hence,
2. Used in the Bible for a miracle. NOTE. Hawaiians supposed there was a class of gods having superhuman power, and next to these were the highest chiefs, who were reverenced as gods. Kamehameha was one.

HA-NE-HA-NE, *v.* To cry; to wail, as the ghosts of the dead were supposed to do.

HA-NE-HA-NE, *s.* The wailing or crying of the spirits; hoopihaia i na leo wawalo o ka *hanehane*, me ka leo uwe; (the air) was filled with the voices of lamentation, and crying out and the sound of wailing.

HA-NU, *s.* The breathing; the natural breath.
2. Breath; spirit. FIG. 2 *Oihl.* 9:4. *Hanu wale*, mere existence without enjoyment; vanity. *Iob.* 7:16.

HA-PAI, *v.* To lift up; to elevate; to take up; to carry.

HE, *art.* The indefinite article, answering somewhat to English *a* or *an.* For its various uses, see *Gram.* § 66, 111, Rule 6th, Syntax, &c.

HE-A, *v.* To call; to give an appellation. SYN. with kapa. *Ioan.* 13:13. To call to one; to call one.
2. To choose; to appoint.

HE-A, *s.* A call; a calling out; a cry.

HE-A, *adv. int.* Which? what? when? where? referring to place, *where*; ka hale *hea?* what or which house? ka manawa *hea?* when? what time? &c.; it is declined like a noun. See *Gram.* § 160 and 165. It takes also other prefixes; as, *auhea? pehea?* &c.

HEE, *v.* To melt; to change from a solid to a liquid substance; to run, as a liquid; to flow, as blood or water.

HEE-HEE, *v.* The 13th conj. of *hee.* To flow or melt away; to disappear; to be-

come liquid : to flee in battle; to dip up water with a cup. *Hoo.* To melt away, as an army ; hence, to flee ; to run.
2. A word used in enforcing the highest kapus.

HEI, *s.* A net; a snare for entangling and taking an animal;` applied to men. *Sol.* 29:5.
2. A draught of fish. *Luke* 5:4.
3. Game caught in hunting.
4. A cat's cradle. *Bul.*

HEI, *v.* To entangle, as in a net. *Habak.* 1:15.
2. FIG. To be insnared or entangled with difficulty. 1 *Tim.* 3:7.
3. To catch and entangle one by the neck or legs ; i mea e *hei* ai ka a-i, ka wawae paha.
4. *Hoo.* To catch in a net. FIG. *Luke* 5:10. To entrap, entangle. &c.; ua makau au i ka mea kii mai ia'u e *hoohei* aku, I am afraid of him who shall come to *entrap* me.

HEI-AU, *s.* A small secret room in the large temple.
2. A large temple of idolatry among Hawaiians ; a temple for the worship of one or more of the gods ; e kukulu oe i mau *heiau* no na akua, no Ku, no Lono, no Kane ame Kanaloa, build thou some *temples* for the gods, for Ku, for Lono, for Kane and Kanaloa.
3. The *heiau* was one of the six houses of every man's regular establishment—the house for the god ; eono hale o na kanaka, he *heiau,* oia kekahi, men had six houses, the *heiau* (temple) was one.
4. In the Bible, a high place of worship. 2 *Nal.* 12:14 ; *Isa.* 15:2.

HE-HE-NA, *v.* To be mad; crazy; insane. *Ier.* 25:16.

HE-LE, *v.* To move in any way to a large or small minute distance; the quality of the motion is expressed by other words.
2. To walk ; to go ; to move.
3. To act; to exhibit moral conduct. 1 *Kor.* 3:3.
4. To stretch, as a string or rope.
5. *Hoo.* To cause one to go or pass on. *Ezek.* 16:21. To desire or pretend to go on; to depart ; aole nae e pono ia laua e *hoohele* wale i na pohaku *hoohele ; hele* kue, to go against, as a enemy. *Lunk.* 1:10. *Hele* wale, to be or to walk about naked. See HELEWALE. *Hele* e, to go before ; ke *hele* aku nei ke keiki, the child grows, i. e., increases in stature ; *hele* liilii, helelei, to scatter ; to separate. See the compounds.

HE-LE, *s.* A noose ; a snare for catching birds. See PAHELE.

HE-LE-LEI, *v. Hele* and *lei,* to throw

away.
1. To scatter, as any small articles ; to spill, as water.
2. To distill, as dew, i. e., to fall upon one, as music or a speech. *Kanl.* 32:2.
3. To slaver with one's spittle. 1 *Sam.* 21:13.
4. To scatter, i. e., to fall, as seed sown. *Mat.* 13:4. *Hoo.* To cast or throw away, &c.

HE-MO, *v.* To loosen; to untie, as a rope ; to cast off.
2. To come out; move away ; depart ; to turn off, as a tenant; to dispossess of one's land.
3. To loosen, i. e., to sail, as a vessel; to set sail.
4. To break loose from restraint or confinement; to break over a boundary. *Puk.* 19:21.
5. To break off a habit ; to wean, as a child ; i *hemo* ke keiki i ka waiu, let the child be *broken off* from the milk, i. e., weaned.
6. *Hoo.* To loosen, &c. ; to put away, i. e., divorce, as married persons ; he wahine i *hoohemoia.* See OKI and HOOKI.

HE-MO-LE-LE, *v. Hemo,* to loosen, and *lele,* to jump or fly off ; to be separate from some other thing ; hence,
1. In a *natural sense* (the defect of a thing is supposed to have been separated), to be complete ; perfect ; fully finished.
2. In a *moral sense,* to break or separate from what is wrong or evil. *Kanl.* 26:19. In this passage the *lele* is evidently used as the intensive of *hemo,* i. e., to be entirely separated. *Oihk.* 19:2.
3. To be perfect ; lacking nothing; completed, as a work. 1 *Ioan.* 2:5. Also in a moral sense. *Kol.* 4:12.
4. To be perfect in moral rectitude. 1 *Nal.* 8:61. To be holy; perfect. 1 *Pet.* 1:15.
5. *Hoo.* To perfect; to finish. *Ezek.* 27:4.

HE-MO-LE-LE, *s.* The perfection of a thing.
2. Virtue ; holiness. *Oih.* 3:12. A separation from what is evil; goodness; a state of glory.

HE-MO-LE-LE, *adj.* Perfect ; faultless ; holy ; complete. *Hal.* 139:22.

HE-WA, *v.* To be wrong ; to be in the wrong ; to act or to be in error.
2. To sin, i. e., to go contrary to right; to transgress. *Isa.* 43:27. To be viciously inclined.
3. *Hoo.* To accuse ; to find fault with ; to complain. See AHEWA.
4. To condemn ; to reprove.
5. To be under a curse ; to be accursed. *Kin.* 3:17.

HE-NE, *v.* To laugh at; to mock; to

deride. See Henehene.

He-wa, *adv.* Erroneously; wrongfully; hele *hewa*, to go wrong ; to miss the right way. Fig. To commit sin.

Hi, *s.* A flowing away ; a purging, as in dysentery.
2. The name of the disease called dysentery ; he *hi* ka mai.
3. A hissing sound, as the rapid flow of a liquid ; *hikoko*, a bloody flux. *Oih.* 28:8. See Hikoko.

Hi-a, *v.* To rub two sticks one upon another to obtain fire. See Aulima and Aunahi. E hana i ke ahi me ka aunahi, a maluna iho ka aulima, alaila kuolo me ka anai ana i mea e a i ke ahi.
2. To reflect ; to think.
3. To run about as wild ; to strut about.
4. To entangle ; to catch, as in a net ; eha ai i ka upena.

Hi-a, *s.* A reflecting ; the act of thinking.

Hi-a. The passive termination of many verbs instead of *ia* ; as, *pauhia* for *pauia*. *Gram.* § 48.

Hi-a-mo-e, *v. Hi*, to droop, *a*, until, and *moe*, to prostrate.
1. To lie asleep; to sleep; to fall asleep.
2. Fig. To rest in sleep; e *hiamoe* i ka make, to sleep in death, i. e., to be dead. 1 *Nal.* 15:8. To die. *Kanl.* 31:16.
3. To fall prostrate, as if asleep. *Dan.*

Hi-hi-a, *s.* A difficulty ; a thing perplexed ; a cause of trouble.
2. A thicket of forest; ka *hihia* paa o ka nahele. *Laieik.* 94.

Hi-ki, *v.* To come to ; to arrive at, as connected with *mai* or *aku*.
2. To be able to do a thing ; to accomplish a purpose ; to prevail. *Hiki* is often used with other verbs as a kind of helping verb. *Gram.* § 171.
3. *Hoo.* To cause to come ; to bring forth : to produce. *Puk.* 8:3.
4. To take an oath ; to affirm a thing. or an event as true.
5. To call or give a name to. *Mat.* 22:43, 45. To name or speak of. with approbation. *Epes.* 5:3.

6. To mention in one's prayers. *Pilem.* 4.
7. To vow ; to consecrate ; to set apart; to promise a thing especially to a god ; to set apart as sacred. 1 *Sam.* 1:11. *Hoohiki ino*, to desecrate ; to treat with contempt ; *hoohiki* wahahee, to swear falsely ; to take a false oath. See Hoohiki, *s. Hiki* wale, to happen : to come by chance.

Hi-kii, *v.* To tie ; to fasten by tying ; to bind, as a person. *Kin.* 22:9. To bind,

Hi-li, *v.* To braid ; to plait, as a wreath ; to braid, as the hair. 1 *Pet.* 3:3. To string, as kukui nuts ; e *hili* kukui.
2. To turn over and over, as in braiding; to twist ; to spin ; to tie on, as Hawaiians formerly tied or braided their kois on to the handles.
3. To deviate from the path in traveling; to wander here and there. *Sol.* 15:22. To miss one's way.
4. To droop; to flag. See Milo and Wili.
5. To smite, as with a sword or the hand.

Hi-li-nai, *v. Hili* and *nai*, to strive for.
1. To lean upon; to lean against. *Lunk.* 16:26.
2. To trust in; to have confidence in one's word. 2 *Nal.* 18:19, 20.

Hi-ne, *adj.* Strutting; proud of one's appearance.

Hi-ni, *v.* To be small; thin; feeble.

Hi-ni-hi-ni, *s.* See Hini. Speaking in a small, thin voice; a whispering ; hanehane.

Hi-ni-hi-ni, *adj.* See Hini and Uhini. Thin ; slender ; pointed.

Ho, *v.* To transfer, i. e., to bring here or carry away, according as it is followed by *mai* or *aku*. See Mai and Aku. *Gram.* § 233 and 234. As, *ho* mai, bring here; *ho* aku, carry away.
2. To bring ; to present. 1 *Sam.* 17:10. To give or put away, as money at interest. *Hal.* 15:5.
3. To carry or cause to be conveyed; to transport ; to remove.
4. To produce; to bring forward, as food on to the table. *Kin.* 43:31.

Ho, *v.* To cry out in a clamorous manner

Ho. This syllable (see the two articles above) has a meaning of its own, and as such may enter into compound words; but very often, as will appear, it is a contraction of *hoo*. (See Hoo.) The contraction is made before all the letters, but mostly where the word commences with some of the vowels, especially with the letter *o*.

Ho-a, *s.* A companion ; a fellow; a friend ; an assistant. It is found in many compounds ; as, *hoapio*, a fellow prisoner ; *hoamoe*, a bed-fellow ; *hoahele*, a traveling companion, &c.

Ho-a, *v.* To strike on the head with a stick.
2. To beat, as kapa with a stick on a stone.
3. To strike, as in fighting.
4. To drive, as cattle.

Ho-a, v. To tie; to secure by tying; to bind; to wind round, as a rope or string; to rig up, as a canoe; a ma ka wa e hoa ai ka waa, he kapu ka hoa ana. See A and HOHOA. Alaila, hoaia ka pou me ka lohelau.

Ho-aa, s. A mistake; a blunder; an error.
2. The kindling, i. e., small pieces of fuel used in kindling a fire.

Ho-a-ai, s. Hoa, companion, and ai, to eat. An eating companion; a guest. 1 Nal. 1:41.

Ho-ai, v. Ho for hoo, and ai, food.
1. To stir up; to mix; to make poi thin with water that it may be fit for eating.
2. To unite two things together, as by stretching or sewing kapas together.

Ho-a-hu, s. An assemblage of things; a collection.
2. A collecting, as of property; a gathering together.

Ho-a-ho, v. Ho for hoo, and aho, breath.
1. To give breath, i. e., deliverance from immediate danger; to put one in safety from danger.
2. To be quick; to hasten; to do quickly.
3. To kindle a fire.

Ho-a-ho, v. Ho and aho, a string.
1. To make or twist strings for a house.
2. To tie aho on to a building. See AHO.

Ho-a-ho, s. Quickness; rapidity.
2. One who has escaped a place of protection.

Ho-a-ho-a, v. See HOA, to strike. The freq. conj. of hoa. To strike or smite frequently.

Ho-a-ka, v. To lift up; to lift up, as a spear in fighting. 2 Sam. 23:18.
2. To drive away; to frighten.
3. To open; to open the mouth in speaking. See OAKA. Hoik. 13:6.
4. To glitter; to shine; to be splendid. Nahum. 2:3.

Ho-a-ka, v. Ho for hoo, and aka, to laugh. To cause one to laugh; to laugh; to be pleased.

Ho-a-ka, s. Brightness; shining; a glittering; a flaming torch. Nahum. 2:3. Glory, as of a people, i. e., their liberty; freedom.

Ho-a-ka-ka, v. Ho for hoo, and akaka, clear; explicit. To make plain; clear; to render explicit; to explain; to interpret.

Ho-a-ka-ka, s. An explanation; an opening of what is intricate.

Ho-a-ka-ku, v. Ho for hoo, and akaku,

a vision. To have a vision with the eyes open. See AKAKU.

Ho-a-la, v. Ho for hoo, and ala, to rise up.
1. To raise up from a prostrate position.
2. To awake from sleep; to cause one to awake.
3. To raise up; to excite; to stir up; applied to the mind.
4. To rouse one to action.

Ho-a-li, v. To shake; to wave an offering made to the gods; to swing: to move to and fro. Puk. 29:24. To wave, as an offering. Nah. 5:26.
2. To offer, as a sacrifice. Nah. 8:21.
3. To stir up, as ashes.

Ho-a-li, adj. That which may be waved. Puk. 29:24. Mohai hoali, a wave-offering.

Ho-a-lo-ha, } v. Ho for hoo, and
Ho-a-lo-ha-lo-ha, } aloha, to love.
1. To love; to fondle; to cherish.
2. To give thanks for something received. 1 Kor. 11:24.

Ho-a-no, v. Ho for hoo, and ano, form.
1. To reverence in the highest degree. Mat. 6:9. To hallow. Oihk. 10:3. To be holy. Oihk. 11:45.
2. To set apart; to consecrate; to lay up, as a sacred deposit; to put by; to keep back. See HOANAE.
3. Hoano e, to set apart for a particular purpose, either good or bad; to keep back; to conceal; to embezzle property.
4. To dare; to venture.
5. To be proud; to be full of self confidence. Rom. 2:17.
6. To change one's appearance; to appear what one is not; to disguise. 2 Sam. 28:8.

Ho-a-no, s. See the verb. Pride; self confidence; a high, daring spirit. See HOANO and AANO. Boasting of one's bravery. See HAANO.

Ho-a-no, adj. Sacred. Puk. 3:5. Devoted to sacred uses. Oihk. 5:15, 16. Consecrated.

Ho-a-pi-li, s. Hoa, companion, and pili, to adhere. One who attaches himself to a chief and goes with him constantly; a friend. Hal. 15:3. An attaché. NOTE.— This was the name given to the late Governor of Maui, from his attachment to Kamehameha I. His original name was Ulumaheihei.

Ho-a-pi-pi, v. To be united together, as two canoes, but not like a double-canoe; he waa aole i hoapipiia, he waa hookahi.

Ho-e-ha, v. Ho for hoo, and eha, pain. To cause pain; to give pain.

Ho-I-KE-I-KE, *v.* *Ho* for *hoo*, and *ike*, to know. To know, more particularly than *hoike;* to make known clearly; to communicate knowledge; to point out truths or facts.

Ho-I-LI, *v.* *Ho* for *hoo*, and *ili*, to strike; to hit.
1. To cause to bring or to come upon one.
2. To place upon, i. e., to put on board a ship.
3. To strike upon, as a ship upon a rock; to go ashore; to strand.
4. To fall to one, as property from a parent; to inherit. See ILI.

Ho-I-LI-I-LI, *v.* *Ho* for *hoo*, and *ilili*, to collect.
1. To collect together, as things of any kind in one place.

Ho-I-NO, *s.* Reproach; contempt. 1 Sam. 17:26.

Hoo. This word is the causative prefix to verbs; as, *malu*, to shade, *hoomalu*, to cause a shade, to overshadow; *pono*, good, right, *hoopono*, to correct, to make right; *akea*, to be broad, *hooakea* or *hoakea*, to cause to be broad, i. e., to extend, enlarge, &c. See *Gram.* § 33 and § 212, and the conjugations 7, 8, 11, 12, 15 and 16.
This prefix, though originally adapted to the verb, continues its influence though the verb with its causative prefix becomes a noun, adjective or adverb. Ua hele oia i ka *hoike*, he has gone to the *exhibition;* he kanaka *hoopunipuni*, a man *causing deception*, i. e., a *deceitful* man; olelo *hooino* iho la, he spoke *causing reproach*, i. e., he spoke reproachfully. Before words whose first letter is a vowel, the last *o* of the *hoo* frequently coalesces with the vowel of the word following, particularly before *a, e* and *o;* as, *hoano* for *hooano; hoole* for *hooole*, &c. (See the preceding pages from the word *hoaa* to *hoo*.) Some words have *haa* for their causative prefix instead of *hoo;* as, *haaheo* for *hooheo* (from *heo*, pride), to be haughty. This seems to come from the Tahitian dialect. A few words take both forms for their causative, as *hoonui* and *haanui*, from *nui*, to be large. *Hoawi.*

Hoo-A-NO-A-NO, *v.* See HOANO. To be solemn, as with the idea that an invisible spirit was present.
2. To solemnize the mind, as for worship, or as in the presence of a spirit; *hooanoano* wale mai no me he haili la e kau iho ana maluna.

Hoo-I-HA-I-HA, *v.* See IHA. To draw tightly, as a rope; to be intent.

Hoo-I-HO, *v.* See IHO, to descend. To cause to descend; to go down; e *hooiho*

Hoo-U-HA, *v.* To draw tightly.

Hoo-U-HA-U-HA, *v.* To fatigue; to tire.

Hoo-U-HA-LU, *v.* To bring out; to unfold.

Hoo-U-HE-NE-HE-NE, *v.* See HENEHENE. To laugh secretly at one; to mock ironically.

Hoo-U-HI, *v.* See UHI, to cover up. To overspread; to cover up; to wrap up; to put out of sight by covering up.

Hoo-U-HI-U-HI, *v.* See UHI as above. To cover up; to conceal in various ways; to cover over: to hide from view.

Hoo-U-HU-HI, *v.* To trouble; to vex.

Hoo-U-NA, *v.* See UNA, to send. To cause one to go on business; to send on an errand.

Hoo-U-NA-U-NA, *v.* Intensive of *una.* To send frequently.
2. To perform some part in the hooplopio or anaana.
3. To ask or urge one to do a thing; aole o'u manao e *hoounauna* aku ia olua. *Laieik.* 21.

Hoo-HA-LA, *v.* See HALA, to miss; to pass on. To cause to miss the mark; to dodge: to turn aside.
2. To transgress; to go beyond. *Nah.* 14:41.

Hoo-HI-KI, *v.* See HIKI, to come to. To arrive at a place, especially at a place designated.
2. To vow; to swear to a fact; to adjure on oath.
3. To swear at; to reproach; to revile; mostly with *ino.*

Hoo-HU-NA, *v.* See HUNA, to conceal. To hide; to secrete; to conceal.

Hoo-KA-HU-NA, *v.* See KAHUNA, a professional man. To act in any profession; to act the artisan, the priest, the doctor, &c.

Hoo-KA-HU-NA-HU-NA, *v.* See HUNA, a small particle. To be little, small or fine. See HUNAHUNA.

Hoo-KE, *v.* See KE, to force; to compel. To crowd together, as at the door of a house (as formerly); to elbow; to edge on by degrees.
2. To get possession in a foreign country without permission; applied to many foreigners who have crowded themselves in; to push aside any person or thing that is in the way.
3. To get one into difficulty; to struggle against opposition.
4. To abstain from; to let alone; to leave untouched.

Hoo-KO, *v.* See KO, to fulfill. To fulfill; to carry out, as a contract; to fulfill, as an

Hoo-ko-i, *v.* See Koi, to urge on; to compel. To speak in a rough harsh voice; to make rough or harsh; to urge; to drive on.

Hoo-ko-i-ko-i, *v.* See Koikoi, heaviness; weight. To make heavy literally or morally; to oppress; to treat with rigor.

Hoo-ko-i-ko-i, *s.* A bearing of a burden; the act of making one sad; putting one in circumstances very disagreeable and grievous to be borne.

Hoo-ku-i, *v.* See Kui, to join. To stitch together, as with a needle; to stitch together, as the five kapas for a pau or sleeping kapas.
2. To pierce, as in sewing cloth or kapa.
3. To join together, as letters in making a word, i. e., to spell.
4. To meet together.

Hoo-ku-i, *s.* A joining or connecting; o kahi mawaena o ka lani ame ka honua, ua kapaia he lewa, he *hookui* ame ka halawai.

Hoo-ku-i-ka-hi, *v.* See Kuikahi, to unite in one. To unite in one; to agree together.
2. To make a treaty of peace and friendship.

Hoo-ku-i-ku-i, *v.* See Kui, to unite. To unite; to join together; to put words together, as in a dictionary.

Hoo-la, *v.* For *hooola.* See Ola, to recover from sickness. To have ease after pain; to recover from sickness.
2. To save from danger; to cure a disease.
3. To deliver or free from death.

Hoo-la, *s.* Used for *hooola.* Safety after danger; deliverance from peril; salvation as of a people. *Puk.* 14:13.

Hoo-laa, *v.* See Laa, to consecrate.

To consecrate; to hallow: to set apart for a particular purpose, especially for religious purposes.

Hoo-laa-laa, *v.* For *hoolala.* See Lala, a branch; a limb. To branch out, as the limbs of trees.

Hoo-lau-a-ka-ne-a, *v.* To hide; to conceal; to go or put away out of sight; to deceive.

Hoo-la-la, *v.* See Lala and Hoolaalaa, to branch out. To branch out, as the branches of a tree; to divide off different ways.
2. To lay the foundation of a work; to commence a job.

Hoo-la-pa-nai, *v.* For *hooolapanai.* See Hoola, to save, and Panai, to redeem. To

save one by redeeming; to buy one's liberty who is in bondage; to redeem.

Hoo-la-pa-nai, *s.* A redeemer. *Isa.* 41:14; *Hal.* 78:35.

Hoo-le-ma-na, *v. Hoole,* to deny, and *mana,* power; authority. To deny one's power or authority, as the people in Liholiho's time denied the authority of the priests and the ancient gods; as the Jews also denied the authority of Jesus Christ.

Hoo-le-pu-le, *v.* See Hoole, to deny, and Pule, prayer; religion. To deny one's authority to act as priest, as the people did after Liholiho had broken the kapu. See Hoolemana above.

Hoo-le-wa, *v.* See Lewa, to swing. To cause to swing; to vibrate; to float in the air.
2. To lift up and carry, as between two persons; to carry in a manele or palanquin.

Hoo-la-na, *v.* See Lana, to float; to hope. To cause to float; to be light; to float upon, as upon water.
2. To offer, as a sacrifice.
3. To listen with attention; e *hoolana* i ka pepeiao.

Hoo-ma, *v.* See Ma, to fade; to wilt. To cause to fade; to wilt, as a flower; to perish.
2. To strike with the hands or paddle, as a man on a surf-board.

Hoo-maa, *v.* See Maa, to accustom. To accustom; to practice; to exercise by practice.

Hoo-ma-lu, *v.* See Malu, a shade, peace, &c. To rule over, especially in a peaceful way; to govern quietly; to make peace.

Hoo-ma-lu, *adj.* Making or causing peace between differing parties: mohai *hoomalu,* a peace-offering. *Puk.* 20:21.

Hoo-ma-lu-le, *v.* To change from one form to another; to metamorphose, as a caterpillar into a butterfly.

Hoo-ma-lu-ma-lu, *adj.* Overshadowing; shading, as clouds that run low; he ao *hoomalumalu.*

Hoo-ma-na, *v.* See Mana, superhuman power. To ascribe divine honors: to worship; to cause one to have regal authority.

Hoo-ma-nao, *v.* See Manao, to think. To turn the mind upon; to call to mind; to cause to consider; to remember that which is past.

Hoo-ma-nao-nao, *v.* See Manaonao, to lament. To call up the past with sorrow; to think or reflect on the past.

Hoo-ma-na-kii, *v.* See Hoomana above and Kii, an idol. To worship idols; to worship any god except Jehovah.

Hoo-ma-na-kii, *s.* The practice of worshipping idols; idolatry; called *figuratively* in Scripture, whoredom. 2 *Nal.* 9:22. Also vanity; a vain service; idolatry. 2 *Nal.* 17:15.

Hoo-pi-li, *v.* See Pili, to adhere to. To adhere to; to stick to; to cling to.
2. To put together the parts of a thing.
3. To attach one's self to another; to adhere to a person, as a servant or retainer; no ka *hoopili* mea ai i loaa mai ka ai ia lakou.

Hoo-pi-li-pi-li, *v.* See Pili and Pipili, to adhere to. To put together two or more things into one; to cause them to adhere closely.
2. To live together in close friendship, as two intimate friends.
3. To put in opposition; to bring into difficulty.

Hoo-wa-le-wa-le, *v.* See Walewale, to deceive. To deceive; to insnare; to plot mischief.

Hoo-wa-le-wa-le, *s.* The deceiver; the tempter.

Hoo-wa-le-wa-le-na-he-sa, *v.* To exercise enchantment. *Kanl.* 18:11.

Hou, *v.* To stab; to pierce. 1 *Sam.* 31:4. To run through the body, as with a spear. *Puk.* 19:13.
2. To exert one's self in casting a spear or javelin. 1 *Sam.* 18:11.
3. To dip, as a pen into an inkstand; *hou* aku la i ka hulu i ka inika; to dip into a liquid. *Rut.* 2:14. To moisten or soak in water.
4. To thrust, as the hand into a hole.
5. To stretch out, as the hand; to draw out; to extend.
6. To search for something, as the mind; *hou* wale aku la ka manao i o, i o, e ake e loaa; i. e., to reach after.

Hou, *v.* See Hou, new. To be new; to be fresh; to be recent. *Iob.* 29:20.
2. To repeat; to do over again. *Kanik.* *Ier.* 3:23. To do again as before. *Lunk.* 20:31.
3. To breathe short; to pant.

Ho-ku, *s.* A star; *hoku* lele, a comet; ka poe *hoku* o ke kaei, the planets. 2 *Nal.* 33:5. The twinkling orbs of heaven.

Ho-ku, *s.* A word; a thought; something rising in the mind; he wahi *hoku* iki ko'u no keia mea.

Ho-la-ho-la, *v.* See Hola, to spread

out. To spread out; to smooth; to smooth, as a kapa or cloth; to make up, as a bed. *Oih.* 9:34.
2. Applied to the mind, to calm; to soothe; to open; to enlighten. See Hohola and Uhola.

Ho-le, *v.* To curse.
2. To peel off; to skin; to flay.
3. To rasp; to file; to rub off.
4. To scratch or break the bark of a tree or skin of the flesh.

Ho-li, *v.* To commence or start first; to go forward.
2. To beg earnestly, in such a manner as that one cannot be denied.

Ho-no, *v.* To stitch; to sew up; to mend, as a garment or a net. *Mat.* 4:21.
2. To join; to unite together by sewing or stitching.

Ho-no-wai, *s.* A uniting; a bringing together and causing a new relationship; mostly brought about by marriage; as, makua *honoai,* a parent by marriage, or a parent-in-law; makua *honoai* kane, a father-in-law; makua *honoai* wahine, a mother-in-law. Note.—The orthography *honoai* is better than *honowai.* See also the word Hunoai.

Ho-nu-a, *adj.* Preceding; going beforehand; olelo *honua,* the foregoing description; pule *honua,* the former religion; i kau kauoha *honua* ana, your charge just given. *Laieik.* 20. Ke makau *honua* e mai nei no. *Laieik.* 180.

Ho-nu-a, *adv.* Gratuitously; without cause; naturally; ua aloha *honua* anei na kanaka kekahi i kekahi? do men *naturally* love each other? No ka pono a ke Akua i waiho *honua* mai ai, for the righteousness which God had *freely* manifested; o ka hoomaka ana, ua like no ia me ke ao ana, i ola *honua* i ka palapala; thoroughly; entirely. *Lunk.* 20:25. Altogether. 1 *Nal.* 11:13.

Ho-pe, *s.* The end or beginning of a thing; the termination of an extremity; the finishing result or termination of a course of conduct.
2. A place; stead; office; successor in a place.
3. The finishing; the close of a period of time.

Hu, *v.* To rise or swell up, as leaven or new poi; to effervesce.
2. To swell and rise up, as water in a pot.
3. To rise up, as a thought; *hu* mai keia manao iloko o'u, this thought *swelled* up in me.

4. To overflow; to run over the banks, as a river. *Isa.* 8:7.

5. To burst out, spoken of affection. 1 *Nal.* 3:26. Or a flow of passion (hence *huhu.*)

6. To shed or pour out, as tears. *Iob.* 16:20. *Hu* ka uhane, to have compassion. *Isa.* 58:10.

7. To ooze out silently.

8. To circulate, as the story of a murder.

9. To miss one's way; to deviate from a direct path.

10. To come, i. e., to heave in sight; to make its appearance, as a ship at a distance.

11. To be unstable; to be inconstant. *Kin.* 49:4.

12. To whistle, as the wind through the rigging of a ship.

13. *Hoo.* To meditate; to indite, as a song. *Hal.* 45:1.

Ho-po, *v.* To fear; to be afraid; to shrink back through fear.

Ho-pu, *v.* To seize upon, as something escaping; to grasp; to catch.

2. To take, as a prisoner; to apprehend, as a criminal. *Lunk.* 21:21. To hold fast, as something caught.

Hu-a, *adj.* See Huwa. Envious; jealous of success in another; quick to find fault.

Hu-a, *v.* To sprout; to bud; to bear fruit, as a tree or vegetable.

2. To grow or increase in size, as fruit; to increase, as a people. *Oihk.* 26:9.

3. To swell up, as the foam of water. See Huahua.

4. *Hua* with *huaolelo,* to speak; to utter; to produce words. *Kin.* 49:21.

5. *Hoo.* To produce fruit.

6. To increase, as a people. *Kin.* 1:28. To be fruitful, as a race. *Kin.* 9:1.

7. Fruit in several senses; as, *hua* o ke kino, children; *hua* o ka aina, increase of the fruits of the land, i. e., means of living; *hua* o na holoholona, flocks, herds, &c.; *hua* ala, spices.

8. A flowing; a going out from; froth; foam, as of one in a fit.

9. A flowing robe; a train. *Isa.* 6:1. *Hua* lole, the skirts of a garment. *Ier.* 13:22, 26.

10. Seed, as of grain for sowing. *Kin.* 47:23.

11. The human testicles. *Oihk.* 21:20.

Hu-i, *v.* To mix; to unite together, as different things; to unite, as an aha with the spectators; hence, *hui* ka aha, to *break up* the assembly. *Laieik.* 47.

2. To add one thing to another. *Kin.* 28:9.

3. To assemble together, as people for business.

4. To agree in opinion; to have a union of thought; ua *hui* pu ka manao.

5. To bend; to turn one way then another, as the voice in rising and falling in reading music.

6. To ache; to be in pain.

7. *Hoo.* To add one thing to another; to connect. *Luk.* 3:20.

8. To unite, as in a treaty; to make affinity. 1 *Nal.* 3:1.

9. To collect together, as men.

10. To meet; to mingle; to come together, as waters.

11. To meet, as persons long separated.

Hu-i, *s.* A uniting; an assembling.

2. A cluster or collection of things; as, *hui* maia, a bunch of bananas; *hui* kalo, a kalo hill; *hui* waina, a cluster of grapes; *hui* niu, a cluster of cocoanuts.

3. The flippers of the sea-turtle.

4. The small uniting sticks in a thatched house, parallel with the posts and rafters and between them.

5. Bodily pain; rheumatic pain; niho *hui,* the toothache.

6. The name of the prayer on the morning after the anaana. See Huihui.

Hu-i, } *adj.* Cool; cold; chilly, as **Hu-i-hu-i,** } the morning air from the mountain; i hoomanawanui ai hoi kaua i ka hau *huihui* o ke kakahiaka; cold, as cold water. *Mat.* 10:42.

Hu-i-o-pa-pa, *s.* The name of a prayer used in or near the luakini; a ma ia ahiahi no haule ka *huiopapa.*

Hu-i-u-na, *s.* Perhaps for *huiana.* A seam; a uniting by sewing together.

Hu-i-hu-i, *s.* A bunch; a cluster of things, as stars.

2. A constellation. *Isa.* 13:10.

3. A bunch; applied to kalo. See Hui 2.

4. The name of the seven stars. See Huhui.

Hu-i-hu-i, *adj.* Cold; chilly. See Hui above.

2. Mixed; manifold; much; many containing the idea of union; aloha *huihui, much* love.

Hu-i-ka-la, *v.* *Hui* and *kala,* to loosen; to forgive. To cleanse, as a disease; to purify.

2. To be purified. *Puk.* 29:23.

3. To sanctify one's self. *Oihk.* 20:7.

4. To cleanse morally. *Kin.* 35:2.

5. To cleanse ceremonially. *Neh.* 12:30. *Huikala* ole, unholy. 2 *Tim.* 3:2.

6. *Hoo.* To cleanse; to purify; to sanctify. *Heb.* 9:13.

Hu-i-ka-la, *adj.* Cleansing; purifying;

wai *huikala*, water of purification. *Nah.* 19:9.

Hu-hu-ki, *v.* See Huki, to pull. To draw frequently ; to pull out, as in drawing cuts. *Laieik.* 72. To pull along.
2. To dry up, as water ; hoomaloo.
3. To cut down, as a tree ; e kua aku.

Hu-ki, *v.* To draw; to pull ; to draw, as with a rope. *Ioan.* 4:7.
2. To raise ; to lift up, as a person by the hand.

Hu-la, *v.* To pry up with a lever.
2. To transplant, as a tree; to plant out, as a young tree.
3. To cut off the tops of plants.
4. To bend over, as a tree; to push over any upright thing; to fall over upon.
5. To shake or tremble for fear of injury from another.
6. To trample and make a beaten path; to tread down ; to trample upon.
7. To shake ; to dance ; to play an instrument and dance; to sing and dance. 2 *Sam.* 6:21. The same as *haa* and *lole* in verses 14:16. Alaila, *hula* iho la kahi poe alii ame kanaka, then danced certain of the chiefs and people.
8. To play on an instrument.
9. To sing ; to sing and dance together.
10. To make sport. *Lunk.* 16:25.
11. To palpitate, as the heart ; to throb, as an artery.
12. To move from place to place.
13. To bore a hole; e *hula* a puka, to bore and pierce through.

Hu-la,) *s.* Music; dancing; singing, &c.
Hu-la-hu-la,)
2. A play in which numbers dance and a few sing and drum.
3. A dance ; a carousal ; the action of dancing. *Puk.* 15:20.
4. A dance; a dancing, an expression of joy. *Kanik. Ier.* 5:15. Note.—The name of the *hula* god was Lakakane.

Hu-la-hu-la, *s.* The name of a good or favorable aha. See Aha, the name of a prayer formerly very sacred.

Hu-la-ni, *v.* *Hu*, to rise, and *lani*, heaven. To praise; to exalt. See Lele-pailani.

Hu-lei, *v.* To place on high; to put up on a precipice ; to be lifted up, as a female's dress by the wind.

Hu-li, *v.* To turn generally in any way; to turn over and about.
2. To change; to turn over, as the leaves of a book ; to search here and there for a thing. *Kin.* 31:37.
3. E *huli* i ka naau, to give attention to a thing.
6. E *huli* i ka manao, to change the mind or opinion ; hence, to repent and change the life.

Hu-na, *v.* To hide ; to conceal; to keep from the sight or knowledge of another. *Kin.* 26:15.
2. To keep back truth in speaking. 1 *Sam.* 3:17.
3. To hide, as a trap or snare.
4. To hide ; to conceal ; with *maka*, to hide the face, i. e., to turn from. *Kanl.* 32:20.
5. To conceal, i. e., to disguise one's self. 2 *Oihl.* 18:29.
6. To protect ; to defend. *Hal.* 64:2.
7. *Hoo.* To conceal, as knowledge or wisdom. *Iob.* 17:4.

Hu-na, *v.* To be small ; to be little ; to be reduced fine, as powder.

Hu-na, *s.* That which is concealed ; kahi *huna*, the private members of the body. *Oihk.* 18:6, 7. Wahi *huna*, same. *Puk.* 20:23.

Hu-na, *s.* A small part of anything. *Luk.* 16:17. A particle of dust ; a crumb of food or other substance. 2 *Oihl.* 1:9. See Huna, to be little. See other words below with their qualities.

Hu-lu-ma-nu, *s.* *Hulu* and *manu*, a bird. A bird-feather. Note.—Bird's feathers were highly valued in former times ; o ka *hulumanu* ka mea i manao nui ia, he waiwai ia.

Hu-na-hu-na, *v.* See Huna, to conceal. To steal away and hide ; to conceal one's self.
2. Fine rain; spray ; fine dust; maluna o na *hunahuna* lepo a pau ma ka honua.
3. Little particles of knowledge ; o na *hunahuna* o ka maano, oia ka i loaa mai ia'u, the *little parts* of knowledge, that is what I have received; eia ke ano o ka *hunahuna*, he wahi mea uuku loa ia.

Hu-ne, *adj.* Destitute of property; naked ; poor; applied to persons.

K the seventh letter of the Hawaiian alphabet. Its sound varies somewhat from the English *k* sound to that of the *t*, according as the enunciation is made at the end of the tongue or near the root. It is difficult to make Hawaiians perceive the difference between the English sounds of *k* and *t*. The natives on the Island of Hawaii generally pronounce the letter with the palate, that is, give it the *k* sound, while the natives of the Island of Kauai pronounce it with the end of the tongue that is, pronounce it as *t*.

Ka in the beginning of a speech is used to call attention.

Ka, *int.* An exclamation of surprise, wonder, disappointment or disgust; also, similar to hark, hush; often repeated. See Kahaha.

Ka! ka! *int.* Enough; sufficient; stop.

Ka in different parts of a sentence, contains something like an assertion with disapprobation; used also on the discovery of a mistake. 1 *Sam.* 28:12. It is·used on expressing opposition of sentiment. *Puk.* 32:17. After a verb it implies oblique absurdity, something unaccountable. *Luke* 23:35. When the contrary takes place from what was expected or attempted. *Isa.* 14:14, 15. He kau malie ka la, o ka honua ka ke kaa nei! it is the sun is it that stands still, the earth *forsooth*, that rolls! *Ka* contains the idea of some supposed error, or something wrongly done or thought. *Oih.* 11:3.

Ka, *art.* The definite article, *the.* Before nouns beginning with the letter *k.* it is changed into *ke* instead of *ka.* See Ke. See *Gram.* § 59, 60, 61. *Ka* as an article often represents not only the article but the noun supposed to belong to it, or it may have *mea* or some other word understood (like, in another sense, the English *what,* as an antecedent and a relative); as, o ka aila ka (mea) iloko o kona lima, the oil the (thing) which, *that which* was in his hand. *Oihk.* 17:11. O ke koko *ka* (mea) i hana i kalahala, the blood the (thing) it makes atonement; that is, the thing *which makes;* o ka pono wale no *ka* i oi mamua o ka hewa, righteousness only is the thing (that which) excels wickedness. *Ka* also as an article stands for *ka mea,* and *ka mea nana,* the person who, or the thing which. See the following passages: John 12:2, 49; Mat. 18:23 ; Mar. 9:7. See also Grammar, Syntax, Rule 6, Note 3.

Ka, *prep.* Having the general sense, of; belonging to; it marks the relation of possession and is used before nouns and pronouns; it is similar in meaning to the preposition *a,* but used in a different part of the sentence. See Grammar § 105, 4. *Ka* (also *ko*) before nouns is similar in meaning to the apostrophic *s* in English, and signifies the *thing* or the *things belonging* to those nouns; as, *ka* ke alii, *belonging* to the chief; *ka* laua, *that of* them two. See Grammar § 105, 4.

Ka, *v.* To bail water, as from a canoe; e *ka* oe i ka liu.
2. To strike ; to dash ; to overthrow. *Puk.* 15:4.
3. To strike, as to strike fire with flint

and steel; *ka* ahi. See Kaka. To block or split off a piece of hard stone for the purpose of making a stone adze in ancient times; o ka poe *ka* koi ka poe i manao nui ia; hele no ka poe *ka* koi e imi i na pohaku paa e pono ai ke hana i koi ; *ka* makau, to fabricate a bone into a fish-hook.
4. To finish or end a thing ; to rest; to escape from pursuit; to flee away; ua *ka* ilaila kuu po auhee.
5. To radiate; to go out from the center, as light from the sun ; as cinders from a red hot iron ; to braid or kuit, as a fish net (o ka poe *ka* upena) from a center point.
6. To go out every way, as from a center. *Kin.* 3:24. See Kaa.
7. To curse ; to express anger at one by wishing evil from God; a low kind of swearing.
8. To doom ; to pass sentence ; ·*ka* ola, *ka* make. to doom to life, to doom to death (according to the pleasure of the gods.)
9. To catch birds in a snare.
10. *Hoo.* To destroy ; cause to perish.
11. To be disappointed ; put to confusion; to be made ashamed.
12. A nolaila e aho hoi ke *ka* i ka nele lua. *Laieik.* 197.

Ka, *s.* A dish to bail water with.
2. A striking against ; a collision.
3. A vine, the branches of which spread and run.

Kaa, *v.* To radiate. See Ka 5. To go out, as rays of light from the sun ; as cinders from a red hot iron ; to turn every way, as bones in a socket joint. *Anat.* 18.

Kaa, *v.* To roll, as a wheel ; e olo *kaa;* to travel about from place to place ; often with *puni.*
2. To operate; to take effect, as an emetic or cathartic.
3. To pass off or out from ; to go out from the presence of one.
4. To fall away ; to leave one party to join another. 1 *Oihl.* 12:19. See Kaana.
5. To remove ; to change one's place ; to be transferred to another. *Nah.* 36:9. To cause to be done ; to be gone ; ua *kaa* na peelua, the worms (peeluas) are done, i. e., the time for them is past. *Isa.* 10:25.
6. To be sick ; to suffer pain in sickness; to lie or be confined with long sickness. *Isa.* 51:20.
7. To mourn, as in the loss of relatives ; *kaa* kumakena na wahine i na kane i kela la i keia la, wives *were sick* with weeping for their husbands every day.
8. To pay a debt ; e emo *kaa* koke ae no ka aie a ke alii, very soon *will be paid* the debt of the chief ; to postpone ; to put off; to put aside. *Oih.* 5:34.
9. *Hoo.* To roll off; to remove.

KAA, *s.* A tradition; a legend. See KAAO.

2. A cross; same as *kea.*

3. Anything that rolls or turns, as a top, a wheel of a carriage, a carriage itself, a cart, wagon or chariot. *Kin.* 46:5. *Kaa* i uhiia, a covered wagon. *Nah.* 7:3. A grindstone.

4. The branch of a vine.

5. A name given to all kinds of foreign timber, except oak.

6. A strand of a cord; a rope; the string that fastens a fish-hook to the line.

7. A path to walk in. *Hal.* 6:11.

8. A shrub.

KAA, *adv.* Gone; absent; no more.

KA-AI, *v.* To bind or tie round; to gird on, as an oriental dress; to tie on, as a fillet on the head, or a girdle around the waist. See KAEI. Paai o haho aku i ke *kaai.*

KA-A-NA, *v.* To make alike; to resemble.

2. To bring over to one's party or purpose; to proselyte. *Mat.* 23:15.

3. To fall away from one party to another. 1 *Oihl.* 12:19. See KAA.

4. To make; to gain.

5. To deceive; to entrap; to outwit.

6. To compare, i. e., to resemble; to make like; to be mingled in with others; ua *kaana* ka iho (kapa) me ka hewa; ua *kaana* mai ka bipi hihiu maloko o ka bipi laka a laua, the wild cattle *were mixed* with the tame.

KAI, *v.* To lift up on the hands and carry; to lift up the foot and walk, as an infant in beginning to walk, or as one recovering from sickness; to step amiss, as a child; generally connected with *hina;* as, *kai* aku la ke keiki a hina iho la.

2. To lead; to guide; to direct; *kai* aku i ke kaa, to drive a cart. 2 *Sam.* 6:3. To direct the ceremonies of the luakini; ke *kai* ana o ka aha. SYN. with oihana.

3. To lead, direct or bring to a place. *Kin.* 2:19.

4. To lead into or entice, as fish into a net, or any animal into a trap or snare.

5. To bring; to take in hand; to do with; to pull up, as kalo.

6. To shove along; to move; to go a journey; to travel slowly.

7. To bring. i. e., to lead; to transfer, as a people from one place to another. *Kanl.* 7:1.

8. *Hoo.* To separate or part asunder, as a cracked part of a canoe; ua *kai* ka pili o ka waa; or as a door so swelled as not to shut; ua *kai* na pili o ka pani; to displace; to put away. *Heb.* 10:9.

9. To take away by robbery; to misspend; to squander. *Luk.* 15:30. To reject; to disregard. See HOKAI.

KAI, *s.* The sea; sea water; a flood; *kai* hooee, an overflowing flood. *Dan.* 9:26. Hence,

2. Brine; gravy of roast meat; broth. *Lunk.* 6:20.

3. The surf of the sea; *kai* ula, the red sea; *kai* piha, the full sea or flood tide; *kai* make, the dead sea or ebb tide; *kai* koo, a very high surf, &c. See these compounds.

4. A current in the sea; he *kai* i Hawaii, a current towards Hawaii.

5. A traveling guard.

KAI, *int.* How; how much; how great. 2 *Sam.* 1:19. *Kai* ka nani! O how glorious! 2 *Sam.* 6:20. *Kai* ka hemolele! how excellent! *Hal.* 8:1. Renowned; wonderful; *kai* ka luhi, what a weariness. *Mat.* 1:13.

KAI-KAI-NA, *s.* The younger of two brothers or sisters; used by a brother when speaking of a brother, or a sister of a sister. But if a brother speak of a sister, or a sister of a brother, it is *kaikunane.*

KAI-KUA-A-NA, *s.* The elder of two brothers or sisters; used by a brother when speaking of a brother, or by a sister when speaking of a sister; but when a brother speaks of an elder sister, it is *kaikuwahine.* When a sister speaks of an elder brother it is *kaikunane.*

KA-I-NA, *v.* See KAI, to take, and ANA. To take; to seize. as a fit; as the influence of a wicked spirit. *Mar.* 9:18.

2. To seize, as a prisoner; to lead away to trial; ua uku i ke dala, ua hanu, ua paa i ka hao, ua *kaina* aku imua o na lunakanawai.

KAI-NA, *v.* To move slowly and softly, as a weak person trying to walk.

KAI-NA, *s.* A younger of two brothers or two sisters; hence, a thing that is after or second to another; pokii *kaina*, the very younger.

KAI-NA, *s.* A sitting to practice sorcery; the practice of sorcery.

KA-O, *v.* To intercede; to mediate; to separate contending parties; to prevent one from accusing or slandering another.

KA-O-HI, *v.* To fix; to establish.

2. To abide; to continue to adhere firmly to a thing or course of conduct; to be steadfast.

KAU, *v.* In an *active sense*, to hang; to hang up; to suspend, as an article to be out of the way; to crucify or hang, as a criminal. *Kin.* 40:22.

2. To hang, tie or gird on, as a sword; *kau i ka pahi kaua. Puk.* 32:27.

3. To put upon or place a thing in some designated place; to put in an elevated situation; to mount a horse; to go on board a ship or canoe.

4. To overhang, as the heavens over the earth.

5. To fall upon; to embrace affectionately, with *ai. Kin.* 46:29.

6. To put upon one, as a heavy burden. *Nah.* 11:11.

7. To set or fix the boundaries of a land or country.

8. To put down, as words on paper. See Kakau. To write; to dot; hence,

9. To give publicity to a thing; to promulgate, as a law; i *kau* aku oukou i kanawai maikai, that you may establish good laws.

10. To set before one, as food.

11. To tempt, as in taking birds with a snare.

12. In a *neuter sense*, to light down upon, as a bird; as the spirit or divine influence upon one. *Nah.* 11:26.

13. To come down upon one unexpectedly.

14. *Kau ponō* kona maka, to set or direct óne's face or desire.

15. To rest upon; to stretch out or over.

16. To come upon one, as a suffering or calamity.

17. To rehearse in the hearing of another that he may learn.

18. A *kau* ka hamere ma kekahi lima, he took the hammer in one hand. *Lunk.* 4:21. To lay or place the hand upon one for evil.

19. *Hoo.* To set against; to resist. *Lunk.* 7:22.

20. To appoint against; to come upon. *Ier.* 15:3.

21. To bring upon; to cause to fall upon.

22. To rest; to place. *Kanl.* 7:23.

23. *Kau* aku i kau hale, to go about from house to house; to go about idly. See definition 11.

Kau, *s.* Season. *Kin.* 1:14.

2. The summer or warm season, in distinction from *hooilo*, the winter months. Note.—The Hawaiians had but two seasons in a year, viz.: the *kau* summer, and *hooilo* winter; hence,

Kau, *pers. pro.* An oblique case of *oe*, second person. Of thee; of thine. *Gram.* § 132, 133. Also a prefix pronoun, thy; thine. *Gram.* § 149, 150.

Ka'u, *pers. pro.* An oblique case of *au*. Of me; mine; belonging to me. *Gram.* § 124, 1. Also a prefix pronoun, my; mine;

Kau-a, *v.* To war; to fight, as two armies.

2. To make war upon or against. *Kin.* 14:2.

3. To fight for. *Puk.* 14:14.

Ka-ua, *pro. dual.* We two; you and I. *Gram.* § 124, 3.

Kau-a-ka, *s.* A person crazy, noisy with constant muscular motion.

Kau-i-la, *v.* To offer sacrifice at the close of a kapu.

Kau-o,) *v.* To draw or drag along;
Kau-wo,) to haul, as a load. *Kanl.* 21:3. To draw morally, i. e., to endure; to incline to do a thing.

2. To conduct, as a prisoner.

3. To pray for a special blessing or favor; applied to the worship at the time of makahiki.

Kau-o,) *s.* Seed; offspring; increase;
Kau-wo,) fruit of marriage. If Nahiena-

Kau-o-ha, *v.* To give a dying charge; to make a bequest or a parting charge. *Isa.* 38:1. Hence, to make a will. Note.— Ancient wills, of course, were verbal; now, by law, they must be written.

Kau-kau, *v.* To set or fix, as a snare or net for birds. See Kau. *Hal.* 141:9.

2. To take counsel; to revolve in one's mind. *Hal.* 13:2.

3. To speak to one, especially to chide; to speak reproachfully; e nuku; to address one, as a petitioner, and in a way of complaint. *Laieik.* 71.

4. To explain; to make clear, i pohihi ole.

Kau-la, *s.* A rope; a strong cord; a cord or tendon in the animal system. *Anat.* 25.

2. *Kaula* uila, a chain of lightning.

3. A bow string. *Hal.* 11:2.

4. A line in a book or written document. *Isa.* 28:10.

5. A stick laid across the rafters of a house or the top of the posts, after the manner of a beam; more properly written *kaola.* See Kaola.

6. In *geometry*, the chord of an arc of a circle. *Anahonua* 28.

7. A lash, i. e., the wound of a lash in whipping; a stripe. 2 *Kor.* 11:24.

Kau-la, *s.* A prophet; one who preaches or announces future events. *Oih.* 3:24.

Kau-ma-ha, *s.* Weight, as of a burden; weariness; heaviness; depression of spirits; nui ke *kaumaha* o kona naau no ko lakou luku wale ana, he was very *sorrow-*

ful at such a slaughter of men.

KĀU-MA-HA, *s.* A sacrifice; a service rendered to God.

KA-HE, *v.* To cut or slit longitudinally; to cut off; with *omaka*, to circumcise after the Hawaiian manner; to castrate; to shave. See KAHI.
2. To bind round the waist; to gird.
3. To begin to wither, as leaves eaten by a worm.

KA-HE, *s.* *Hoo.* A flowing; a flowing of blood; he poko ma kauwahi, he la ma kauwahi, he hauoki ma kauwahi, he *kahe* ma kauwahi.

KA-HE-A, *v.* See HEA, to call. To call any one for any purpose. *Oihk.* 1:1.
2. To cry to one for help; to call upon one, as in prayer. *Puk.* 14:15.
3. To speak; to call aloud.
4. To cry out, as in pain.

KA-HI-HI, *s.* Entanglement; perplexity.

KA-HI-KO-LU, *s.* Three in one; the Trinity; used only in the Scriptural sense; the Godhead, Father, Son and Holy Spirit.

KĀ-HO-A-KA, *s.* The spirit or soul of a person still living, supposed to be seen by priests; nona ia *kahoaka* e hihia nei, he uhane, he haili, he uhane kakaola.

KA-HOI, *v.* To hinder; to keep back.

KA-HOO-KU-I, *s.* A union; a joining; a uniting. See KUI and HOOKUI.

KA-HU, *s.* An honored or upper servant; a guardian or nurse for children. *But.* 4:16. Hence, a feeder; a keeper; a provider; *kahu* hipa, a shepherd.

KA-HU-KA-HU, *v.* To offer a sacrifice to the gods; to sacrifice; to worship the god of fishermen, to the aumakua.

KA-HU-KA-HU, *s.* The sacrifice offered to the gods.

KA-HU-NA, *s.* *Kahu* and *ana*, a cooking. Hence, a general name applied to such persons as have a trade, an art, or who practice some profession; some qualifying term is generally added; as, *kahuna* lapaau, a physician; *kahuna* pule, a priest; *kahuna* kalai laau, a carpenter; *kahuna* kala, a silversmith; *kahuna* kalai, an engraver. *Puk.* 38:23. NOTE.—Generally in Hawaiian antiquities, the word *kahuna* without any qualifying term, refers to the priest or the person who offered sacrifices. *Puk.* 18:1. O ka mea pule i ka ke alii heiau, he *kahuna* pule ia. See the above and others in their own places.

KA-HU-NA, *v.* To exercise a profession; to work at one's appropriate business.

2. *Specifically*, to be or act the priest. *Lunk.* 18:19.
3. To sprinkle salt on a sacrifice; e kapi i ka paakai i awaawa ole. See KAHUNA-HUNA.
4. *Hoo.* To sanctify or set apart to the priests' office. *Puk.* 28:41.

KA-HU-NA·AO, *s.* *Kahuna*, and *ao*, to teach. A preacher; a pulpit teacher; one whose business it is to impart knowledge to men.

KA-HU-NA-A-NA-NA, *s.* *Kahuna* and *ana-ana*, sorcery. One who uses divination or sorcery. *Kanl.* 18:10.

KA-HU-NA-HAI, *s.* *Kahuna* and *hai*, to speak. One who speaks or declares publicly; a preacher. *2 Tim.* 1:11. The full form is *kahunahai olelo.*

KA-HU-NA-HOO-PIO-PIO, *s.* *Kahuna* and *hoopiopio*, to practice sorcery. A priest or one who practices sorcery in connection with his priest's office.

KA-HU-NA-HU-NA, *v.* To sprinkle; to sprinkle a little salt upon meat; to sprinkle salt or water in small quantities; e kapi awaawa ole i ka paakai. See KAHUNA 2.

KA-HU-NA-KA-LAI, *s.* *Kahuna* and *kalai*, to hew. One who hews out canoes; a carpenter generally.

KA-HU-NA-LA-PA-AU, *s.* *Kahuna* and *lapaau*, to heal. A physician; a doctor of medicine.

KA-HU-NA-PE-LE, *s.* *Kahuna* and *pele.* The priest or priestess of Pele.
2. The worshipers of Pele.

KA-HU-NA-PU-LE, *s.* *Kahuna* and *pule*, prayer. A priest; one who publicly officiates in the exercises of religion.

KA-HU-PU-AA, *s.* *Kahu* and *puaa*, swine. One who tends or feeds swine; a swine herd. *Mat.* 8:33.

KA-HU-WAI, *s.* *Kahu* and *wai*, water. One who has the charge or oversight of the division of water.

KA-KA, *v.* *Ka*, to strike; to dash. To beat; to whip.
2. To cut and split or break wood (this was anciently done, not with an axe, but by striking sticks against stones or rocks.)
3. To wash, as dirty clothes (this is done by Hawaiians by beating them.)
4. To strike, as fire with flint and steel; ka or kaka ahi.
5. To thrash, as grain. *Rut.* 2:17.
6. To rip open. *2 Nal.* 18:12.
7. To dip or bail out water. See KA.

KA-KA, *s.* Fruits that grow in clusters, as grapes; much fruit in one place.

KA-KAA, *v.* See KAA, to roll. To roll; to turn this way and that.

KA-KA-O-LA, *s.* The spirit or soul of a living person as seen or pretended to be seen by the kahuna kilokilo or juggling priest. If many spirits were seen in company they were called *oio.* The ghost of a single deceased person was called *kinowailua,* which see.

KA-KOU, *pers. pron.,* first person plural. We; spoken of more than two, including the speaker and the persons addressed. *Gram.* § 124, 125 and 130.

KA-KU-A, *v.* To bind or fasten on, as a pa-u.
2. To tie on, as a kihei. 2 *Sam.* 20:8. To put round, as a cincture or girdle. See KAKOO.

KA-KU-A, *v.* To ascribe power to the gods; to magnify; to offer sacrifice to the gods.

KA-KU-A, *s.* The worship of the gods, ascribing to them power; worship.

KA-KU-AI, *v.* To worship the gods; to pray in a particular manner.

KA-KU-AI, *s.* The constant daily sacrifice offered at every meal. NOTE.—The offerings were mostly of bananas.

KA-LA, *v.* To loosen; to untie, as a string or rope; to let loose, as an animal. *Mar.* 11:2.
2. To unloose; to put off, as clothes from a person; to undress; to put off, as armor. 1 *Sam.* 17:39.
3. To open half way, as a door or book.
4. To absolve from a contract.
5. To put away; to take away, i. e., to forgive sin or a crime; to pardon. *Puk.* 34:7.
6. To forgive, as a debt; to release one from payment. *Mat.* 18:27.
7. To spare; to save from punishment. 2 *Sam.* 21:7.
8. *Hoo.* To whet; to grind or sharpen on a grindstone or hone. *Kanl.* 32:41.
, 9. To run out the tongue, as a serpent; to sharpen the tongue, i. e., to speak against or injure one. *Ios.* 10:21.
10. To sharpen, as a sword. *Hal.* 7:12.

KA-LA, *v.* To proclaim, as a public person the will of his sovereign; to cry, as a public crier.

KA-LA-HA-LA, *v. Kala,* to pardon, and *hala,* guilt. To loose or absolve one from guilt or sin; to pardon sin.
2. To take away the ground of an offense, or to answer for it.
3. *Hoo.* To make an atonement. *Puk.* 29:36.

KA-LE-WA, *s.* A swing; a pendulous machine for moving back and forward, like *kowali.*
2. A place near or in the luakini where the king and a few people were separated from the multitude.

KA-LE-WA, *adj.* Hanging; swinging, as a weight on a pole; flying, as clouds; lying off and on, as a ship.

KA-LI, *v.* To wait; to tarry; to stay. *Puk.* 12:39.
2. To sojourn with one.
3. To wait for something; to lie in wait.
4. To hesitate in speaking.
5. To expect; to look for.
6. To gird; to tie; to fasten on.
7. *Hoo.* To waste away with disease.

KA-LO, *s.* The well known vegetable of the Hawaiian Islands; a species of the *arum esculentum;* it is cultivated in artificial water beds, and also on high mellow upland soil; it is made into food by baking and pounding into hard paste; after fermenting and slightly souring, it is diluted with water, then called poi, and eaten with the fingers. NOTE.—The origin of the *kalo* plant is thus described in Hawaiian Mythology (see *Mooolelo Hawaii* by Dibble, p. 37): ulu mai la ua alualu la, a lilo i *kalo,* the fetus grew (when it was buried) and became a *kalo.*

KA-LO, *s.* One of the class of gods called akua noho; Opua ame *Kalo* kekahi akua makau ia.

KA-LO-KA-LO, *v.* To pray to the gods; to supplicate favors.
2. (In a *modern christian sense*) to call upon God; to ask for assistance; aka, e *kalokalo* aku kakou i ke Akua, a nana e lileuli lelewae, but let us call upon God, and he will blot out and wash away (our sins); e hoi a *kalokalo* aku i ka mea nani hiwahiwa o ka lanikolu.

KA-MA, *v.* To lead or direct.
2. To bind or tie up, as a bundle. See

KA-MAA, *s.* Sandals; shoes, i. e., shoes for the bottom of the feet.

KA-NA, *pron.* An oblique case of the personal pronoun, third person singular of *ia. His; hers;* its (seldom used in the neuter.) *Ke* is a preposition, of. More often it signifies possession, where in English the apostrophic *s* would be used. See Grammar § 137, 138 and 139.

KA-NA, *v.* To see; to appear; to get a sight of; to obtain what one wished; i nana aku i ka hana i ka hale o ke alii, aole i *kana* mai, o ko'u hilahila no ia mea, I went to see the house of the ohief, I did not see it (get sight of), I was ashamed.

KA-NAE, *s.* *Ka* and *nae*, hard breathing. Hence, fear; a holding the breath from fear.

KA-NAE-NAE, *v.* To observe; to watch.
2. To pray to the gods; to offer sacrifice to the gods; e *kanaenae* i ke akua.
3. To appear angry.

KA-NA-KA, *s.* A man; one of the human species; one of the genus *homo*; the general name of men, women and children of all classes, in distinction from other animals.
2. A common man, in distinction from alii or chief.
3. People generally; persons; mankind.
4. In a *vulgar*, *low sense* as sometimes used by foreigners, a Hawaiian, a native, in distinction from a foreigner.
5. Own; self; person; aka, i makau ia kakou *kanaka* iho, but they feared us our *own persons*; *kanaka* e, another man, i. e., a stranger. *Puk.* 12:19.

KA-NE, *s.* The male of the animal species; opposite to *wahine.*
2. A husband; he *kane* mea wahine, a husband having a wife; *kane* hou, a man lately married; a bridegroom; also, *kane* mare, a bridegroom.
3. The name of a stone god.
4. White spots on the flesh.
5. The god of living water; he akua nana ka wai ola.
6. The name of certain gods, Kane and Kanaloa.
7. The name of a small insect. See ANE.
8. Name of a day of the month; ma ia ao ae. o *Kane* ia la.

KA-NE, *v.* To be or act the part of a husband. 1 *Tim.* 3:2.

KA-PA, *v.* To call; to name; to give a name to. *Kin.* 3:2. To give an appellation.

KA-PA, *s.* The cloth beaten from the bark of the wauki or paper mulberry, also from the mamaki and other trees; hence,
2. Cloth of any kind; clothes generally; *kapa* komo, a coat; a dress.

KA-PAE, *v.* To pervert; to turn aside; to make crooked morally, i. e.. to turn aside from moral rectitude. 1 *Nal.* 9:6.

KA-PU, *s.* A general name of the system of religion that existed formerly on the Hawaiian Islands, and which was grounded upon numerous restrictions or prohibitions, keeping the common people in obedience to the chiefs and priests; but many of the *kapus* extended to the chiefs themselves.

The word signifies,
1. Prohibited; forbidden.
2. Sacred; devoted to certain purposes. *Nah.* 6:7.
3. A consecration; a separation. (See Hawaiian History and D. Malo on *kapus.*) Eha na po *kapu* ma ka malama hookahi, there were four *tabu* nights (days) in a month: 1st, *kapuku*, 2d, *kapuhua*, 3d, *kapukaloa*, 4th. *kapukane.*

KA-PU, *v.* To set apart; to prohibit from use; to make sacred or holy.

KE, *def. art.* The. See KA, *art.* This form of the article (*ke*) is used before all nouns beginning with the letter *k.* A few nouns beginning with the letter *p* have *ke* also for their article. and a still smaller number beginning with the letter *m.* Nouns whose first letter is *a* have both *ka* and *ke* for their article; that is, some nouns take one and some the other, but no one noun, without a radical change of meaning, takes both forms of the article. Nouns beginning with *o*, like *a*, take both forms of the article. Before all other letters, whether vowels or consonants, *ka* is the form of the article. See Grammar § 59, 60.

KE, *particle*, before a verb and *nei* after it, marks the present tense of the indicative mood; but *ke* with the subjunctive mood marks the future tense. After the verbs *hiki*, always, and *pono* generally (both used as auxiliary verbs), *ke* is used before the infinitive instead of e. *Gram.* § 203.

KE, *interj.* An exclamation of surprise, indeed! 1 *Kor.* 15:36. See KA. *Ke* is often used in beginning a reply to what one has said, and expresses astonishment at what had been advanced; sometimes disgust and the greatest contempt; e manao ino me ka henehene.

KE, *v.* Mostly with *hoo.* To force; to compel; to urge on. *Lunk.* 1:34.
2. To be intent upon; to press forward; to go ahead in any affair; *hooke* loa mai la o Keoua me ka manao e lawe i ko Kamehameha mau okana nona, Keoua *was intent* upon the idea of taking Kamehameha's districts for his own.
3. To thrust; to push or drive at. *Hal.* 118:13.
4. To obstruct one as he goes along; to get a person or persons into difficulty; to struggle against; to be troubled. 2 *Kor.* 4:8.
5. To crowd together at a door or about a person; to assault one's house; to press upon.
6. With *ai*, food, to push away, as food without eating; to abstain from food; hence,
7. To fast. 2 *Sam.* 12:16. NOTE.—Voluntary fasting among Hawaiians requires

the exercise of some force.

KE-A, s. A cross; the form of a cross, viz.: one post upright, the other transverse. See AMANA.

KE-A, v. To hinder; to object to. See KE. v.. and KEAKEA below.

KE-A-KE-A, v. See KEA, to hinder. To hinder. 1 Sam. 14:6. To stand in the way of.
2. To object to that which would be to the advantage of another.
3. To keep back; to restrain one from doing a thing. Nah. 24:11. To prohibit; to resist. Oih. 13:10.

KE-A-KE-A, adj. See KEA, cross, above. In the form of several crosses, as sticks under a piece of timber to carry it; a keakea a amo aku.

KE-A-KE-A, s. See KEA 4 above. The semen masculinum; the semen of all males. See KEKEA.

KE-LA, adj. pron. From ke, the, and la, there. That; that person; that thing; that fellow (more emphatic and definite than ia); he; she; it. It is used in opposition to keia, this; it is used when the noun to which it refers has just before been used. Gram. § 152.

KE-LA, v. To exceed; to go beyond. 1 Nal. 10:7.
2. To project out beyond another thing.
3. To be more. Ier. 7:26.
4. To cause to exceed; to be more. Hal. 119:98. E hookela i ke aloha, to love more. Mat. 10:37.

KI, v. Modern. To pull the trigger (ki) of a gun; hence, to shoot a gun; alaila ki mai la na haole i koe i ka pu; to discharge fire-arms; ina e ae oe i kuu lio, e ki koke aku au ia oe i ka pu, a make oe.
2. To squirt water, as with a syringe.
3. To sift; to strain.
4. To make fine by separating the coarse.
5. To blow from the mouth into the sea, as fishermen blow from the mouth a kind of oily nut chewed up in order to quiet the surface of the sea, so that they can look deep down into the water.

KI, s. The name of a plant having a saccharine root, the leaves of which are used for wrapping up bundles of food; the leaves are used also as food for cattle and for thatching; dracœna terminalis.

KI-E-KI-E, v. See KIE. To be lofty; to be high.
2. To be lifted up; to be raised high, as a material object.
3. To be high, as the mind; to be proud; to be self-exalted; to think one's self above or better than others.

KII, v. To go after a thing; to go for the purpose of bringing something; to fetch. 1 Nal. 12:3.
2. To come to one; to approach; to meet.
3. To send for a person or thing; to send away.
4. To take from another; to procure for one. Kin. 34:4.
5. To require of one. Ezek. 3:18, 20.
6. Hoo. To pine away, as in the consumption; to cause to grow thin in flesh.
7. To starve; to suffer starvation.
8. To mourn; to suffer. Hal. 88:9.
9. To make thin, i. e., to deprive of; i hoonele a i hookiiia oukou i ka ike.

KII, s. An image; a picture; i ko lakou ike ana i ke kii o ko lakou mau hale; an idol; a statue; kii kalaiia, a graven image. Puk. 20:4. Kii palapalaia, a picture. Nah. 33:52. Kii hoobeeheeia, a molten or cast image. Nah. 33:52. Kii akua, images of gods for worship. 1 Nal. 14:23. He laau ke kii no na kanaka ame na 'lii; the common people and the chiefs have idols of wood; kii ku, a standing image. Oihk. 26:1. Kii pohaku, an image of stone; kii onohi, pupil of the eye.

KII-A-KU-A, s. See the foregoing. An image representing a god.

KI-HAE, v. To fade; to decay; to corrupt, as dead vegetables or animals; kihae oho o ka lau ki o Luakaka.
2. To be inspired or possessed of some god.
3. To become a god and go above.

KI-HAE-HAE, v. To tear to pieces; to rend into small parts. See HAEHAE.

KI-HE, v. See KIHAE, to wilt. To fade; to wilt, as a plant.
2. To be weak; to faint, as a person.
3. To become a demi-god.

KI-HE-HE, v. To be or become deified; to pass or live invisibly in the air.

KI-KI, v. A frequentative and intensive of ki, to shoot or squirt. To spurt, as water pressed through a small orifice.
2. To eject black matter, as the squid.
3. To practice masturbation.
4. To flow swiftly, as water from the bottom of a full barrel.
5. To do a thing with vehemence; to run very swiftly; to fly furiously at, as one cock at another, or as a hen in defense of her young. NOTE.—Kiki is used as an intensive adverb in various senses. See below.

KI-KI, v. To paint the face or hair white with lime or with clay (palolo.)

KI-KI, s. Bundles done up for carrying on a stick, of which a man carries two.

Kɪ-ʟᴏ, v. To look earnestly at a thing.
2. To look at and watch the stars.
3. To prognosticate events by looking at the stars; to foretell what the weather will be.
4. To act as a sorcerer.
5. To be or act as a judge between man and man.

Kɪ-ʟᴏ-ᴋɪ-ʟᴏ, adj. Practicing enchantment; divining; fortune telling.

Kɪ-ʟᴏ-ᴋɪ-ʟᴏ-ᴜ-ʜᴀ-ɴᴇ, s. Kilo and uhane, the spirit. To foretell the condition of one's soul as being safe or near death, as living or as about to suffer; a species of necromancy based upon falsehood, much practiced in former times.

Kɪ-ʟᴏ-ᴡᴀ-ʜɪ-ɴᴇ, s. Kilo and wahine, a woman. A prophetess; a sorceress. Isa. 57:3.

Kɪ-ɴᴀ, s. A blemish, as in a person or body of an animal. Kanl. 15:21.
2. Sin; error; wickedness; kina ole, without fault; sinless.

Kɪ-ɴᴀɪ, v. To quench; to extinguish, as fire. Oihk. 6:12.
2. To put out a light; na kinai loa ia ka malamalama.
3. To extinguish, as life; to kill by strangling, striking or piercing, as oo keiki.
4. To make bitter with bitter ingredients.
5. To kill by poisonous medicines.

Kɪ-ɴᴏ, s. The body of a person or other substance as distinguished from the limbs or other appendages.
2. The body of a person in distinction from uhane, the soul; okoa ke kino, okoa ka uhane.
3. A person; an individual; one's self; kuhi oia me kona kino iho, he thought with himself.
4. The body; the substance; the principal part of a thing; he keokeo ke kino o ko'u kapa.
5. A stalk of grass; the body of a tree; that which is the substantial part of matter. See Oɪᴡɪ.
6. In grammar, person; as, kino kahi, first person; kino lua, &c.

Kɪ-ɴᴏ, v. Hoo. To take a body; to take shape; to embody, as a shapeless mass; hookino ka honua, the earth took shape (from chaos.) Mel. of Creation.

Kɪ-ɴᴏ-ᴀ-ᴋᴀ-ʟᴀᴜ, s. Kino and akalau, a spirit or ghost. The spirit or ghost of a person not yet dead. See Wᴀɪʟᴜᴀ, Aᴋᴀʟᴀᴜ and Kɪɴᴏᴡᴀɪʟᴜᴀ. Nᴏᴛᴇ.—There were persons formerly. mostly priests, who pretended to see the ghosts or souls or spirits of others while still living, and would inform the living persons that they had seen their spirits, and that it was a sign of some great calamity about to befall them; this the priests did to extort something valuable from them. I aku la kela (ke kahuna),

Kɪ-ɴᴏ-ʜɪ, } s. The beginning; the first
Kɪ-ɴᴏ-ʜᴏᴜ, } of a series.
2. Primitive; the first in time.
3. The beginning of the world.
4. The name of the first book of the Bible, Genesis, from the first word. Nᴏᴛᴇ.—Kinohi never takes the article.

Kɪ-ɴᴏ-ʜᴏᴜ, adv. At first; before. 1 Nal. 20:9.

Kɪ-ɴᴏ-ʜɪ-ɴᴏ-ʜɪ, adj. Printed, as calico; spotted; kikokiko, onio.

Kɪ-ɴᴏ-ᴍᴀ-ᴋᴇ, s. Kino and make, dead. A dead body. Oihk. 5:2. A corpse of a man or animal. See Kᴜᴘᴀᴘᴀᴜ.

Kɪ-ɴᴏ-ᴘᴜ, s. The effluvia or smell or strong scent of tobacco; o ka poe a pau i lawe i ke kinopu, ua okiia ka lakou mau ipu.

Kɪ-ɴᴏ-ᴡᴀɪ-ʟᴜ-ᴀ, s. Kino and wailua, a ghost. A poetical name for a spirit or ghost of one seen while living, distinct from and in a different place from his body. See Kɪɴᴏᴀᴋᴀʟᴀᴜ and Kᴀᴋᴀᴏʟᴀ.

Kᴏ, prep. Of; the sign of possession or property, answering often to the apostrophic s in English, thus: ko na, of him, of her, of it, that is, his. hers or its (seldom however in the neuter); ko kakou, of us, that is. our, ours; ko lakou, of them, theirs, &c. It has the same meaning as o, but is placed in another part of the sentence. Ko is used also before nouns proper and common in the same way. Sometimes ko and o are both used; as, ko o nei poe kanaka, of, or what belongs to the people here, or the o may be taken as a noun of place. Gram. § 69, 1, 2. 3.

Kᴏ, v. To accomplish; to fulfill; to bring to pass, as a promise or a prophecy. Lunk. 13:17. To fulfill, as an agreement; opposite to haule, to fail. Ios. 23:14. To fulfill, as a threat; to be avenged. Ier. 5:29. To obtain; to conquer; to overpower.
2. To win in a bet; olioli iho la ka poe i ko, so those who winned in a race rejoiced; to prevail, as one party over another. Luk. 23:23. To obtain what one has sought after; to succeed in a search. Laieik. 63.
3. To proceed from, as a child from a parent; to beget, as a father. Ier. 16:3.
4. To conceive, as a female; to become pregnant; e hapai, e piha. Kin. 16:4.
5. To draw or drag. as with a rope; e kauo, e huki. 2 Sam. 17:13.

6. *Hoo.* To fulfill an engagement. *Laieik.*
109. To perform what has been spoken.
Nah. 23:19.
7. To put a law in force; e *hooko* i ke
kanawai. 2 *Sam.* 8:15. That is, cause to
fulfill the law.

Ko, *adj.* Drawn ; dragged, &c.

Ko, *s.* Sugar-cane; hence, sugar; mo-
lasses.
2. In *music*, the second ascending note.

Ko-a, *v.* To be dry; to be without moisture ; maloo, mauu ole.
2. To be unfruitful ; to bear no fruit, as
a plant or tree ; e hua ole mai i ka hua.
3. To speak unwittingly; to speak in
jest; not meaning exactly what one says.
4. To miss ; to make a mistake in speaking; e olelo kikoola; to throw words carelessly together without thought.

Ko-i, *v.* To use force with one, either
physical or moral.
2. To urge ; to entreat one to do or not
to do a thing ; to compel by entreaty.
3. To tempt: to be led to do a thing.
Kanl. 4:19. *Koi* ae la lakou ia ia (ia Liholiho) e aie, they *urged* him (Liholiho) to go
in debt.
4. To drive; to urge with violence; to
compel by force ; to insist on a thing ; to
practice any athletic exercise ; e *koi* mau
a mama i ka holo.
5. To ask or invite one to go in company
with him.
6. To take aside to ask a favor.
7. To carry a bundle on the shoulders of
two men on a stick between them.
8. To drive or force in, as a nail or spike
into wood; to force one thing into another.
9. To flow or rush like rushing water
over a dam or any obstruction.
10. To put in the stick or vine on which
kukui nuts are strung ; e *koi* i ke kukui.

Kou, *adj. pron.* Thy; thine; of thee;
of you ; of yours ; an oblique case of *oe.*
Gram. § 132 and 133, 3d. See Kau. Note.
It has the diphthongal sound.

Ko'u, *adj. pron.*, first person. My; mine;
of me ; an oblique case of *au* or *wau*, and
formed like the foregoing. See Grammar
§ 124, 1st, and § 126, 3d. *Ko'u* is distinguished from *kou* by a slight break in the
pronunciation between the preposition *ko*
and the *u* and indicated in writing by an
apostrophe. It is doubtless a contraction

Ko-ho, *v.* To choose generally ; to select without regard to number.
2. To choose one of two persons; to make
choice among two or more objects. *Ios.*
24:15, 22.

Ko-hi, *v.* To dig; to make a hole or
cavity in the ground ; to dig, as a well.
Puk. 7:24. To dig in the ground. *Isa.* 5:2.
Syn. with eli.
2. To take up ; to separate, as the kalo
from the hull.
3. To prevent ; to hinder ; to hold back.
4. *Haa.* To travail in birth ; to endure

Ko-ko, *v.* To feel; to squeeze; to press,
as in lomilomi.
2. To set a broken bone ; to replace a
bone.
3. To go about from place to place without object.
4. To pull this way and that; to pull or
drag along ; to tie up the koko or strings
of a calabash. See Koko, *s.*, 3. To push ;
to jostle, as in a crowd.
5. To be inconstant; to be fickle.
6. To fill; to fulfill; to fill up a specified
time. *Iob.* 39:2. See Ko, *v.*

Ko-ko, *s.* Blood; the red flow in the
arteries and veins of animals; *koko* hala
ole, innocent blood. 2 *Nal.* 24:4.
2. A species of shrub or bush used for
fuel.
3. The netting or net work of strings
around a calabash.

Ko-ko-e, *v.* To divide; to separate into
parts ; to divide out.
2. To cut with a sharp instrument. 1
Nal. 18:28.
3. To be in advance or ahead of another;
to hasten forward ; to set or fix one's eyes
upon ; *kokoe* aku la na maka, i ka ike i
kona enemi. *Laieik.* 120.
4. To strike, injure or disfigure the eyes
of one when angry.
5. *Hoo.* To scratch or dig at one's eyes
in order to injure them ; mai *hookokoe* i na
maka a ka mea i alohaia, o ku ia oe ia ala
hookahi.

Ko-ko-i, *v.* See Koi. To spurt; to eject,
as water ; to cast out suddenly.

Ko-ku-a, *s.* Help; assistance; what is
given in charity; entertainment: hospital-
ity; epithet of the Holy Spirit. *Ioan.* 14:26.
The Comforter.

Ko-mo-ko-mo, *s.* The act of fitting a garment to a person until it fits well.
2. A disease, epilepsy ; a demoniacal
possession perhaps.
3. The name of a play or game.

Ku, *v.* Note.—This word has two distinct meanings and yet they run into each
other ; as, first, *ku* to rise up ; second, *ku*
to stand.
1. To arise ; to rise up, as from a sitting
posture. *Ioan.* 11:29. To stand erect.
2. To rise, as war. 1 *Oihl.* 20:4. To rise
up to do a thing or for a specified purpose.

Ioan. 1:2.

3. To stand against; to resist; to act contrary to.

4. *Hoo.* To excite; to stir up, as an insurrection.

5. To raise up, as an eminent person. *Kanl.* 18:15, 18.

6. To raise up; to propagate. *Kanl.* 25:7.

Ku, v. To stand, i. e., to stop still; to let down, as an anchor (generally written *kuu*); *ku* iho la makou ia nei, we anchored (stood, stopped) at this place; to stand against or opposite to.

2. To hit; to strike against; to pierce, as a spear; a *ku* oia i ka poe panapua.

3. To hit, as the foot in walking; to stumble. *Rom.* 9:32.

4. To stand, as a ship, i. e., to come to anchor.

5. *Hoo.* To cause to stand, i. e., to hold up; to stretch out, as the hand. 1 *Nal.* 8:22.

6. To be placed or set in a state or condition. *Iob.* 20:4.

7. To fit; to be like; to resemble; to agree with; ua *ku* ke keiki i ka makua, the child *resembles* the parent; aole e *ku* i ke kanawai, it is not according to law.

8. To fit, as a garment. The following are miscellaneous uses:

9. With *pono*, to be opposite to; holo mai la lakou a *ku* pono i Honaunau, they sailed till *opposite to* Honaunau.

10. *Ku* e, to resist; to oppose.

11. Ka *hooku* ole i ka hala, not condemned.

12. *Ku* i ka wa, to stand in a space (between two parties); hence, to be free; to be uncommitted. 1 *Kor.* 9:1.

13. *Ku* o ka hao, to be fitted of iron, i. e., to be bound with iron. *Mat.* 8:28.

14. To be suitable; to be proper; to be fit. *Luk.* 3:8.

15. To extend; to reach from one place to another; ua *ku* ko'u pilau mai Hawaii a Kauai, my evil influence (ill savor) *has reached* from Hawaii to Kauai.

16. To come to one, as a report or information; *ku* mai ia Poliahu ka ike no Aiwohikupua mau hana.

Ku-a, v. To strike in a horizontal direction; hence,

1. To cut or hew down, as a tree with an axe: alaila *kua* laau ala o Kalaninoku, then Kalaninoku cut down sandal-wood.

2. To hew, as wood or stones. *Kanl.* 7:5.

Ku-a, s. The back of a person or animal in distinction from the face. *Puk.* 33:23. He kahi mahope o ke poo o ke kanaka, a o ka holoholona.

2. The top of a ridge or high land.

Ku-a-ha, s. An altar for sacrifice. *Kin.*

8:20. *Kuaha* okoa, a whole altar. 1 *Nal.* 6:22. He wahi e hoomoa ai na mohai.

Ku-e, v. *Ku*, to stand, and *e*, opposite. To be opposed; to be contrary; to be strange.

2. To act contrary to authority; to oppose the civil government.

3. *Hoo.* To set against; to oppose. *Ier.*

Ku-i, v. To stick together; to join.

2. To stitch or sew together. *Kin.* 3:7. E *kui* lehua, to braid lehua blossoms into a wreath. *Laieik.* 145.

3. *Hoo.* To splice; to join on; to add or attach one thing to another. *Iob.* 34:37.

Kuu, v. To let go; to loosen; to release; to slacken, as a rope that is too tight; to let down, as by a rope: to let down from the shoulder. *Kin.* 24:18.

2. To dismiss or send away, as on an errand; to send away, as a messenger; to allow to come. *Lunk.* 13:8.

Kuu-la-la, v. To be beside one's self; to be out of one's right mind; e pupule, e hehena; to go here and there; to be lawless.

Kuu-la-la, s. Great ignorance; stupidity; a want of common sense views; no ke *kualala* loa o ko onei poe kahiko i na olelo lalau.

Ku-hi, v. To think; to suppose; to imagine. *Sol.* 17:28. *Kuhi* lakou he lokoino ko na kanaka o Hawaii, they thought the people of Hawaii of bad disposition.

2. To point out; to point at with the finger.

Ku-he-a, v. *Ku* and *hea*, to call. To call; to cry aloud; to call for one; to make a noise; to call out. See KAHEA.

Ku-hou-a-na, s. *Ku*, to rise, *hou*, again, and *ana*, participial termination. A rising anew; a rising again; a resurrection.

Ku-ka-ku-ka, v. See KUKA, to think. To think; to reflect.

2. To hold a consultation. 1 *Nal.* 12:6. To consult together how to manage a difficult matter. *Luk.* 19:30.

3. With *naau* or *iho*, to consult or think within one's self; to muse; to think. *Luk.* 3:15.

4. To devise good or evil. *Ezek.* 11:2.

Ku-ke, v. *Ku* and *ke*, to drive off. To drive or force away.

2. To hunch or push off, i. e., to give a hint with the elbow to go.

3. *Hoo.* To cast out; to expel; to drive away. *Nah.* 32:21.

4. To be angry at.

Ku-lu, *v.* To drop, as water; *kulu* ka lani, the heavens dropped water, that is, it rained. *Lunk.* 5:4. To drop, as tears; na waimaka o kela mea keia mea e *kulu* i lalo; to distill from. *Mel. Sol.* 5:5. Hence,
2. To leak, as the roof of a house.
3. To flow, as water.
4. To fall down ; to tumble over.
5. To be asleep ; to dream ; to be in a trance.
6. To be in a pleasant frame of mind.
7. To be near or quite midnight; ua *kulu* ka po ; ua *kulu* ke aumoe.
8. To be near night ; kokoke po ka la.

L A, name of the eighth letter of the Hawaiian alphabet. It represents the sound of a liquid as in other languages ; hence it is easily assimilated to such of the other liquids as are similarly pronounced, viz. : *n* and the smooth American *r* in foreign words. Thus, *nanai* for *lanai;* on the contrary *lanahu* is used for *nanahu,* &c. *L* is inserted sometimes, for the sake of euphony, between a verb and its passive termination *ia;* as, *kaulia* for *kauia;* manao*lia* for *manaoia.* The letter *h* is used in a similar manner. See H and Grammar § 48.

The name of the letter *la* instead of *el* is required by a law of the language, viz. :

that every syllable must end with a vowel sound.

LA, a particle following verbs, mostly in some preterit tense, and generally connected with either *mai, aku, iho* or *ae. Gram.* § 239 and 240. It is also used with nouns and adverbs and seems to have a slight reference to place ; similar, but not so marked or strong as the French *la.*

LA, *s.* The sun; he mea e malamalama ai i ke ao, ke alii o ka malamalama, that which gives light to day, the king of light.
2. Day or light, in distinction from *po,* darkness.
3. A particular or appointed day; *la* ka*lahala,* day of atonement. *Oihk.* 23:27. A particular day of the month or year.
4. The effects of the heat of the sun, i. e., a drought; ka *la* nui, a great drought; heat ; warmth. Stifling heat is *ikiiki.*

LAA, *v.* To be holy; to be set apart for holy purposes ; e hookaawale i na waiwai i hoanoia. *Puk.* 30:29.
2. To be devoted to any person ; to be consecrated to a particular use or purpose, generally religious ; to be under or bound by an oath. *Laieik.* 38. By a kiss. *Laieik.* 126.
3. To be devoted to destruction or death. *Ios.* 6:17. A ike mai la na ilamuku o Liloa ua *laa* keia keiki no ka ae ana ma kahi

kapu, and the sheriffs of Liloa saw that the child *was devoted* (had forfeited his life) on account of his climbing over a kapu place (fence.)
4. To be defiled ; to become impure by mixing one plant with another of a different kind. *Kanl.* 22:9.
5. *Hoo.* To sanctify; to be sanctified; to be devoted ; to be set apart as sacred, or for sacred purposes. *Puk.* 13:2. To make sacred or holy ; to revere ; to dedicate, as a temple or image. *Dan.* 3:2. To devote. *Oihl.* 18:11.

LAA, *adj.* Sacred; devoted, i. e., given up or set apart to sacred purposes; hence, holy ; mea *laa,* a consecrated or holy one. *Puk.* 16:23. He lahui kanaka *laa,* a consecrated nation. *Puk.* 19:6.
2. Accursed ; devoted to destruction. *Ios.* 6:18. (See the verb in the same verse.)

LAA, *adv.* Also; together with others ; so ; like *pela;* besides all this ; oia mea a pau e *laa* me keia, all that thing *together* with this ; o ka launa nui aku i ka wahine e, e *laa* me ka wahine i ke kane e. See ELAA.

LAA, *s.* Width; breadth. SYN. with laula.

LA-AU, *s.* A general name for what grew out of the ground ; o na mea e ulu ana ma ka honua ua kapaia he *laau.*
1. Wood ; trees ; timber ; but not often fire-wood, which is *wahie.*
2. A forest ; a thicket of trees : ka mea ulu ma na kuahiwi.
3. Fig. Strength ; firmness ; hardness.
4. *Laau* palupalu, herbs ; tender vegetables. *Mat.* 13:32.
5. Medicine; that which is taken in case of sickness. NOTE.—The ancient Hawaiian medicines were numerous, and consisted mostly of mixtures of leaves of trees, barks, roots, &c., and some were exceedingly nauseous, and others very acrid; but the physicians depended more on their enchantments, their invocations to the gods, the sacrifices offered, or the prices paid, than on the virtue of their medicines.

LA-AU-A, *adj.* See LAA, devoted. Devoted to destruction, as for having broken kapu.

LA-AU-A-LA, *s. Laau,* wood, and *ala,* odoriferous. Sandal-wood, an odoriferous wood formerly in great abundance in the mountainous regions.

LA-AU-KE-A, *s. Laau* and *kea,* a cross. A cross of wood.

LAE-LAE, *v.* See LAE, *v.* To enlighten, i. e., to make visibly clear or plain by means of a light.

2. To make clear or explicit by words, as a statement or assertion.

3. To be free to move; to be unfettered; to be loose; to be separate from another. Lāe-lae, *adj.* Bright; bright shining.

La-kou, *pers. pron.* The third person plural of the personal pronouns. They; used mostly of persons. *Gram.* § 122 and § 139, 3.

La-ko-la-ko, *v.* See Lako. To enrich, &c. *Hoo.* To furnish; to provide for, as for family use, or for any occasion. *Mat.* 12:54.

La-la, *v.* To begin a piece of work or a job.

2. To draw the outline of a piece of land desired; to mark out the plan or lines of what is to be done.

3. To set a copy for writing, as a teacher.

4. To make straight; to straighten, as a stick of timber that is sprung.

5. See La, sun. To bask in the sunshine.

6. To be hot, as the sun.

La-la, *s.* The limb or branch of a tree; *lala* laau, branches of trees.

2. A limb of the human or animal frame.

La-na-la-na, *v.* See Lana. To make light; the opposite of heavy; e hoomama; to cause to float; to be buoyant.

La-ni, *s.* The upper air; the sky. *Kin.* 1:15. The visible heavens; kahi i kau nei na hoku; na ao o ka *lani*, the clouds of heaven; na manu o ka *lani*, the fowls of heaven; equivalent to na manu o ka *lewa*.

2. Heaven; a holy place. *Kanl.* 26:15. Anything high up *literally* or by dignity of character: haui ka *lani*, ke alii kiekie.

La-ni-ku-a-kaa, *s.* The highest heaven; nothing beyond. *Laieik.* 194.

La-pu, *s.* An apparition; a ghost; the appearance of the supposed spirit of a deceased person. *Hal.* 88:10. Na mea *lapu*, the ghosts: the dead. *Isa.* 34:14. A o kou inoa, he *Lapu*, a o kau mea e ai āi, o na pulelehua, thy name shall be Ghost (*Lapu*), thy food the butterflies (the judgment against Kaonohiokala for his crimes.)

2. A night monster.

Lei, *s.* Any ornamental dress for the head or neck.

1. A string of beads; a necklace; a wreath of green leaves or flowers.

2. A crown for the head. See Leialii. *Lei* bipi, the bow of an ox yoke; the garland for crowning a god.

3. Any external ornamental work. *Puk.*

Le-o, *s.* A voice; a sound, mostly of a person or an animated being; hookahi

Le-le, *v.* To fly; to jump; to leap; to fly, as a bird; a ike aku la au i ka *lele* ana o ka manu.

2. To burst forth, as fire in a conflagration.

3. To move, as a meteor through the air.

4. To depart from one, as the spirit of a dying person; *lele* ke aho.

5. To come upon, as an officer upon a criminal; to fly or rush upon one, as an

8. *Haa.* for *hoo.* To leave; to forsake; to leave one place of residence or business for another.

9. To reject as not fit for use; *lele* liilii, to scatter; to disperse; to scatter entirely.

Le-le, *s.* An altar for sacrifice; he wahi e kau ai i ka mohai kuni i ke kuahu.

Le-le-pau, *v.* To trust in; to trust to something. *Ilul.* 4:5. To lean upon. .

2. To apply the mind; to give heed; to attend to. *Heb.* 2:1. *Lelepau* i ka manao.

3. To think much of another; e manao nui ia hai.

Li, *adj.* Trembling, as from cold; shaking, as with an ague fit.

Li-a, *v.* To ponder; to think; to contemplate.

2. To fear; to be afraid; to start suddenly, as a dog in catching a fly.

3. To desire greedily; to lust after; to ponder or run, as the mind on something foolish.

4. To be cold; to shiver with fear or cold; to have the sensation of cold.

Li-a, *s.* A shaking or trembling through fear.

2. Fear or dread, as when one supposes he sees a spirit.

Li-lo, *v.* To transfer or be transferred in various ways.

1. To become another's; to pass into the possession of another; *lilo* mai, to obtain; to possess; *lilo* aku, to be lost; to perish.

2. To turn; to change; to be lost; to be gone indefinitely.

5. To bring under one's dominion or authority.

6. To change from one thing to another.

Lo-a, *adj.* Long; spoken of time, of space or measure.

Lo-a, *adv.* An intensive word of general application; much; very; exceedingly; it is connected with nouns, adjectives and verbs.

Lo-a-a, *v.* Anomalous. *Gram.* § 232. To obtain; to find; to receive; to have, i. e., to have obtained; to meet with; to happen; to befall; to be overtaken; to be caught; to be seized; to be possessed of.

Lo-hi-a, *v.* Seé Loohia. To happen to one; to fall upon; to befall, as a calamity or disease. *Mat.* 4:24.
2. To unite; to come together, as two things.
3. To overtake.

Lo-hi-a, *adj.* Overtaken; seized; possessed of, as by a spirit; overcome, as by sleep; overtaken by a fault.

Lo-lo-lo, *v.* To think; to reflect; to reason; to turn over in one's mind.

Lu, *s.* That which is thrown away or scattered.

M is the ninth letter of the Hawaiian alphabet. It is a liquid, and yet it is interchangeable with *k*, a mute; as, *makia, kakia*, &c.

Ma. The syllable *ma* is used for several purposes.
1. *Ma* is formative of many nouns, in which case it seems to imply fullness, solidity, addition, &c., to the original word.
2. It often carries the idea of accompanying, together, &c. See Malana, Mamamake, to die together, &c.
3. *Ma* is used in swearing or taking an oath (1 *Sam.* 17:43, 55). and signifies *by.* See the preposition *ma.*
4. *Ma* is also used sometimes like the emphatic *o* in such phrases as this: *na kela mau mea elua, ua loaa paka no i na kanawai.*

Ma, *prep.* At; by; in; through; unto; by means of; according to, &c. *Gram.* § 67 and § 68, 1. *Ma laua o,* together with; *haalele oia i ka aina o Wailuku ma laua o Waibee,* he forsook the region of Wailuku *together with that of* Waihee; in this case it is synonymous with *laua me* and *a me.*

Ma, *adj.* or a *particle,* which mostly follows proper names of persons, and signifies *an attendant upon,* or *persons belonging to.* or *accompanying;* as, ke alii *ma,* the chief *and his train;* an officer *and his posse;* the master of a family with his children and domestics; Hoapili *ma,* Hoapili and *those known to be about him.* It includes persons in all capacities from an equal with the one named to all connected with him, even to his servants. *Nah.* 16:8. Note.—It is possible that the double *ma* or *mama* which enters most of the numeral adjectives both cardinal and ordinal above umi or ten, should be referred to this particle.

Ma, *v.* To fade, as a leaf or flower; to wilt.
2. To blush, as one ashamed.
3. To wear out, as a person engaged in too much business. *Puk.* 18:18.
4. *Hoo.* To fail; to perish, as a person or thing.

Maa, *v.* To accustom; to be accustomed to do a thing, as a work; to be easy in one's manners; to be polite; to be friendly; e walea, e launa; to be used; to be accustomed; to have practice. *Ier.* 2:24.
2. To accustom one's self; applied to the knowledge of a road often traveled.
3. To gain knowledge by practice.
4. To sling, as a stone; to cast a stone from a sling. *Lunk.* 20:16. To throw or cast away, as a sling does a stone. *Ier.* 10:18.
5. To be small or little, as a substance.

Maa, *s.* A sling. 2 *Oihl.* 26:14. An offensive weapon of war formerly in use among the Hawaiians. 1 *Sam.* 17:40. He kaula hoolele i ka pohaku.
2. A string of a musical instrument; he kaula hookani.
3. Ease of manners; politeness gained by practice.
4. Experience; long use; frequent trial.
5. A going about here and there; ka hele wale i o ia nei.
6. The name of a sea breeze at Lahaina; the same as aa.

Mai, *v.* See Mae, to fade, &c. To be or to fall sick. 2 *Sam.* 12:15. To be diseased; to be unwell. *Ioan.* 11:1, 3.

Mai, *s.* Sickness generally; illness; disease; *mai ahulau, mai luku,* a pestilence; *mai eha nui,* a painful disease; *mai pehu,* the dropsy.

Mai, *prep.* From, as from a person, place or thing *spoken of.*
2. Towards a person, place or thing *speaking,* and repeated after the noun when the motion is *towards* the person speaking; otherwise *aku* or *ae* is used; as, *mai Kauai mai, from* Kauai (here) this way; *mai* Honolulu *aku* a i Kailua, *from* Honolulu *onward* to Kailua. *Gram.* § 75.

Mai, *adv.* An adverb of prohibition; before a verb it is used imperatively for prohibiting; *mai hele oe, don't* you go; *mai hana hou aku, do it not* again. It is often used with *noho a* in a prohibitory sense; as, *mai noho oukou a hana kolohe, do not* do mischief. See Noho.

Mai-kai, *v.* To be handsome; to be externally good; to be pleasing to the sight.
2. To be of use; to be useful; to benefit; to be good.
3. *Hoo.* To make good; to repair what has been wasted, lost or destroyed. 2 *Oihl.* 24:4. To supply a deficiency; to set things in order; to regulate.
4. To treat kindly; to speak favorably of. *Kin.* 12:15.
5. To bless; to praise, as in worship.

6. *Passively*, to cause to be blessed to pronounce a blessing upon.

7. To honor; to reverence, as a worthy character. *Puk.* 20:12.

8. To exalt; to extol; to glorify.

Mau, *v.* To repeat often or frequently, as in counting; to do over and over the same thing; ua *mau* ka ua o Hilo.

Ma-ka, *s.* The eye; the organ of sight; aole e ike ka *maka* i kona pula iho, the *eye* does not see its own mote. *Proverb.* The face; the countenance; he *maka* no he *maka*, face to face. *Ezek.* 20:35.

2. The point or edge of an instrument, as a knife or sword; *maka* o ka pahi kaua; the blade of a knife or sword in distinction from the handle. *Lunk.* 3:22.

3. The bud of a plant.

Ma-ka-la, *v. Ma* and *kala*, to loosen. To open what is closed; to separate a little.

2. To draw out; to extract.

3. To open a little, as a door; to open, as a book that has clasps on it.

4. To untie; to loosen; to set at liberty.

5. To remit, as a debt; to forgive, as an offense; e *makala* mai i kuu hala, *forgive* my offense. See **Kala.**

Ma-ka-po, *v. Maka* and *po*, night. To be blind naturally; unable to see; to be blind morally. *Puk.* 23:8.

Ma-ke, *v.* To die; to perish; to be killed; to suffer, as a calamity.

2. *Hoo.* To put to death; to deaden; to cause to die; to be slain. *Ezek.* 11:6. To mortify; to kill. *Oihk.* 20:4.

Ma-ke, *v.* To desire; to wish for; to wish; e manao nui, to think much upon; to desire often; to love.

Ma-ke, *v.* Used impersonally. To need; to have necessity; it is necessary; generally a negative; aole *make* kukui, *there is no need* of a lamp.

2. To be proper; to be fit; to be right; aole *make* hookuke ia Kalaiwahi, *it is not proper* to banish Kalaiwahi.

3. To be; to exist; to be present; aole *make* hau maluna iho ou, *let there be* no dew

Ma-ku-a, *adj.* Full grown; of full age; mature; kanaka *makua*, a full grown man.

Ma-ku-a, *v.* See **Maku** above, to be large. To enlarge; to grow. *Hoo.* To increase; to be full; to be thick set.

2. To strengthen; to sustain. *Hal.* 18:35.

3. To call one father or master; to honor. *Mat.* 23:9.

Ma-ku-a-hi-ne, ⎫ *s. Makua,* parent,
Ma-ku-wa-hi-ne, ⎬ and *wahine,* female.
Ma-ku-a-wa-hi-ne, ⎭ A mother, &c., subject to all the figurative ideas of *makua, s.*

Ma-la-ma-la-ma, *v.* See **Ma** and **Lama,** a torch; also **Malama.** To shine; to give light, as the sun or a luminous body.

2. *Hoo.* To enlighten; to cause light. *Kin.* 1:14, 15.

Ma-la-ma-la-ma, *s.* Light; the light of the sun or of the heavenly bodies; the light of a lamp or of a fire.

2. *Fig.* Supernatural light; light of the mind; knowledge; knowledge of salvation; opposite to *pouli* o **ka naau.**

Ma-lo, *s.* A strip of kapa or cloth girded about the loins of men; in former times the *malo* was the only dress worn by men when at work; a covering for the nakedness of men; ka wawae e paa'i ka mai.

2. *Fig.* Ua loheia mamua ka olelo a kekahi alii, e kaohi a e moku ka ka *malo.*

Ma-lo, *adj.* See **Maloo.**

Ma-loo, *v.* To dry up, as water.

2. To wither, as a tree.

3. To become dry, as a river. *Ios.* 3:16.

4. *Hoo.* To cause to dry up, as the sea. *Ios.* 2:10. To dry or season in the sun.

Ma-lu, *s.* A shade; the shadow of a tree or anything that keeps off the sun.

2. Peace; quietness; protection.

3. Watchfulness; care.

Ma-lu, *adj.* Secret; not openly; contrary to order; without liberty; unlawful; olelo *malu*, secret conversation. *Lunk.* 3:19.

Ma-lu, *adv.* Secretly; unlawfully.

Ma-lu, *adj.* Overshadowed; protected;

Ma-mu-li, *comp. prep. Ma* and *muli,* after. Behind; afterwards; hereafter; soon; by and by; after; according to; after the example of. *Gram.* § 161.

Ma-na, *s.* Supernatural power, such as was supposed and believed to be an attribute of the gods; power; strength; might. See *Oihk.* 26:19. Applied under the christian system to divine power. *Lunk.* 6:14.

2. Spirit; energy of character. 2 *Nal.* 2:9. Official power or authority; o kona mau kaikuahine ka *mana* kiai. *Laieik.* 101.

3. Glory; majesty; intelligence; ka ihiihi, ka nani, ka ike.

4. A branch or limb of a tree; the cross piece of a cross; a limb of the human body.

5. A line projecting from another line. *Puk.* 37:19. See **Manamana.**

6. Food while being chewed in the mouth, children were fed by taking the food from the mother's mouth and putting it into the child's; a mouthful of food.

7. The name of the place of worship in a heiau; a house in the luakini; hence,

Ma-na, *adj.* Powerful; strong. 1 *Sam.* 2:4.

Ma-na, *v.* To branch out; to be divided; to be many.
2. To chew food for infants; e *mana* aku i ka ai na ke keiki.
3. *Hoo.* To reverence or worship, as a superior being, i. e., of superhuman power; a *hoomana* aku la i na alii la e like me ka *hoomana* akua, they *worshiped* that chief as if they *worshiped* a god.
4. To worship; to render homage to. *Puk.* 20:5.

Ma-na, *s.* *Hoo.* Worship; reverence; adoration.

Ma-na-o, *v.* *Ma* and *nao*, root not found.
To think; to think of; to call to mind; to meditate; *manao* io, *manao* oiaio, to believe as true; to credit; to have full confidence in; to wish; to will. *Rom.* 9:18.
2. *Hoo.* To remember; to consider; to call to mind; to please to do a thing; to will.

Ma-na-o, *s.* A thought; an idea; a plan; a device; a purpose; a counsel; a stratagem; *manao* kiekie, a high thought; pride; *manao* io, faith; belief; confidence; *manao* oiaio, the same; *manao* kuko, lust; *manao* lana, hope; expectation; *manao* akamai, spirit of wisdom. *Puk.* 28:3.

Ma-nao-ia, *s.* or *part. pass.* What is believed, thought or supposed.

Ma-nao-i-o, *v.* *Manao* and *io*, real; substantial. To believe: to credit what one says. *Kin.* 15:6. To have confidence in. *Puk.* 14:31. The same as *manao* oiaio, to think to be truth or true.

Ma-nao-i-o, *s.* Faith; verity; full confidence.

Ma-nao-la-na, *v.* *Manao* and *lana*, to float. To be buoyed up, as the mind; not to sink, in opposition to *manao poho*, to sink; to despond; hence,
2. To hope; to trust in; to expect. *Hal.* 71:5.

Ma-nao-la-na, *s.* Hope; expectation; a buoyancy of mind.

Ma-nao-li-a, *s.* See Manaoia, *l* inserted. What is thought of, or destined, or purposed. *Gram.* § 48.

Ma-nao-nao, *v.* Freq. of *manao*, to think. To think over; to turn over and over in one's mind; to meditate. *Hal.* 63:6.
2. To lament; to grieve; to pity one; to mourn for one; kumakena.

Ma-nao-nao, *s.* A meditating; a turning over in the mind; grief; sadness on parting with friends. *Laieik.* 194. Mourning; sadness for the death of one.

Ma-nao-paa, *s.* *Manao* and *paa*, fast.

Ma-na-ka, *v.* To be discouraged; to be disheartened in doing a thing.
2. To become indifferent as to the result; to be lazy; to work slackly and carelessly.

Ma-na-ma-na, *v.* See Mana, a branch. To branch out; to grow into branches; to form several divisions; to part asunder, as several things from each other.

Ma-na-ma-na, *s.* A branch; a limb of a tree or of a person.

Ma-na-ma-na, *adj.* Branching; projecting in parallel or radiated lines; divided; split, as limbs of trees, twigs of branches, &c.

Ma-na-ma-na-li-ma, *s.* I. e., the branching of the arm; the finger. *Puk.* 29:12.

Ma-na-ma-na-nu-i, *s.* The thumb or the great toe as it is connected with the *lima* or the *wawae.*

Ma-na-nao, *s.* See Manao. Thought; opinion; view of a matter; eia ka *manao* o ka poe pono ia lakou. Ina hoi i ole ka pepa, heaha ka pono e loaa mai no ka noonoo ana i *mananao?*

Ma-na-na-lo, *v.* To be pure; to be simple, as a liquid; without mixture of ingredients. *Hoik.* 14:10.

Ma-na-na-lo, *adj.* See Manalo. Insipid; tasteless, as pure cool water; slightly brackish; hence,
2. Sweet, as water. *Sol.* 9:17. Okakai, kockoe.

Ma-na-wa, *s.* Feelings; affections; sympathy. *Kin.* 43:30.
2. A spirit; an apparition.
3. The anterior and posterior fontanel in the heads of young children; the soft place in the heads of infants. *Anat.* 9.
4. A time; a season; a space between two events; a space of place between two material objects, between two localities, &c.; he *manawa* ole, instantly; immediately. *Laieik.* 102. See Wa.

Me, *simp. prep.* With; accompanying; as; like; like as; besides; so. *Gram.* § 68 and 72.

Me-a, *s.* A thing; an external object; a visible or invisible substance.
2. A circumstance or condition.
3. A person; a thing in its most extensive application, including persons; amo kolaila poe *mea* a pau, and all the *things* belonging to them. *Kin.* 2:1.
4. Having the quality of obtaining or possessing something; as, he wahine *mea* kane, a woman *having* a husband. *Kin.* 20:3.

Me-a, *v.* To do; to say; to act.
2. To have to do; to meddle with. *Kanl.* 22:26.

3. To touch; to injure; to meddle with. *Kin.* 22:12.

ME-LE, *v.* To chant; to cantillate; to sing singly.
2. To sing in chorus or concert. *Puk.*

MI-HI, *v.* To be sad in countenance; to express the feeling of sadness or grief in the countenance.
2. To feel or have regret for past conduct.
3. To repent of a past act or acts.
4. To change or break off from a sinful course of life.

MI-KI-LI, *v.* See MAKILI. To perceive internally; to perceive, as the mind; i ka lua o ko'u noonoo ana, *mikili* iki mai la ka maka o ka manao maloko o ko'u naau, on my second thought, the eye of my mind within me *perceived*.

MI-KO-LE-LE-HU-A, *adj.* Thoughtful; skillful; having the power of reflecting pertaining or applying to the subject on hand; ua huli au, ua noke au, ua noii au i mauao *mikolelehua* no'u, a.

MO-E-U-HA-NE, *s.* *Moe,* to sleep, and *uhane,* soul; spirit. A dream. *Kin.* 20:3. A dreamer. *Ier.* 27:9. A vision; a trance; he akaku; eia keia mea nui, he *moeuhane* na ka wahine o Liliha, here is a thing of importance, a *dream* by a woman of Liliha.

MOO, *s.* A general name for all kinds of lizards. *Oihk.* 11:30. Hence, a serpent; a snake; the lizard god of Paliuli, whose name was Kihanuilulumoku, ka *moo* nui. *Laieik.* 104.

MO-HAI, *v.* To break, as a stick; to break in two; to break off.
2. To sacrifice to the gods; to offer a sacrifice; to present a gift at the altar.

MO-HAI, *adj.* Broken; fractured; broken in two.

MO-HAI, *s.* An expiatory sacrifice; a sacrifice generally; a general name of an offering to the gods, of various kinds and for various purposes. NOTE.—The most of the following kinds of sacrifices are common to the Levitical and to the ancient Hawaiian priesthood.

MO-HAI-AI, *s.* A meat offering. *Puk.* 40:29.

MO-HAI-A-HI, *s.* An offering made by fire. *Puk.* 29:25.

MO-HAI-A-LA-O-NO, *s.* A sweet-smelling offering. *Oihk.* 3:5.

MO-HAI-A-LO-HA, *s.* A free-will offering. *Kanl.* 12:6.

MO-HAI-HA-LA, *s.* A sin offering. *Nah.* 15:25, 27.

MO-LU-LO-LE-A, *s.* The voice or wail of a ghost.

N, the tenth letter of the Hawaiian alphabet. It represents the same liquid in Hawaiian as in most European languages. It is often commuted for *l* (see the letter L); as, *nanai, lanai; nanahu, lanahu, &c.*.

NA, *simp. prep.* Of; for; belonging to. Placed before nouns or pronouns, it conveys the idea of possession, property or duty. It has the relation to *no* that *a* has to *o,* or *ka* to *ko.* *Gram.* § 69, 1, 2, 3.

NA, *art.,* standing before nouns, represents the plural number; as, *ke* alii, the chief; *na* alii, chiefs or *the chiefs.* *Na* often answers the double purpose of a plural article (that is, a plural for all the other articles which are singular), and the sign of the plural number of the noun. As an article, it is both definite and indefinite. *Gram.* § 67; also, § 83, 86 and 87.

NA. A particle somewhat frequent, adding strength to an expression either positive or negative; aole *na* he wahine e, o ka moopuna *na* a Waka, she is not *certainly* any other woman, she is *certainly* the grandchild of Waka. *Laieik.* 128.

NA, *v.* To be quiet; to be pacified, as a child; ua *na* ke keiki, the child is *quiet;* to be comforted, as one in affliction. *Ier.* 31:15.

NA-AU, *s.* The small intestines of men or animals, which the Hawaiians suppose to be the seat of thought, of intellect and the affections.
2. The internal parts, i. e., the inwards of animals. *Oihk.* 1:13. The bowels. 2 *Oihl.* 21:15. Alua ano o na *naau,* o ka mea nui ame ka mea liilii, the *intestines* are of two kinds, the large and the small. *Anat.* 51. Hence,
3. The affections; the mind; the moral nature; the heart; the seat of the moral powers. *Mat.* 22:37. Synonymous in many cases with *uhane,* the soul. NOTE.—The *naau* of animals were formerly used by Hawaiians as strings for various purposes; ka *naau* i mea aha moa, the *intestines* for strings to tie fowls. See the compounds of *naau* below.

NA-AU-AO, *s.* *Naau,* the mind, and *ao,* instructed. An enlightened mind.
2. Instruction; knowledge; learning; wisdom. *Kanl.* 4:6. He ike, he noonoo, he noiau.

NA-AU-PO, *s.* *Naau* and *po,* night. Ignorance; darkness of mind; without intelligence or instruction; a cloudy mind; awkwardness.

NA-O-NA-O, *v.* See NAO. To thrust in

the hand; to take hold of; to seize; to steal.

2. To look earnestly at; to contemplate. See Manao.

Nau, *pers. pron.* An oblique case (the *auipaewa*) of the personal pronoun, second person singular of *oe.* For thee; to thine; thine; belonging to thee, &c. *Gram.* § 132.

Na'u, *pers. pron.* An oblique case (*auipaewa*) of *au*, first person singular of the pronouns. For me; belonging to me; mine. *Gram.* § 124.

Na-lo, *v.* To be lost; to vanish. *Luk.* 24:31. To be concealed from one; aka, aole ia i *nalo* ia Papa, but he *was* not *concealed* from Papa.

Na-lu, *v.* To be in doubt or suspense; to suspend one's judgment.

Na-nao, *v.* See Nao. To thrust the hand or fingers into some unknown receptacle.

2. To think deeply; to penetrate, as the mind.

3. To seize hold of, as the mind.

4. To be slippery; to be led astray; to turn aside.

Na-nau-ha, *v.* To force; to compel with strength; to belch or throw up from the throat or stomach. See Kakauha.

Ni-kii, *v.* To tie, as a rope; to fasten; to tie tightly. See Nakii.

Ni-kii-kii, *v.* To tie in knots; to fasten by tying; to bind; to tie fast with ropes or strings. 2 *Sam.* 3:34. See Hikiikii.

Ni-nau-u-ha-ne, *adj. Ninau* and *uhane*, ghost. Having familiar spirits; talking with or getting information from ghosts. *Oihk.* 19:31.

Ni-nau-ku-pa-pau, *s. Ninau* and *kupapau*, a corpse. One who consults the dead or the spirits of the dead. *Isa.* 8:19.

No, *s.* A hole in the ground which draws off water from kalo patches.

No, *v.* To leak, as water under ground from a kalo patch; e u aku, to ooze out.

No, *adv.* An affirmative particle; truly; indeed; even so.

2. An intensive, strengthening the idea, connected both with verbs and nouns.

No, *prep.* Of; for; belonging to; concerning; similar in meaning to *o* and *ko*, but used in a different part of the sentence. *Gram.* § 69, 3.

No-a, *v.* To be released from the restrictions of a kapu; to take off the kapu or prohibition; ko lakou makemake, i *noa* loa na lealea, ame na hana uhauha, their wish was that pleasure and licentiousness *should have no restraint.*

No-e, } *v.* To sprinkle a little, as
No-e-no-e, } fine rain; to be damp in the air, as a fog; to rain, yet scarcely discernible to the eve.

No-i, *v.* To beg; to beseech; to ask for a thing; to ask earnestly; to entreat; to ask, as in prayer; *noi* ikaika lakou, i pu, a i pauda, they *begged strongly*, give us guns, give us powder.

No-i-au, *s.* See Noeau. Wisdom. *Iob.* 12:2. Knowledge. *Sol.* 1:2. Skill in language; he akamai i ka olelo.

Noo-noo, *v.* See Noo. To think; to reflect; to consider in order to give an opinion.

Nou, *pers. pron.*, second person. An oblique case of *oe*, thou. Thy; thine; of thee; for thee, &c. *Gram.* § 132. *Nou* ka nou, or *nau*, yours is the fault; none to blame but yourself.

No-ho, *v.* To sit; to dwell; to tarry in a place.

2. To be in a certain condition or to exhibit a certain character; e *noho* malie, to live quietly, or to hold one's peace; e *noho* pio, to be in bondage; e *noho* like, to be at peace, as between two people. *Lunk.* 4:17. I. e., to have equal privileges. *Noho* in some positions seems almost to carry the idea of existence; ua *noho* oluolu oia, he *lived* comfortably.

Nu-i, *v.* To be great; to increase in size; to swell; to be more; to enlarge; to raise, as the voice; heaha kou mea e *nui* nei kou leo? *Laieik.* 22.

2. *Hoo.* To add to; to increase; to multiply. *Isa.* 59:12.

3. To magnify; to extol, as one's kindness. *Kin.* 19:19.

4. *Haa.* To speak proudly; to vaunt; to brag.

Nu-hou, *v.* To appear, as a new thing; to spring up in the mind, as a new thought or desire.

P the eleventh letter of the Hawaiian alphabet. It represents, as in English, a *labial* sound. Hawaiians are apt to use it for *b* in words derived from English, as *pipi* for *bipi*, or as it should be written, *bipi*, neat cattle, from the word *beef.* It is often used also for *f* in the word *piku* for *fiku*, a fig. &c.

Pa. A distributive particle prefixed to other words, as nouns, adjectives and verbs; mostly however to numeral adjectives; as,

48

pakahi, one by one, each one ; *pahua* or *papalua*, two by two, two-fold, double ; *pakolu*, each of the three, three-fold ; *pahiku*, by sevens, seven-fold, &c., and so on to any number. These words are sometimes constructed in the sentence as verbs, and thus become verbs; as, *na pahiku* mai la oia i ka ia ia makou, he *divided* to us the fish *by sevens ;* e *paumi* aku ia lakou. *give* them *ten each.*
  2. As a *particle. pa*, like *ka. ma. na.* &c., is prefixed to a great many words, but the definite meaning of such particles has not yet been ascertained.

PA, *s.* The name of any material having a flat surface, as a board (see PAPA), a plate. a server. a pan ; *pa* wili ai, a poi *board ; pa* holoi, a *basin* to wash in ; *pa* hao, an iron *pan.* NOTE.—With this meaning, *pa* takes *ke* for its article.

  2. The extremity ; the furthest point of a thing. *Mar.* 13:27.
  3. A remnant or piece ; the same as *apana.* NOTE.—This meaning also takes *ke* for its article.
  4. The wall of a city ; an inclosure, including the fence and the space inclosed ; *pa* pohaku, a stone *wall ; pa* laau, a stick *fence ; pa* hipa, a sheep *fold.*
  5. A hall ; an open court.
  6. A pair ; as, *pa* bipi, a *pair* or yoke of oxen ; *pa* kamaa, a *pair* of shoes, &c. See also PAA.
  7. A kind of fish-hook for taking the aku or bonito.
  8. A species of yam.
  9. A kind of shell-fish somewhat large, of the clam or muscle kind.
  10. A brazen grate ; he *pa* keleawe, manamana, *pukapuka.*

PA, *adj.* Barren, as a female ; applied to men or animals. 1 *Sam.* 2:5.
  2. Dry ; parched ; cracked, as land ; broken.

PA, *v.* To divide out to individuals, as several things to two or more ; e *pa* lima ae oe ia lakou. *divide out five apiece* to them. See PA. particle.

PA, *v.* To touch ; to tap lightly ; to strike gently. *Puk.* 19:12.
  2. To beat ; to strike heavily : to strike suddenly, as a gust of wind. *Iob.* 1:19. Ke *pa* mai nei ka makani, the wind *strikes* us.
  3. To strike, i. e., to bite. as a serpent.
  4. To strike, i. e., to hit, as a stone thrown.

PAA, *v.* To be tight ; to be fast ; to make tight ; hence, to finish a work. *Kin.* 2:1. Ua *paa* ka waha, the mouth *is shut ;* he *is silenced. Mat.* 22:34.
  2. To confirm ; to establish ; to continue permanently the same.

  3. To lay hold of ; to retain ; to secure.
  4. To retain in the memory ; to keep a secret.

PAU, *adj.* All ; *a pau loa,* all ; every one ; everything.
PAU, *adv.* Entirely; wholly; completely. NOTE.—Use has rendered the meaning of this word like the French *tout.* as in *tout le mond,* all the world, everybody, when only a small part is intended.

PAU-LE-LE, *v.* To trust in ; to lean or rely upon ; to believe or credit what one has said ; to put confidence in ; to desire with the whole heart ; to believe fully.
PAU-LE-LE, *s.* Confidence ; faith. *Luk.* 7:9.

PA-HAO-HAO, *adj.* Changed in appearance ; transfigured ; having another external form.
  2. That which cannot be laid hold of; not material ; not substantial, as a ghost ; he mea *pahaohao,* a *bodiless* thing.

PA-HE-A-HE-A, *s. Pa* and *hea,* to call. The voice of whispering like a ghost; a small, thin voice just audible.

PA-LE, *v.* To refuse ; to stand in the way ; to hinder.

PA-LE-O-PU-A, *v.* To pardon one's offenses, as the priest in former times by offering a sacrifice ; e kala, e wailua, e *paleopua.*

PA-NAI, *v.* To put one thing in the place of another, i. e., to compensate for something lost.
  2. To give a substitute; to redeem. *Puk.* 13:13.

PE, *adv.* Thus ; so ; as ; in this way ;
PE, *v.* To anoint ; to apply odoriferous. ointment.
  2. *Hoo.* To anoint ; to pour on odoriferous ointment.
  3. FIG. To scent, i. e., to give tone and character to one's life ; applied also to the soul : o ke kupaoa ia e *hoope* ai na uhane. See KUPAOA.

PE, *v.* To humble ; to crush ; to pound fine. See PEPE.
PE, *adj.* Broken or flatted down ; depressed ; crushed.

PE-A, *v.* To make a cross ; to set up timbers in the form of a cross ; to make four arms or four prominent points ; to be opposed to.
  2. *Hoo.* To accuse through envy. *Mat.* 27:18. To punish for little or no crime ; ame ka *hoopea* wale o ka poe koikoi i ka

poe liilii, and the great *accused* (punished) the small.

3. To be in bonds; to suffer, as a prisoner. *Kol.* 4:3. To bind one's hands behind his back or to a post; ua *peaia* kona mau lima i kona kua, no ka aihue.

10. A cross or timbers put cross wise thus ✕, formerly placed before the heiau as a sign of kapu (taboo); e *kau pea*, to place in the form of a cross. See **Kha.**

Pe-a-hi, *s.* The bones of the hand distinct from the arm; e malama i kona mau iwi ame na *peahi* lima.

2. The open hand: an open hand as a symbol of power. *Hal.* 44:3.

3. A fan. *Mat.* 3:12. The sign or picture of a fan marked on anything; he *peahi* ko kona poe kanaka, oia o lakou hoailona: ua kakauia ma ko lakou papalina.

4. A gentle fanning breeze; a soft wind, as though made with a fan; he koaniani.

Pe-a-hi, *v.* To fan; to sweep; to brush; to make wind with a fan.

2. To motion or beckon to one with the hand or otherwise.

Pe-ua, *adj.* Uniting; joining; adhering.

Pe-he-a, *adv. inter. Pe*, as, and *hea*, how? In what manner? how? why? what?

Pe-he-a, *v.* See the adverb above. To ask how or in what manner a thing was done; to inquire how a person is; alaila, *pehea* iho la kela? pane mai la ia, *pehea* hoi, then that person *asked how it was done?* he answered, *how indeed.*

Pe-le, *s.* The name of the fabled goddess of volcanoes.

Pi, *v.* To sprinkle, as water. *Oihk.* 6:27.

2. To throw water with the hand. See Pipi, Kapii and Kapipi.

3. To cause water to flow drop by drop; to flow in very small quantities.

4. *Hoo.* To be stingy; to be close; to be hard upon the poor.

Pi-li, *v.* To coincide; to agree with, as boards jointed.

2. To cleave or adhere to, as persons good or bad as friends; to lay a wager; to bet; a *pili* nui mai i ko lakou waiwai a pau; *pili* kekahi wahine i kona kino iho, a lilo i ka pu.

3. To become one's to account for or to take care of.

4. To agree together, as witnesses.

5. To belong to; to accompany; to follow.

6. *Hoo.* To join company with; to adhere to one; applied to persons.

7. To seal up, as a document. *Dan.* 12:4.

8. To approach to one of the opposite sex for defilement.

9. To be united to; to adhere to each other, as husband and wife.

10. To add something else to a thing. *Kanl.* 4:2.

11. To treat badly; to reproach; to cast up to one.

Pi-li, *adj.* Of or belonging to a person or thing; ka *pili* ana o ke ahiahi, first of evening; after dark.

2. United; joining.

3. Things adhering or coming in contact that ought not: hence.

Pi-li-ki-a, *s.* A difficulty; a hindrance; a perilous situation; extreme danger, as in distress.

Pi-li-lo-ko, *v. Pili* and *loko*, internal. To belong to that which is internal; to go close to.

Po, *s.* Night; the time after the going down of the sun; the time of the twenty-four hours opposite to *ao*, day.

2. Darkness; the time when the sun gives no light.

3. Chaos; the time before there was light; mai ka *po* mai, from chaos (darkness) hitherto, that is, from the beginning, from eternity.

4. The place of departed spirits; the place of torment. Note.—Hawaiians reckon time by *nights* rather than by days; as, *Po akahi*, first night, i. e., Monday; *Po alua*, second night, Tuesday. *Po* was counted as a god among the poe akuanoho.

Po-e, *s.* A company; a number of persons or animals, from three to any indefinitely large number. It is not so often applied to *things* as to persons and animals; but the idea is that of a certain company or assemblage as distinct from some others. A cluster; a bunch. It is often synonymous with *pae* and *puu.*

Po-i, *v.* To make clear or explicit.

2. To excite; to stir up; to hurry.

3. To cover; to shut, as a door or book; to cover over; to protect.

Poi, *s.* The paste or pudding which was formerly the chief food of Hawaiians, and is so to a great extent yet. It is made of kalo, sweet potatoes or breadfruit, but mostly of kalo, by baking the above articles in ovens under ground, and afterwards peeling and pounding them with more or less water (but not much); it is then left in a mass to ferment; after fermentation, it is again worked over with more water until it has the consistency of thick paste. It is eaten cold with the fingers.

Po-iu, *v. Po,* intensive, and *iu,* sacred; consecrated. To be under the protection or care of some one having power to protect.

2. To be prohibited or forbidden; to be under a kapu.

3. To be consecrated; to be holy. See Iutu.

Po-iu, *adj.* Afar off; at a great distance.

2. Grand; solemn, as a sacred place; glorious.

3. Precious: desirable.

Po-i-na, *v.* To forget; to be forgotten. *Kin.* 41:30. Note.—In this form, it is used only in a neuter or passive sense.

2. *Hoo.* To cause to forget; to pass from the mind or memory.

3. To forget a person or an event. *Kin.* 40:23. To forget God. *Lunk.* 3:7.

Po-i-no, *v. Po,* intensive, and *ino,* bad; evil. To be in distress; to be in miserable circumstances.

2. To suffer from some cause; to suffer an injury; to be injured.

3. To be ill-fated or destined to suffer.

Poo, *s.* Takes the article *ke.* The head; the summit, &c.; ke *poo* o ka mauna, the *top* of the mountain.

2. The head of a person; the seat of thought; the seat of the intellectual powers: he wahi e noho ai ka noonoo, ka noho ana o ka uhane.

Poo-noo, *v. Poo* and *noonoo,* to think. To think; to reflect; to turn over and over in the mind.

Po-ha-la, *v.* To be healed; to recover from sickness. *Iak.* 5:16.

2. To recover from a swoon or fainting; alaila, *pohala* ae la kona manao. *Kin.* 45:27. Used also with *naau.*

3. To breathe freely and easily after being relieved from severe pain.

4. To be freed from constraint; to break loose from confinement.

Po-ni, *v.* To besmear; to daub over.

2. To anoint. *Ioan.* 12:3. To consecrate by anointing, as a priest. *Puk.* 23:41. To anoint, as a king. *Lunk.* 9:8. Mea *poni,* an anointed one.

3. To rub over some odoriferous matter; to cause a pleasant odor.

5. The anointing of a chief or god; ka hamo ana i ka mea ala i alii, i akua; ointment. *Ioan.* 12:3.

Po-no, *s.* Goodness; uprightness; moral good; rectitude of conduct.

2. That which is right or excellent; *abstract,* righteousness; excellency.

Pu, *v.* To come forth from; to come out of, as words out of the mouth; to draw out or move off, as a canoe from the place where it was dug out; alaila hele mai ke kahuna e *pu* ia ka waa.

2. To hold water in the mouth and try to talk; to mumble; to suck wind into the mouth.

3. To call; to call out; to proclaim; to call upon inanimate matter, as to call upon the mountains.

4. To cast lots; to choose by lot. See *Puu.* This was done usually by doubling the hand and one telling whether anything was in it or not.

5. *Hoo.* To sit with the knees bent up and the hands over them; to sit idly; to do nothing.

Pu-a-lu, *v. Pu,* together, and *alu,* to combine. To work together; to combine in aid of one or of each other; to act in concert; to work like a multitude at one kind of business.

Pu-o-pu-o, *v.* To clap together the hollow hands with a sound. See Hoopuopuo.

Puu, *v.* To collect together; to lay by, particularly in heaps.

Puu, *s.* Any round protuberance belonging to a larger substance.

2. A small round hill; a peak; a pimple; a wart; the knuckles; the ankle joints; the Adam's apple of the throat; hence, the throat; a knop; an ornament of a candlestick. *Puk.* 25:3.

3. The material heart. 2 *Sam.* 18:14.

Pu-ka, *v.* To enter or pass through a hole, crevice, a gate or door-way.

2. To enter in or to pass out, according as it is followed by *mai* or *aku.* With *aku* it signifies to go out; to go from one place to another; to go forth. 1 *Nah.* 19:11.

8. To pass from one state or condition to that of another, as from ignorance to knowledge; o kakou hoi ka poe i *hoopukaia* noloko mai o ka pouli.

9. To end; to finish; e hoopau aku.

10. To separate from; to go away; e hookaawale aku.

Pu-ka, *s.* A door-way; a gate-way; an entrance; a hole; *puka* o ke kui, *puka* o

Pu-le, *v.* To pray; to supplicate; to worship; to call, with adoration, upon some invisible being; e kahea aku, me ka mahalo aku i ka mea ike maka ole ia.

Pu-le, *s.* The act of worshiping some god; conversation with an invisible being; religious service; begging some favor from heaven.

Pu-lo-u, *s.* A veil; a covering for the

head. *Eset.* 5:12.

PU-PU-LE, *v.* To be mad; to be crazy; to act insanely; to be infatuated. *ler.* 50:38. To make one mad. *Kekah.* 7:7.

W the twelfth letter of the Hawaiian 9 alphabet. The real sound represented by it is one between the English *w* and *v*. In Tahitian the *v* sound is most universal; in Hawaiian the *w* sound predominates. In many cases the letter *w* is superfluous, the vowel *u* before *a, e, i, o,* producing the same sound as is made by the use of *w*; as, *uwala, uala; uwao. uao; uwa, uä; uwe, uë; uweke, uëke; uwi, uï; uwila, uila; uwo, uö; kawowo, kauowo,* &c. In other places the *w* is an important letter, and sometimes, if the orthography of the language were fully settled, its use would serve to make a distinction in the meaning of words, as *kaua,* war, and *kauwa,* a servant, &c.

WA, *s.* A space between two objects, as between two rafters or two posts of a house; hence.

2. A space between two points of time.

3. A definite period of time, as the lifetime of a person; i ka *wa* i hiki mai ai o Vanekouva, at the *time* Vancouver arrived; *wa* kamalii, *time* of childhood; ka *wa* ana

ao (see WANAAO), the early dawn of the morning. NOTE.—The Hawaiian year was formerly divided into two *was.* Elua no *wa* o ka makahiki hookahi, o ke *kau* a o ka *hooilo,* there are two *was* (periods) in one year, the *kau* (summer) and the *hooilo* (winter.)

4. In *grammar,* a tense.

5. A situation without friends or connexions, as in the phrase *ku i ka wa,* independent. He alii e noho wale ana i ka *wa,* a chief without subjects.

WA, *s.* Private talk or gossip concerning the characters of others.

WA, *v.* To reflect; to think; to reason. *Mat.* 16:7, 8.

2. To seek to know; to wish. PASS. To be the subject of conversation. *Laieik.* 87.

3. To say to one's self; to ponder; to revolve in one's mind; to consider.

4. To hit as a stone hits a mark; to compass, as a man his designs.

WAE, *v.* To select; to pick out; to choose. *Puk.* 12:21.

2. To sort out the good from the bad; to separate; to set aside; to draw out some from among others; *uae ae la ke kuhina* i na waa kupono ke holo. *Laieik.* 100.

3. To break and separate, as the parts of a thing.

4. To dwell upon, as the mind in thinking of an event.

5. To think; to reflect; to consider a case. See WA.

WAI, *s.* A general name for what is liquid; fresh water in distinction from *kai,* salt water; *wai maka.* tears; *wai kahe,* running water; *wai u,* milk; *wai eleele,* ink; *wai hooluu,* dye; *wai puna.* spring water, &c. See the compounds.

WAI-U-A, *s. Wai* and *ua,* rain. Rain water; water from the clouds; also *wai maoli* in distinction from well or spring water, which is *wai kai.*

WAI-HA, *v.* To desire or request of the gods, as in prayer; pela ka'u *waiha aku* ame ka'u waipa aku ia oe e ke akua.

WAI-HI, *s. Wai* and *hi,* to flow down. A cataract; a cascade; a waterfall. See WAILELE.

WAI-LU-A, *s.* A ghost or spirit of one seen before or after death, separate from the body. See KINOWAILUA and KINOAKALAU.

WAI-PA, *v.* See WAIHA. To desire; to request from the gods in prayer; pela ka'u waiha aku ame ka'u *waipa aku* ia oe e ke akua.

WAU, *pers. pron.,* first person. I. *Gram.* § 122, 124. NOTE.—The *w* in this word seems unnecessary: it is formed by the coalescence of the emphatic *o* and *au,* the pronoun proper; thus the simple form *au,* emphatic *o au.* pronounced quickly becomes *wau.* The several forms are *au, o au, wau* and *owau.*

WAU-A-HA, *adj.* In prayer; entire deliverance, freedom from, &c.; pali *wauaha* kua makani holo uka.

WA-HA, *s.* A mouth; an opening generally.

2. The mouth of a person; e olelo he *waha* no he *waha,* to speak *mouth* to mouth.

WA-HA, *v.* To carry on the back, as a child, or a person, or a bundle.

2. To dig a furrow or a ditch, especially a long one. See WAHA, *s.*

WA-HA-HEE, *adj.* Lying; deceitful; deceiving.

WA-HI-NE, *s.* A female in distinction from *kane,* male.

2. A woman; a wife. The term is applied to men and animals, and when applied to animals it merely marks the feminine gender. In *grammar,* ano *wahine,* feminine gender. *Wahine,* he mea ia e nani ai ke kane, he lei alii maikai no ke kane, *woman,* she gives honor to the man, she is

a crown of beauty for the husband.

WA-LE, *adv.* A state of being or existing without qualification; used mostly in an adverbial sense; only; alone; gratuitous, &c.; as, e noho *wale*, to sit *only*, i. e., to sit *idly;* e hana *wale*. to work *only*, i. e.. to work *without reward, gratuitously;* e olelo *wale*, to speak *without effect;* e hele *wale*, to go *as one is*, i. e., to go *naked.* As *wale* has no corresponding term in English, it is difficult to define, the idea must be gained by the connection.

WA-LE-A, *v.* To indulge in ease; to please one's self; to dwell in quiet free from care.
2. To be satisfied with one's circumstances. *Puk.* 2:21.
3. To be accustomed or habituated to a thing; to do often.

WA-LE-WA-LE, *v.* See **WALE.** To be deceived; to be led astray by one. *Isa.* 36:14. To deceive; to entrap; to get the advantage.

WA-LU-NA, *s.* A prophecy.

WA-NA-NA, *s.* A prophecy; the declaration of the kilo or of the kaula; a declaration made before hand of what is to be, which was known by its fulfillment.

WA-WAE, *s.* The leg of a person or animal; the foot. NOTE.—Hawaiians have no separate words for leg and foot, *wawae* includes both; so *lima* includes both hand and arm. See **LIMA.**

WA-WA-HI, *v.* See **WAHI,** to break. To break to pieces; to break down; to demolish, as a house or building. 2 *Nal.* 21:3.
2. To break, as bread; to break open, as a box or chest.
3. To split; to break up, as rocks. 1 *Nal.* 19:11.
4. To break up, as a boat; *wawahiia* hoi ka waapa i kui houhou. the boat also *was broken up* for the nails to make awls.
5. To break down, as idols. *Puk.* 23:24.
6. To break up, i. e., to take down, as a tent. *Nah.* 10:17.
7. To break down. as a tower. *Lunk.* 8:9.

WE-HE, *v.* To open, as a door; to open, as the dawn or advance of light in the morning; a *wehe* ae la ke alaula o ke ao, pau ka pouli.
2. To uncover what is covered up; to uncover, as the head. *Oihk.* 10:6. To uncover for illicit purposes. *Oihk.* 18:6, 7.
3. To strip off the clothes from one.
4. To open, as the eyes. FIG. To open, as the heart.
5. To open, as a well or cave. *Ios.* 10:22.
6. To open, as a book; to unfold, as a

scroll. *Neh.* 8:5.
7. To loosen; to untie, as a string or rope.
8. To disregard or disbelieve one's word.
9. To reject a favor. NOTE.—The passive is sometimes written *wehea* instead of *weheia.*

WE-LA, *s.* The heat of fire or of the sun. FIG. The heat of anger. A burning, as of a sore. *Oihk.* 13:25. Warmth. FIG. Strong feelings.

WE-LI-WE-LI, *v.* See WELI, *s.*, 5. To tremble with fear : to fear; to dread.
2. To be astonished; to be amazed. *Puk.* 15:15.
3. To fear; to reverence as a child should a parent. *Oihk.* 19:3.
4. To fear and obey, as God. *Oihk.* 25:17.
5. To be in anguish through fear. *Kanl.* 2:25.
6. To be afraid of an enemy. *Kanl.* 20:3.
7. *Hoo.* To cause one to tremble; to put one in fear.
8. To give one a charge; to threaten severely in case of disobedience. See OLELO HOOWELIWELI, to threaten. *Oih.* 4:17, 21.

Additional Words

Ai-hu-e, *v.* *Ai*, food, and *hue*, to steal. Lit. To steal food. But *ai* represents property of all kinds. See Ai, *s.* Note.— Hence, to steal generally; to take another's property secretly and without leave; to steal a person. *Kanl.* 24:7.

Ai-hu-e, *s.* A thief; one who steals.

Ao-ao, *s.* The side of a thing, as land, country : the coast of a country. Ma ka aoao o Puna a me Kau ka holo ana, along the shore of Puna and Kau was the sailing.

A-wa, *v.* To converse earnestly.

A-wa, *s.* Name of a plant, of a bitter acrid taste, from which an intoxicating drink is made,
2. The name of the liquor itself expressed from the root of the plant; the drinking of awa causes the skin to crack and flake off for a time ; i ka manawa e inu ai kekahi i ka awa, he maikai kona ili ke nana aku ; a mahope, mahuna ka ili, nakaka, puehoeho, inoino loa ke nana aku.
3. Bitterness, from the name of the plant.

A-wa, *s.* Fine rain; mist; he ua awa, ma ka mauna la ua.

E-e, *adj.* Out of sight; at a great distance. See E, *adv.*

E-e, *adv.* Opposite to ; adversely ; against. 1 Tim. 6:20.

E-li-ma, *num. adj.* Five ; the number five ; also alima. See Lima.

E-lu, *v.* To crumble to pieces.

E-lu-a, *num. adj.* Two ; the number two. See Alua and Lua.

I-li-hu-ne, *adj.* *Ili*, skin, and *hune*, poor, i. e., poor to the skin. Poor ; destitute of property ; without clothing.

I-li-hu-ne, *v.* To be poor; without property. 2 Sam. 12:1. The opposite of waiwai. Hoo. To make or cause one to become poor. 1 Sam. 2:7.

I-li-na, *s.* A burying place where many are buried (where only one is buried, it is called hunakele) ; a grave. 2 Oihl. 34:4. With kapapau, a burying place. Kin. 49:30. A sepulchre. Neh. 2:5. A tomb ; same as hale kupapau.
2. Hoo. An inheritance. Kanl. 18:2. A possession. Kin. 48:4.
3. An heir ; one to whom an estate or inheritance has fallen or is to fall ; he mea e hooili ai ka waiwai a ka mea i make.

O-o-o, *v.* To crow, as a cock. *Mat.* 26:74, 75. Syn. with kani.

O-o-o, *s.* Any small vessel for containing water to drink ; he ooo no ka wai, he kioo, kiahaaha.

O-o-o, *v.* To shrink away.
2. To be very careful of one's person or property.

O-ka, *v.* To move the lips, as in speaking, but without sound ; e oka wale ana no ka waha, the mouth only was moving.
2. To blow the nose.

O-ki, *v.* To cut off; to cut in two, as any substance; as, oki laau, oki pohaku.
2. To end or finish any talk or business. Kin. 11:8.
3. To cut up root and branch ; to destroy in any way.
4. To stop ; put an end to ; e oki i ke kamailio, to cease talking. Kin. 17:22.
5. To cut off; to separate from privileges ; to punish. Oihk. 7:20.
6. To cut grain, as a harvest. Kanl. 24:19.
7. To cut off one's head.

O-ki-o-ki, *adj.* Cutting; dividing, &c.; oia ka moku i loaa mai ai ka pahi okioki, that was the vessel from which was obtained the cutting knives.

O-ma-ka, *s.* The fountain head of a stream.
2. The springing up of vegetables. See Maka, the eye, the bud, &c.
3. The nipples of a female. Ezek. 23:3. Omaka waiu, the breast. Kanik. 4:3.
4. The foreskin in males that was cut off in circumcision. Kanl. 10:16. Note.—Circumcision was formerly practiced among Hawaiians.
5. Ka omaka wai o ka niu ; ka omaka, ka omua ke poo ; na halu ka omaka wai i kai, ua lepo ka omaka wai i kinohi. See Olomua.

O-no, *v.* To be or become sweet ; to relish, as food ; to have a like or relish for sweet food. Kin. 27:4. To have a sweet taste.
2. To be sweet, that is, good to eat ; eatable. Kin. 3:6.
3. To desire greatly to taste or eat a thing ; ono iho la kekahi mau kanaka i ka ia.
4. To be savory ; ua ono, ua mikomiko, ua onoono.
5. Morally, to have a relish for virtue.

O-no, *adj.* The ordinal of six; the sixth; used with the article. Gram. 115:4. Aono, eono, six.

HA-O, v. To wonder at; to be astonished; mostly *huohao*.

HA-HA, v. See HA. To breathe hard; to pant for breath, as in great haste.
2. To feel of; to move the hand over a thing. *Kin.* 27:12, 21.
3. To feel, as a blind person; to grope; to feel, as if searching for something. *Isa.* 59:10.
4. *Hoo.* To manipulate; to manufacture; *hoohaha paakai*, to manufacture or make salt.

HA-HAI, v. To follow; to pursue. *Puk.* 14:4. To chase; to follow literally.
2. To follow one's example; ua *hahai* nui na kanaka a pau mamuli o na 'lii e noho ai, all men generally *followed* after the chiefs for the time being.
3. To break; to break to pieces; to break, as a law. See HAE and HAHAE.

HA-HAI, v. See HAI, to speak. To tell; to talk about; e *hahai* ana no lakou i na moeuhane, they were *telling* their dreams. *Laieik.* 143.

HA-HAI, s. A breaking; a disjoining; a separating. See HAE.

HA-HAI, s. Name of a disease on the

HI-LA-HI-LA, v. To be ashamed; to be put in confusion; to be ashamed of. *2 Nal.* 2:17.
2. *Hoo.* To cause shame; to make ashamed.
3. To have that quick agitation which arises from shame; confusion, suffusion of the face.

HI-WA-HI-WA, v. See HIWA, *adj.* To be greatly loved; mostly with hoo.
2. To be pleased with; to be satisfied with, as a god with an offering; to be acceptable to; e *hoohiwahiwa* kakou i ka hana, let us make the work acceptable.
3. To pet; to treat a child, a servant or an animal with delicacy. *Sol.* 29:21.

HI-WA-HI-WA, s. A person or thing greatly beloved; applied mostly to animals or children; a pet; a beloved one. *Hanl.* 33:12. The beloved one. *Luk.* 23:35.

HI-WA-HI-WA, *adj.* See HIWA. Thick; dense; black, as a cloud; glossy black.
2. Acceptable; desired by any one.
3. Very precious; greatly esteemed. 1 *Tes.* 2:8. Greatly beloved. *Isa.* 5:1.
4. Meek; docile; he keiki *hiwahiwa* ia.

HOO-I-LI-I-LI, v. See ILI and ILIILI, to collect. To collect in store; to gather together; to gather in heaps.

HOO-I-LI-NA, s. See ILINA, burying place. An inheritance; property falling to one from the death of a person.
2. An heir; an inheritor of the property of a deceased person. *Kin.* 15:3, 4.
3. A burying place.

HOO-KAU-WA, v. See KAUWA, a servant. To make a servant of; to cause one to serve or to be a servant; to act in the capacity of a servant.

HOO-KU-MA-KAI-A, v. To cause an ambuscade; to betray; to accuse an innocent person.

HOO-LA-KO, v. See LAKO, a sufficiency. To supply; to cause a supply; to be furnished; to supply for an emergency; to prepare; to get ready.

HOO-LA-KO-LA-KO, v. Freq. of the above.

KAA-WI-LI, v. *Kaa* and *wili*, to twist. To writhe; to writhe in pain.
2. To mix together, as different ingredients; mea *kaawili* laau, an apothecary. *Puk.* 37:29.
3. To knead, as bread. *Ier.* 7:18.
4. *Hoo.* To torture; to cause to writhe in pain; to give pain to. *Ier.* 4:19.
5. To tear; to rage, as a foul spirit. *Mar.* 1:26.

KAA-WI-LI, s. A pain; a torture; a writhing pain.
2. A mixture of things.
3. A school of fish; *kaawili* iheihe, *kaawili* auau, *kaawili* pukiki.

KAU-NA, s. Four; the composite number four. *Oih.* 12:4. See Grammar § 116, 5.

KAU-WA, v. See KAUA, v., 5. A servant; in the most general sense, one who serves or does the business or labors for another.

KA-HE, v. To cut or slit longitudinally; to cut off; with *omaka*, to circumcise after the Hawaiian manner; to castrate; to shave. See KAHI.
2. To bind round the waist; to gird.
3. To begin to wither, as leaves eaten by a worm.

KA-HE, s. *Hoo.* A flowing; a flowing of blood; he poko ma kauwahi, he la ma kauwahi, he hauoki ma kauwahi, he *kahe* ma kauwahi.

KA-HI, v. To rub gently with the thumb and finger.
2. To comb, as the hair. NOTE.—The idea is from the *motion* of rubbing, polishing, sawing, &c.

3. To cut; to shave, as the beard. 2 *Sam.* 10:4.

4. To cut, that is, to tear; to lacerate. *Iunk.* 8:7. See KAHE, to cut, &c. Mea *kahi* umiumi, a barber.

5. To cut, as the hair. *Iunk.* 16:17. From the old manner of sawing off the hair with bamboo knives.

6. To slit open, i. e., cut longitudinally;

KA-HI-LI, *v.* To brush; to sweep, as with a broom; to sweep, as a house. *Mat.* 12:44. To wipe.

2. To sweep away, as the wind blows away light substances; hence,

3. To destroy.

4. To change; to be changeable.

KA-HI-LI-HI-LI, *v.* To scatter away; to brush off, as small dust or light substances.

KAI-KAI, *v.* See KAI. To lift up, as the hand. *Nah.* 20:11. To lift or raise up, as the eyes to heaven. SYN. with leha. To lift up or raise, as the voice in complaint; *kaikai* i ka leo. *Nah.* 14:1.

2. To take up; to bear; to carry upon. *Kin.* 7:17. To carry off; *kaikai* no laua i ka pahu a hiki ma ka hakae.

3. To take off, as a burden; to carry away; to lift, as a weight. *Isa.* 40:15.

4. To carry tenderly, as a child. *Puk.* 19:4.

5. To promote; to exalt; to favor, as a king a subject. *Eset.* 3:1.

6. To be led or urged on, as by strong desire or lust; a na keia kuko, *kaikai* kino hou ia mai la. *Laieik.* 196.

KA-KA-O-LE-LO, *s.* *Kaka* and *olelo*, word. A counsellor; an adviser; a lawgiver; a scribe; one skilled in language; kekahi poe kanaka akamai i ke *kakaolelo*, certain men skillful in judgment.

KE-I-KI, *s.* *Ke*, article, and *iki*, little, small, i. e., the little one. The *ke* has now become assimilated to the word *iki* and takes another article.

1. A child, male or female.

2. The offspring of one, whether a child or grown person.

3. A descendant of any number of degrees.

4. The young of animals or vegetables; *keiki* maia.

KO-KO-HU, *v.* See KOHU. To spot; to mark; to daub.

2. To have a form; to take the garb or assume the manners of another.

KO-LU, *num. adj.* The simple form for the number three; with the article, ke kolu, the third. The common forms are *akolu* and *ekolu*.

KU-AI, *adj.* Of or belonging to trade; he hale *kuai*, a house for sale, or a house where sales are made, i. e., a store; waiwai *kuai*, goods or property for sale.

2. To barter one thing for another. NOTE. This was the ancient idea of selling and buying, as Hawaiians formerly had no common circulating medium.

3. To traffic or exchange one commodity for another: after coin began to circulate, *kuai* lilo mai signified to buy, and *kuai* lilo aku, to sell. *Puk.* 21:16. At present, the phrase is contracted into *kuai* mai, to buy, and *kuai* aku, to sell; ina i make kahi kanaka, a *kuai* ia oia i ke akua kii.

KU-HA, *v.* To spit; to spit upon. *Nah.'* 12:14. To eject saliva from the mouth.

KU-HA, *s.* Saliva; spittle; water from

KU-MA, *s.* *Kuma* is a word used for *standing in company with.* See KU, to stand, and MA, implying some persons not mentioned. See MA. Hence, it implies *an addition to, an enlarging.* It is found in the compounds of numerals above ten; thus, *umi*, ten; *kuma*, increased or standing with *kahi*, one, that is *eleven;* the second *ma* may be used for euphony's sake for *me*, with. *Gram.* § 115, 4.

KU-MA-KA-IA, *v.* To betray; to ambuscade.

2. To accuse an innocent person.

3. To allure: to entice to sin; to offend against one. *Hal.* 73:15.

4. To revile; to reproach.

KU-MA-KA-IA, *s.* A traitor; one who is apparently friendly, but is in reality an enemy.

KU-PAI, *v.* To send away by water; *imperatively*, get away; be off.

KU-PAI-A-NA-HA, *adj.* Wonderful; unaccountable; strange, as a story or the relation of an event good or bad; it is used as an intensive. See KUPANAHA.

KU-PA-PAU, *s.* A dead body; a corpse; a deceased person; lawe aku la lakou i ke *kupapau* o Lono, the people carried away the dead body of Captain Cook; eia ke kauoha a ke *kupapau* ia'u, here is the last charge of the deceased to me.

KU-PA-PAU, *adj.* Of or belonging to a dead body; hale *kupapau*, a tomb.

KU-WA-LA, *v.* See KUALA. To turn over, as a man or other substance.

2. To add to a price agreed on, as for delay in payment.

3. To take something else in pay in lieu if the thing agreed on is not sufficient; *kuwala* i ka waiwai e, i ka puaa paha ke lawa

LA-WA, *v.* To work out even to the edge or boundary of a land, i. e., to leave none uncultivated.

2. To fill a container up to the brim; hence,

3. To suffice; to be enough. *Puk.* 36:7. To satisfy.

4. *Passively,* to be satisfied; to have enough. *Ioh.* 6:7.

5. *Hoo.* To supply what is wanting. 1 *Tes.* 3:10.

6. To fulfill, as a task; to complete, as a job. *Puk.* 5:13.

LA-WA, *s.* The full finishing of a work.

2. The filling up of a vessel or container to the brim.

3. An enough; a sufficiency; a supply.

4. The name of a disease concerning which it is said, paapu ka opu i na iwi aoao.

5. A white fowl; he moa keokeo; such as was offered in sacrifice. *Laieik.* 49.

6. Name of a hook for catching sharks; he lawa ka makau mano.

7. The name of an office in the king's train.

LA-WA, *adj.* Sufficient; enough.

2. Full to the brim.

3. White; shining; he moa *lawa,* a white fowl. *Laieik.* 14.

LA-WA-IA, *v.* *Lawa* for *lawe,* to take, and *ia,* fish. To catch fish, i. e., to exercise the calling of a fisherman, by understanding the places and times of the appearance of different kinds of fish and the art of taking them; in more modern time the word was applied also to the taking of birds. See LAWAIAMANU.

LA-WA-IA, *s.* A fisherman; one skilled in catching fish, and whose occupation it is. *Mat.* 4:18.

LA-WA-LA-WA, *v.* See LAWA, to hold fast; to bind tightly. To bind, as a grass house or anything in danger of floating or being blown away by the wind; e *lawa-lawa* i ka hale a paa.

2. To stretch cords from one place to another to fasten something.

3. To bind round and make fast; e *lawa-lawa* i ka ukana ma ka waa. NOTE.—The force of this word and *lawakua* consists in the completeness with which the fastening is done, as we say, *do it up all snug.*

2. To transfer from one place to another.

3. To take away from, or out of.

4. To carry in any way.

5. To take, as a wife, i. e., to marry; e *lawe* i ka wahine. *Nah.* 12:1.

6. *Hoo.* To take out of, a smaller number from a larger, as in subtraction. SYN. with unuhi.

LA-WE, *v.* The passive is often written *lawea* instead of *laweia.* To take; *particularly,* to take and carry in the hand.

LA-WE-LA-WE, *adj.* Pertaining to work, service or office; ka poe *lawelawe,* servants, waiters, &c.

LI, *v.* To hang by the neck. *Eset.* 2:23. To strangle by hanging; to hang; to furl, as a sail; ela ko kakou pea e *li.*

2. To see; to observe. *Hal.* 48:5.

3. To fear; to be afraid; to shrink back with dread.

LI, *s.* The chill or shake of an ague fit; the ague. *Kanl.* 28:22. Any sickness connected with the chills; *li* nui, inflammation. *Kanl.* 28:22. In *music,* the third note of the scale; na. ko. *li.*

LI-MA-LI-MA, *v.* See LIMA, hand. To handle; to employ the hands. *Hoo.* To hire; to bargain for work to be done; to agree with one concerning wages.

LO, *s.* The fore part of the head.

2. A species of bug, long and with sharp claws.

3. The name of some chiefs who lived on the mountain Helemano and ate men; he mau alii ai kanaka no uka o Helemano.

LO-I, *s.* A water kalo patch; an artificial pond where kalo is cultivated.

LO-I, *v.* To sneer at or ridicule another's opinion.

LO-I, *s.* Disapprobation or contempt

LO-KO, *s.* The inner part; that which is within; applied to persons or things.

1. To persons, the internal organs.

2. The moral state or disposition of a person, either good or bad, according to its compounds; as, *loko* maikai, *loko* ino, &c.

3. Applied to things, the within; the interior; that which belongs within; the inwards; ia po no. ai no i ka *loko* o ka ilio noa, on that night indeed, they ate the *inwards* of a dog not forbidden; he mau mea e pili ana maloko o ka naau; ia *loko,* the within. *Mat.* 23:26. NOTE.—The Hawaiians believed that the moral powers or dispositions had their seat in the small intestines. See NAAU.

LO-KO, *adj.* Inner; what is within; pahale *loko,* the inner court. 1 *Nal.* 6:36.

LO-KO, *prep.* In; within; inner, &c.; compounded with the simple prepositions o, ko, no, i, ma and mai. *Gram.* § 161. See each in its place. *Ia loko* is used in *Mat.* 23:26.

LO-KO, *s.* A pond; a lake; a small collection of water ; ho wai lana malie i puni i ka aina.

Lo-ko-mai-kai, v. Loko, disposition, and maikai, good. To feel and act benevolently;'to be kindly disposed towards one; to be favorable to one.

Lo-ko-mai-kai, } s. Grace; favor; spe-
Lo-ko-mai-kai-ia, } cial favor; good will. Kin. 39:4.

Lo-ko-mai-kai, adj. Merciful. Puk.34:6. Disposed to do good ; generous ; obliging; kind.

Lo-lo, v. To punish; to fine for delinquency.
2. To ordain ; to appoint.

Lo-lo, s. The brain of a person or animal ; lolo poo. Anat. 49.
2. The marrow of the bones ; lolo iwi.
3. The seat of thought ; ke kumu o ka manao ma ke poo. Note.—This is a modern idea : the ancient Hawaiians supposed the seat of thought to be in the naau.
4. The palsy ; feebleness or disuse of one's limbs. Mat. 4:24.
5. A person afflicted with the palsy.
6. A person very awkward at doing anything as though he had not the use of his limbs.
7. The sheath that surrounds a young cocoanut.

Lo-lo, s. The name of the hog sacrificed on the finishing of a canoe ; alaila, lolo ka waa, hoomana hou no i ke akua ; e hoolohe mai oe i ka maikai o ka lolo ana o ka waa.

Lo-lo, adj. Palsied; lying helpless.
2. Indolent ; lazy.
3. Crazy ; insane.
4. Tall ; slender, as a man.

Lu-e-hu, adj. Soft ; yielding, &c.

Lu-e-lu-e, v. Freq. of lue. To loosen; to destroy ; to break up, &c.

Lu-e-lu-e, adj. Loose; flowing; long, as a large loose kapa; lole hooluelue, a long loose robe. Esel. 8:15. He lole e uhi ana mai luna a hala loa ilalo.

Lo-le, s. Cloth, particularly foreign cloth ; he aa haole.
2. A garment. Lunk. 8:25. Lole komo, a garment; wearing apparel; lole hana,

Ma-ha, v. To exercise affection towards one ; to acknowledge or treat one as a friend ; to be complaisant towards one; to love ; to cherish.
2. To make a rent or hole in, as in a kapa : to tear in two.
3. To hide a thing away ; to steal.

Ma-ha, s. Rest ; repose ; respite or relief from pain or sickness ; convalescence ; relief from any calamity. Puk. 8:11. Rest; peace.
2. The wing of an army ; the fore fins of a fish.
3. The side of the head ; the temple. Lunk. 4:21. See Mahamaha.

Ma-ha, adj. Easy ; quiet ; resting, as from labor ; free from pain ; ceasing from anger.

Ma-ha-la, } v. Ma and halo, to look
Ma-ha-lo, } out ; to turn the eyes upon. To admire ; to wonder at ; to magnify the goodness or virtues of a person or thing.
2. To be glorious; magnificent to behold.
3. To approve ; to praise ; to honor ; to glorify.

Ma-ha-lo, s. Wonder; surprise; admiration.
2. Approbation ; blessing ; honor given to one.
3. The act of blessing or praising God ; ua like ka mahalo me ka hoonani.

Ma-hu, s. A man who assimilates his manners and dresses his person like a woman.
2. A hermaphrodite ; a eunuch.

Ma-hu, adj. Silent; indisposed to conversation ; silent, as a deserted place.

Mo-ku, v. To divide in two; to cut, as with a sword ; hahau mai la i ka pahi, a moku kekahi alii, he struck with a sword and cut a certain chief; to cut off, as a member of the body.
2. To break asunder, as a cord, rope or chain. Oihk. 26:13.
3. To break, as the neck ; a moku ko Kiwalao a-i a make no ia, he broke Kiwalao's neck and he died.
4. To cut off, as with a sword at a single blow.
5. To rend or tear in pieces, as a furious beast. Mat. 7:6.
6. To crack; to burst open with a noise.
7. To hold fast, as an anchor holds a ship.
8. To cast or throw into the sea; mokuia i ke kai, aole e make.

Mo-ku-a-ha-na, v. To be divided, as a kingdom, a city or a family into two or more contending parties ; to be split, as a community into factions. Hal. 55:9. To set one against another, as parties.

Mo-ku-a-ha-na, adj. Split into parties or factions, as a people ; divided ; unfriendly ; opposed.

Ma-lu-na, comp. prep. Ma and luna, above. Upward; upon; over, either as to place or office; oia no *maluna* o **ka pee kaua.** *Gram.* § 161.

Ni-ni-ni, *v.* See Nini. To pour out, as a liquid; to pour out upon; to give; to imbue; to suffuse.

2. To pour out grain, as from a bag. *Kin.* 42:35.

3. To pour out, as from a bottle. *Puk.* 29:7.

4. Fig. To pour out, as the desires of the heart. 1 *Sam.* 1:15. To pour out, as a complaint, sorrow, weeping. *Iob.* 3:24.

5. In a *religious sense*, to pour out, as the Holy Spirit. *Oih.* 2:17.

6. To exhibit anger, i. e., to pour out fury. 2 *Oihl.* 34:21.

7. To throw away; to squander; e hoolei, e hoopau.

8. To count out, as money. 2 *Nal.* 22:9.

Pai, *s.* A row; a line.

2. A quantity of food done up in a globular form in ki leaves: he *pai* ai; a ball; a round loaf of bread; he *pai* palaoa; cakes, &c. *Nah.* 6:15.

3. A cluster or bunch; as, he *pai* maia, a *bunch* of bananas; he *pai* huawaina, a *bunch* of grapes.

4. A striking; a stamping; an impressing, i. e., a printing, as kapa is printed, or as paper is printed in a press.

5. *Hoo. Hoopai*, a punishment; a judgment. *Puk.* 7:4.

6. A kind of snail shell-fish, said to be poisonous to the touch.

7. A blight; a fading and dying of the leaves of vegetables; the act of decay in vegetables.

8. A shell or cup for scooping up the oopu; he *pai* oopu.

Pa-hao-hao, *v. Pa* and *haohao*, to wonder at. To have another form; to be transfigured. *Luk.* 9:29.

2. To change one's appearance externally; to be changeable.

3. To change one's character.

4. *Hoo.* To transform. *Rom.* 12:2.

Pa-pa, *v.* To prohibit; to forbid. Note. The language or the words of the prohibition generally follow. To rebuke; to reprove. *Kin.* 37:10. To adjure; to request in strong terms. *Nah.* 11:28.

2. To erect a shade or screen to prevent the light or heat of the sun. See Papai, *s.*

3. To shine, as the sun, i. e., to create light and heat.

Po-e, *v.* To break up; to mash; to pound, as in pounding poi.

Pu-ni, *v.* To surround as water does an island.

2. To inclose; to be hemmed in, as one person by multitudes.

3. To surround, i. e., to get round one by deceit; to prevail over; to get the better of.

4. To be surrounded; to be deceived; to be insnared; to be taken.

5. To go around; to encircle; hence,

6. To finish; to complete; to terminate..

7. To close, as an appointed period of time; as the end of the year. 1 *Nal.* 20:22.. To finish the period of gestation. 1 *Sam.* 4:19.

8. To gain possession of; hee o Kalanikupule ia Kamehameha, a *puni* Oahu a me Molokai, a me Lanai a me Maui a me Kahoolawe, Kalanikupule fled before Kamehameha. and he *came in possession of* Oahu and Molokai and Lanai and Maui and Kahoolawe.

9. To covet; to desire greatly. See Note below.

10. To be addicted to; to be influenced by, as pleasure or gain; ua *puni* na 'lii ame na kanaka i na hana ino loa, the chiefs and people *were addicted* to very evil practices.

11. *Hoo.* To give false testimony; to deceive.

12. To surround for protection. *Iob.* 1:16.

Note.—*Puni* is connected with many other words and signifies, *influenced, led by*, or *addicted to*, as well as *deceived; puni* lealea, *addicted* to pleasure; *puni* waiwai, *greedy* of property; *puni* hula, *given to* the practice of the hula, &c.

Pu-ni, *s.* Name of fish nets with small meshes.

2. The termination of a fixed period, as the end of the year; ka *puni* o ka makahiki; the termination of the period of gestation, &c.

3. A desire; a strong inclination for the possession of a thing, or a particular course of conduct; he kii ka *puni* o ua wahine la, an image was the *great desire* of that woman.

Pu-ni, *adv.* Around; on every side; a *puni*, around about.

2. An intensive. Greatly; exceedingly; hotly, as in anger; mai ulu *puni* mai kou huhu, be not *exceedingly* angry. *Puk.* 32:22. See Ulu.

Wai-wai, *s.* Goods; property; that which is possessed or owned; property in distinction from money or cash; *waiwai*

Wi-li, *v.* To twist; to wind; to turn, as a crank; to grind at a hand-mill. *Lunk.* 16:21. To bore, as with an auger or gimlet. 2 *Nal.* 12:10.

2. To writhe in pain.

3. To mix, as liquids of different qualities, i. e., to stir them round and round.

16 A o kekahi poe, e hoao ana ia ia, ⁵ nonoi aku la i hoailona ma ka lani.

17 ʰ Aka, ua ike hoi ⁱ oia i ko lakou manao, i mai la ia lakou, O ke aupuni i mokuahana ia, ia iho, e pau ia, a o ka hale i ka hale iho, e hina ia.

18 A ina i mokuahana o Satana ia ia iho, pehea la e ku paa ai kona aupuni? no ka mea, ke olelo nei oukou, ma o Belezebuba la i mahiki aku ai au i na daimonio.

19 Ina paha ma o Belezebuba la wau i mahiki aku ai i na daimonio, ma owai la hoi ka oukou poe keiki e mahiki aku ai? Nolaila hoi o lakou ko oukou poe nana e hooponopono.

20 Aka, ina ma ᵏ ka manamanalima o ke Akua i mahiki aku ai au i na daimonio, oia hoi, ua hiki mai no ke aupuni o ke Akua io oukou nei.

21 ˡ O ka mea ikaika a makaukau hoi i na mea oi, i na wa i kiai ai oia i kona hale, ua maluhia kana waiwai:

22 Aka, ᵐ i hiki mai io na la ka mea i oi aku kona ikaika mamua o kona, a lanakila ia maluna ona, alaila e kaili aku ia mai ona aku, i na mea oi ana i hilinai ai, a e haawi i kana waiwai pio.

23 ⁿ O ka mea aole ma o'u nei, oia ke ku e mai ia'u; o ka mea hoiliili pu ole me au, oia ke lu aku.

24 ᵒ A i puka aku ka uhane ino mai loko aku o ke kanaka, hele no ia mawaena o na wahi panoa, e imi ana i kahi e maha'i; a loaa ole, olelo iho la ia, E hoi au i kuu hale a'u i puka mai ai.

25 A hiki mai ia, ike i ka hale ua kahiliia a ua hoolakolakoia hoi.

26 Alaila kii aku la a lawe mai i kekahi poe uhane e ehiku, ua oi aku ko lakou hewa i kona iho, a komo hoi lakou a noho malaila; a ua oi aku ka hewa o ᵖ hope o ua kanaka la i ko ka noho ana mamua.

27 ¶ Eia kekahi, ia ia e olelo ana

ᶠ Mat. 12. 38. & 16. 1.
ʰ Mat. 12. 25. Mar. 3. 24.
ⁱ Ioa. 2. 25.

ᵏ Puk. 8. 19.

ˡ Mat. 12. 29. Mar. 3. 27.

ᵐ Is. 53. 12. Kol. 2. 15.

ⁿ Mat. 12. 30.

ᵒ Mat. 12. 43.

ᵖ Ioa. 5. 14. Heb 6. 4. & 10. 26. 2 Pet. 2. 20.

---

16 And others, tempting him, ⁵ sought of him a sign from heaven.

17 ʰ But ⁱ he, knowing their thoughts, said unto them, Every kingdom divided against itself is brought to desolation; and a house divided against a house falleth.

18 If Satan also be divided against himself, how shall his kingdom stand? because ye say that I cast out devils through Beelzebub.

19 And if I by Beelzebub cast out devils, by whom do your sons cast them out? therefore shall they be your judges.

20 But if I ᵏ with the finger of God cast out devils, no doubt the kingdom of God is come upon you.

21 ˡ When a strong man armed keepeth his palace, his goods are in peace:

22 But ᵐ when a stronger than he shall come upon him, and overcome him, he taketh from him all his armour wherein he trusted, and divideth his spoils.

23 ⁿ He that is not with me is against me; and he that gathereth not with me scattereth.

24 ᵒ When the unclean spirit is gone out of a man, he walketh through dry places, seeking rest; and finding none, he saith, I will return unto my house whence I came out.

25 And when he cometh, he findeth it swept and garnished.

26 Then goeth he, and taketh to him seven other spirits more wicked than himself; and they enter in, and dwell there: and ᵖ the last state of that man is worse than the first.

27 ¶ And it came to pass, as he

17 Olelo aku la ka wahine, i aku la, Aohe a'u kane. I mai la o Iesu ia ia, He pono kau i i mai nei, Aohe a'u kane;

18 No ka mea, elima ae nei au mau kane, a o kau mea i keia manawa, aole ia o kau kane; he oiaio kau i i mai nei.

19 Olelo aku la ua wahine la ia ia, E ka Haku, [h]ke ike nei au he kaula oe.

20 Maluna o [i]keia mauna ko makou poe makua i hoomana'i; aka, ke olelo mai nei oukou, aia ma [k]Ierusalema kahi pono e hoomana aku ai.

21 Olelo mai la o Iesu ia ia, E ka wahine, e manaoio mai i ka'u, e hiki mai auanei ka manawa, [l]aole ma keia mauna, aole hoi ma Ierusalema e hoomana aku ai oukou i ka Makua.

22 Ke hoomana nei oukou i [m]ka mea a oukou i ike ole ai; ke hoomana nei makou i ka mea a makou i ike ai: no ka mea, no na Iudaio mai [n]ke ola.

23 Aka, ua kokoke mai ka manawa, a o nei hoi ia, o ka poe hoomana oiaio, e hoomana lakou i ka Makua me [o]ka uhane a me [p]ka oiaio: no ka mea, oia ka poe a ka Makua i makemake ai e hoomana aku ia ia.

24 [q]He Uhane ke Akua; a o ka poe hoomana ia ia, he pono no lakou e hoomana aku ia ia me ka uhane a me ka oiaio.

25 Olelo aku la ka wahine ia ia, Ua ike no au e hele mai ana ka Mesia, ka mea i oleloia o Kristo; aia hiki mai ia, [r]nana no e hoakaka mai na mea a pau ia makou.

26 Olelo mai la o Iesu ia ia, [s]Owau no ia, ka mea e kamailio pu ana me oe.

27 ¶ Alaila hoi mai la kana poe haumana, a kahaha iho la ko lakou naau i kana kamailio pu ana me ka wahine: aole nae kekahi i ninau aku ia ia, Heaha kau e imi nei? a no ke aha la kau e kamailio pu me ia?

h Luk. 7. 16. & 24. 19. mo. 6. 14. & 7. 40.
i Lun. 9. 7.
k Kan. 12. 5, 11. 1 Nalii 9. 3. 2 Oihlii 7. 12.
l Mal. 1. 11. 1 Tim. 2. 8.
m 2 Nalii 17. 29.
n Is. 2. 3. Luk. 24. 47. Rom. 9. 4, 5.
o Pil. 3. 3.
p mo. 1. 17.
q Kor. 3. 17.
r pau. 29, 39.
s Mat. 26. 63, 64. Mar. 14. 61, 62. mo. 9. 37.

17 The woman answered and said, I have no husband. Jesus said unto her, Thou hast well said, I have no husband:

18 For thou hast had five husbands; and he whom thou now hast is not thy husband: in that saidst thou truly.

19 The woman saith unto him, Sir, [h]I perceive that thou art a prophet.

20 Our fathers worshipped in [i]this mountain; and ye say, that in [k]Jerusalem is the place where men ought to worship.

21 Jesus saith unto her, Woman, believe me, the hour cometh, [l]when ye shall neither in this mountain, nor yet at Jerusalem, worship the Father.

22 Ye worship [m]ye know not what: we know what we worship; for [n]salvation is of the Jews.

23 But the hour cometh, and now is, when the true worshippers shall worship the Father in [o]spirit [p]and in truth: for the Father seeketh such to worship him.

24 [q]God *is* a Spirit: and they that worship him must worship *him* in spirit and in truth.

25 The woman saith unto him, I know that Messias cometh, which is called Christ: when he is come, [r]he will tell us all things.

26 Jesus saith unto her, [s]I that speak unto thee am *he*.

27 ¶ And upon this came his disciples, and marvelled that he talked with the woman: yet no man said, What seekest thou? or, Why talkest thou with her?

hope o'u, e Satana, no ka mea, aole i like kou manao me ko ke Akua.

34 ¶ A kahea mai la ia i kanaka, a i kana poe haumana no hoi, i mai la ia lakou, O ᵘka mea make-make e hahai mai mahope o'u, e hoole oia ia ia iho, a e kaikai i kona kea a e hahai mai ia'u.

35 O ˣka mea manao e malama i kona ola nei, e lilo auanei kona ola, a o ka mea haalele i kona ola no'u nei, a no ka euanelio, e loaa ia ia ke ola.

36 Heaha la uanei ko ke kanaka pomaikai ke loaa ia ia ke ao nei a pau, a lilo aku kona uhane?

37 Heaha la hoi ko ke kanaka ku-mu e haawi aku ai, e loaa hou mai ai kona uhane?

38 ʸO ka mea e ᶻhilahila mai ia'u a me ka'u olelo, i keia hanauna kolohe a hana hewa, e hilahila no hoi ke Keiki a ke kanaka ia ia i kona wa e hele mai ai me ka nani o kona Makua, me na anela hemo-lele.

MOKUNA IX.

I MAI la oia ia lakou, ᵃOiaio ka'u e olelo aku nei ia oukou; ke ku mai nei kekahi mau mea, aole la-kou e make e, a ike no lakou i ka hele ana mai o ᵇke aupuni o ke Akua me ka mana.

2 ¶ ᶜA hala ae la na la eono, kono ae la o Iesu ia Petero, a me Iakobo, a me Ioane, alakai aku la ia lakou i kahi mehameha, ma ke-kahi mauna kiekie, hoopahaohao iho la ia imua o lakou.

3 Alohi ae la kona kapa, a ᵈkeo-keo loa e like me ka hau; aole e hiki i kanaka hoomaemae lole ma-luna o ka honua ke hookeokeo pela.

4 Ikea mai la e lakou o Elia, laua o Mose e kamailio ana me Iesu.

5 Olelo aku la o Petero i aku la ia Iesu, E ka Haku e, nani wale kakou e noho ai ia nei; e hana

hind me, Satan: for thou savourest not the things that be of God, but the things that be of men.

34 ¶ And when he had called the people *unto him* with his disciples also, he said unto them, ᵘWhoso-ever will come after me, let him deny himself, and take up his cross, and follow me.

35 For ˣwhosoever will save his life shall lose it; but whosoever shall lose his life for my sake and the gospel's, the same shall save it.

36 For what shall it profit a man, if he shall gain the whole world, and lose his own soul?

37 Or what shall a man give in exchange for his soul?

38 ʸ Whosoever therefore ᶻshall be ashamed of me and of my words, in this adulterous and sinful gen-eration, of him also shall the Son of man be ashamed, when he com-eth in the glory of his Father with the holy angels.

CHAPTER IX.

AND he said unto them, ᵃVerily I say unto you, That there be some of them that stand here, which shall not taste of death, till they have seen ᵇthe kingdom of God come with power.

2 ¶ ᶜAnd after six days Jesus taketh *with him* Peter, and James, and John, and leadeth them up in-to a high mountain apart by them-selves: and he was transfigured before them.

3 And his raiment became shining, exceeding ᵈwhite as snow; so as no fuller on earth can white them.

4 And there appeared unto them Elias with Moses: and they were talking with Jesus.

5 And Peter answered and said to Jesus, Master, it is good for us to be here: and let us make three

Center column references:

u Mat. 10 38. & 16. 24. Luk. 9. 23. & 14. 27.

x Ioa. 12. 25.

y Mat. 10. 33. Luk. 9. 26. & 12. 9.
z See Rom. 1. 16.
2 Tim. 1. 8. & 2. 12.

a Mat. 16. 28. Luk. 9. 27.

b Mat. 24. 30. & 25. 31. Luk. 22. 18.
c Mat. 17. 1. Luk. 9. 28.

d Dan. 7. 9. Mat. 28. 3.

19.95 curlers
1(800) 632-1700